Navigating the Winding Road
Family Law and Estate Planning in Illinois

Navigating the Winding Road
Family Law and Estate Planning in Illinois

Written By
Sterk Family Law Group, P.C.

Contributing Authors
Alyssa A. Blando
Amy M. Bravo
Amanda N. Engelman
Arianna A. Fleckenstein
Terrence M. Fogarty
Kelly L. Garver
Jennifer J. Hanik
Laura A. Kennard
Kelli M. Lardi
Nicole L. Morales
Jennifer S. Nolen
Ragan Pattison
Crystal S. Pavloski
Amy A. Schellekens
Frederick M. Smithhart
Gwendolyn J. Sterk
Jackie L. Sulich
Joan van Oss
Monika L. Wolniak

ISBN: 978-1-7357148-0-6

© Copyright 2020
Sterk Family Law Group, PC
Printed in the United States of America
All Rights Reserved

Koru
Legal Publishing, LLC

DEDICATION

THIS BOOK IS DEDICATED TO YOU

At Sterk Family Law…the team members section of our website includes our clients. In like manner, we dedicate this book to YOU…the reader. Obviously...you chose to read this book, because you need information, and knowledge is power.

The text is not individual legal advice and should not be construed as such, but it does give you the opportunity to empower yourself to gain a general understanding of the legal process.

If you are about to embark through any of these issues, we urge YOU…the reader...to take an active role in your litigation.

We suggest arming yourself with any and all possible resources you will need to move forward in a positive direction and to emerge stronger and more empowered than you ever thought you could be.

YOU CAN DO THIS!

ACKNOWLEDGEMENTS

This publication was made possible by hard work from the following team members at **Sterk Family Law Group, P.C.:**

- Alyssa A. Blando - Receptionist / Legal Assistant
- Arianna A. Fleckenstein - Discovery Paralegal
- Amy A. Schellekens - Attorney at Law
- Amy M. Bravo - Litigation Paralegal
- Amanda N. Engelman - Senior Paralegal
- Crystal S. Pavloski - Senior Paralegal
- Frederick M. Smithhart - Copy Editor
- Gwendolyn J. Sterk - Attorney at Law
- Jennifer J. Hanik - Discovery Paralegal
- Jackie L. Sulich - Managing Paralegal
- Jennifer S. Nolen - Attorney at Law
- Joan van Oss - Attorney at Law
- Ragan Pattison - Attorney at Law
- Kelly L. Garver - Business Development and Marketing Manager
- Kelli M. Lardi - Attorney at Law
- Laura A. Kennard - Senior Paralegal
- Monika L. Wolniak - Graphic Designer / Office Assistant
- Nicole L. Morales - Discovery and Docket Manager / Paralegal
- Terrance M. Fogarty - Attorney at Law

OTHER ACKNOWLEDGEMENTS

We would like to thank our other team members: Stephanie Daniels and Robin Mattman for their support and encouragement in creating this book. Thank you to Lauren Kilmartin for your assistance as well.

Thank you to Sterk Family Law Group's therapy dog, Duke Sterk, for his support and cuddles to provide some distraction, when we faced a bit of writer's block.

We are forever grateful to K.P. Lynne for her loyalty and assistance throughout the process of creating this book. Her support and guidance was crucial in making this book come to life.

Empower Yourself With Options

Gwendolyn J. Sterk has been practicing family law since 1989 and successfully started her own law firm, Sterk Family Law Group, P.C., in 2015 in Orland Park, IL. The team believes in a holistic approach to the practice of family law and estate planning and strives to not only serve a client's legal needs, but also to help manage a client's emotional and overall well-being. The Family Law team works hard to establish connections with a vast network of counselors, support groups, and other various non-traditional service providers within our communities for their unique resource center, which provides clients with access to help prepare for the next steps in their lives.

In 2017, Sterk Family Law Group was the founding sponsor of the free community program called "Building Hope for the Future" to provide the community with access to resources similar to the law group's inhouse resource center. The Building Hope for the Future program is held each month to offer public programs about a variety of life topics ranging from anxiety and depression, to bullying, financial planning, human trafficking, special needs, and more.

The members of the Sterk Family Law Group team are advocates for providing ongoing education and are often involved in sharing their knowledge by speaking to business chambers, mental health organizations, mental health providers, and educational institutions. The Sterk Family Law Group's YouTube page serves as another avenue for the firm to share information to the world via video podcasts, co-hosted by Gwendolyn J. Sterk and various professionals, to discuss a plethora of trending topics, issues and laws.

The Sterk Family Law team strives to provide clients and the community with the tools they need to be empowered by their life changes and encouraged to move on with integrity and dignity.

Sterk Family Law Group, P.C.

www.sterkfamilylaw.com

info@sterkfamilylaw.com

815-600-8950

Stay Connected Via Facebook, YouTube, LinkedIn and Instagram: Sterk Family Law Group
For Press or Media Inquiries, Contact Kelly L. Garver, Business Development and Marketing Manager

LEGAL DISCLAIMER

The content of this publication has been prepared by Gwendolyn J. Sterk and the Family Law Group, P.C. for informational purposes only and does NOT constitute legal advice, nor does it create or constitute an attorney-client relationship.

You must personally contact an attorney for individual advice regarding your specific situation. Do not send us information until you speak with one of our attorneys and secure authorization to send information to us.

We cannot represent you until we know our representation of you will not result in a conflict of interest and an agreement is reached between you and us as to the terms of your engagement with our firm. This book was created to provide general information only.

This book may include links or references providing direct access to other resources including websites. Gwendolyn J. Sterk and the Family Law Group, P.C. is not responsible for the accuracy or content of information contained in these outside sources.

Links, articles, or references from Gwendolyn J. Sterk and the Family Law Group, P.C. to third-party sites or providers do not constitute an endorsement by Gwendolyn J. Sterk and the Family Law Group, P.C. of the parties or their products and services.

Gwendolyn J. Sterk and the Family Law Group, P.C. has been granted Limited Licensing for stock images. All images and other content in this publication (collectively the "Content"), as well as the selection and arrangement of the Content, are protected by copyright, trademark, patent, trade secret and other intellectual property laws and treaties (collectively, "Intellectual Property Laws").

Any unauthorized use of any Content may violate such laws and the Terms of Use.

Gwendolyn J. Sterk and the Family Law Group, P.C. does not grant any express or implied permission to use any Content. You agree not to copy, republish, frame, link to, download, transmit, modify, adapt, create derivative works based on, rent, lease, loan, sell, assign, distribute, display, perform, license, sublicense or reverse engineer sites or any content contained within this book. All images are protected by United States and International copyright laws and treaties.

TABLE OF CONTENTS

Introduction……………………………………………………………………...7

The First Steps……………………………………………………………….....10

Holistic Options For Family Law and Estate Planning………………………17

You've Been Served……………………………………………………..….22

Overview of the Legal Process…………………………………………….....25

Children First……………………………………………………………………..38

Knowledge is Power: Disclosing Your Financial Picture……………………60

Family Support Basics……………………………………………………….....116

Slicing the Pie……………………………………………………………….....132

You Mean I Have To Share My Retirement?...144

Whose Business Is This?..164

You Spent What? Follow the Money…………………………….…………..171

Make Sure You're Covered…………………………………………………...178

Get Out of My Head: Mental Health Protection……………………………..183

Abuse Is Serious……………………………………………………..…………193

I'm Too Old For This………………………………………………………….205

Nothing Is Free: Who Foots the Bill For This?..225

Never Married, But Bonded By Shared Children……………………………239

Diverse Families and Unique Issues………………………………………...247

Planning Your Legacy……………………………………..……………....254

Keeping A Watchful Eye……………………………………………………….261

Special Needs and Circumstances……………………………………..…..274

To Sign or Not To Sign? Basics of Pre and Post-Nuptial Agreements……288

Agreements When Cohabitating To Protect A Couple's Interests………....298

Glossary…………………………………………………………..……… 301

Closing………………………………………………………………….309

INTRODUCTION

To navigate, one must have a planned course of action for their route. As much as we may try to plan or navigate our paths and future lives, it is inevitable that we will encounter a twist in the road, or even face a roadblock or two. When one encounters a hurdle that feels too ominous to cross, it is natural to feel like things are unfurling and you may feel like you have an overwhelming loss of control. The basic definition of unfurling means to unravel, unwind, or to spread out from a folded state. When things unfurl, many people have a tendency to let the negatives outweigh the positives, because "change" and the fear of the unknown can be very frightening.

Change is something that is inevitable and often unpredictable. Some change in life is good, some is mediocre, and some may just feel plain dreadful. In life, every decision we make will determine an outcome and how we decide to react to those changes, affects those outcomes. As we travel the many roads of life, we will encounter many people, adventures and situations. As children, we are taught many lessons, and a lot of those lessons were passed down from our parents or guardians, from their parents, and so forth, to keep us on course. We may pick up their habits, and sometimes old habits die hard, but sometimes habits evolve. We will move on and age and start to pave our own paths by the decisions, opinions, habits and relationships we make with people who may lead us down a different path or winding road.

Relationships come in many forms, whether it be with our parents, family, a partner, friends or our children. Many people may enter into a marriage wearing rose colored glasses and are oblivious to the major life change they are embarking on. People who decide to marry typically join every aspect of their lives together emotionally, physically, mentally, financially and socially.

As a couple progresses in their relationship, they may choose to create a family together, whether it be through natural or adopted children, and for some people...pets. Property may be purchased to supplement the lives you are creating together. Businesses may be a part of your future goals together. Financial plans, retirement plans, and accounts may be made to plan for your future. As part of your plan, you will likely want to make sure that your loved ones are cared for in the event you face a medical situation or to plan a legacy after you pass.

But...what happens when the path you thought you paved suddenly changes direction? As we all know, not every relationship is always eternal, besides taxes, aging and death there may be snags in the road. Your marriage may deteriorate and you or your spouse may be contemplating divorce. Your aging parents or family members may need you to be an advocate for their health and finances. If you have a child with special needs, how can you help ensure that their well-being is protected now and after you are gone? How can you protect yourself, your children, and everything you have worked so hard for all these years?

When life tosses you a wrench you feel you cannot turn by yourself, know that you need not face it alone! Friends or family may be there to support you or you may find solace in resources such as a financial planner, a mental health professional, or a support group. In the event that you are facing a legal situation, finding an advocate in the form of a legal professional, or an attorney, can also be a stressful process in itself. Be sure to do your research to find a legal team you can trust to advocate for you and your family's best interests.

The Value of a Free Legal Consultation

Who says you can't get something for nothing? We all tend to be skeptical of anything that is "free", but in the world of Family Law or Estate Planning, a free consultation is both valuable and free of charge. The definition of value in this particular case can really be summed up in one word-knowledge.

The decision to consult a family law or estate planning attorney is usually one that is not reached overnight. It could involve months or even years of evaluating. The mental process of questioning the fate of a relationship, the well-being of your children, the stability of your finances or the overall fear of the unknown can create waves of indecision. Riding those waves can be challenging and upsetting when you don't understand you have options.

The true value of a free consultation is knowledge. Knowledge is power. This power comes in the form of an understanding of your current options and a capability to make an educated decision. The ultimate decision may be to move forward with legal action or it may be to reconcile the matter at home. Either way, the decision can be made with clarity.

Resources: A Comprehensive Approach

In addition to finding a legal team you trust, recovery from divorce, managing child related matters, or preparing an estate plan, is case specific and each person will have different needs. Family law and estate planning involve not only legal but emotional issues. Matters such as divorce are often prompted by triggers in the family such as domestic violence, loss of a loved one, hoarding, a special needs child, etc. You may want to consider finding support you need by way of outside resources and professional resources. These resources range from counselors, to educational institutions, to financial planners, and the like.

Ask your attorney for trusted referrals to local resources for assistance. In addition, researching professionals or businesses in your local chamber of commerce could be another valuable tool to help you locate the resources you require.

Are you ready for change or presently facing a change? There are many reasons why a life-changing decision like divorce, or establishing an estate plan, may feel imminent, but there's no clear understanding of how to get there. If you're wondering what to do next and learn the various steps of this process in Illinois, you're in luck as this book can help. Although this book provides a great deal of general information, it is not to be construed as legal advice and should be viewed as more of a road map. It is important to understand your rights and responsibilities and to be fully informed of your choices before taking any legal action. Empowering yourself with options is the key!

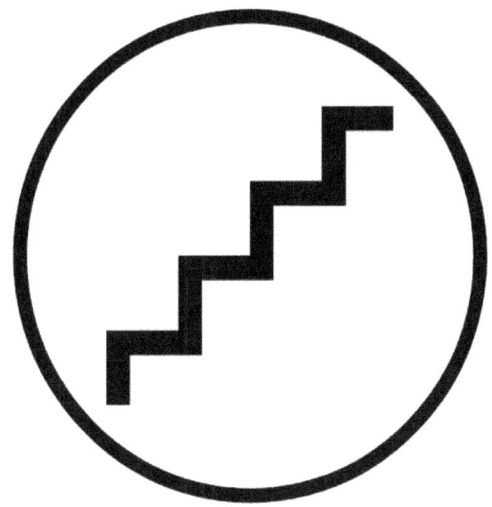

THE FIRST STEPS

Scheduling a Consultation and Choosing an Attorney

Where does one draw the line and say enough is enough? Not everyone is exactly eager to consult an attorney over their personal matters, however, there may come a time in your life when you may need to speak to a lawyer about your options. The decision to consult a family law attorney is not one that is taken lightly or decided overnight. This could be something that you have been contemplating for months or even years. You may have been finding yourself questioning the safety and wellbeing of your children, the fate of your relationship, the solidity of your finances, and the overall fear of the unknown.

You're not happy with your current situation and you are looking for a change. These questions could be constantly in the back of your mind and possibly keeping you up at night. While some couples try to work amicably to resolve their issues, others do not have a reasonable bone in their body, taking on the, "It's my way or the highway", kind of attitude. When you find that you have exhausted every avenue, and made every reasonable concession, it's time to take that step and reach out to a family law attorney to find out what your rights are and what options you legally have.

Beginning Your Search For An Attorney

So where do you start? How do you go about finding a good family law attorney? Finding an attorney is no different than finding a doctor, or a nanny, or even choosing a university to attend. You wouldn't hire a nanny that you don't feel comfortable with, doesn't listen to your directions, and has little to no experience to watch and care for your children, would you? You wouldn't pick a university without doing a thorough investigation of all they have to offer…would you? Well, selecting a family law attorney is no different. Whether you are contemplating divorce or potentially have a parenting battle on your hands, you will want to seek a competent attorney who will listen to your needs and that has years of experience.

When you first start your search, a good way of finding a lawyer is asking for a referral from within your personal network. Ask and see if a trusted family member, friend or another working professional has a referral for you. Hopefully, this will help point you in the right direction. It is recommended, before you even meet with an attorney, that you go online and check the reviews for that attorney or law firm that you are considering speaking to. Keep in mind that attorneys cannot respond to these reviews and sometimes the author of the review may not have been the attorney's own client. You should also be on the lookout to see if there are any cases against that attorney or firm for professional misconduct.

Obviously, that should raise a red flag and should be avoided. You should only seek out an attorney that exclusively handles family law cases because chances are your opponent will hire a lawyer that strictly practices family law and you do not want to find yourself at a disadvantage. After all this is your life and your future and you don't want to take mediocre legal advice from someone that doesn't have experience handling family law cases. When investigating attorneys, most firms and attorneys have a website and it is highly advantageous for you to review their website in detail and read the attorney's mini bios. This will tell you what the attorney's background is, what they focus on and how long they have been practicing that area of law.

Seek an attorney that has experience in your area of needs, especially if you have a complicated case. For example, if your case is involved with the Department of Child and Family Service, also known as "DCFS", you should seek an attorney that has years of experience helping family cases in that regard. If your marriage owns multiple businesses, properties, and financial assets you should seek an attorney that has handled high net-worth litigation cases and that will be able to recommend a good business evaluator to determine the business' worth.

You will want the best outcome of your case, your future and your children's future, that is why it is crucial to do your due diligence and make a thorough search before hiring your attorney. You will also want to seek a firm and/or an attorney that offers a free, no obligation consultation.

Preparing for Your Consultation

Most people are skeptical when taking things for free but when it comes to family law, a free consultation is both free of charge, as well as valuable. This consultation is usually an hour long, a face to face confidential interview with an attorney, where you present all of your case facts and information, ask questions, and in return get sound legal advice. The ultimate value of a consultation is knowledge and we all know, knowledge is power. You will gain power in understanding what your options and legal rights are and have the ability to make an educated decision with clarity for your future.

When scheduling a consultation, you will normally be asked some general questions, such as the county you reside in and the name of the other party. The law firm will have to do a conflict check, meaning a scan of their database to ensure they haven't already spoken to or previously represented any other involved parties. The meeting is one hundred percent confidential. A client's right to privacy is absolute and all attorney-client communications are protected. During the consultation, the attorney will open the dialogue by discussing such things as grounds for divorce and the possibility of reconciliation.

They will discuss with you your parental responsibilities, child support, parenting time, division of the marital estate, maintenance, business interests, inheritance, etc. The attorney will go over filing fees, as well as educating you on the general court process. During your consultation you are normally asked to complete a form or questionnaire and now would be the time to ask all those questions that have troubled you. Legal papers and documents that bear on your situation should also be brought to this meeting. The more information and details that you provide will give the attorney a better understanding of your situation and your case.

When the time comes for your consultation, you should ask a series of general questions to get familiar with the operation of his or her practice. How many attorneys work at the firm? Will the attorney you are meeting with be the one that solely works on your case if you decide to retain their services or, will a different attorney be assigned? Does the firm have a team approach?

While most of this information can usually be found on their website, it is still best to ask all of these questions in person so that you can better gauge the attorney and/or law firm. An extremely important question to ask is, how long have they been practicing family law? Experience is key when finding a knowledgeable attorney.

You need to know how long they have been practicing, how many cases they have handled, and how long they have been practicing in your area or county. How familiar is the attorney with the courthouse where your case will be handled? How well do they know the judges? If your case is assigned to a judge already, how has that judge ruled on matters similar to their situation in the past? Does that Judge tend to sway a certain way? If your opponent has an attorney, do they know that lawyer? Have they worked with that attorney on cases together in the past? Do you think that attorney will work with them to settle your case? Is there anything that would prevent them from working with the opposing attorney? These are good questions you need to ask when you are in the interviewing process to help you determine if they are a good fit for your case.

Another important question you need to ask is, what percentage of their cases have gone to Trial. You will want to find a lawyer that has a low percentage of Trial cases because you are looking for a good negotiator that will settle your case without a long expensive court battle. In the event that your case is greatly litigated and the judge sets your matter for Trial, you need to ask if the attorney is willing to go to Trial, if the case cannot be settled.

What is their retainer fee, hourly fees, billing format and are there different fees and rates for Trial? How often will you be billed? Do they set up payment plans? Going through this process can be costly and you should have a clear understanding about how the attorney's billing system works. You will also want to make sure you provide the attorney all of the case facts and the likelihood of you and your spouse coming to an agreement on all matters in order for the attorney to predict the longevity of the case. However, no attorney can truly predict what the final cost or time frame of a case will be as it is nearly impossible to predict how the opposing party will act, react, and how the negotiations will unfold. The only thing that an attorney can help control is their client's own actions.

Divorce is a rollercoaster ride and family law attorneys understand the consequences and danger of decisions that are made out of spite. Any attorney you meet with should make you fully aware of all of all your rights, obligations, and options and they should respect your choices while also safeguarding your best interests. The best family law attorneys understand that this may be the most emotionally terrifying time of your life and they should never leave you in the dark looking for answers. This is why two-way communication is of utmost importance.

They should be able to effectively communicate with you in a way that you can fully understand. When you decide to move forward with a particular attorney or law firm, they should be able to provide you with quick, responsive service and respond in some way to emails and phone calls within at most 24 to 48 business hours. Some clients may have needs outside of normal business hours so it is always good to know if the attorney you are choosing provides off-hour communication on the weekends for when you may potentially need it most. Ask what the best method is to communicate with them. What is the best form of communication and the most cost-effective way to communicate? You need to know exactly how you are going to communicate with the attorney that will be representing you should you choose to retain their services.

A good family law attorney should hear your concerns, empower you with options and develop a case strategy that will get you from point A to point B. Divorce and all of its connected life changes can be nerve wracking but a good family law attorney will get you through it, using a holistic approach. Family law cases, unlike any other area of law, have an intimate and emotional nature and your attorney or law firm will play a unique role in your life as you start on this new journey. They should be attentive to detail, caring and recognize the deeply personal nature of your case.

A solid understanding of the negotiating points in your case and attention to emotional balance is the winning combination for change. Divorce affects all areas of your life and a good attorney should be able to provide you with various resources such as counseling, financial planners, divorce coaches, estate attorneys etc. for specialized advice to help you along your journey. Your attorney should not only be able to help negotiate difficult legal situations but navigate you through them as well.

About the Divorce Process

Everyone knows that going through a divorce can be complicated and expensive. Everything you once had together as a family, now must be divided. You have to discuss and divide your home, all of your belongings, your time with your children, and of course, money. If a couple is able to communicate effectively and come to an agreement on these matters, less time and money will be spent on court and attorney's fees. There are five issues when it comes to filing for divorce that must be addressed and have in writing no matter if you think it is a non-issue or not. During the consultation, the attorney will go over the five main issues of divorce as well as the process. The main issues consist of grounds for divorce, the allocation of parental responsibilities and parenting time, child support, maintenance, and property plus debt.

Grounds for divorce is what is the cause for ending your marriage. In the past, if you decided to file for divorce you had to state to the court why you are entitled to be divorced based upon the grounds set forth in the law. In 2016, Illinois eliminated grounds and now it is a no-fault state.

If you have children from the marriage, the attorney will address with you the allocation of parental responsibilities and parenting time. Under the Illinois Marriage and Dissolution of Marriage Act, if the two of you do not come to an agreement, a court will determine the responsibilities of the parents. Parental responsibilities controls who has the significant decision making of the children's or child's education, healthcare, religion, and extracurricular activities. This also applies to couples who are not married or do not have a relationship with the other parent. The attorney will discuss with you what the current situation with your child or children is and what your ideal plan would be going forward. They will also discuss parenting time, formally known as visitation, which determines the schedule that is created for when a parent has time with their child including all holidays. Regular parenting is usually based around the parent's work schedule and who is available to care for the children. While holidays may be divided between even and odd years.

Along with parenting time and responsibilities comes the topic of child support. If provided enough financial information and income of both parties, an attorney should be able to run some soft calculations at the consultation to give you an idea how much each parent will have to contribute to the economic support of their children. Similarly, this will also be done when calculating maintenance, formerly known as alimony or spousal support. Maintenance is widely based on spousal income. Whoever the breadwinner of the marriage is, will be paying their ex-spouse maintenance in order for them to support themselves going forward. The duration of how long you have to pay maintenance is based on the duration of the marriage.

When dividing property, debt, and all financial assets, anything that either party owned prior to the marriage is considered premarital and all property, debt, and assets that came throughout the marriage is marital. During the consultation, the attorney will ask and go over with you all of the properties, financial accounts, debts, inheritances, retirement accounts, businesses, etc. In a lot of marriages one spouse controls the parties' finances. If this is not you, before you meet with an attorney you should try to gather as much information regarding your finances prior to meeting with an attorney. The attorney will take all of the collected information and develop a case strategy that best fits your needs, rights and wishes.

Each attorney or law firm that you meet with will offer you a different strategy for your case. You should make every effort to interview at least two to three attorneys or law firms before deciding on which one will represent you. It is your responsibility to retain a competent attorney who is not only good at his or her job but one whose personality and outlook are compatible with yours. You will be spending a lot of time together making life changing decisions. Choose an attorney that you can carry a good working relationship with that can explain your options, rights and responsibilities in a clear competent manner and will advocate for you.

Divorce May Not Be the Answer

Now, when you are meeting with an attorney to get legal advice on your relationship, it does not mean that the marriage is over and that you need immediate representation. Sometimes you just need to speak to an attorney about your situation because you need guidance and need to know what your legal rights and options are. What if you're not ready for divorce or ready to retain an attorney at all? That is completely okay. Utilize the free consultation and gather as much information and legal advice as possible. A good lawyer will help identify with you, all of the issues that your marriage has and will also help direct you where the marriage could use improvement if there is a possibility for reconciliation. You can speak to an attorney without your spouse ever knowing as it all remains confidential. An attorney may actually turn you away themselves, if there are other options and avenues for you to try first before you decide that divorce is the answer. Some couples may still love each other dearly but there are other strains on their relationship that are taking a hefty or deadly toll on the relationship.

A major reason for divorce between couples is financial issues. More often than not, when couples have financial hardship the weight that it carries over the relationship can be burdensome and threatening. After meeting with an experienced attorney, they may direct you to a financial planner and/or a marriage counselor if they believe this could help improve the parties' marriage. If the other spouse has an addiction problem whether it be gambling, a shopping addiction, or drug or alcohol related, there are professionals that can help and the most caring family law attorneys will provide you with good referrals so that they can seek the help or treatment that your spouse or family needs. Marriage is sacred and couples shouldn't jump to divorce when things get tough. Remember, you once took a vow together to love each other for better, for worse, for richer, for poorer, in sickness and in health, to love and to cherish, till death do you part. Unless you simply are no longer in love with your partner anymore, you should do everything in your power to make the marriage work. And when all else fails then it may be time to start the divorce process.

Now just to be clear, just because you decide to retain an attorney doesn't necessarily mean that you have to file for divorce right away either. Sometimes it is good to have an attorney in your corner to ensure that you are legally doing everything in the correct manner and to develop case strategy. This also applies to those that are not married but have children together. The attorney can draft letters and settlement proposals using specific legal terms on your behalf before filing. In the event you do need to move forward and file you are already ahead of the game if you have legal counsel. Your spouse may also choose to not hire an attorney at all. Rest assured the case can still settle amicably using your attorney to draft, file and enter court orders on your behalf so long as the other spouse files his or her own appearance with the court. When filing your own appearance with the court, that means you represent yourself as a Pro Se litigant and you make your own arguments without the use of an attorney. This is a very cost-effective option to proceed with divorce and usually occurs with short marriages with little assets.

You may also decide that you are ready to move forward and to retain an attorney but you do not have the financial means to retain them at that current point in time. Be straightforward with the attorney you would like to move forward with and let them know what your ideal plan is. If you need a few weeks, a few months or a year to get all of your ducks in a row and come up with the funds for the retainer fee that is completely fine too. Everyone needs to take the process at their own pace and if you spend time gathering all of the financial documents before you retain them then there will be a less time-consuming discovery process. You should take some time to weigh all of your options. Every attorney that you meet with will have a different background, knowledge, experience and fees. Go with your gut and choose the attorney that best fits you and your needs.

HOLISTIC OPTIONS FOR FAMILY LAW AND ESTATE PLANNING

Family law touches on all relationships from divorce, to child custody, to adoption and to orders of protection. When it comes to divorce specifically, divorce affects all areas of your life. Not only are you ending your marriage with your spouse, but you are splitting up a family and potentially affecting your relationship with your children, the friendships associated with the marriage, in-law relationships, your living situation, property, financials, the list can go on and on. All of these major life changes can be overwhelming and may be hard to bear alone. Having an attorney that has a holistic approach to family law is of utmost importance. Everyone has unique family dynamics, values, and are on their own emotional rollercoaster. You have to look at the big picture especially when it comes to divorce. That is why having a holistic approach to your case is crucial to your divorce journey and your journey moving forward after divorce.

So, what does holistic mean? Most people when they hear the word holistic are familiar with the concept of holistic medicine. Holistic medicine is a form of healing that considers the whole person and the circumstances surrounding them, not just specific parts of the body. In the quest for optimal health and wellness, a holistic doctor, which also may be known as a Naturopathic doctor or physician, will examine a patient and provide multiple forms of health care from conventional medication to alternative therapies to nutritional information. They will evaluate both subjective and objective information necessary to uncover a patient's potential susceptibilities to future disease. A holistic doctor's ultimate goal is to heal and balance the patients mind, body, and spirit for the long term.

Holistic treatment means "taking into account mental and social factors, rather than just the symptoms of the disease"— so holistic mental health isn't merely an attempt to alleviate the fatigue, anger and anxiety that often come along with mental and emotional struggles, but to address the roots of the disorders. "Holistic spirituality is about fully acknowledging and encompassing every aspect of life, including our shadows, denials and ultimately death. And, most of all, it involves embracing the shadow side of spirituality itself, including God.

Holistic health doesn't solely look at the physical body. Holistic health combines five aspects of health, including physical, emotional, social, spiritual, and intellectual. When combined, these five areas enable a person to live their life to its happiest and fullest.

Generally, holistic means relating to the idea that things should be looked at as an entire whole rather than dealing with a specific part or component of a larger system. An attorney that has a holistic approach to family law will have the ability to look at the entire family dynamic or situation.

They understand the various components that make up a family and have the knowledge, sensitivity and compassion to successfully navigate you through your family law matter. Most families struggle with co-parenting challenges and conflicts, and they only become amplified when a family goes through a major transition such as divorce, remarriage or separation.

A lawyer with a holistic approach will not only advise you on your legal rights but will provide healthy options and sustainable solutions for your case. They will also have the ability to provide you with professional referrals and resources. Whether that be a counselor, divorce coach, real estate agent, or financial advisor, their goal is to provide you with the assistance that you need for you to continue to move forward with your life both during and after the divorce process.

Holistic law is a style of practice. It is not an area of law like divorce; however, it is a detailed client centered approach to the legal practice. Holistic lawyers, like traditional lawyers, provide legal advice and legal information about the specific legal problem. But holistic lawyers provide an additional service by helping clients focus on the many ways in which this legal problem can be solved by looking at health, economic, and therapeutic resources.

A holistic approach during a divorce means that you will need to consult with a financial planner, make an estate plan, and reconnect/connect with your religious leader.

But it all starts with the client. Similar to a holistic doctor, an attorney with a holistic approach knows the importance of their client's overall personal wellbeing. Whether you are going through a divorce or a child custody dispute, or are experiencing domestic violence, it affects a person inside and out. During what could be a time of great uncertainty, it can absolutely take a toll on your mental health. You may find yourself in a state of depression, frustration and worry.

Your attorney will listen to you and guide you, and may refer you to a counselor, therapist, or psychologist if you are not already speaking to one. You will need to gain control of your state of mind in order to make hard decisions and negotiations that will affect you and your children's life going forward.

When you enter the realm of family law, you are seeking change in some way, shape or form. Change for anyone, negative or positive, you must possess sufficient energy for the adaptation process to unfold. The capacity to adapt to change involves the mental, emotional, and physical means to incorporate new behaviors and mindsets. You must be open to change in order to move forward with your life and the lives of your children.

When you decide to empower yourself with options and make the decision to change your life, it can be a frightening process, and you will need some assistance to come out of this stronger and better than ever before.

Self-Care During the Divorce Process

When going through the process of divorce, getting out of bed each morning can be, for some, a daunting task. To maintain a healthy lifestyle, it is essential for one to sleep eight hours a night, eat at least three nutritious meals a day, and drink 8 glasses of water daily as well as fit in daily exercise. As simple as that may sound, completing that on a day-to-day basis can be overwhelmingly difficult for many and not many adults can accomplish that on a regular basis, divorce or not. When you actually think about it, humans have a lot of upkeep. We have to constantly groom ourselves, i.e. brush your teeth, wash your face, shower, style your hair, shave, etc. We have to constantly hydrate and feed ourselves and many struggle with consuming healthy meal choices that have the nutrients our body needs. You have to constantly grocery shop, clean, do laundry, exercise, sleep, etc. And if you have children, you have to make sure their basic daily needs are met as well as get them to and from school, activities and other appointments.

Mind, body and soul are important to maintain during the divorce process. Get back in touch with your spirit, whatever that may be. Whether it is with church, a support group, a pastor, get that spirit back. Mental self-care will assist you to think clearer, focus, concentrate, manage time, plan, make decisions and remember. For your mental care, avoid negative people, rethink your new obligations, don't be self-critical, and go out on a limb and do something different.

If divorce is taking a toll on your mental health and you find yourself in a depressed state of mind, getting out of bed is just the first challenge. You could be sleeping too little or too much, stress eating anything and everything, or have no appetite to eat at all. Everyone handles stress, depression and change differently, but every single person needs to take responsibility and strive for their basic care needs in order to get healthy or maintain their health. Make goals for yourself to at least go for a walk a day, fresh air and sunshine will do wonders. If the weather does not permit, do some indoor stretching and exercises to maintain good health. Eat nutritious meals containing lots of vegetables and fruit and drink water constantly above everything else. These basic steps may seem simple for some but hard for others. It is alright to cry, just take one day at a time. Take baby steps towards these goals and you will get there.

Self-care is often overlooked while this struggling process is going on. It is ok to be vulnerable, give yourself a break, you are human. You are encouraged to join a support group, surround yourself with friends and loved ones, exercise, and enjoy life. Have you tried yoga or meditation? It may not be a bad time to start a journal, write letters, or write a book. Give yourself permission to change your hair color or length. With daily positive affirmations and a reduction of stress (as much as you can), you can be well on your way to reinventing a new you after the storm.

Tips for Breaking the Divorce to Children

Divorce is an ending of your marriage, and it could be a very complex and difficult process. It is often an overwhelming and emotionally devastating experience. Some of the tips listed will help the parties and will enable them to assist the children through this process. First and foremost, let your children know it is not their fault. While divorce almost always feels like it is someone's fault, it is typically just the path two people's lives take.

If you encourage kids to share their feelings, this will let them express what they are feeling inside. Whether it is anger, sadness or confusion, expressing these feelings will make them feel free. You may want to inform the spouse of some news or you may be feeling that you want to gather some information to or from one party to another. Don't use kids as messengers to go between parents. This will make them simply feel bad. You have to discuss a remedy that will not involve the kids. This will relate to not using the kids as pawns. Do not make them feel bad going back and forth between parents.

Keep adult conversations, visible conflict, heated discussions and legal talk out of the child's ears and between adults. Minimize the disruptions to the daily routines. Keep the same flow to your daily schedules. Encourage counseling and attend counseling as individuals and together. Seek support from professionals, friends, family, clergy and others, not the children. Do not rely on the children for support. Utilize your own outlets as the children need their own separate outlets and support systems. Confine negativity and blame to private therapy sessions or conversations with friends and or family outside of the home. Even though you may not be together as a couple, keep both parents a positive part and stay involved in their lives. They will be able to depend on both of you and that will bring comfort and reassurance.

Talking to your kids about the decision to divorce or live separate can be devastating. Practice how you are going to report this news to the family and children. Try to have both parents at this conversation and keep your discussion simple and to the point. However, for older children, you may have to explain more and be prepared to answer specific questions. At this time, you can again continue to reassure children that you recognize and care about their feelings, let them know what they are feeling is alright.

You may not be ready for this but be prepared to see your children upset and emotional. It is important to let them express their fears. During this turbulent time, and at any stage, be prepared to answer a lot of questions from your children like, who will I live with, where will I go to school, will I see my friends again, and the list goes on.
Try to leave feelings of anger, blame or guilt out of the conversation. Do not become angry or upset during the conversation and fit the conversation to the child's age and maturity. At this point offer a lot of reassurance and provide as much information as possible. Try to be as truthful as you can. In the long run the children will find out anyway, one way or another. This will assist you in the long run with the children knowing they can trust you and look to you for assistance.

Children Coping After the Divorce

It is best to ensure privacy when you discuss divorce details and keep your interactions with the ex (or soon to be ex) as civil as you can and maintain this attitude when you interact with the children. This is an excellent coping skill, and the better you cope, the better it is for the children to model. When you go to exchange the children, this can be a difficult time and difficult transition. It will be tempting to spat and throw curve balls at each other. To make this easier, you have to be willing to change the visitation schedule, have peaceful transitions with child exchanges, when you say goodbye, say it with a wave and a smile and when the child comes home have a good welcome home -

do not concentrate on what they were doing at the ex's house. Coming together for the sake of the children and their long-term mental status is difficult to do, especially when you are in the moment. Think of the long-term picture.

During this stage and process there are signs and things to look for, to be on the alert that your child may be having difficulties. You should watch their behavior, watch for anger, sadness, and fears. Watch and discuss changes to behavior and trust your instincts and watch their routines. If you watch interactions, you will have a better handle on what may be going on as far as negative behaviors. Watch for behavioral changes in your children and signs of anxiety, sadness, mood swings, acting out, lack of sleep or appetite, and changes to social life.

Try not to argue, or have hostility such as screaming, fighting, arguing, and violence, verbal or physical, behaviors while going through this time. You can be an example at this juncture and stage of your lives. This will enable you and your children to navigate the different feelings you or they may be having. Children tend to keep things to themselves, and many people tend to think that divorce is prevalent, that it does not affect children, but how will the children respond to the divorce. Don't make your child feel torn. You do not want your child to favor one parent or relationship over the other and listen to your children and continue to explain - they deserve an explanation.

There are several books, videos, and tools that can be used in order to help families cope with divorce and separations. Books, videos, and other media outlets can be helpful to the parent, child, and therapist to utilize during the divorce process. Start these early on in the divorce process, if not immediately, with smaller children. This will give the children a chance to absorb things. This will give them time to sort things out on their own. They will need their own time to process.

A divorce is one of the most difficult transitions in life that anyone may go through, especially when both parties are experiencing anger or hurt and there are children involved. These tips can help ease the pain out of divorce and make the proceedings run smoother for a financially, emotionally, and physically improved outcome.

Remember to take care of yourself during the process. Take care of your financials, estate planning, and all other important matters that will be impacted by the change in your life. Look at the whole picture and not just the snapshot. Get educated and do research on how the divorce process works. Learn about divorce mediation- peaceful options and choose an experienced and competent professional to guide you. You have to take responsibility and actively participate in the divorce negations. Get emotional support and learn how to lower your emotional reactivity and to help you focus on the big picture.

YOU'VE BEEN SERVED

When the Petitioner files the underlying pleading on a matter, they are responsible for serving the opposing party with said documents. When filing the pleading with the court, a summons is filed on or about the same time. A summons is an official notice of your complaint/pleading. It is given to the opposing side/Respondent so that they know and are given the opportunity to defend themselves. This notification procedure is called service of process.

Once the Summons is filed with the Court, the Summons is valid for 30 days which means there are 30 days to have the Respondent served with the pleadings. Ill. Sup. Ct. R. 102(b). There are several ways to obtain service including a waiver of service, sheriff's service, or service by a private process server. Ill. Sup. Ct. R. 102(b), 735 Ill. Comp. Stat. Ann. 5/2-213(d) (LexisNexis through P.A. 101-631). The preferred way for most is a Waiver of Sheriff's Service. A Waiver of Sheriff's Service is when the Respondent waives being formally served and accepts the underlying pleading without formal service by sheriff or process server. Generally, the Petitioner notifies the Respondent of the filing so there are no surprises, but this is not required. Another way to serve a party is to have a member of your legal team reach out to Respondent and notify them and give them the option to come into the office to execute the Waiver of Sheriff's Service in person. If the Respondent does not consent to the waiver, service by sheriff or process server is the next plan. This Waiver is an option and cannot be forced if the Respondent does not cooperate.

Service by the sheriff is also an option; however, not always the best option depending on the case. If this route is taken, once the pleading is filed, all necessary documents will need to be delivered to the sheriff's office with an address for service, along with payment for same. The sheriff will then attempt to serve the Respondent within the 30-day timeframe. Sometimes this method is least preferred since the sheriff serves on their own time and the Petitioner or their attorney isn't notified when service is about to be attempted or directly after service is completed. Since every case is different, in our experience most clients like to be given a forewarning when service is about to be attempted. If that's the case, service by sheriff will not be the best option. There is a fee for this method, which is different from county to county, however, it is generally more cost efficient than using a special process server.

The last customary means of service on Respondent is by way of special process server. When the Respondent becomes uncooperative with the Waiver of Sheriff Service option, this method tends to be Plan B. This method allows a selection of a specific time of day or specific day of the week that is preferred for the service to be attempted as a private process server has more flexibility in service. Whether they need a service job done before the Respondent leaves for work at 6:00 a.m. or want them served when the children are not present.

Every process server is different, so be sure to talk with him or her about their rates and how many times they will attempt service before hiring them to do this. All counties allow a process server to be hired; however, in Cook County you will need to file a Motion for Appointment of Process Server before one can be used because Cook County has a population of more than 2,000,000. 735 Ill. Comp. Stat. Ann. 5/2-202(a) (LexisNexis through P.A. 101-631). Once the Judge approves said Motion, you then can go about using your process server.

For smaller County cases, a process server can be used at any time and no Motion needs to be filed for permission for this means of service. *Id.* The requirement of the Motion for Appointment of Process Server is governed by statute based upon the population of the county and therefore it will be updated as populations fluctuate. *Id.* If a service needs to occur outside the State of Illinois, a process server can still be located. 735 Ill. Comp. Stat. Ann. 5/2-208(a)-(b) (LexisNexis through P.A. 101-631). Whether we use a sheriff or special process server, the Respondent can be properly served the following ways:

- *By handing the Summons and underlying pleading to the Respondent personally at their residence or any preferred location; or*
- *By going to the Respondent's residence and giving the Summons and underlying pleading to someone who lives with the Respondent, who is at least 13 years or older.*

735 Ill. Comp. Stat. Ann. 5/2-203(a) (LexisNexis through P.A. 101-631).

Please note that the appropriate age for service may change from state to state. Further in Illinois, the person receiving documents has to be informed of the contents, and the person making service is also required to mail the document to the Respondent at their usual place of abode.

The first method is called personal service, because the Respondent themselves was served. The second method is called substitute or abode service. Rules vary from state to state, and you do not want your case to be thrown out because you did not actually get proper service on the Respondent or have them served by an approved individual.

If none of the service options can be completed in the 30-day timeframe and more time is needed, an Alias Summons will need to be filed before additional attempts at service can be done which incurs another fee. Ill. Sup. Ct. R. 103(a). An Alias Summons gives you an additional 30 days for service. This does not need to be filed right after your original Summons expires or 'goes stale', you can wait to file this until you're ready to complete your service again. Note that the longer you wait, the longer it will take to get movement on your case. Once you receive the file stamped copy of your Alias Summons, you can go about your service as mentioned above. Sometimes you need to get permission from the Court to issue an Alias.

In some cases, locating the Respondent could be impossible which means getting them served is just not an option. Even though you may know this, you still need to show the courts all your attempts at service by sheriff and/or process server.

The last means of service is service by publication which means that notice is published in a newspaper in the area where the Summons and underlying pleading was filed. 735 Ill. Comp. Stat. Ann. 5/2-206(a) (LexisNexis through P.A. 101-631). In order to have such notice published in a newspaper, you will need to file a Motion for Leave to Serve by Publication and an Affidavit for Service by Publication before being allowed to give service through the newspaper; all counties work differently so make sure you or your attorney are looking up the rules/law for same. *Id.* Generally, this requires you to show the court the efforts you have made in order to obtain the Respondent's whereabouts. *Id.* Make note that even though the Petitioner cannot get the Respondent properly served, does not mean they will get everything they asked for in their underlying Petition. For example, you might jump through some hoops to be able to get divorced; however, getting a judgment against the opposing side for monies owed such as child support or maintenance is unlikely, as there are certain things that cannot be dealt with in a Judgment for Dissolution of Marriage if the Respondent is defaulted for failure to appear. 750 Ill. Comp. Stat. Ann. 5/405 (LexisNexis through P.A. 101-631).

After Respondent has been properly served with the documents, proof of service will need to be filed with the court, whether a Waiver of Sheriff's Service, Sheriff's sworn statement on the Summons or Affidavit of Special Process Server. Ill. Sup. Ct. R. 102(d). After this step is completed, Respondent then has 30 days to file their Answer to the pleading and/or file their Appearance on the matter as an unrepresented litigant or hire an attorney. Ill. Sup. Ct. R. 101(d). Usually the first 30 days of initially filing your underlying pleading is getting the opposing side served with all the necessary documents. Now that the opposing side has been served, you can move forward with your case.

Just because the opposing side has been served with the underlying pleadings, does not mean you may not need service in the future. You can still hire a process server throughout the litigation of your case. For instance, say you served a witness a Subpoena for Appearance in Court and they 'rejected' your certified mail and it was returned to you. Technically your Subpoena was not served, so you need to go about service on this another way, the process server way. Or let's say, the opposing side was served the initial documents; however, they chose not to file their appearance on the case and you want to file a Motion with the court. More than likely your first attempt can be done by email and/or mail; however, once you appear before the court, the Judge may require you to serve the new pleadings to the opposing side to ensure they received your documents before they will rule on your Motion. This is not unusual and can happen. If the Respondent hires an attorney or the party files an unrepresented litigant appearance, you will more than likely not need to hire a process server in the future to have them served. Just remember, as previously stated, that you are checking your counties local rules on whether personal or substitute service will be accepted.

OVERVIEW OF THE LEGAL PROCESS

Starting a divorce proceeding feels like beginning any difficult task, you simply want it to be over as quickly as possible. Dissolving a marriage rarely happens quickly. With so much to research, it can be very overwhelming for most. Family law cases have a particularly intimate and emotional nature.

The divorce process is as unique as your marriage. You need an experienced attorney near you to guide you, inform you, and advocate for you. Get help throughout all the steps of the divorce process by hiring an attorney that focuses on family law.

Family law attorneys help clients negotiate difficult situations and decisions, and ultimately move forward with reformed relationships. They can help you break down the steps and make a plan for the future. People in need deserve a family law attorney who recognizes the deeply personal nature of their cases.

As the parties move through a process of separation there are consistent steps to follow. Taking a step-by-step approach makes the process more manageable.

The General Process

No two cases are alike. Each case and parties are unique. A major mistake people make is to believe that their case will follow a direct pattern of their neighbor's case. While there are general operating procedures placing the actors and facts into the mix make each situation different.

Unexpected delays like a contested case involving children in front of you may have an impact on the timing of your case. The best way to describe the process is that it is like a chess game meaning that depending on where party A moves a piece, party B will then decide what to do.

That being said, some general steps are as follows.

Preparing to File

Make the decision on how you'll proceed into the legal process of filing for divorce. You may wish to handle the divorce process on your own or receive assistance from a mediator or family law attorney. Filing a petition for divorce is a serious action that has legal and personal consequences, so take time to prepare for those changes, as well. You may have to consider new living arrangements, schedules or new modes of communication. It helps to have plans in place, or at a minimum, giving it some forethought.

Filing

You must file in the jurisdiction where you live. 750 Ill. Comp. Stat. Ann. 5/401(a) (LexisNexis through P.A. 101-631). There are certain forms that must be filed. There are notifications that must be done. You will enter a phase of negotiations on matters such as financial and personal assets, determine spousal support, child support, parenting and allocation of parental responsibilities. Finding mutual agreements on these issues can be a lengthy process, though the duration is typically determined by the parties themselves and their attitude about working in cooperation toward finalization.

Settlement and Moving Forward

After making an agreement on the terms you must appear before a judge and ask for the contract to be affirmed and the divorce granted. The judge can ask questions, call witnesses, and then suggest or order changes in the divorce agreement. If the parties are truly not able to reach an agreement, the Judge will ultimately set the case for trial and make the decisions for the parties.

Once all elements of the agreement are settled and approved by the court, the petition of dissolution of marriage is granted by the court. However, that's not where the divorce process ends.

The parties are now obligated to the terms of the divorce agreement and must take actions to fulfill them.

One person can ask the court for a divorce, without permission from the other spouse. One of the spouses must have been a resident of Illinois for 90 days before filing the petition for dissolution of marriage. 750 Ill. Comp. Stat. Ann 5/401(a) (LexisNexis through P.A. 101-631). The parties may request a divorce based upon the ground of irreconcilable differences. Illinois is a "no fault" state, meaning that the state has rejected the concept of divorce based upon fault.

Some commons forms used in divorce cases are:
- Petition for Dissolution asks the court for a divorce and gives information needed to begin a divorce case:
- Certificate of Dissolution of Marriage – lists information about your case that is sent to the Illinois Department of Public Health after your divorce is final;
- Summons-tells your spouse that you are asking the court for a divorce;

- Appearance-completed by your spouse to tell the court that they do not need to receive a Summons or is completed by your spouse after being served with a Summons;
- Parenting Plan: lists who is responsible for decision making for the children and a schedule for when the children are with you and when they are with the other parent;
- Certificate of Agreement-used if you and your spouse have agreed on what will be in the Judgment and Parenting Plan;
- Qualified Domestic Relations Order (QDRO): is used to divide a pension or retirement plan. You will need this if a Judge orders that a QDRO be prepared.

Getting the Case Before the Court

A Petition for Dissolution of Marriage is the initial filing in a dissolution proceeding. This is the document in which you will be asking for a Judgment of Dissolution from the Court (final judgment or decree). It requests that the court make decisions involving the care, allocation of decision-making, and control of the parties' minor child (ren), the division of the real and personal property, division of the debt and obligations of the parties and any other additional matters the parties need resolved. The party filing for the divorce is referred to as the Petitioner. The other party is referred to as the Respondent. The Petition needs to outline several points. You must incorporate all information regarding the parties, the marriage, any children, assets, and debts in order to inform the court as much as possible. The more information that you provided to the court the easier it will be able to reach an equitable decision.

The first portion of the Petition should address where the Petition will be filed and that it is the proper venue. All proceedings should be held in the county where the Petitioner or Respondent resides. 750 Ill. Comp. Stat. Ann. 5/104 (LexisNexis through P.A. 101-631).

The Petition will outline basic background information of the parties i.e. age, address, date of marriage, and occupation. 750 Ill. Comp. Stat. Ann. 5/403(a)(1)-(6) (LexisNexis through P.A. 101-631). This will help the court get to know the parties. The address can help with jurisdiction and also will determine where the Respondent will be served. It is required in the Petition for Dissolution of Marriage in Illinois that both parties are residents of the state of Illinois and that they have been doing so in excess of ninety (90) days. 750 Ill. Comp. Stat. Ann. 5/401(a) (LexisNexis through P.A. 101-631). Residency means to live in a locality making it a fixed and permanent home.

Next, you need to state in the Petition for Dissolution of Marriage the grounds for which a party is seeking the dissolution. *Id.* In Illinois the only grounds for divorce is irreconcilable differences. *Id.* All divorces are granted because of irreconcilable differences. Irreconcilable differences means you and your spouse do not get along anymore and you do not want to be married. *Id.* Those irreconcilable differences must have caused an irretrievable breakdown of the marriage. *Id.* Meaning that those differences have caused such a problem between the two spouses, that there is no chance that the differences can ever be resolved.

If the parties have children, they should be listed in the Petition for Dissolution of Marriage, along with their ages. 750 Ill. Comp. Stat. Ann. 5/403(a)(4) (LexisNexis through P.A. 101-631). It is also important to list in the Petition whether the wife is or is not pregnant at the time of the filing. *Id.* All children should be listed regardless of whether they were born of the parties or adopted by them. *Id.* The Petition should make a specific request regarding allocation of the minor child (ren) and parenting time with the child (ren) of the non-custodial parent. 750 Ill. Comp. Stat. Ann. 5/403(a)(5) (LexisNexis through P.A. 101-631). The court can decide decision-making, parenting time and support only for the children listed in your Petition for Dissolution.

The Petition will also address the matter of marital property and the equitable division of that property. 750 Ill. Comp. Stat. Ann. 5/403(a)(6) (LexisNexis through P.A. 101-631). The parties will generally have a marital residence, joint bank accounts, retirement accounts, pensions, automobiles, furniture and other personal property that will need to be divided upon the dissolution of the marriage. The Petition will not get into specific assets, rather it will generally state that there are assets to be divided between the parties. *Id.* The division of said marital property will later be incorporated into a Marital Settlement Agreement which will be incorporated into the Judgment for Dissolution and filed with the court.

The Petition should mention marital debts and the allocation of payment of debts. *Id.* The Petition will merely mention that there is marital debt that needs to be addressed between the parties and a Marital Settlement Agreement is where the specific division will occur.

The Petition should mention if you are seeking maintenance (formerly known as alimony). *Id.* Maintenance is money paid from one spouse to the other on a regular basis. Maintenance is based on each spouse's income and the duration is determined by the length of the marriage. To determine the calculation of the same, see the chapter entitled Maintenance and Child Support.

Finally, it should include language to claim dissipation. *Id.* Dissipation occurs when one spouse destroys, wastes, or hides property or money while the marriage is undergoing an irretrievable breakdown. If you fear that your spouse may have or may try to hide or transfer assets to deny you your fair share you must enter the language about dissipation. It could protect you from debt that your spouse may recklessly run up.

The Petition for Dissolution of Marriage is only the first step in a divorce proceeding. The Respondent/spouse must be personally served with the Petition for Dissolution of Marriage. Service is simply the process of providing your spouse with copies of the divorce documents that have been filed in the case. Illinois law allows the filing spouse to "serve" the other spouse by the sheriff's office or a private process server. When filing your Petition for Dissolution you will also file a Summons. A Summons is an official notice of a complaint being filed. Then, you will have the summons and the Petition for Dissolution of Marriage served on the other party. Every county has specific rules regarding service. You have the option to have the Sheriff, Private Process Server or you can even make arrangements for the other party to pick up the document(s) themselves from your attorney's office and have them sign a Waiver of Sheriff's Service. The person who is filing for divorce cannot simply hand the documents to their spouse, this is not considered proper service. If you choose to use a Special Process Server to serve your spouse, some counties require that a Motion/Order for Special Process server be filed. In

Illinois, the law requires appointment of a process server in counties with a population of 2,000,000 or more. 735 Ill. Comp. Stat. Ann. 5/2-202(a) (LexisNexis through P.A. 101-631). This realistically means that only in Cook County must you appoint a process server. In Cook County, a judge must issue an order appointing the server before they can serve the opposing party. Once service to your spouse has been made you must file the documents with the court stating this has been completed. Ill. Sup. Ct. R. 102(d). If a person does not properly serve the documents the divorce can be dismissed. Once a summons is property served on the other party, then the parties will move forward and go to court to present their case. A Summons is valid for 30 days, this means that you are giving the other side 30 days to file an appearance. Ill. Sup. Ct. R. 101(d). If the person is not able to be served, the person who filed the petition must now file and serve an alias summons. Ill. Sup. Ct. R. 103(a). This is just a second summons. The service of this summons is just like the original summons. A person cannot move forward with their case until the opposing party is served. The cost for serving a summons will vary depending on how you serve the summons.

The Respondent/spouse must file an appearance with the court, either as pro se (representing oneself), or through an attorney. Often, an individual representing oneself is now referred to as a self-represented litigant.

The Respondent (or the respondent's attorney) must file a document known as answer or response in which they will admit or deny any allegations stated in the Petition for Dissolution of Marriage.

The court may find that the respondent is in default and the petitioner may be awarded a divorce if the respondent does not file an appearance or an answer. 735 Ill. Comp. Stat. Ann. 5/2-1301(d) (LexisNexis through P.A. 101-631). The extent of the authority of the Court in the event of a Default Judgment varies and should be addressed by your attorney.

If you are the Respondent in a divorce proceeding, you should always file a Counter-Petition for Dissolution of Marriage. This is similar to the Petition for Dissolution of Marriage in that you are also asking the court to hear your case and grant you a divorce. The Counter-Petition for Dissolution of Marriage should be filed at the time of filing the Appearance and Answer/Response to the Petition for Dissolution of Marriage. Once you file your Counter-Petition you are known as the Respondent/Counter-Petitioner. The Petitioner must respond to the Counter-Petition for Dissolution of Marriage either by admitting or denying the facts listed. If no response is filed, the court will assume that the Petitioner agrees with all of the factual claims being made. It is important to file a Counter-Petition of Marriage because you are making your own requests of the court. By filing the Counter-Petition this is a safeguard in a sense that you will be permitted to claim additional facts and request your own relief from the court. It also ensures that the Petitioner does not voluntarily dismiss or withdraw their petition. Even if the Petitioner voluntarily dismisses their petition, the Respondent can then move forward with their Counter-Petition without having to go through the process of re-filing a new Petition. There is a filing fee for filing an Appearance and Counter-Petition for Dissolution of Marriage. If no counter petition is filed and the underlying Petition is dismissed, the case will have to be re-filed changing the date of filing and jeopardizing the time from which maintenance is calculated (maintenance calculated from date of marriage until filing of Petition for Dissolution of Marriage).

Once you have filled out all the required forms for your particular county, you'll need to file them with the clerk of the court. Each county has their own requirements as to what forms must be filed. All documents must be electronically filed. Be prepared to pay your filing fee when you submit your documents. Costs vary, depending on your county. The clerk will file-stamp the documents with the case number which you will use during the pendency of your divorce and for any post-decree issues. The original copy will remain at the courthouse. You can find forms on the county clerk's websites. If you cannot afford to pay the fees, you can ask the court to file for free. Ill. Sup. Ct. R. 298. Fill out the Application for Waiver of Court Fees to ask the court for a fee waiver.

Once all of the initial court documents and pleadings are filed, the case is at issue and the Court as well the parties can proceed with the next steps. This stage of the litigation can proceed at different speeds but is really the first hurdle to cross.

Temporary Relief

Temporary relief is defined as temporary orders regarding what has been referred to as child custody and visitation, (now called Allocation of Parenting Time and Parental Responsibilities), as well as child support and maintenance. Within this broad term of temporary relief there are different types, those being: custody, support, or maintenance. 750 Ill. Comp. Stat. Ann. 5/501(a)(1), (3) (LexisNexis through P.A. 101-631). You are allowed to ask for temporary relief in situations like divorce proceedings, paternity proceedings, and proceedings to modify maintenance, child support, or custody. The temporary relief continues until the end of the case unless the court modifies the relief. 750 Ill. Comp. Stat. Ann. 5/501(d)(2)-(3) (LexisNexis through P.A. 101-631). A Petition for Temporary Relief can be filed at any stage during the divorce process, but it is typically filed in the beginning. A party might seek temporary relief to provide for the children of the marriage and the household expenses. Also, if one party does not work (stay at home mom or wife for example), a temporary relief pleading can provide for personal expenses of the non-working party. The "status quo" of the financial resources of both parties and the family should stay intact during a divorce proceeding.

Temporary issues regarding parenting time and decision-making comes down to what is in the best interest of the child. 750 Ill. Comp. Stat. Ann. 5/603.5(a) (LexisNexis through P.A. 101-631). During the requested hearing both parties are able to present evidence. According to 750 ILCS 5/602.10, "All parents, within 120 days after service or filing of any petition for allocation of parental responsibilities, must file with the court, either jointly or separately, a proposed parenting plan. The time period for filing a parenting plan may be extended by the court for good cause shown. If no appearance has been filed by the respondent, no parenting plan is required unless ordered by the court." 750 Ill. Comp. Stat. Ann. 5/602.10(a) (LexisNexis through P.A. 101-631).

A motion requesting temporary maintenance as a form of temporary relief is accompanied by an affidavit with the facts for the relief that is being requested. 750 Ill. Comp. Stat. Ann. 5/501(a)(1) (LexisNexis through P.A. 101-631). This is when the financial affidavit comes into play. The Financial Affidavit must be completed and exchanged between the parties and provided to the Judge before any maintenance or child support hearing can proceed. Support calculations are submitted to the court to help guide the Judge's decision or the parties' agreement for temporary support. This evidence includes things such as tax returns, paycheck stubs, and bank statements. 750 Ill. Comp. Stat. Ann. 5/501(a)(1) (LexisNexis through P.A. 101-631). The court will consider different factors. Some factors when determining temporary maintenance include:

- The income of both parties
- The property of both parties
- Any impairment on the ability to seek employment
- The duration of the marriage
- The standard of living during the marriage

750 Ill. Comp. Stat. Ann. 5/505(a) (LexisNexis through P.A. 101-631).

After considering these the court will award maintenance in an amount they see fit.

Temporary child support is the same basis as final child support. Child support is based on the incomes of both parties along with the parenting time schedule. 750 Ill. Comp. Stat. Ann. 5/501(a) (LexisNexis through P.A. 101-631). Some factors that are considered are the number of overnights per year for the non-residential parent. If each of the parents is responsible for the child for at least 146 overnight stays per year, Illinois law considers this a "shared parenting situation." 750 Ill. Comp. Stat. Ann. 5/505(a)(3.8) (LexisNexis through P.A. 101-631). Illinois child support is calculated differently in "shared parenting situations" than in non-shared parenting situations. In shared-parenting situations, the total amount of child support for which the parents are responsible is increased by a factor of 50% and the amount of time each parent spends with the child is factored into the calculation of each parent's obligation. *Id.* In shared-parenting situations, the more time the obligor parent spends with the child, the less he or she will be required to pay in child support. See the chapter on calculating support for further explanation on the child support calculation.

Similar to temporary orders for child support and maintenance, the Court also has the discretion to award a litigant some amount of attorneys' fees, upon the presentment of a proper petition and a hearing after the exchange of financial information. 750 Ill. Comp. Stat. Ann. 5/501(c-1) (LexisNexis through P.A. 101-631). Additionally, the Court has the power to force the sale of a marital asset, such as a house. 750 Ill. Comp. Stat. Ann. 5/501(a)(3) (LexisNexis through P.A. 101-631). Under the statute, 750 ILCS 5/501, the Court tries to help the divorcing parties preserve their marital estate during the divorce. Yes, even when one spouse just wants to get divorced amicably and the other wants to burn it down. The Court can preserve resources by ordering the sale of the marital residence, during the divorce process. *Id.* You can imagine how in some cases the spouse with the higher earning power may plan to leave the other spouse penniless, but the Court can forbid wasting all the money paying an expensive mortgage on a house that neither can afford separately.

A temporary restraining order (TRO) is a legal document issued by the court requiring someone to do, not do, or stop doing something. Temporary restraining orders are injunctions lasting for ten days or less and are usually granted without notice to the opposing party. 735 Ill. Comp. Stat. Ann. 5/11-101 (LexisNexis through P.A. 101-631). Illinois divorce law states "the court may issue a temporary restraining order without requiring notice to the other party only if it finds, on the basis of the moving affidavit or other evidence that irreparable injury will result to the moving party if no order issued until the time for responding has elapsed." 750 Ill. Comp. Stat. Ann. 5/501(a)(2) (LexisNexis through P.A. 101-631). When a temporary restraining order is granted without notice it should be:

- Indorsed with the date and the hour of signing
- Shall be filed in the clerk's office
- Shall define the injury and state why the order was granted without notice
- Shall expire by its terms within such time after signing the order
- Not exceed 10 days

735 Ill. Comp. Stat. Ann. 5/11-101 (LexisNexis through P.A. 101-631).

Typically, courts will use a 2-part test to determine whether to issue a temporary restraining order:

1. If it clearly appears from specific facts shown by an affidavit or by verified complaint that immediate and irreparable injury, loss, or damage will result to the applicant before the adverse party or that party's attorney can be heard in opposition;
2. The applicant's attorney certifies to the court in writing and efforts, if any, which have been made to give the notice and the reasons supporting the claim that notice should not be required.

Temporary Restraining Order, CORNELL LAW SCHOOL LEGAL INFORMATION INSTITUTE, https://www.law.cornell.edu/wex/temporary_restraining_order (last visited Jul. 7, 2020).

Although temporary restraining orders typically last ten days or less they can be converted to permanent injunctions by the court.

Other temporary orders may include: an Order restraining one parent from removing a child from the state; enjoining both parents from concealing a child from the other parent; allocating fees and costs of mediation during the divorce; awarding one spouse exclusive possession of the marital residence (evicting the other spouse); and enjoining both parties from making extraordinary expenditures. 750 Ill. Comp. Stat. Ann. 5/501(a), (b), (c-1), (c-2) (LexisNexis through P.A. 101-631). All temporary orders are just, well, temporary, but they can be very helpful if you are the spouse with the lower earning power and the divorce takes, say, two years to complete.

Motions vs. Pleadings

A motion is a written request or proposal to the court to obtain and ask for order, ruling, or direction. A Pleading is a formal, written document filed with the court that asks, or pleads with, the court to grant some type of relief. Generally, a "pleading" is used to describe something that is filed that creates an entirely new cause of action. 750 Ill. Comp. Stat. Ann. 5/105(d) (LexisNexis through P.A. 101-631). An example of this is the Petition for Dissolution of Marriage that starts a divorce proceeding. A motion is a request for relief within the umbrella of the entire case—such as a motion to compel discovery, or motion to set trial dates. *In re Marriage of Wolff*, 355 Ill. App. 3d 403, 407 (Ill. App. Ct. 2d Dist. 2005). The title of a Pleading or Motion may vary depending on the reason it is being filed, but they include complaints, petitions, answers, responses, replies and motions. Either party files both Motions and Petitions during the course of the divorce proceedings and they request the Judge to give a ruling on issues the parties are unable to agree on or that are an emergency. Motions can be ruled on during the litigation or they can also be held over until trial, per the Judge.

In Illinois, the distinction between a Motion and a Pleading is of great importance in that under the law a Motion is not subject to a Motion to Strike or Dismiss while a pleading is subject to relief pursuant to a Motion to Strike or Dismiss. *Id.* While a Motion is still subject to legal defenses, the distinction is important in the speed in which a Motion can be addressed by a Court.

Pretrials

A Pre-Trial is a meeting between parties to a case that happens prior to the beginning of a trial. This will take place in the Judge's chambers and usually only the Judge and attorneys are involved in this process. Generally self-represented litigants do not participate in pre-trial conferences with the Court. At this meeting, the attorneys present to the judge the progress of the divorce settlement and discuss any remaining issues that need to be resolved between the parties. Most Judges require a Pre-Trial Memorandum and this will list the history of the case and the party's position. During the conference, judges may make suggestions regarding the settlement and give indications as to how they might rule on various issues raised by the attorneys. This is something that can help the parties when it comes to the big cost of litigation by narrowing the issues that are worth and not worth going to trial over by getting an idea of what the Judge's position is on the specific issues. The attorneys in a pre-trial have a little bit more leeway to discuss issues without worrying about the rules of evidence. A Pre-Trial is not a court proceeding that is put on the record.

Following a pretrial, the parties have the right to accept or reject the Court's recommendations. While litigants often feel that they are left out of this process, the pretrial procedure is a simple, quick and inexpensive way to gauge how a Judge may rule on a matter.

Prove Ups

A Marital Settlement Agreement is a document that the parties can enter into by agreement. It contains many different provisions such as disposition of property, maintenance, child support, allocation of parental responsibilities for decision- making and parenting time. Just like most contracts it is just best to have everything in writing. The Court will incorporate the Marital Settlement Agreement into the Judgment for Dissolution of Marriage as long as the Court does not find the Marital Settlement Agreement to be unconscionable (or shockingly unjust or unfair). *Unconscionable*, Black's Law Dictionary (5th pocket ed. 2016). Settlements can be reached at any stage of the litigation process. Some parties are able to resolve their differences after an initial mediation session. Some parties decide to settle after hearing their Judge's pre-trial recommendations and other parties decide to take their issues all the way to a trial.

After making an agreement on the terms of separation, the divorcing parties appear before a family court judge and ask for their contract to be affirmed and their divorce granted. This is called a prove up where the parties affirm that they have in fact reached an agreement and these are the terms of the agreement.

Once all elements of the agreement are settled and approved by the court, the court grants the petition of dissolution. However, that's not where the Illinois divorce process ends. The parties are now obligated to the terms of the divorce agreement and must take actions to fulfill them. This involves voluntarily providing the funds, assets, time and access mandated by the legally binding agreement. It may also require the parties to revisit issues, as necessary if the agreement requires updating due to changes in employment or living situations.

Trials

If the parties are not able to come to an agreement, then the Judge will set the matter for Trial. The Judge will now decide how to allocate the assets and obligations of the parties. The word trial brings to mind images of attorneys yelling at witnesses in front of a tense jury and a packed courtroom. In reality, Illinois family law trials are held in front of one Judge. Because courtrooms are open to the public, anyone could come in to observe the trial. The goal of a trial is to persuade the Judge to accept your position and issue a ruling that best advances your interests. Trials are handled differently in different counties. Trials that involve minor children trump divorces without children, when a trial is being scheduled. This can sometimes result in trials that don't involve minor children being pushed out or rescheduled due to other cases that are dealing with parenting issues. In some counties, trials can go day-to-day, start to finish. In other counties, scheduled dates from a court order are usually set. In yet other counties, there are only scheduled trial dates by an Order and you could get assigned a whole new judge for trial.

Appeals

If either party disagrees with the ruling, they may file an appeal within a specific timeframe. An appeal is typically only filed after the trial in a dissolution proceeding. Appeals can be filed during a divorce process as well based on the Judge's ruling or ruling made during the litigation and before there is a trial, however, are not required. When an appeal is filed for rulings in a family law case, it follows the same procedure as appeals for any other type of case. If someone does file a Notice of Appeal, it must be done within 30 days of the final order being appealed from. Ill. Sup. Ct. R. 303(a)(1). If you want to appeal a final decision by a Court, it is a good idea to make sure you do your research or consult with an attorney. It is very important to ensure that all the Appellate Court Rules are followed, as failure to follow the rules could result in an appeal being dismissed. It should be noted that as a general rule, only rulings of the Judge can be appealed and therefore, if the parties actually entered into a settlement, an Appeal is less likely.

The Illinois Supreme Court Commission on Access to Justice has released a publication with basic information about appeals for self-represented litigants. *Guide for Appeals to the Illinois Appellate Court for Self-Represented Litigants*, ILLINOIS COMM'N ON ACCESS TO JUSTICE
https://courts.illinois.gov/CivilJustice/Resources/Guide_for_Appeals_to_the_IL_Appellate_Court.pdf (updated August 2018).

There are a number of steps to the appeals process which may vary depending on the kind of order being appealed from, and may include:

1. File a notice of appeal with the clerk of the circuit court.
2. Contact the circuit court clerk to request preparation of the record on appeal, and to confirm and pay any related fees. Submit written requests to the circuit court reporters for them to prepare transcripts of the hearings held in your case and pay the reporters' fees for that preparation.
3. File a notice of filing with the clerk of the appellate court. Include proof of service that says you have sent copies of that document to the other parties.
4. Pay the $50 filing fee and file the docketing statement with the appellate court, together with copies of your requests to the circuit court and the court reporters for preparation of the record on appeal and the transcripts. The circuit court clerk will file the record on appeal with the appellate court.
5. File your brief.
6. Other side (the appellee) files its answering brief, if it chooses to do so.
7. File your reply brief. (Optional)
8. The appellate court issues its decision.
9. File a Petition for Rehearing if you believe the appellate court decision should be reconsidered by the court. (optional)
10. File a Petition for Leave to Appeal to the Illinois Supreme Court. (optional)

The appeal must be specific as to the ruling made by the Judge that is being requested for appellate intervention. Appeals are expensive and time consuming and they are not to be made just because one does not like a Judge's ruling. Judges must make an error in deciphering the law while making a ruling on a motion or petition or trial in order for an Appeal to be filed. The Appellate Court may hear oral arguments on your Appeal. If neither party requests an oral argument, then it is not likely that the Appellate Court will call the matter for oral argument. An oral argument is when both parties to the appeal (or their attorneys) appear in front of a panel of Appellate Court Judges and argue why the trial court made an error in deciphering or applying the law. At the end of the appeal process, when the appellate court releases their opinion, they may affirm or reverse a trial court's decision. If the decision is affirmed, then the Appellate Court agrees with the trial court's application of the law, and nothing further will happen unless the party filing the appeal wishes to file a Petition for Rehearing or Petition for Leave to Appeal to the Illinois Supreme Court. If a trial court's decision is reversed and remanded, that means the Appellate Court does not agree with what the trial court did, and reverses the order, requiring the trial court to conduct new proceedings with certain instructions to follow.
Structure of the Courts

Article VI, the Judicial Article of the Illinois Constitution of 1970, provides for a unified, 3-tiered judicial - Circuit Court, Appellate Court, and Supreme Court. Ill. Const. art. VI. § 1. The Illinois Supreme Court is the highest court in the State. The Supreme Court has original and exclusive jurisdiction in matters that involve legislative redistricting and determining the ability of the Governor to serve in office. Ill. Const. Art. VI § 9. The Supreme Court also has discretionary original jurisdiction in cases relating to State revenue and writs of mandamus, prohibition, or habeas corpus. Ill. Const. Art. VI § 4. The

Illinois State Supreme Court comprises 7 Justices; 3 represent the First Appellate Judicial District (Cook County) and 1 each represents the remaining 4 Appellate Judicial Districts. Ill. Const. art. VI §3. A majority vote of 4 is required to decide a case. *Id.*

The Appellate Court is divided into Judicial Districts. Cook County is the entire First Appellate District, with the rest of the State being divided into the remaining 4 appellate districts of "substantially equal population, each of which shall be compact and composed of contiguous counties." Ill. Const. art. VI § 2. The appellate court affirms the trial court decision or they may reverse the trial court decision and set a new trial.

The State of Illinois is divided into 23 Judicial Circuits. *ABOUT THE COURTS IN ILLINOIS*, ILLINOIS COURTS, http://www.illinoiscourts.gov/General/CourtsInIL.asp (last visited July 1, 2020). Each Judicial Circuit consists of one or more contiguous counties. Circuit Courts, also known as trial courts, are established within each judicial circuit. These are courts of general jurisdiction.

Conclusion

We know that divorce in Illinois doesn't happen quickly, but taking a step-by-step approach makes the process more manageable. It may be helpful to view the number of steps in the Illinois divorce process as having basic major components. The process begins with making some decisions about how you'll proceed into the legal aspect of filing for divorce. You may wish to handle the divorce process on your own or receive assistance from a mediator or family law attorney.

There is no way to know how long the divorce process will take, because the length of time depends on many things. Generally, if there are minor children, the Court is expected to enter judgment within eighteen (18) months of the filing of the petition. Ill. Sup. Ct. R. 922. Sometimes, divorcing couples will resolve the allocation of parenting decision-making and parenting time first, then focus on resolving their financial differences. The courts like to finalize parenting issues and the Allocation Judgment foremost before property distribution.

In many cases, the cost of the Illinois divorce process is far less than the cost of an inequitable settlement. Your divorce process may include: a business valuation, or perhaps your spouse obtained a loan, using non-marital property as collateral, and then acquired new property with the loan proceeds. Your divorce process may include a neutral court expert to value assets or conduct forensic work. Your Illinois divorce process is unique to you. Become familiar with the questions that the court will consider.

Ask questions when you first meet with your divorce attorney, and as new issues come up, discuss the standards and the changes so that you are well-informed and not confused when the court makes important decisions concerning your divorce.

The Illinois law governing divorce is the Illinois Marriage and Dissolution of Marriage Act. According to the Act, the Court must:
- Protect children from harm resulting from their parents' divorce
- Quickly resolve the allocation of parental decision-making and parenting time, and
- Protect and promote children's relationships with both of their parents.

If you are getting a divorce and you have minor children, or children who have reached the age of eighteen but are not emancipated, your divorce process includes a careful analysis of which parent's residence will be used for school purposes, which parent will be making substantial decisions in the areas of religion, health, education and extracurricular activities, and how the parents may be dividing up the parenting time. If you are getting a divorce, and your children have all emancipated, the divorce process will be substantially quicker for you.

CHILDREN FIRST

Illinois adopted its first joint custody law in 1982. This law defined both "joint legal custody" and "joint physical custody." The law was revised in 1986 to no longer distinguish between legal and physical custody. In an Illinois Fourth District Appellate case, *In re the Marriage of Seitzinger*, the Court defined joint custody as follows: "[joint custody means joint responsibility and not shared physical custody. It is simply a tool to maximize the involvement of both parents in the life of a child." *In re Marriage of Seitzinger,* 333 Ill. App. 3d 103, 109 (Ill. App. Ct. 4th Dist., 2002). The word "custody" is what caused problems and still does today. All child decisions usually fell to one parent and this was usually the mother. The law was again changed in 2016 to replace "custody" with "decision-making" and identifying four significant issues: education, health, religion, and extracurricular activities. 750 Ill. Comp. Stat. Ann. 5/602.5(b) (LexisNexis through P.A. 101-631).

In all divorce cases involving minor children and all parentage cases, a Proposed Parenting Plan must be filed by each parent. Within 120 days after service or filing of an appearance, each parent must file with the court, either jointly or separately, a proposed parenting plan. 750 Ill. Comp. Stat. Ann. 5/602.10(a) (LexisNexis through P.A. 101-631). This time period for filing a parenting plan may be extended by the court for good cause shown. *Id.* If the respondent has filed no appearance, no parenting plan is required unless ordered by the court. *Id.* If the parents agree on a proposed parenting plan, then the parenting plan must be in writing and signed by both parents. 750 Ill. Comp. Stat. Ann. 5/602.10(d) (LexisNexis through P.A. 101-631). However, the parents may agree upon and submit a parenting plan to be entered by the Court at any time after the commencement of a proceeding until prior to the entry of a judgment of dissolution of marriage or final order in a parentage case. *Id.* The agreement is binding upon the court unless it finds, after considering the circumstances of the parties and any other relevant evidence produced by the parties, that the agreement is not in the best interests of the child. *Id.* If the court does not approve the parenting plan, the court shall make express findings of the reason or reasons for its refusal to approve the plan. *Id.* The court, on its own motion, may conduct an evidentiary hearing to determine whether the parenting plan is in the child's best interests. *Id.* An evidentiary hearing is a court proceeding that involves testimony relevant to the case and may also involve physical pieces of evidence such as documents.

If parents cannot agree, each parent must file and submit a written, signed parenting plan to the court within 120 days after the filing of an appearance, except for good cause shown. 750 Ill. Comp. Stat. Ann. 5/602.10(a) (LexisNexis through P.A. 101-631). The court's determination of parenting time should be based on the child's best interests. The filing of the plan may be excused by the court if:

- *The parties have finished mediation for the purpose of formulating a parenting plan;*
- *The parents have agreed in writing to extend the filing time and the court has approved; or*
- *The court orders otherwise for good cause shown.*

750 Ill. Comp. Stat. Ann. 5/602.10(e) (Lexis Nexis through P.A. 101-631).

Today, parents are awarded joint decision or sole decision power for the four significant decision-making areas. 750 Ill. Comp. Stat. Ann. 5/602.5(b) (LexisNexis through P.A. 101-631). Joint responsibility and decision making is when the two parents can make decisions about the children jointly in the best interest of the child. *Id.* Sole decision-making is when the parents cannot make decisions jointly, and one parent has the authority to make decisions without the other parent. *Id.* Even in a sole decision-making judgment, in some cases the parent with the decision making must keep the other parent informed as to issues involving the minor child(ren).

The broad term once known as "custody" is now known as "allocation of parental responsibilities." Under Illinois law, married parents going through a divorce, and unmarried parents going through proceedings to establish parentage are to have an Allocation Judgment/Parenting Plan. According to 750 ILCS 5/602.10, an Allocation Agreement or Parenting Plan is a written agreement that allocates significant decision-making responsibilities, parenting time, or both." 750 Ill. Comp. Stat. Ann. 602.10(f) (LexisNexis through P.A. 101-631). After this document has been executed by the Judge, the parenting plan is then valid and enforceable until the child becomes an adult, or until a modification is required or a change has been made with the court. Within this document, the responsibilities of each parent will be highlighted. *Id.* There are many different parts that make up this document.

The term parenting responsibilities means both parenting time and significant decision-making with respect to a child. 750 Ill. Comp. Stat. Ann. 5/600(d) (LexisNexis through P.A. 101-631). The term parenting time means the time during which a parent is responsible for exercising caretaking functions and non-significant decision-making responsibilities with respect to a child. 750 Ill. Comp. Stat. Ann. 5/600(e) (LexisNexis through P.A. 101-631). Each parent will get input on what they think would be the best schedule for the minor child/children. The term parenting plan means a written agreement that allocates significant decision-making responsibilities, parenting time, or both, this is the point of the actual Allocation Judgment/Parenting Agreement. 750 Ill. Comp. Stat. Ann. 5/600(f) (LexisNexis through P.A. 101-631).

The allocation of parenting time is all in the best interest of the child. 750 Ill. Comp. Stat. Ann. 5/602.7(a) (LexisNexis through P.A. 101-631). Unless the parents present a mutually agreed written parenting plan and the court approves that plan, the court shall allocate parenting time. It is presumed both parents are fit and the court shall not place any restrictions on parenting time as defined in Section 600 and described in Section 603.10 of the Marriage and Dissolution of Marriage Act, unless it finds by a preponderance of the evidence that a parent's exercise of parenting time would seriously endanger the child's physical, mental, moral, or emotional health. 750 Ill. Comp. Stat. Ann. 602.7(b) (LexisNexis through P.A. 101-631). The 'preponderance of the evidence' standard means that it is more likely than not.

Allocation of Parental Responsibilities

As stated in 750 ILCS 5/600, there are different definitions of what goes into the Allocation Judgment/Parenting Plan. Starting with the "caretaking functions" this means that there are different tasks that involve interaction with a child. 750 Ill. Comp. Stat. Ann. 5/600(c) (LexisNexis through P.A. 101-631). Caretaking functions involve the following: managing a child's bedtime and wake-up routines, caring for a child when the child is sick or injured; being attentive to a child's personal hygiene needs, including washing, grooming, and dressing; playing with a child and ensuring the child attends scheduled extracurricular activities; protecting a child's physical safety; and providing transportation for a child. *Id.* These caretaking functions ensure that a child's various developmental needs are addressed. *Id.*

To ensure the parent is providing discipline and giving instructions, it is also important to make sure that the child attends school, including remedial and special services appropriate to the child's needs. *Id.* It is also critical to ensure the child attends medical appointments and is available for medical follow-up and meeting the medical needs of the child in the home. *Id.* If the parent is not available, then they need to make sure there is a plan for alternative care in place. Overall, all of these things are simply to make sure the child will be taken care of.

The courts will allocate decision-making responsibilities according to the child's best interests. 750 Ill. Comp. Stat. Ann. 5/602.5(a) (LexisNexis through P.A. 101-631). Unless the parents otherwise agree in writing on an allocation of significant decision-making responsibilities, or the issue of the allocation of parental responsibilities has been reserved under Section 401, the court shall make the determination. 750 Ill. Comp. Stat. Ann. 5/602.5(b) (LexisNexis through P.A. 101-631). The court shall allocate to one or both of the parents the significant decision-making responsibility for each significant issue affecting the child. *Id.* The significant issues include education, health, religion, and extracurricular activities. 750 Ill. Comp. Stat. Ann. 5/602.5(b)(1)-(4) (LexisNexis through P.A. 101-631).

The first major area for decision-making is education. 750 Ill. Comp. Stat. Ann. 5/602.5(b)(1) (LexisNexis through P.A. 101-631). This area includes many different types of decisions, such as where the child will attend school and tutors. *Id.* Both parties will be listed as the parent of the child on all school records. This way they can both access any online grading systems and or newsletters.

The second major area of decision-making is health. 750 Ill. Comp. Stat. Ann. 5/602.5(b)(2) (LexisNexis through P.A. 101-631). This includes things such as non-emergency care vs. emergency care. When it comes to non-emergency care, typically each party shall notify the other of any issue that arises relative to the non-emergency medical care of the child and they shall respond to the same within seventy- two hours. Should the child require emergency care, including emergency surgery, necessary for the preservation of life or to prevent a further serious injury while the child is with a parent, the parent in possession of the child shall immediately make all reasonable efforts to contact and consult with the parent not in possession of the child by all reasonable means, to include telephone (at work, home, and cellular phone), email, and text message. However, in no event shall this provision be construed so as to prevent either parent from unilaterally making emergency health care decisions if medical necessity dictates that such decisions be made and treatment rendered prior to an opportunity to contact the parent not in possession of the child. In such case, the parent not in possession shall be notified immediately or as soon as practicable.

With regard to Religion, the courts can allocate decision- making responsibility for the child's religious upbringing with any express or implied agreement between the parties. 750 Ill. Comp. Stat. Ann. 5/602.5(b)(3)(A) (LexisNexis through P.A. 101-631). The court will consider evidence of the parents' past views as to the child's religious upbringing when allocating these responsibilities. 750 Ill. Comp. Stat. Ann. 5/602.5(b)(3)(B) (LexisNexis through P.A. 101-631). The court shall not allocate any aspect of the child's religious upbringing if it determines that the parents do not or did not have any agreement for such religious upbringing or that there is insufficient evidence to demonstrate a course of conduct regarding the child's upbringing that could service as a basis for any order. 750 Ill. Comp. Stat. Ann. 5/602.5(b)(3)(C) (LexisNexis through P.A. 101-631).

Extracurricular activities will be determined based on the child's best interests and the child's previous participation in the activity. 750 Ill. Comp. Stat. Ann. 5/602.5(b)(4) (LexisNexis through P.A. 101-631). This is something that the parties need to agree on. Usually the parties will split the costs of the extracurricular activities 50/50 unless it is not equitable based on the parties' incomes. The parties shall jointly determine what extracurricular activities the child will participate in, and either party may file a Petition to review the same if there is no such agreement like after mediation of the issues. A party shall not unreasonably withhold his or her consent for the child to participate in an extracurricular activity.

Parenting Time

Under the umbrella of parenting time there are different things that will be addressed. Starting with the school year schedule, this will be the schedule for the majority of the year. The Allocation Judgment will need to determine who will drop the child off at the bus stop or at school and who will pick the child up. School break parenting times, including spring and winter breaks when the children are out of school for a long period of time, are usually alternated between the parties. Holiday schedules are structured around traditional ways of celebration, some families celebrate more holidays than others. The big six include New Year's, Labor Day, 4th of July, Memorial Day, Thanksgiving, and Christmas; and some others, like: the child's birthday, Mom and Dad's birthday, MLK Day, President's Day, St. Patrick's Day, Pulaski Day, Valentine's Day, and Halloween. When it comes to vacations, normally each parent would get a certain amount of weeks for travel, or to stay at home with the children while they are out of school.

The term, "in the best interests of the child," is used a lot in connection with the determination of parenting time and allocating decision-making responsibilities. There are factors that go into deciding what is truly in the best interest of the child. When determining the child's best interest, the court will consider all relevant factors, including:

1. *The wishes of each parent seeking parenting time;*
2. *The wishes of the child, taking into account the child's maturity and ability to express reasoned and independent preferences as to parenting time;*
3. *The amount of time each parent spent performing caretaking functions with respect to the child in the 24 months preceding the filing of any petition for allocation of parental responsibilities or, if the child is under 2 years of age, since the child's birth;*
4. *Any prior agreement or course of conduct between the parents relating to caretaking functions with respect to the child;*
5. *The interaction and interrelationship of the child with his or her parents and siblings and with any other person who may significantly affect the child's best interests;*
6. *The child's adjustment to his or her home, school, and community;*
7. *The mental and physical health of all individuals involved;*
8. *The child's needs;*
9. *The distance between the parents' residences, the cost and difficulty of transporting the child, each parent's and the child's daily schedules, and the ability of the parents to cooperate in the arrangement;*
10. *Whether a restriction on parenting time is appropriate;*
11. *The physical violence or threat of physical violence by the child's parent directed against the child or other member of the child's household;*
12. *The willingness and ability of each parent to place the needs of the child ahead of his or her own needs;*
13. *The willingness and ability of each parent to facilitate and encourage a close and continuing relationship between the other parent and the child;*
14. *The occurrence of abuse against the child or other member of the child's household;*
15. *Whether one of the parents is a convicted sex offender or lives with a convicted sex offender and, if so, the exact nature*

> *of the offense and what if any treatment the offender has successfully participated in; the parties are entitled to a hearing on the issues raised in this paragraph (15);*
>
> 16. *The terms of a parent's military family-care plan that a parent must complete before deployment if a parent is a member of the United States Armed Forces who is being deployed; and*
>
> 17. *Any other factor that the court expressly finds to be relevant.*

750 Ill. Comp. Stat. Ann. 5/602.7(b) (LexisNexis through P.A. 101-631).

During the pendency of a divorce or parentage proceeding, the court may order a temporary Allocation of Parenting Responsibilities in the child's best interest before the entry of the final Allocation Judgment. 750 Ill. Comp. Stat. Ann. 5/603.5(a) (LexisNexis through P.A. 101-631).

The allocation judgment should also deal with the right of first refusal. According to 750 ILCS 5/602.3, a "right of first refusal" means that if a party intends to leave a child with a substitute care-giver (a baby-sitter, current spouse, other family member, neighbor, etc.) for a significant period of time, that parent must first offer the other parent an opportunity to personally care for the child. 750 Ill. Comp. Stat. Ann. 5/602.3(b) (LexisNexis through P.A. 101-631). This means that one party intends to leave the minor child or children with a substitute care taker for a significant period of time. If this is the case, then that party must first offer the other party an opportunity to personally care for the minor child or children. The court can make this decision to have a right of first refusal on behalf of the parties if it is in the best interest of the child. *Id.* When invoking the right of first refusal the party must share the length and kind of child care requirements, notification to the other parent, transportation requirements, and anything else that is in the best interest of the child. *Id.* The right of first refusal is terminated upon the termination of the allocation of parental responsibilities or parenting time. 750 Ill. Comp. Stat. Ann. 5/602.3(d) (LexisNexis through P.A. 101-631).

Today, parents with a majority of, or equal, parenting time may relocate relatively short distances away, even out-of-state, and it's no big deal. If they move beyond a certain distance, however, they must follow relocation rules spelled out in the law. 750 Ill. Comp. Stat. Ann. 5/609.2(b) (LexisNexis through P.A. 101-631). There are two different terms: relocating and merely moving. Merely moving is a term to describe situations where Illinois' relocation law doesn't apply. Other rules may apply, but those are defined in your Allocation Judgment/Parenting Plan or court orders . . . not in the law. To help keep things clear, lawyers and judges use the term "relocating" to describe only those situations where the relocation rules are triggered and a parent needs to take specific steps in court prior to relocating. The term "relocating" is the change of residence from the child's current primary residence to a new residence outside of a certain distance from the child's current residence; depending in which county the child resides. 750 Ill. Comp. Stat. Ann. 5/600(g) (LexisNexis through P.A. 101-631). The new residence must be within this State that does not exceed more than a certain number of miles from the child's current residence, an Internet mapping service measures this distance. *Id.* Relocation means a change of residence from the child's current primary residence located in the counties of Will, DuPage, Kane, Lake, McHenry or Cook to a new residence within this State that is more than 25 miles from the child's current residence; a change of residence from the child's current primary residence located in a county other than Will, DuPage, Kane, Lake, McHenry or Cook to a new residence within this State that is more than 50 miles from the child's current primary residence; or a change of residence from the child's current primary residence to a residence outside the borders of this State that is more than 25 miles from the current primary residence. *Id.*

If you are planning to relocate with the child, you must send a notice of relocation to the other party at least 60 days prior to the planned date of relocation. 750 Ill. Comp. Stat. Ann. 5/609.2(d) (LexisNexis through P.A. 101-631). There must be a copy of notice to relocate filed with the court. 750 Ill. Comp. Stat. Ann. 5/609.2(c) (LexisNexis through P.A. 101-631). This date is recorded so that the judge will know if the 60-day requirement has been made.

The notice must include the date that you are planning to move, your new address, if the relocation is permanent or temporary. 750 Ill. Comp. Stat. Ann. 5/609.2(d)(1)-(3) (LexisNexis through P.A. 101-631). If it is temporary it must include the expected duration of time you will be staying there. 750 Ill. Comp. Stat. Ann 5/609.2(d)(3) (LexisNexis through P.A. 101-631). If the non-relocating parent agrees to the relocation then they will sign the notice and update the Allocation Judgment and present it to the judge to sign off on. 750 Ill. Comp. Stat. Ann. 5/609.2(e)(LexisNexis through P.A. 101-631). If there is no agreement this process will include more work. If they happen to object and refuse to sign the notice, then the party planning on moving must file a petition asking the court to relocate. 750 Ill. Comp. Stat. Ann. 5/609.2(f) (LexisNexis through P.A. 101-631). The court will consider factors such as:

- *The circumstances and reasons for the intended relocation;*
- *The reasons, if any, why a parent is objecting to the intended relocation;*
- *The history and quality of each parent's relationship with the child and specifically whether a parent has substantially failed or refused to exercise the parental responsibilities allocated to him or her under the parenting plan or allocation judgment;*
- *The educational opportunities for the child at the existing location and at the proposed new location;*
- *The anticipated impact of the relocation of the child;*
- *Whether the court will be able to fashion a reasonable allocation of parental responsibilities between all parents if the relocation occurs;*
- *The wishes of the child; taking into account the child's maturity and abilities to express reasoned and independent preferences as to relocation;*
- *Possible arrangements for the exercise of parental responsibilities appropriate to the parents' resources and circumstances and the developmental level of the child;*
- *Minimization of the impairment to a parent-child relationship caused by a parent's relocation; and*
- *Any other relevant facts bearing on the child's best interests.*

750 Ill. Comp. Stat. Ann. 5/609.2(g) (LexisNexis through P.A. 101-631).

After entry of an Allocation Judgment, the Court may restrict parenting time or restrict allocation of parental responsibilities. There could be a restriction of parental responsibilities, meaning if the court finds that a parent engaged in any conduct that has endangered the child's mental, moral, or physical health or that significantly impaired the child's emotional development, the court then enters orders as necessary to protect the child. 750 Ill. Comp. Stat. Ann. 5/603.10(a) (LexisNexis through P.A. 101-631). Some orders may include:

- *A reduction, elimination, or other adjustment to the decision-making responsibilities or parenting time, or both decision-making responsibilities and parenting time;*
- *Supervision, including ordering the Department of Children and Family Services to exercise continuing supervision under Section 5 of the Children and Family Services Act;*
- *Requiring the exchange of the child between the parents through an intermediary or in a protected setting;*
- *Restraining a parent's communication with or proximity to the other parent or the child;*
- *Requiring a parent to abstain from possessing or consuming alcohol or non-prescribed drugs while exercising parenting time with the child and within a specified period immediately preceding the exercise of parenting time;*
- *Restricting the presence of specific persons while a parent is exercising parenting time with the child;*
- *Requiring a parent to post a bond to secure the return of the child following the parent's exercise of parenting time or to secure other performance required by the court;*
- *Requiring a parent to complete a treatment program for perpetrators of abuse, for drug or alcohol abuse, or for other behavior that is the basis for restricting parental responsibilities under this Section; and*
- *Any other constraints or conditions that the court deem necessary to provide for the child's safety or welfare.*

750 Ill. Comp. Stat. Ann. 5/603.10(a)(1)-(9) (LexisNexis through P.A. 101-631).

You can modify an order to restrict parenting time or decision-making. The order can be changed because either there has been a change in circumstances that occurred after the entry of the order or there is conduct that the court was previously unaware that seriously endangers the child. 750 Ill. Comp. Stat. Ann. 5/603.10(b) (LexisNexis through P.A. 101-631). Some factors that go into changing the order are:

- *Abuse, neglect, or abandonment of the child;*

> - *Abusing or allowing abuse of another person that had an impact upon the child;*
> - *Use of drugs, alcohol, or any other substance in a way that interferes with the parent's ability to perform caretaking responsibilities;*
> - *Persistent continuing interference with other parent's access to the child, except for actions taken with a reasonable way of protecting the child.*

750 Ill. Comp. Stat. Ann. 5/603.10(b)(1)-(4) (LexisNexis through P.A. 101-631).

Separation and divorce disrupt the lives of more than just the two people involved. The ripple effect most significantly affects children, who are faced with new home structures, changing rules and an uncertain future dynamic. Many parents use a shared allocation of parental responsibilities as a way to maintain the greatest amount of continuity in their children's lives. It offers an agreement that allows parents to make decisions as equal parties. Even with the best intentions, however, this type of co-parenting is challenging for individuals who decide to separate, especially when the circumstances are less than amicable. Regardless of their feelings about one another, however, two people can successfully co-parent their children during and after divorce or entry of an Allocation Judgment, by holding on to some central tenets.

You can't get past it; it's part of the word. The prefix "co-" means together, mutually, in common. Two parties who have mutual children are equally responsible morally and legally for the children, whether or not they're a romantic couple. An agreement extends to co-parents far beyond an equal separation of time, energy and money expended toward your children. Real co-parenting involves working together to make decisions and solve problems in exactly the same way you would if you were still a couple. Without communication, your co-parenting ship will inevitably sink. For a co-parenting relationship to be successful, both parties must commit to maintaining open lines of communication. While communication includes logistics such as schedules, health updates, extra-curricular activities, and discipline issues, it is helpful to also have the ability to communicate on a sincerely interpersonal level about fears, wins, frustrations, and hopes. Remember to include your children in co-parenting communication the same way you might have when you were together. This presents a united front and offers an example of good cooperation for your children. Example: "Dad and I have discussed it, and we decided your curfew can be extended to 11 p.m. on the weekends. It's the same whether you're at his house or mine."

Children thrive on consistency, taking comfort in a sense of practical and emotional routines. They are bound to feel some insecurity about their changing life situation; don't compound that anxiety with a wobbly co-parenting arrangement. Set your ground-rules and general agreements and establish consistency within those bounds. There's time for gradual change along the way. Also, though you're going through a difficult experience, provide as much emotional stability as possible for your child.

The fact is you don't always get your way as a parent who is part of a couple. So, don't expect your decisions to always be met with agreement in co-parenting after your relationship ends. You'll be put in the position of needing to compromise frequently. Remember to check your priorities. You should make decisions because they're in the best interests of your children, not your need to be dominant or prove a point to your ex-partner. If you enter a new relationship, do not allow your new romantic interest to influence your parenting decisions, but do be considerate of their concerns.

For most people, this is the most difficult aspect of co-parenting. To make co-parenting work for your children, you have to support your ex-partner, even if it hurts. Your children will work through successful and failed relationships in the course of their lives, and they will learn as much from the way you conduct yourself in separation as they would if you had stayed together. Having compassion for your co-parent doesn't mean you have to like them or be their shoulder to cry on. It does involve remembering they are a human being dealing with changes and challenges in much the same way you are. It involves not putting them down—and, in fact, building them up—in front of your mutual children. And, yes, it might involve going for the occasional cup of coffee to figure out a drop-off and pick-up calendar. Just remember that your positive attitude and supportive behavior now will benefit your children in the future.

There has been a movement toward equal parenting time. In 2018, the 50/50 parenting time bill was proposed in Illinois and this created some controversy. The fathers' rights movement pushed for enactment of a statute creating a 50/50 parenting time presumption in Illinois, and that came through in House Bill 185, and Committee Amendment No.1. H.B. 185, 101st Assembly (Ill. 2018). The purpose of this Act is to recognize that the involvement of each parent for equal time is presumptively in the children's best interests. The proposal also deletes language providing that nothing in the Act requires that each parent be allocated decision-making responsibilities. Additionally, the proposed bill also provides that there is a rebuttable presumption in favor of equal parenting time. Provisions listing factors for the court to consider in determining a child's bests interests for purposes of allocating parenting time. In specific situations, the court is required to issue a written decision stating its specific findings of fact and conclusions of law in support of its ruling if it goes against the 50/50 presumption.

Illinois lawmakers are considering a bill that would dramatically impact families in the state who are involved in shared parenting situations. House Bill 185 is a proposed amendment to the Illinois Marriage and Dissolution of Marriage Act, and it changes the way courts approach the allocation of parenting time. In its legal definition, the bill proposes that equal parenting time is "presumptively in the best interests of the children," and that if a court diverges from that assumption, it shall issue a "written decision stating its specific findings of fact and conclusions of law in support of the deviation from the presumption." Illinois House Bill 4113 never went anywhere, because it was not finished in the 2017- 2018 session. House Bill 185 is the current one at this time.

According to the Bill, this act shall be applied to promote its underlying purposes:

- Provide procedures for the solemnization and registration of marriage;
- Strengthen and preserve the integrity of marriage and safeguard family relationships;
- Promote the amicable settlement of disputes that have arisen between parties to the marriage;
- Mitigate the potential harm to spouses and their children caused by the process of an action brought under this act, and protect children from conflict and violence;
- To ensure predictable decision making for the care of the child;

- Recognize the right of children to a healthy relationship with parents and;
- Acknowledge the best interest of the children.

In practical terms, if the bill becomes law it will instruct family courts to presume that it is in a child's best interest to spend equal time with each of his or her parents. A judge could still decide to deviate from the equal time presumption to give one parent more time with the child. However, setting a fairly high standard, the proposed law would require a judge to specifically outline what facts and legal basis support deviating from an "equal time" decision.

House Bill 185 concludes it is in all children's best interests to spend equal time with each parent. Based on the families we've assisted throughout Will, DuPage and Cook counties, we find that while equal parenting time can work, it can be difficult in many situations. While there are cases in which parents come together to successfully implement an equal parenting schedule, disputes often arise over issues of time.

This bill's focus of 50/50 parenting time appears to shift the focus away from the needs of children and onto a requirement to make parents "equal." Changing the tenor of "custodial" or "parenting" determinations to that which seeks to make parents equal may take the emphasis away from the needs of the children. A child's upbringing is based on feelings of safety, consistency and intimate connections with their parents, and divisions of time are matters to be handled with great delicacy and thoughtfulness.

In some situations, either mother or father primarily raised the child during the parents' relationship. Regardless of a parent's competence or connection with their child, we know that routines and consistency make kids feel safe. A sudden shift in parenting time can cause an upheaval in a child's life, causing confusion and feelings of rejection and resentment.

Even children who adapt well still emotionally struggle with the inconsistency of constantly switching between households. Tracking two separate sets of household procedures, rules and relationships can be taxing for anyone, especially a child. Only those families who establish a solid co-parenting plan successfully maneuver through this complex arrangement. When people divorce, one or both parties often move out of a shared home and into a new place, sometimes in a different town or even another state. Especially for families with school-age children, a physical distance between parents can make it burdensome or even prohibitive to work out an effective co-parenting schedule based on equal time.

Likewise, an equal time decision can be unrealistic in light of parents' work situations. Schedules that overlap, run overnight, push into overtime, take parents out of state or constantly change — all these things can run counter to the logic that equal time automatically works best for all families.

From a legal perspective, the new law would change the very standard used to determine the allocation of parenting time and parental responsibilities. If passed into law, House Bill 185 would shift the burden from the judge to the parents, who would have to "fight it out" to prove who is more deserving of time. This could incite increased litigation and ugly mudslinging between parents. In large part, this change would affect those parents who are responsible for the majority of parenting time. The burden would be on them to prove why the other parent shouldn't have equal time.

Determining the allocation of parenting time and parental responsibilities REQUIRE that decisions be made while taking into consideration the best interests of the child. Sometimes this could be a presumption that equal parenting time is in the child's best interests but it may not actually account for the child's best interests.

This change could make legal procedures even more difficult for families experiencing domestic violence. A victim of domestic violence who does the majority of parenting may not want to risk going against their abuser in court to argue against equal time. Although they know it may be in the child's best interests, a victim may still be afraid to speak up because they fear retaliation against them or their children.

For parties who are responsible for the majority of parenting time, the proposed law could threaten their financial stability. A presumption of equal parenting time may cause a reduction or even elimination of child support payments for a parent who may genuinely need financial assistance with the rearing of the parties' mutual children.

Within the state's new child support guidelines, an automatic presumption of equal parenting time would put the parties into the "shared parenting" calculation. Effectively, this would decrease the amount of child support a parent receives.

This can be an issue for parents who were primarily not working outside the home during the course of the marriage and raising the children, while the other parent worked on a full-time basis to support the household. In those cases, the former primary custodians would be awarded lower amounts of child support, making it unlikely that they will be able to earn enough to care for themselves and children.

While House Bill 185 appears to seek a standard of equity within parenting hearings, it could create difficult issues for families in which an equal division of time simply isn't safe or practical. The outcomes may be known if and when the Illinois legislature passes the bill.

Guardians ad Litem, Child's Representatives, Attorneys for the Child

In cases where the allocation of parental responsibility is contested, the judge may appoint an experienced family law attorney to serve as an "Attorney for the Child," a "Guardian ad Litem," or a "Child Representative." Those appointments come with different responsibilities, powers, privileges, and abilities. (For purposes of this section, we will use children (plural) to indicate a family law matter involving one child or more than one child).

When family law cases begin to look like they might present a contest regarding allocation of parental responsibilities and decision making on behalf of the children, the courts will consider appointing an attorney on behalf of the children. Likewise, if the parents cannot agree between themselves as to what is in the best interest of their kids, the court will consider appointing an attorney to make a recommendation for the children's best interests. This could also be the case after entry of an Allocation Judgment (i.e. Parenting Agreement) that may have been agreed to by parents without contest during the initial divorce proceeding, but where children's issues arose post-divorce. An appointment of a children's attorney doesn't happen in every Family Law case involving children, and Judges avoid it when possible, and prefer (and strongly encourage) parents to work out any differences amongst themselves. A finding in *In re the Marriage of Wycoff* noted the following:

> *In most cases the child's interests are adequately protected by one or the other parent, or by the court, and it is difficult to see how the presence of another lawyer could improve the process enough to be worth the cost. (2 H. Clark, The Law of Domestic Relations in the United States § 20.3, at 492-93 (2d ed. 1987)).*

In re: Marriage of Wycoff, 266 Ill.App.3d 408, 417 (Ill. App. Ct. 4th Dist., 1994).

However, in some cases there are serious concerns about one party's ability to adequately care for his or her children; such as cases where physical, emotional, or substance abuse may be a factor. Or other cases where no serious endangerment is at play, but the parties get caught up in emotion and sometimes see more time with their kids as a "win" against the other parent, thereby forgetting or foregoing what may actually be in their children's best interests. In these cases where parents lose sight, the court must do something to look out for the kids.

When it comes to "looking out for the kids", Illinois law (750 ILCS 5/506) allows for three options:

- an "attorney for the child".
- a Guardian ad Litem (GAL); and
- a Child's Representative (CR).

750 Ill. Comp. Stat. Ann. 5/506(a)(1)-(3) (LexisNexis through P.A. 101-631).

Either party may ask the court to appoint an attorney to serve in one of these three capacities. 750 Ill. Comp. Stat. Ann. 5/506(a) (LexisNexis through P.A. 101-631). We will break down the different functions of an Attorney for the Child, a GAL and a CR later on. However, each act as an advocate for the children only (not the parents), and in each capacity, these individuals are charged with investigating and determining the "best interests of the children". It is also important to note that if a case is highly contested, the Court can appoint any one of these three advocates on its own, without either party requesting it. *Id.* The Court (or Judge) has the authority to make this appointment even over one (or both) parent's objections.

In cases where a parent/litigant is specifically requesting an advocate for the children be appointed, that parent (or moving party) will typically identify a specific individual to be appointed by the Court. The parties may also independently agree to use a particular attorney in a particular capacity; however, the Court must still approve of the parties' selection, as well as the scope of the individual's role in the case.

So, what's the difference between an attorney for the children, a GAL and a CR? It really comes down to this . . . in what capacity should an attorney serve your children and their best interests? Here's what they do and how do they do it:

Attorney for the Child (AFC): An Attorney for the Child is just that: AN independent attorney who represents the children's interests just like the attorneys who represent each parent's interests. 750 Ill. Comp. Stat. Ann. 5/506(a)(1)(LexisNexis through P.A. 101-631). Like all attorneys, an AFC is an advocate . . . for the children. Communications between the children and the attorney (if any) are confidential. *Id.* The

AFC may file pleadings and motions on behalf of the children, conduct discovery, and call and cross-examine witnesses just like an attorney for either adult party. *Id.*

Guardian ad Litem (GAL): A GAL is "the eyes and ears of the court." Once appointed, a GAL conducts an investigation of the parties, the children, each parent's individual situations (at home, at work, and historically in caring for the children), and anything else that is relevant to the children's best interests. 750 Ill. Comp. Stat. Ann. 5/506(a)(2) (LexisNexis through P.A. 101-631). After their investigation, the GAL prepares a written report for the Court to review and consider. *Id.* This report includes a custody recommendation, which we now call a recommendation for the "allocation of parental responsibility". The report is submitted to the judge and is shared with both parents and their attorneys. The GAL is also able to testify in Court about any finding in their report, their personal observations of the parties and the children, all content reviewed from either party prior to making a final determination, as well as their specific reasons for the recommendations contained in their report. *Id.* A GAL is also subject to cross-examination by either party. *Id.* It should be noted that although a GAL is considered "the eyes and ears of the Court" a Judge is not bound by the GAL's recommendations; however, because a GAL is charged with performing a thorough investigation of the parties and the children, their determination as to the best interests of the children usually weighs heavily in any final determination of parental responsibility and parenting time schedule ordered by the Court.

Additionally, GAL's have the authority to file pleadings and motions seeking relief on behalf of the children. GAL's additionally have the authority to issue subpoenas as part of their investigation. GAL's may even call and cross-examine witnesses at the trial if he or she feels that would serve the children's best interests. A GAL can also file post-trial motions to protect the children and enforce their rights after the conclusion of the initial Family Law matter is concluded.

Child's Representative: A Child's Representative is an advocate but does not submit a recommendation for the allocation of parental responsibility, nor a written report to the court (unlike a GAL). 750 Ill. Comp. Stat. Ann. 5/506(a)(3)(LexisNexis through P.A. 101-631). Further, a CR may not be called as a witness at Trial. *Id.* Instead of making a recommendation or submitting a report to the Court following an investigation of the parties and the children, the CR is to "offer evidence-based legal arguments" only. *Id.* The specific role of a CR is trickier to define than that of a GAL and the two are often confused. If the Court specifically appoints a Child's Representative on behalf of the children, that CR cannot and should not perform the same function as would an appointed GAL. *Id.* Although any appointed CR should interview the children and the parties and perform a thorough investigation (similar to a GAL) the current Statute prohibits a CR from preparing a written opinion report as to the children's best interest. *Id.* The Statute also prevents a CR from testifying as a Witness at Trial. *Id.* A CR is limited to "offering evidence-based legal arguments" as to the children's best interest. *Id.* Confused? Me too. A CR's role vs. a GAL's role in Family Law Cases was so unclear that the Statutes controlling GAL and CR functions were amended.

The Supreme Court in <u>De Bates</u> examined this very issue, and this precedent setting case attempted to more clearly define the role of a CR: In the case *In re: Marriage of De Bates*, the appointed Child's Representative submitted a written report (like a GAL would) to the Court, but the mother was prevented from cross-examining the Child's

Representative. *In re: Marriage of De Bates*, 212 Ill.2d 489, 509 (2004). The Illinois Supreme Court held that allowing the CR's report into evidence without allowing the mother the opportunity to cross-examine the CR deprived the mother of due process. Because (the old) Section 5/603 prohibited the cross-examination of the Child's Rep., the Illinois Supreme Court held that allowing the CR to submit a report or make a recommendation was unconstitutional. *De Bates*, at 514-15. The Illinois legislature responded in 2006 by amending 750 ILCS 5/506(a)(3) to say "[t]he child representative shall not render an opinion, recommendation, or report to the court and shall not be called as a witness, but shall offer evidence-based legal arguments." 750 Ill. Comp. Stat. Ann. 5/506(a)(3) (LexisNexis through P.A. 101-631).

So, what can a CR do? A Child's Representative may file motions to affect the course of the case, including motions to establish or modify temporary parental responsibilities, decision-making, and a temporary parenting schedule. 750 ILCS 5/506(a)(3) (LexisNexis through P.A. 101-631). The CR can make a recommendation about the allocation of parental responsibilities, decision-making, the parenting schedule, and other elements of the Parenting Plan in a pre-trial memorandum submitted to the judge and shared with the parents. *Id.* The CR advocates for what he or she thinks is best for the children -- but only after taking into consideration the children's wishes. *Id.* Like with an attorney, communications between the children and the CR are confidential. *Id.* Unlike a GAL, the CR MUST meet with the children (and the parents), and as stated above, he or she is expected to conduct an investigation much like a GAL would. *Id.* However, a GAL does not necessarily have to interview the parties' children. For example, if a child or children in a particular case are too young to actually be interviewed independent of their parents, a GAL can forgo meeting with the parties' children altogether.

However, because a CR must (by law) interview the children, they are typically only appointed in cases where the children are old enough and mature enough to articulate their concerns and wishes.

The law was amended in 2006 and again in 2016, but the changes to the relevant portion are not substantive (changing "power and authority" to "authority and obligation" in the 2006 amendment which was retained in the 2016 amendment):

> *The question here is whether the "power and authority" of the child's representative to "take part in the conduct of the litigation as does an attorney for a party" includes the ability to file motions for changes in temporary custody. Interpreting section 506(a)(3) in accordance with its plain meaning ... the child's representative, pursuant to his powers as an attorney, must be "able and obligated to conduct necessary discovery, file appropriate pleadings, depose and present witnesses, and review experts' reports." See Davis & Yazici, 12 Illinois Practice of Family Law 750 5/506 (2005-06 ed.) (discussing the role of an attorney for the child in dissolution of marriage proceedings). Further, section 603(a) of the Act provides that "[a] party to a custody proceeding * * * may move for a temporary custody order." 750 ILCS 5/603(a) (West 2004).*

> *Because the child's representative is to have the same power and authority to take part in the litigation as an attorney for the parties, and an attorney for the parties may move for a temporary custody order, we find that section 506(a)(3) does endow the child's representative with the authority to file motions for changes in temporary custody. If we were to hold otherwise, the child's representative would be unable to advocate for the best interest of the child during the dissolution of marriage proceedings. (See 750 ILCS 5/506(a)(3) (West 2004)).*

In re: Marriage of Kostusik, 361 Ill.App.3d 103, 115 (Ill. App. Ct. 1st. Dist., 2005).

An Attorney for the Child (if so appointed) is not required to conduct an investigation, submit a report or make a recommendation, and is also not required to meet with the child and parents simultaneously. An AFC is simply acting as an attorney for the child. An AFC is not typically appointed unless the child or children in question are older and able to articulate his or her wishes because they have reached an appropriate level of maturity that allows their wishes to bear significant weight on which parent would be best suited to act in their best interest. For purposes of the rest of this section, we will focus on GAL's and/or CR's as they are the most widely used in Illinois Family Law matters.

Some judges assign a GAL or CR to nearly every case involving children where the parents cannot independently agree; others only do so at the request (via Motion) of one of the parties. However, as previously stated, any Judge can appoint a GAL or CR on his or her own Order, even if both parents object. 750 Ill. App. Comp. Stat. Ann. 5/506(a) (LexisNexis through P.A. 101-631).

So, if a GAL or CR is appointed, who pays the fees? Well, it's up to the Judge. The law says the court may order "either or both parents . . . any other party or source . . . the marital estate or the child's separate estate" to pay the appointed GAL/Attorney for Child/CR's retainer and continuing fees, costs, and disbursements. 750 Ill. Comp. Stat. Ann. 5/506(b) (LexisNexis through P.A. 101-631). The appointee must submit invoices to the court (and the parties) at least every 90 days after appointment. *Id.* The Court reviews the invoices and has the ability to approve or disapprove the reasonableness of the fees. *Id.*

The factors the court considers in allocating fees incurred by the AFC/GAL/CR are those applied to attorney fee awards for the parties under 750 ILCS 5/501 and 750 ILCS 5/508 (see Chapter on Attorneys' Fees set forth herein). *Id.* The allocation of the cost of the appointed attorney is left to the discretion of the Court. *McClelland v. McClelland*, 231 Ill.App.3d 214, 227 (Ill. App. Ct. 1st Dist., 1992).

In McClelland the Court identified the following factors in determining each party's obligation to pay GAL fees: "Judith's income was approximately $16,000, 50% less than the previous year, as a result of the impact of the litigation. However, the amount did not include the $6,000 received in child support from Donald. Donald's income was reported at $25,000 to $30,000, less the $6,000 for an approximate net of $19,000 to $24,000. Thus, the parties' relative ability to pay the fees was about equal." *McClelland*, at 228-29.

A GAL, CR or AFC has been appointed in my case, now what?

It is important to keep in mind that the GAL and/or the CR's recommendations enjoy substantial deference by the court, and many judges defer to the GALs/CRs in terms of deciding or formulating the best interests of children in a case. Therefore, professional collaboration and interaction with the GAL/CR is of utmost importance. Further, it is important that clients understand the whole process of a GAL/CR appointment, and that they are prepared and comfortable to be in a position to best assist the GAL/CR with their investigation of child related issues.
You and your attorney should seek to establish and sustain a good relationship with the appointed GAL/CR. Your attorney should also be a buffer between you and the GAL/CR. As soon as the GAL/CR is appointed, he or she will frequently try to identify first what issues exist between the parents.

Frequently custody is an issue (now called allocation of parental responsibilities), sometimes visitation or parenting time. Sometimes the matter at issue is whether one parent is preparing to move with the child outside the State of Illinois or outside of the school district or county where the other parent lives. Occasionally, abuse allegations are a factor.

A GAL/CR's investigation will likely require looking into private matters of the parents and the minor children. The GAL may ask about your family's history, what brought you to the present disputes, what is currently going on, and what can be forecasted for the future with respect to your children's needs and the present or ongoing issues between you and the other parent.

Sometimes, but not always, it is additionally necessary to involve third parties, such as teachers, neighbors and doctors. In fact, you may be asked to sign releases for medical and school related records. The ultimate goal of the investigation is to help bring about a quick and fair resolution of all of the issues involving your children.

Usually, the GAL/CR will schedule at least one visit to the children's residence (or to both parent's residences if the parties live separately) to meet and interview all those who live there and perhaps one or more visits with each parent and the child will be scheduled. This is commonly called a home-study.

Frequently, the Guardian ad litem's investigation extends to speaking with some third parties usually identified by the parents such as relatives, schoolteachers, neighbors, or others who may have information pertaining to the children's welfare and the parent's involvement with the children. Occasionally, a Guardian ad litem will ask for a background check, a criminal background check, a fingerprint check, or a drug screening.

Remember, a GAL/CR is charged with advocating for the best interests of your children. In other words, the safety and security of your kids, as well as the objective of ensuring the least amount of disruption to their routines as possible post litigation are top priorities. So, honesty and candidness are key when communicating with the GAL/CR. This person is also looking to determine which parent is most adept at fostering a positive relationship with the kids and the other parent.

GALs and CR's are typically attorneys with family law experience, who must undergo some type of minimal training in order to be certified to be on the "list" of GALs/CRs in each judge's courtroom. Many judges have preferences to appoint certain individuals in their cases, as there can be a belief with some judges that certain GALs tend to be more successful settling contested cases than others.

The Illinois State Bar Association (ISBA) does have guidelines for GAL's and CR's upon each appointment. Helen W. Gunnarsson, *ABCs for GALs*, Illinois State Bar Association, November 2010 at 572. Those guidelines emphasize that a GAL or CR is to be neutral and base his or her investigation on specific facts unique to each situation. *Id.* The relationship between the GAL/CR and the parents is not meant to be adversarial in any way, as the GAL/CR is to act only in the best interest of the child. *Id.* The long-term goal is always for the parents to work together in achieving the best interests of their child or children. *Id.*

In an extremely contested custody situation, a parent, a GAL/CR or the Court could additionally appoint a Custody Evaluator and order the parties and the children to undergo a Custody Evaluation., now often referred to as a Parenting Evaluation.

Illinois Parenting Evaluations

When the parents cannot agree to a joint Parenting Plan as stated above, it is left to the court to allocate parental responsibilities and decision-making authority. Nothing in the law requires that each parent be allocated decision-making responsibilities. These contested cases are difficult -- for the parents, for the lawyers, and for the judges:
During any contested custody case a judge may order a child custody evaluation. 750 Ill. Comp. Stat. Ann. 5/604.10(d) (LexisNexis through P.A. 101-631). An appointed evaluator (typically a psychologist or psychiatrist), will study you, the other parent and your children to give an official custody recommendation.

In the first reported decision involving custody of a child (see 1 Kings 3:16), Solomon, vested with plenary powers and unhampered by precedent, rendered a judgment which has been cited through the ages as incontrovertible evidence of his great wisdom. 1 Kings 3:16.

Today, a trial judge is almost daily presented with custody problems which are far more complex. *Elbe v. Elbe*, 100 Ill. App. 2d 221, 225-26, (Ill. App. Ct. 5th Dist., 1968). Parental Responsibility and Decision-Making awards must be decided "according to the child's best interest." 750 Ill. Comp. Stat. Ann. 5/602.5(a)(LexisNexis through P.A. 101-631). When allocating between the parents' significant decision-making responsibilities, Illinois law directs the court to consider "all relevant factors, including" fifteen specific factors. 750 Ill. Comp. Stat. Ann. 5/602.5(c) (LexisNexis through P.A. 101-631). (Note: The law presents fifteen factors in a numbered list. The prior law had a similar, ten-item, list. The current law adds seven new factors, deletes two old factors, and rearranges the order of the others. That fact may presume that the legislature wants courts to give greater consideration to factors appearing higher on the list and less consideration to factors appearing lower on the list. The factors are listed below in the order in which they appear in the current law.)

There are three types of evaluations you should be aware of: 604.10(b), 604.10(c) and Illinois Supreme Court Rule 215. These specific number and letter combinations come from the State Codes (or Statutes) that govern each type of evaluation.
604.10(b)

A 604.10(b) evaluation is the standard evaluation that can be ordered by a Judge, again, typically only in extremely contested custody cases. 750 Ill. Comp. Stat. Ann. 5/604.10(b) (LexisNexis through P.A. 101-631). A 604.10(b) evaluation may be ordered if the capacity of one or both parents to adequately care for their children is called into question. A concern in this regard could be due to mental illness of one or both parents, substance abuse allegations, physical or mental abuse allegations or any other serious endangerment issue one or both parents may raise about the other's ability to care for the children. This type of evaluation not only is an investigation of the parties and the children, but also psychological tests are performed on each parent to determine their mental fitness to adequately care for their children. 750 Ill. Comp. Stat. Ann. 5/604.10(b) (LexisNexis through P.A. 101-631).

750 ILCS 604.10(b) states as follows:

> *The court may seek the advice of professional personnel, whether or not employed by the court on a regular basis. The advice given shall be in writing and made available by the court to counsel. Counsel may examine, as a witness, any professional personnel consulted by the court, designated as a court's witness. Professional personnel consulted by the court are subject to subpoena for the purposes of discovery, trial, or both. The court shall allocate the costs and fees of those professional personnel between the parties based upon the financial ability of each party and any other criteria the court considers appropriate. Upon the request of any party or upon the court's own motion, the court may conduct a hearing as to the reasonableness of those fees and costs.*

750 Ill. Comp. Stat. Ann. 5/604.10(b) (LexisNexis through P.A. 101-631).

As stated, this provision of the statute is most frequently used to appoint custody evaluators. A custody evaluator can be appointed when the parties to a divorce fail to reach an agreement regarding custody, parenting time or removal of the child from the state of Illinois on a permanent basis. Courts (i.e. Judges) tend to give great weight to the recommendations of the evaluator, though a Court may either accept or reject the recommendations of the Custody Evaluator.

If you find fault with a court-ordered 604.10(b) evaluation, you can request a 604.10(c) evaluation. The only difference between the two is the evaluator. When a party requests a 604.10(c) evaluation, they select the evaluator and pay all associated costs without any contribution from the other parent. 750 Ill. Comp. Stat. Ann. 5/604.10(c) (LexisNexis through P.A. 101-631).

A 215 evaluation investigates the mental or physical fitness of a parent. Ill. Sup. Ct. R. 215(a). Often, the evaluator only needs to meet with the parent once before submitting a report. There are differences of opinion as to whether these types of evaluations are appropriate in parenting cases in Illinois.

Common Reasons for Evaluations

The Court will order a 604.10(b) evaluation when more information about a family's circumstances would help decide the best parenting arrangement for a child or children. The judge may also order an evaluation if either parent or the appointed GAL/CR requests one. As stated above, concerns about the following often prompt custody evaluations:
- Domestic violence;
- Substance abuse;
- Mental illness;
- A child with special needs;
- A parent moving a child out of state;
- Mental health issues; and
- Questionable parenting.

Selecting and Paying an Evaluator

Evaluators are licensed professionals who meet state standards (psychologists or psychiatrists). The judge may assign an evaluator to your case or you may choose one from a court-approved list. Your evaluator must be a neutral third party with no connection to you or your family.

Evaluations can cost several thousand dollars. The judge may order parents to split the evaluator's fee based on their relative incomes, or have one parent assume most or all of the costs. Evaluations can last weeks or months while the evaluator studies the dynamics between the children and each parent in multiple ways. The evaluator may:
- Interview the children and parents individually;
- Conduct psychological testing on the family;
- Observe the family at home; and
- Interview friends, relatives and others involved with the family (like teachers or doctors)
- The evaluator may interview each person multiple times.
- The evaluator may interview the children multiple times.
- The evaluator may request to meet with each parent in their home if the parents live apart, or individually in the shared home if the family still lives together.
- You may need to submit personal health documents and take part in psychological testing.

The Evaluator's Report

At the end of the process, the evaluator will submit a report for the judge to review before your judge issues a final judgment regarding the allocation of parental responsibilities (formerly custody). 750 Ill. Comp. Stat. Ann. 5/604.10(b) (LexisNexis through P.A. 101-631). This report should detail the strengths and weaknesses of each parent, the relationships among the parties, and a recommendation for the division of parental responsibilities and parenting time. 750 Ill. Comp. Stat. Ann. 5/604.10(b)(4)-(5) (LexisNexis through P.A. 101-631). A 604.10(b) Evaluator must weigh the best interest of the child factors that are identified in the Statute and must base his or her recommendation on each parent's fitness to parent their children pursuant to these factors. If a 604.10(b) Evaluator is appointed by the Court, the Evaluator will testify as the Court's witness, and may be cross examined by the parties. 750 Ill. Comp. Stat. ann. 5/604.10(b) (LexisNexis through P.A. 101-631). If a 604.10(c) Evaluator is hired by one of the parties, then either party may call the Evaluator as a witness at trial, and the party calling the Evaluator as a witness will be required to pay the Evaluator's fees and costs for trial, unless the Court orders otherwise. 750 Ill. Comp. Stat. Ann. 5/604.10(c) (LexisNexis through P.A. 101-631).

The factors for the courts to observe for making a ruling on the allocation of decision making and other parental responsibility were detailed early on within this chapter.

Here are a few tips for parents going through an evaluation:

- Meet with your attorney before meeting with the evaluator to understand the process.
- Take all interactions with the evaluator seriously. Arrive on time, dress neatly; be prepared with documents, etc.;
- Always show that your children are a priority in your life. Keep their interests and needs at the forefront, rather than your own;
- Remember your words and actions will go into a report. Treat the evaluator with respect, and don't argue;
- Be honest. Recognize both your strengths and your weaknesses as a parent;
- Try not to speak negatively about the other parent;
- Don't coach your children;
- Be forthcoming with any questions you have; and
- Remember that the first impression is often the lasting impression.

While an evaluator is required to be as objective and unbiased as possible, parents should also be aware that their first impression may have an impact on the outcome of the evaluation. Know that a spotless home and perfect physical appearance is not what the evaluator is looking for, but some effort to pick up and dress appropriately may be noticed.

Being organized can also give a good first impression, and parents should try to have all required documentation in one place. Scrambling to find papers can be distracting, so having them close at hand can make it easier to stay calm and relaxed during the process. Evaluations add complexity to an already-complex process.
Throughout your case, you may need to create a parenting plan, draft parenting time schedules, track time with your children, keep a log about interactions with the other parent, and more.

Honesty is Key

For some parents, it can be tempting to try to lie about certain issues in order to get what is wanted out of the evaluation. However, most evaluators are trained to pick up on the signals or behaviors that can show when someone is not being honest. If dishonestly is discovered, it would likely be included in the report provided to the judge, which could have negative consequences in the final outcome.

Regardless of mistakes made in the past, it is important to be fully and completely honest throughout the entire evaluation. It may be wise to come up with straightforward answers to anticipated questions before any interviews so as to avoid sidestepping the issue or trying to make justifications.

Separate marital issues from kid's issues

A bad spouse is not always a bad parent and bringing up issues during an evaluation that have nothing to do with parenting or custody can create greater problems. Keeping spousal concerns between the parents and away from the children is the best way to promote the positive atmosphere that is more likely to result in better custody arrangements.

When an evaluator observes a parent, who is unwilling to separate his or her anger and frustration with an ex-spouse, it may be determined that the bitter spouse may attempt to prevent interactions between the other parent and the children. A judge wants to see parents who are willing to cooperate on behalf of their children without letting other concerns get in the way.

Your evaluator will watch for signs of parental alienation, which is when a parent manipulates their child's relationship with the other parent through false claims. It is important to remember that the parent who is best able to facilitate a relationship with the children and the other parent is a parent who is typically deemed to be able to put his or her own feelings aside and serve the best interests of the children.

A parent who is unable to identify the other parent's strengths may appear to be exhibiting alienating tendencies. If the evaluator detects alienation, he or she may recommend family therapy, and/or reductions in parenting time may result. The alienated parent may receive sole parental responsibility or parenting time that increases gradually. Therefore, it is imperative to keep a level head throughout the evaluation process.

Consult with your legal team

Words, actions and attitudes can impact the results of a child custody evaluation. A family law attorney can provide parents advice throughout the process, giving reminders on how to act and behave. While parents should not pretend to be someone that they are not, they may also want to put their best foot forward, and always lead with the best interests of their children in mind. If questions or concerns come up before or during an evaluation, legal counsel may be able to offer suggestions and guidance.

The first choice for separating parents and their children should be for moms and dads to work together to develop a parenting plan that best serves the best interests of their children. However, in those cases that are highly contested and parents are unable to agree, or other issues are present like mental illness, substance or physical abuse, the courts have legal remedies to protect the rights of children.

KNOWLEDGE IS POWER:
DISCLOSING YOUR FINANCIAL PICTURE

Whether you are filing for a divorce (pre-decree), having issues after a divorce (post-decree), or experiencing parenting issues with another party, either after a divorce or if you were never married, you may be required to answer 213 Interrogatories and gather documents for a Response to a 214 Notice to Produce. Both of these items are frequently referred to by using the Illinois Supreme Court Rules that authorize their usage, Illinois Supreme Court Rule 213 and Illinois Supreme Court Rule 214.

The Discovery Process

Discovery is a formal process of sharing and exchanging information between the parties before any trial takes place. In discovery, the parties (or their attorneys) are trying to get answers to questions about each parties' version of events, what their witnesses may say, what documents or other evidence they have to prove their case, and specifically in a family law case, what assets, income, and debts there are to be dealt with. Also, through discovery, the parties are trying to gather evidence and proof of their claims or defenses.

Financial Affidavits

The financial affidavit is a legal document, a formal declaration of the party's income and debts. It is a sworn statement that portrays a complete picture of your financial situation. It is a statement that shows your income, expenses, debt and assets. The process of completing a financial affidavit varies by state but nonetheless, a financial affidavit reveals to the court everything about your financial situation. This can be the most important process of a court case.

The financial affidavits give the court and the parties a clear and accurate picture of the finances of the marriage and of both parties individually. Illinois law requires a Financial Affidavit to be completed in every case. It can be a snapshot of the current parties' financial picture. It also requires both sides to swear that they are telling the truth about their financial situations as it is completed under oath. The Supreme Court has authorized one form for use in all domestic relations, and family law cases in Illinois.

The court needs this information to make orders about child support, maintenance, legal fees, and awards from investments and retirement accounts. The financial affidavit is also called the financial statement, net worth statement, financial disclosure, and statement of financial affairs. This can vary state to state.

Thorough research will be required in order to gather supporting evidence in each individual case. There will have to be detailed paperwork and supporting documentation when the financial affidavit is compiled and submitted to the Court to support the specific evidence.

Typically, you will disclose your monthly amounts of income and expenses. This will give the court and parties in the case a clear and accurate picture of the finances of the parties. This will entail how much you earn, how much you spend, how many assets you own, how much debt you have and what your investment and retirement assets are.

This may seem like an easy task; however, the financial disclosure statement is very detailed and accuracy is incredibly important. The financial disclosure statement is one of the key documents that the Court will review at a trial and/or hearing regarding finances. If a statement includes inaccurate figures, the Court will begin to question the accuracy of the remaining figures. One key for represented parties in a case is to turn to your attorney's office in completing the disclosure form. If there is a question about how something should be portrayed or how to calculate an amount, the attorney's office is there to advise you. Turning to them is appropriate and each attorney handles the preparation of these disclosures differently.

You will need to review your affidavit, your spouses' affidavit and all supporting documents to note any inconsistencies. If you find any, you will need to bring this to the attorney's attention. Perhaps someone is hiding assets or stating their income incorrectly to try to avoid certain consequences. Your attorney and the court will be looking for these mistakes or omissions and the difficulty lies in finding them. Once you do, you will have to prove whether they were intentionally made or just simple mistakes. This is where the supporting documents come in which will either support the affidavit or reveal errors. .

The financial affidavit also shows whether property is marital. As discussed elsewhere, if property is marital it is subject to division. The financial affidavit should include assets that you believe are marital and non-marital. Labeling something as non-marital on the Financial Disclosure Statement does not meet the burden of proving something is non-marital, however, it still needs to be labeled as such if that is going to be the claim. The Court and the attorneys use this information to see if either party received a gift or inheritance or a monetary settlement from a lawsuit. The court will assign the financial responsibility based on all data presented. You can also use a process called discovery, as discussed in this section to uncover additional information related to both parties. This process is separate from the financial affidavit, but it can be looked at as an extension of the financial affidavit. This process will be more intensive and will require a larger amount of paperwork and supporting documents to complete. Usually one statement as a snapshot such as a pay stub or a copy of your most recent tax returns along with credit card statements will be included with the financial affidavit, while the discovery process compels the production of multiple documents.

When filling out the financial affidavit you should include information such as

- the parties' names, county and case number
- income from all sources
- expenses
- gifts or inheritances
- deductions related to taxes
- extracurricular expenses
- health care costs
- debts
- assets

Supporting documents are needed to complete the financial affidavit, such as, pay stubs, tax forms, credit card statements, checking account statements, savings account statements, money market or credit union account statements, certificates of deposit, cash and prepaid debit cards, stocks, bonds, options and ESOP's, Investment/brokerage accounts, mutual funds, and secured or unsecured notes, real estate/mortgage and or HELOC information, vehicle information, business interests, life insurance policies, retirement benefits, deferred compensation, annuity, IRA, 401k, 403b, SEP, lawsuit/claims, workers' compensation, disability information, valuables, transfers or sale of property and information for other assets and property. Again, these are the most recent or back up documents but not all of the available statements for each asset.

Don't procrastinate when it comes to filling out the affidavit. There is usually a local court rule as to the due date. There can also be a court ordered due date for completion of same. Once the financial affidavit is completed and the supporting documents are submitted you will now be ready to submit the financial affidavit to both parties or to opposing counsels and the court.

A financial affidavit will identify the following elements:

1.) Affiant: the person making the affidavit
2.) Employer: the name and address of the person or company employing the affiant
3.) Sources of income: all sources of income of the affiant, including rental, investment, self-employment, unemployment or disability income
4.) Salary deductions: the monthly deductions from the affiant's salary, including federal income tax, social security, state income tax, Medicare, health insurance, and more depending what your deductions are.

Everyone's payroll is different, however, to complete the Financial Affidavit, everything must be listed in a monthly snapshot. Therefore, despite the frequency of paychecks, the amounts must be converted to a monthly amount. In order to do so if paychecks are received weekly, take the weekly check times 52 (the amount of weeks in a year) and then divide by twelve for a monthly average. If paychecks are received biweekly, take the paycheck amount times 26 (which is the number of checks that will be received during a year) and then divide by twelve for a monthly average. If paychecks are received twice a month (on set days, generally the 15th and last day or the 1st and the 15th), then simply double the paycheck. These formulas are simply for salaried employees but can be different if an hourly wage is earned or the person is only employed seasonally. Another twist is people who are not paid year around, like some educational staff for example. One basic rule of thumb to think about is that the Court is looking for an average or what is typical of what you have to spend during a month. Therefore, seasonal employees should average what they have made year to date for example, because that is likely what they are going to have to do to budget as well.

There are some specific instructions for completing the Illinois specific form that might be helpful as you move along. The current form follows:

This form is approved by the Illinois Supreme Court and is required to be used in all Illinois Circuit Courts.

STATE OF ILLINOIS, CIRCUIT COURT _____ COUNTY	**FINANCIAL AFFIDAVIT** (FAMILY & DIVORCE CASES) ☐ Pre-Judgment ☐ Post-Judgment	For Court Use Only
Instructions ▼ Enter above the county name where the case was filed. Enter name of the Petitioner, the Respondent, and the case number as listed in the initial Petition or Complaint. Enter the Case Number given by the Circuit Clerk.	Petitioner (First, middle, last name) _____ v. _____ Respondent (First, middle, last name)	Case Number

IMPORTANT: (1) If you intentionally or recklessly enter inaccurate or misleading information on this form, you may face significant penalties and sanctions, including costs and attorney's fees; and (2) If you need more room to complete this form, complete and attach the *Additional Information for the Financial Affidavit* form.

1. I am the ☐ Petitioner ☐ Respondent in this case.

2. I swear or affirm the information in this *Financial Affidavit* and all attached documents is true and correct as of _____.
                                                               Date

In 3a-d, check the boxes of the documents you are attaching to this form as evidence of your income, assets, and debts. If you select 3d, enter the names of the additional documents you are attaching.

3. I attached the most recent copies of the following documents *(check all that apply)*:
   a. ☐ income tax returns
   b. ☐ pay stubs or other proof of income
   c. ☐ bank statements
   d. ☐ other supporting documents: _____

In 4, do not complete 4b and 4c if your information is protected because of domestic violence or abuse.

4. Information about myself:
   a. Name: _____
           First   Middle   Last
   b. Phone Number: _____
   c. Home Address: _____
           Street Address, Apt.
   _____
   City   State   ZIP
   d. Date of Birth: _____

In 5b, if you are already divorced from each other, enter the date the divorce was granted.

In 5c, if you do not live together, enter the date you separated.

5. Information about this relationship:
   a. We were married or united: ☐ Yes _____ ☐ No
                                           Date
   b. We are divorced: ☐ Yes _____ ☐ No
                             Date
   c. We currently live together: ☐ Yes ☐ No _____
                                                   Date

DV-A 120.2   (09/16)

Enter the Case Number given by the Circuit Clerk:_____

6. **Information about other household members:**
   I currently live with another adult who is not the Petitioner or Respondent in this case who helps pay my expenses: ☐ Yes ☐ No

> In **7b**, check the box to indicate who each child of this relationship lives with. Check both boxes if the child lives with both parents. If the child does not live with Petitioner or Respondent, do not check either box.

7. **Children:**
   a. Children were born or adopted as a result of this relationship: ☐ Yes ☐ No
   b.

	Name of Child of this Relationship	Date of Birth	Lives with	
1.			☐ Petitioner	☐ Respondent
2.			☐ Petitioner	☐ Respondent
3.			☐ Petitioner	☐ Respondent
4.			☐ Petitioner	☐ Respondent
5.			☐ Petitioner	☐ Respondent

   c. Other children not of this relationship live with me: ☐ Yes ☐ No

> In **8a**, check all that apply. Provide all information requested about your jobs, including all full-time, part-time, temporary, contract, or other work. If you need more room to list additional employment, complete and attach *Additional Information for the Financial Affidavit*.

8. **My employment:**
   a. I am ☐ unemployed ☐ self-employed ☐ employed by someone else
   b. Employer name: _____
   c. Employer address: _____
      Street Address, Apt.

      _____
      City   State   ZIP

   d. Number of paychecks per year: ☐ 12 *(monthly)* ☐ 24 *(two times a month)*
      ☐ 26 *(every two weeks)* ☐ 52 *(weekly)*
      ☐ I am paid in cash

> In **8e**, enter your total gross income from all sources from January 1 of this year through the date you list.

   e. Gross income *(before taxes and deductions)* so far this year $_____
      as of _____
         Date

> In **9a**, check only one.
>
> In **9a-d**, enter the information you submitted on last year's IRS tax return. If you did not file a tax return for last year check **Did not file**, leave **a-d** blank but still complete **9e**.

9. **My gross income and taxes from last year:**
   a. Tax filing status: ☐ Married *(Joint)* ☐ Married *(Separate)* ☐ Single
      ☐ Head of Household ☐ Did not file
   b. Number of dependent exemptions claimed: _____
   c. Total number of exemptions claimed: _____
   d. Amount of most recent tax refund: $_____ or amount owed $_____
   e. Gross income *(before taxes and deductions)* last year: $_____

10. **Bankruptcy in the last 5 years:**
    I filed for bankruptcy in the last 5 years: ☐ Yes ☐ No

> For help in calculating monthly amounts, see *How to Complete a Financial Affidavit*.

11. **My gross monthly income** *(before taxes and deductions)* **is:**

> In **11**, **Regular employment earnings** mean the monthly gross income you receive on a regular basis from employment.

Regular employment earnings *(salary, wages, base pay, etc.)*	$_____
Overtime	$_____
Commission	$_____
Tips	$_____
Bonus	$_____

DV-A 120.2 — Page 2 of 9 — (09/16)

Enter the Case Number given by the Circuit Clerk:_____

Income other than **Regular employment earnings**, such as **Overtime**, **Commission**, or **Bonus** should be listed separately.	Pension and other retirement benefits	$_____
	Annuity	$_____
	Interest income	$_____
	Dividend income	$_____
	Trust income	$_____
	Social Security: ☐ SSI ☐ SSDI ☐ retirement *(check all that apply)*	$_____
For **Educational funds** include fellowships, stipends, grants, scholarships, etc.	Unemployment benefits	$_____
	Disability payment *(not Social Security)*	$_____
	Workers' compensation	$_____
	TANF and SNAP	$_____
	Military allowances	$_____
	Investment income	$_____
	Rental income	$_____
	Partnership income	$_____
	Distributions and draws	$_____
In **Other**, list other income from all sources, including amounts from the *Additional Information for the Financial Affidavit* form, if any.	Royalty income	$_____
	Educational funds *(include payments made directly to the school)*	$_____
	Maintenance	$_____
	Child support for children of this relationship	$_____
	Child support for children not of this relationship	$_____
	Gifts of money	$_____
	Other _____	$_____
In **Total Gross Monthly Income**, add the amounts in **11** together and enter the	**Total Gross Monthly Income**	$_____

12. **My monthly deductions are:**

For help in calculating monthly amounts, see *How to Complete a Financial Affidavit*.	Federal tax	$_____
	State tax	$_____
	FICA *(or Social Security equivalent)*	$_____
In **12**, use information from your paystubs, tax records, and other sources to identify all properly calculated deductions.	Medicare tax	$_____
	Mandatory retirement contributions *(by law or condition of employment)*	$_____
	Union dues	$_____
	Health insurance premiums *(medical, dental, vision)*	$_____
	Life insurance premiums to secure child support	$_____
	Child support actually paid under a court order in a different case	$_____
	Maintenance actually paid under a court order in a different case	$_____
	Maintenance actually paid or payable under a court order in this case	$_____
In **Total Monthly Deductions**, add the amounts from **12** together and enter the total.	Expenditures for repayment of debts that represent reasonable and necessary expenses for the production of income including, but not limited to, student loans, medical expenditures necessary to preserve life or health, reasonable expenditures for the benefit of the child and other parent, exclusive of gifts.	$_____
	Foster care payments paid by DCFS	$_____
	Total Monthly Deductions	$_____

Enter the Case Number given by the Circuit Clerk:_____

For help in calculating monthly amounts, see *How to Complete a Financial Affidavit*.	
In **13a**, enter the amount your household spends on each item each month.	

13. My monthly living expenses are:

a. Household Expenses

Mortgage or rent	$ _____
Home equity *(HELOC)* and second mortgage	$ _____
Real estate taxes	$ _____
Homeowners or condo association dues and assessments	$ _____
Homeowners or renters insurance	$ _____
Gas	$ _____
Electric	$ _____
Telephone	$ _____
Cable or satellite TV	$ _____
Internet	$ _____
Water and sewer	$ _____
Garbage removal	$ _____
Laundry and dry cleaning	$ _____
House cleaning service	$ _____
Necessary repairs and maintenance to my property	$ _____
Pet care	$ _____
Groceries, household supplies, and toiletries	$ _____
Other _____	$ _____

In **Other**, list other Household Expenses from all sources, including amounts from the *Additional Information for the Financial Affidavit* form, if any.

In **Subtotal Monthly Household Expenses**, add the amounts in **13a** together and enter the total.

Subtotal Monthly Household Expenses $ _____

In **13b**, enter the amount you spend monthly on each type of transportation expense.

b. Transportation Expenses

Car payment	$ _____
Repairs and maintenance	$ _____
Insurance, license, and city stickers	$ _____
Gasoline	$ _____
Taxi, ride-share, bus, and train	$ _____
Parking	$ _____
Other_____	$ _____

If you have other transportation expenses not listed in **13b**, describe the expense in **Other** and enter the amount.

Subtotal Monthly Transportation Expenses $ _____

In **Subtotal Monthly Transportation Expenses**, add the amounts in **13b** together and enter the total.

In **13c**, enter the amount you spend monthly only for yourself on each type of expense. Do not include expenses you are reimbursed for through insurance or your employer.

c. Personal Expenses

Medical *(out-of-pocket expenses)*

Doctor visits	$ _____
Therapy and counseling	$ _____
Dental and orthodontia	$ _____
Optical	$ _____
Medicine	$ _____

Life insurance *(not required by law to secure child support)*

Life *(term)*	$ _____
Life *(whole or annuity)*	$ _____
Clothing	$ _____
Grooming *(hair, nails, spa, etc.)*	$ _____
Club membership dues	$ _____

Enter the Case Number given by the Circuit Clerk:_____

	Entertainment, dining out, and hobbies	$
	Newspapers, magazines, and subscriptions	$
	Gifts	$
	Donations *(political, religious, charity, etc.)*	$
	Vacations	$
	Voluntary trade or professional association dues	$
	Professional fees *(accountants, tax preparers, etc.)*	$
	Other _____	$
	Subtotal Monthly Personal Expenses	$

> In **Other**, list other Personal Expenses from all sources, including amounts from the *Additional Information for the Financial Affidavit* form, if any.
>
> In **Subtotal Monthly Personal Expenses**, add the amounts in **13c** together and enter the total.
>
> In **13d**, enter the amount spent monthly on the minor and dependent children of this relationship.

d. Minor and Dependent Children Expenses

Clothing	$
Grooming *(hair, nails, spa, etc.)*	$
Education	
Tuition	$
Books, fees, and supplies	$
School lunch	$
Transportation	$
School-sponsored trips and special events	$
Uniforms	$
Before and after-school care	$
Tutoring and summer school	$
Medical *(out-of-pocket expenses)*	
Doctor visits	$
Therapy and counseling	$
Dental and orthodontia	$
Optical	$
Medicine	$
Allowance	$
Childcare and sitters	$
Extracurricular activities and sports *(including equipment, uniforms, etc.)*	$
Summer and school-break camps	$
Vacations *(children only)*	$
Entertainment, dining out, and hobbies *(children only)*	$
Gifts children give to others	$
Other_____	$
Subtotal Monthly Children Expenses	$

> In **Medical**, do not include expenses you are reimbursed for through insurance or your employer.
>
> If there are other child-related expenses not listed in **13d**, describe the expense in **Other** and enter the amount.
>
> In **Subtotal Monthly Children Expenses**, add the amounts in **13d** together and enter the total.

Total Monthly Living Expenses *(add the subtotals from above)* $ _____

> In **Total Monthly Living Expenses**, add the Subtotals from **13a-13d** together and enter the total.

DV-A 120.2   (09/16)

Enter the Case Number given by the Circuit Clerk:_____

In **14**, enter your debts including credit cards and past due bills. Do not include debt payments previously listed in **13** above, such as your mortgage or car payment.	**14. My debts:**	

	Creditor Name	Describe Nature of Debt *(household goods, attorney's fees, etc.)*	Amount Owed	Monthly Payment Being Made
1.			$	$
2.			$	$
3.			$	$
4.			$	$
5.			$	$
6.			$	$

In **Total Monthly Debt Payments**, add the **Minimum Monthly Payment** amounts from **14** together and enter the total. Include any debts listed on the *Additional Information for the Financial Affidavit* form, if any.

Amount from the *Additional Information for the Financial Affidavit (if any)* $ _____

Total Monthly Debt Payments $ _____

15. Total Income Available Per Month:

In **Total Gross Monthly Income**, enter the total from **11**.

In **Total Monthly Deductions**, enter the total from **12**.

Subtract **Total Monthly Deductions** from Total **Gross Monthly Income** and enter the total.

   a. Total Monthly Net Income

     Total Gross Monthly Income $ _____

     Total Monthly Deductions   − $ _____

     Total Monthly Net Income   = $ _____

In **Total Monthly Living Expenses**, enter the total from **13**.

In **Total Monthly Debt Payments**, enter the total from **14**.

Add **Total Monthly Living Expenses** and **Total Monthly Debt Payments** and enter the total.

   b. Total Monthly Living Expenses and Debt Payments

     Total Monthly Living Expenses $ _____

     Total Monthly Debt Payments   + $ _____

     Total Monthly Living Expenses and Debt Payments   = $ _____

In **Total Monthly Net Income**, enter the total from **15a**.

In **Total Monthly Living Expenses and Debt Payments**, enter the total from **15b**.

Subtract **Total Monthly Living Expenses and Debt Payments** from **Total Monthly Net Income** and enter the total.

   c. Total Income Available Per Month

     Total Monthly Net Income $ _____

     Total Monthly Living Expenses and Debt Payments   − $ _____

     Total Income Available Per Month   = $ _____

Enter the Case Number given by the Circuit Clerk: _____

16. My assets:

In 16a, enter your cash and cash equivalents. Do not list account numbers.

a. Cash and Cash Equivalents

Checking, Savings, Money Market, and Other Bank or Credit Union Accounts

	Name of Bank or Institution	Name on Account	Account Type	Balance
1.				$
2.				$
3.				$
4.				$
5.				$

Certificates of Deposit

	Name of Bank or Institution	Name on Account	Balance
1.			$
2.			$
3.			$
4.			$

Cash and Prepaid Debit Card

	Location of Cash/Card	Held By	Balance
1.			$
2.			$
3.			$

b. Investment Accounts and Securities

In 16b, enter information for your investments and securities.

Stocks, Bonds, Options, and ESOPs

	Company Name	# Shares	Type	Owner	FMV
1.					$
2.					$
3.					$
4.					$
5.					$

FMV means Fair Market Value throughout this form.

Investment/Brokerage Accounts, Mutual Funds, and Secured or Unsecured Notes

	Description of Asset	Owner	Balance
1.			$
2.			$
3.			$
4.			$

DV-A 120.2   Page 7 of 9   (09/16)

Enter the Case Number given by the Circuit Clerk: _____

> In **16c**, enter information for your real estate.
>
> In **16c** and **16d**, in **Balance Due**, enter the total amount remaining on your loan.

c. Real Estate

	Address	Name on Title	FMV	Balance Due
1.			$	$
2.			$	$
3.			$	$
4.			$	$

> In **16d**, enter information about your motor vehicles.

d. Motor Vehicles *(cars, boats, trailers, motorcycles, aircrafts, etc.)*

	Year, Make, and Model	Name on Title	FMV	Balance Due
1.			$	$
2.			$	$
3.			$	$
4.			$	$

> In **16e**, enter information about your business interests.
>
> In **Type**, enter whether the business is a corporation, S Corp, or LLC, etc.

e. Business Interests

	Name of Business	Type	% of Ownership	FMV
1.				$
2.				$
3.				$

> In **16f**, enter information about each life insurance policy you have for yourself, the other party, or your children.

f. Life Insurance Policies

	Name of Insurance Company	Type of Policy	Death Benefit	Cash Value
1.			$	$
2.			$	$
3.			$	$

> In **16g**, enter information about retirement benefits (vested and non-vested).

g. Retirement Benefits and Deferred Compensation *(pension plan, annuity, IRA, 401(k), 403(b), SEP)*

	Name of Plan	Type of Plan	FMV or Account Balance
1.			$
2.			$
3.			$
4.			$

> In **16h**, enter information about your federal and state tax returns for the last 2 years. Check **Refund** if you received money or check **Amount Owed** if you owed additional taxes.

h. Income Tax Refunds or Amounts Owed for the Last 2 Years *(federal and state)*

	Tax year	Federal: ☐ Refund ☐ Amount Owed	State: ☐ Refund ☐ Amount Owed
1.		$	$
2.		$	$

DV-A 120.2

Enter the Case Number given by the Circuit Clerk: _____

	In **16i**, enter information about lawsuits and claims you filed or intend to file. If you did not recover anything, enter $0, or if your case is still pending or has not yet been filed, enter unknown.

i. Lawsuits and Claims (*workers' compensation, disability, etc.*)

	Case Number	Date Lawsuit or Claim Filed	Amount Recovered
1.			$
2.			$

In **16j**, enter information for valuable collectible items.

j. Valuable Collectibles (*coins, stamps, art, antiques, etc.*)

	Description	FMV
1.		$
2.		$

In **16k**, enter information for assets or property you transferred or sold in the last 2 years with a FMV of at least $1,000. Do not include income items listed above in **11**.

k. Transfer or Sale of Assets or Property Within the Last 2 Years With a FMV of at Least $1,000

	Description	Transferred or Sold to	Date of Transfer	Amount
1.				$
2.				$

In **17a-i**, enter information about health insurance you have for yourself and your family.

In **17b**, enter all carriers if more than one.

17. Health insurance:
   a. I have health insurance: ☐ Yes ☐ No
   b. The insurance carrier is: _____
   c. The type of insurance is: ☐ Medical ☐ Dental ☐ Optical
   d. Deductible: Per individual: $ _____ Per family $ _____
   e. It covers: ☐ Me ☐ My spouse/partner ☐ My dependents
   f. Type of policy: ☐ HMO ☐ PPO ☐ Full indemnity
   g. Provided by: ☐ Employer ☐ Private policy ☐ Other group
   h. Monthly cost is paid by: ☐ Employer ☐ Employee ☐ Other
   i. Total monthly cost : $ _____

In **18**, if you need more room to complete this form check yes, and complete and attach the *Additional Information for the Financial Affidavit* form.

18. There is an *Additional Information for the Financial Affidavit* form attached:
   ☐ Yes ☐ No

IMPORTANT: If you intentionally or recklessly enter inaccurate or misleading information on this form, you may face significant penalties and sanctions, including costs and attorney's fees.

Under the Code of Civil Procedure, 735 ILCS 5/1-109, making a statement on this form that you know to be false is perjury, a Class 3 Felony.

I certify that everything in the *Financial Affidavit* is true and correct. I understand that making a false statement on this form is perjury and has penalties provided by law under **735 ILCS 5/1-109**.

After you finish this form, sign and print your name and date it.

Your Signature   Your Name

Date

DV-A 120.2

PRINT FORM   **SAVE FORM**   **RESET FORM**

This form is approved by the Illinois Supreme Court and is required to be used in all Illinois Circuit Courts.

STATE OF ILLINOIS, CIRCUIT COURT	ADDITIONAL INFORMATION FOR THE FINANCIAL AFFIDAVIT (FAMILY & ',925&(CASES)	For Court Use Only
_____ COUNTY	☐ Pre-Judgment ☐ Post-Judgment	

Instructions ▼

Enter above the county name where the case was filed.

Enter name of the Petitioner, the Respondent, and the case number as listed in the initial Petition or Complaint.

Enter the Case Number given by the Circuit Clerk.

Petitioner *(First, middle, last name)*

v.

Respondent *(First, middle, last name)*

Case Number

When adding information for a particular section on the *Financial AffidaYLW*, include the section number and all of the information the section requests.

Complete and attach this document to the *Financial Affidavit*.

DV-AI 121.1   Page 1 of 1   (04/16)

PRINT FORM   **SAVE FORM**   **RESET FORM**

Here are some tips for completing the Financial Affidavit (numbers and letters refer to which section of the above Financial Affidavit are being referenced):

- On Page 1. Enter the county the case was filed in. Enter the name of the petitioner, the respondent and the case number, enter the case number that was provided when the case was filed and can be found on the top right-hand corner of the filed Petition.
- 3 a-d check the boxes of the documents you are attaching to this form for evidence and to support the financial affidavit. There are actually instructions within the form to help you.
- 3d enter the names of any additional documents you may provide. This may be retirement accounts or a collection of valuables.
- In 4 do not complete 4b and 4c if your information is protected because of domestic violence or abuse. If that is the case, there will be specific rules applying to your case and specific orders that will need to be recognized by the Court before the exception can apply.
- 5 b if you are already divorced from each other enter the date the divorce was granted.
- In 5c if you do not live together enter the date you separated.
- 7 b check the box to indicate who the children of this relationship live with. Check both boxes if the child lives with both parents. If the child does not live with the petitioner or the respondent do not check either box.
- 8a check all that apply. Provide all information requested about your job, including all full time, part time, temporary contracted or other work. If more room is needed, complete the attached form, "Additional information for the financial affidavit."
- 8e enter your total gross income from all sources form January 1st of this year through the date you list.
- 9a enter the information to submit on last year's IRS tax return. If you did not file a tax return for last year, check did not file.
- 9c. For help calculating income and monthly amounts please refer to the above discussion.
- 11. Regular employment earnings means the monthly gross income you received on a regular basis from employment. Earnings other than regular employment such as overtime, commissions and bonus should be listed separately. For educational funds you receive include fellowships, stipends, grants, scholarships, etc. If you have other monthly income not listed in 11, list the income source under other. In total gross monthly income, add the amounts in 11 together and enter the total.
- In 12 use the information from your pay stubs, tax documents, and other documents to identify all sources and properly calculate deductions. In total monthly deductions add the amounts together and enter the total.
- 13 enter the amounts your household spends on each item each month. If you have additional monthly living expenses not listed in 13a, fill out the expenses in other and enter the amount. In subtotal monthly household expenses add the amounts in 13 a together and enter the total.

- 13 b enter the amount you spend monthly on each type of transportation expense. If you pay other transportation expenses not listed on 13 b describe the expense in other and enter the amounts. In subtotal monthly transportation expenses add the amounts in 13 b together and enter the total.
- In 13 c enter the amounts you spend monthly only for yourselves on each type of expense. Do not include expenses you are reimbursed for through your insurance or your employer. If you have other personal expenses not listed in 13 c describe the expense in other and enter that amount. In subtotal monthly personal expenses, add the amounts in 13 c together and enter the total.
- 13 d enter the amount spent monthly on the minor and dependent children of this relationship. In medical, do not include expenses paid for through insurance or your employer. If there are additional related items not listed in 13 d describe the expense in other and enter the amount. In subtotal monthly children expenses, add the amounts In 13 d together and enter the total. In total monthly living expenses, add the subtotals from 13 a and 13 d together and enter the total.
- In 14 enter your debts including credit cards and past due bills. Do not include debt payments previously listed in 13 above such as your mortgage or car payment. In total monthly debt payments add the minimum monthly payment amounts from 14 together and enter the total. In total gross monthly income enter the total from 11. In total monthly deductions add the total from 12. Subtract total monthly deductions from total gross monthly income and enter the total. In total monthly living expenses enter the total from 13. In total monthly debt payments enter the total from 14. Add total monthly debt payments and total monthly living expenses and enter the total. In total monthly net income enter the total from 15 a. in total monthly living expenses and debt payments enter the total from 15 b. Subtract total monthly living expenses and debt payments from total monthly net income and enter the total. In 16a enter your cash and cash equivalent.
- 16 b enter information for your investment securities. FMV means fair market value throughout this form. 16c enter information for your real estate. 16 c and 16 d in balance due, enter the total amount remaining on your loan. 16 d enter information about your vehicles. 16 e enter information about your business interests. In business type, enter whether the business is a corporation S or LLC, etc. In 16 f enter information about each life insurance policy you have for yourself, the other party or your children. 16 g enter information about retirement benefits. Vested or not vested. 16 h enter information about your federal and state tax returns for the last 2 years. Check refund or amount owed where applicable. 16 I enter information about lawsuits and claims you filed or intended to file. If you did not recover anything, enter zero or if your case is still pending or had not yet been filed enter unknown. 16 j and 16 K enter information for assets or property you transferred or sold in the last 2 years with a fair market value of at least 1,000.00. Do not include income items listed above in #11.

- In 17 a-I enter information about your health insurance for you and your family. 17 b enter all carriers of insurance if more than one.
- 18 if you need more room to complete this form check yes and attach the additional information to the financial affidavit form.

It is likely that the first thing the Judge will review in your case is the Financial Disclosure Statement. That is why this is an extremely important process. Additionally, the Financial Disclosure Statement is often the basis for setting temporary support orders and the like. Ensuring that time is taken to accurately complete this affidavit is imperative.

Formal Discovery Requests

The discovery process is an important stage of the litigation process and aside from the required Financial Disclosure Statement, there are other avenues of discovery. The most commonly used discovery requests in family law are a Notice to Produce and Marital Interrogatories. It is required that parties use good faith in responding to all discovery requests that are properly issued. It is very important to complete these requests because the discovery is an integral part of the case. The discovery responses are heavily relied upon in court by both the attorneys and the Judge. It is best to get the requests completed and sent to the requesting party within the 28-day time frame authorized by the Illinois Supreme Court Rules, as much as practical.

One reason litigants often wish to delay producing discovery is out of frustration with the other party. Delaying production of the requested discovery because the other party isn't producing the documents requested of them only further delays the case. This could cause an increase in attorney's fees for continual follow up and the potential that a Motion to Compel Discovery is filed against you because of the lack of response. A Motion to Compel is a formal motion filed with the Court where the party requesting discovery, alleges you have not complied with the requests and is requesting that the Court enforce those discovery requests. Additionally, delays may occur in scheduled hearings because of the failure to comply with discovery. There is an option to request an extension from opposing counsel under certain circumstances. Extensions are common and attorneys are required by the Illinois Supreme Court Rules to attempt to resolve discovery differences amongst themselves before seeking Court intervention. There might be reasons why an extension is not practical, however, like an upcoming financial hearing or a reciprocal deadline needing to be met.

If a party does not respond to Interrogatories or Notice to Produce within the 28 days, then the proper procedure is for the issuing attorney to send a request for compliance. This is often referred to as a 201(k) request because Illinois Supreme Court Rule 201(k) requires counsel for the party seeking those answers to requests a conference with opposing counsel to discuss and attempt to resolve the dispute before Court intervention. Ill. Sup. Ct. R. 201(k). Following the conference, if there continues to be a dispute or non-compliance issue, the requesting party can file a Motion to Compel as discussed above. One of the available remedies in a Motion to Compel that the non-compliant party is sanctioned, which are usually monetary penalties assigned to the party, however, there are other non-monetary sanctions available as well. Ill. Sup. Ct. R. 219(c).

There are times when objections to the requests are proper. There must be a basis for the objection, however, and not simply because the party does not wish to comply. One basis that is common is that the issuing party is requesting documents that are too far remote in time. Any Objections must be filed with the Court within the 28-day time period from the date of receipt of said requests, even if an extension regarding the remaining requests is granted. Ill. Sup. Ct. R. 214(c).

There is a continuing duty to disclose information when new or different information is discovered or revealed. Ill. Sup. Ct. R. 214(d). Discuss your disclosure obligations early with your attorney so that you can promptly gather the necessary documents.

213 INTERROGATORIES

Pre-decree Interrogatories

Pre-decree matrimonial interrogatories are written standardized questions that the opposing party wants you to answer. Oftentimes, the questions appear redundant and might relate to information that was also requested in the 214 Notice to Produce, however, it is still necessary that the request is completed. One way to reduce attorneys' fees, is to complete the interrogatories as completely as possible to reduce the time it takes the attorney's office to fill in the missing information.

The rule governing these requests states as follows:

> *(a) Directing Interrogatories. A party may direct written interrogatories to any other party. A copy of the interrogatories shall be served on all other parties entitled to notice; (b) Duty of Attorney. It is the duty of an attorney directing interrogatories to restrict them to the subject matter of the particular case, to avoid undue detail, and to avoid the imposition of any unnecessary burden or expense on the answering party; (c) Number of Interrogatories. Except as provided in subparagraph (j), a party shall not serve more than 30 interrogatories, including sub-parts, on any other party except upon agreement of the parties or leave of court granted upon a showing of good cause. A motion for leave of court to serve more than 30 interrogatories must be in writing and shall set forth the proposed interrogatories and the reasons establishing good cause for their use; (d) Answers and Objections. Within 28 days after service of the interrogatories upon the party to whom they are directed, the party shall serve a sworn answer or an objection to each interrogatory, with proof of service upon all other parties entitled to notice. Any objection to an answer or to the refusal to answer an interrogatory shall be heard by the court upon prompt notice and motion of the party propounding the interrogatory. The answering party shall set forth in full each interrogatory being answered immediately preceding the answer. Sworn answers*

to interrogatories directed to a public or private corporation, or a partnership or association shall be made by an officer, partner, or agent, who shall furnish such information as is available to the party; (e) Option to Produce Documents. When the answer to an interrogatory may be obtained from documents in the possession or control of the party on whom the interrogatory was served, it shall be a sufficient answer to the interrogatory to produce those documents responsive to the interrogatory. When a party elects to answer an interrogatory by the production of documents, that production shall comply with the requirements of Rule 214; (f) Identity and Testimony of Witnesses. Upon written interrogatory, a party must furnish the identities and addresses of witnesses who will testify at trial and must provide the following information; (1) Lay Witnesses. A "lay witness" is a person giving only fact or lay opinion testimony. For each lay witness, the party must identify the subjects on which the witness will testify. An answer is sufficient if it gives reasonable notice of the testimony, taking into account the limitations on the party's knowledge of the facts known by and opinions held by the witness; (2) Independent Expert Witnesses. An "independent expert witness" is a person giving expert testimony who is not the party, the party's current employee, or the party's retained expert. For each independent expert witness, the party must identify the subjects on which the witness will testify and the opinions the party expects to elicit. An answer is sufficient if it gives reasonable notice of the testimony, taking into account the limitations on the party's knowledge of the facts known by and opinions held by the witness; (3) Controlled Expert Witnesses. A "controlled expert witness" is a person giving expert testimony who is the party, the party's current employee, or the party's retained expert. For each controlled expert witness, the party must identify: (i) the subject matter on which the witness will testify; (ii) the conclusions and opinions of the witness and the bases therefor; (iii) the qualifications of the witness; and (iv) any reports prepared by the witness about the case; (g) Limitation on Testimony and Freedom to Cross-Examine. The information disclosed in answer to a Rule 213(f) interrogatory, or in a discovery deposition, limits the testimony that can be given by a witness on direct examination at trial. Information disclosed in a discovery deposition need not be later specifically identified in a Rule 213(f) answer, but, upon objection at trial, the burden is on the proponent of the witness to prove the information was provided in a Rule 213(f) answer or in the discovery deposition. Except upon a showing of good cause, information

> *in an evidence deposition not previously disclosed in a Rule 213(f) interrogatory answer or in a discovery deposition shall not be admissible upon objection at trial. Without making disclosure under this rule, however, a cross-examining party can elicit information, including opinions, from the witness. This freedom to cross-examine is subject to a restriction that applies in actions that involve multiple parties and multiple representation. In such actions, the cross-examining party may not elicit undisclosed information, including opinions, from the witness on an issue on which its position is aligned with that of the party doing the direct examination; (h) Use of Answers to Interrogatories. Answers to interrogatories may be used in evidence to the same extent as a discovery deposition; (i) Duty to Supplement. A party has a duty to seasonably supplement or amend any prior answer or response whenever new or additional information subsequently becomes known to that party; (j) The Supreme Court, by administrative order, may approve standard forms of interrogatories for different classes of cases; (k) Liberal Construction. This rule is to be liberally construed to do substantial justice between or among the parties.*

Ill. Sup. Ct. R. 213.

There may be numerous questions that relate to your situation where the answers are out there, but you do not have possession of the information. If that is the case, it is okay to answer, unknown or explain that the information is in someone's possession. If you are not sure of an answer(s), please state "Unknown." Also, there will be questions that request information for items you do not have. In that case, it is okay to answer none or n/a.

As far as references to the terms "non-marital" or "marital" property, these are answers best left to be formulated by you in conjunction with your attorney's office. Likewise, with answers which seek information regarding "contribution or dissipation" and witnesses who will be testifying at trial. These require some legal strategy in formulating the answers and are best reviewed with your attorney's office to appropriately develop answers.

At times, litigants feel overwhelmed with the discovery requests and feel that the opposing party already knows the answers. While this might be the case, remember the attorney for your spouse (and maybe even your attorney) does not have all the information and requires the information to move forward in the case. By gathering the information now, it will help to educate all the participants and may help facilitate an early settlement.

The purpose of discovery is to ensure that both you and your spouse have access to the same information. This way, you can either negotiate a fair agreement or have all of the facts and documents to present to the judge at trial. The discovery process enables you and your spouse to meet on a more level playing field when it comes to settling your case or taking it to trial. You and your spouse both need the same information if you hope to reach agreement on any of the issues in your divorce. Similarly, a judge must know all of the facts to make a fair decision.

While compiling this information, keep in mind that it is not just useful for the other party. Your attorney should be using this to help you formulate an offer for settlement, evaluating their offer for settlement, negotiating during a mediation or settlement conference, and lastly arguing at trial.

The discovery process may seem tedious at times because of the need to obtain and to provide lots of detailed information. Completing it, however, can give tremendous clarity about the issues in your divorce. Trust your attorney's advice about the importance of having the necessary evidence as you complete the discovery process in order to reach your goals in your divorce.

The State of Illinois has created standard interrogatories for divorce cases which are as follows:

1. *State your name, current address, date of birth and social security number. If you are known by any other names, please state.*
2. *List all employment held by you during the preceding three years and with regard to each employment state:*
    a. *The name and addresses of each employer;*
    b. *Your position, job title or description;*
    c. *If you had an employment contract;*
    d. *The date on which you commenced your employment and, if applicable, the date and reason for the termination of your employment.*
    e. *Your current gross and net income per pay period.*
    f. *Your gross income as shown on the last W-2 tax and wage statement received by you, your social security wages shown on the last W-2 tax and wage statement received by you, and the amounts of deductions shown thereon; and*
    g. *All additional benefits or perquisites received from your employment stating the type and value thereof.*
3. *During the preceding three years, have you had any source of income other than from your employment listed above? If so, with regard to each source of income, state the following:*
    a. *The source of income, including the type of income and name and address of the source;*
    b. *The frequency in which you receive income from the source;*
    c. *The amount of income received by you from the source during the immediately preceding three years; and*

d. The amount of income received by you from the source for each month during the preceding three years.
4. Do you own any interest in real estate? If so, with regard to each such interest state the following:
   a. The size and description of the parcel of real estate, including improvements thereon;
   b. The name, address, and interest of each person who has or claims to have an ownership interest in the parcel of real estate;
   c. The date your interest in the parcel of real estate was acquired;
   d. The consideration you transferred or paid for your interest in the parcel of real estate;
   e. Your estimate of the current fair market value of the parcel of real estate and your interest therein; and
   f. The amount of any indebtedness owed on the parcel of real estate and to whom.
5. For the preceding three years, list the names and addresses of all associations, partnerships, corporations, enterprises or entities in which you have an interest or claim any interest, the nature of your interest or claim of interest therein, the amount of percentage of your interest or claim of interest therein, and an estimate of the value of your interest therein.
6. During the preceding three years have you had any account or investment in any type of financial institution, individually, or with another, including checking accounts, savings accounts, certificates of deposit and money market accounts? If so, with regard to each such account or investment, state the following:
   a. The type of account or investment;
   b. The name and address of the financial institution;
   c. The name and address of each person in whose name the account is held; and
   d. Both the high and the low balance of the account or investment, stating the date of the high balance and the date of the low balance.
7. During the preceding three years, have you been the holder of or had access to any safety deposit boxes? If so, state the following:
   a. The name of the bank or institution where such box is located;

- b. The number of each box;
- c. A description of the contents of each box during the immediately preceding three years and as of the date of the answer; and
- d. The name and address of any joint or co-owners of such safety deposit box or any trustees holding the box for your benefit.

8. During the immediately preceding three years, has any person or entity held cash or property on your behalf? If so, state:
   - a. The name and address of the person or entity holding the cash or property; and
   - b. The type of cash or property held and the value thereof.

9. During the immediately preceding three years, have you owned any stocks, bonds, securities or other investments, including savings bonds? If so, with regard to each stock, bond, security or investment state:
   - a. A description of the stock, bond, security or investment;
   - b. The name and address of the entity issuing the stock, bond, security or investment;
   - c. The present value of such stock, bond, security or investment;
   - d. The date of acquisition of the stock, bond, security or investment;
   - e. The cost of the stock, bond, security or investment;
   - f. The name and address of any owner or owners in such stock, bond, security or investment; and
   - g. If applicable, the date sold and the amount realized therefrom.

10. Do you own or have and incidents of ownership in any life, annuity or endowment insurance policies? If so, with regard to each such policy state:
    - a. The name of the company;
    - b. The number of the policy;
    - c. The face value of the policy;
    - d. The present value of the policy;
    - e. The amount of any loan or encumbrance on the policy;
    - f. The date of acquisition of the policy; and
    - g. With regard to each policy, the beneficiary or beneficiaries.

11. Do you have any right, title, claim or interest in or to a pension plan, retirement plan or profit-sharing plan, including, but not limited to, individual-retirement accounts, 401(k) plans and deferred compensation plans? If so, with regard to each such plan state:
    a. The name and address of the entity providing the plan;
    b. The date of your initial participation in the plan; and
    c. The amount of funds currently held on your behalf under the plan.
12. Do you have any outstanding indebtedness or financial obligations, including mortgages, promissory notes, or other oral or written contracts? If so, with regard to each obligation state the following:
    a. The name and address of the creditor;
    b. The form of the obligation;
    c. The date the obligation was initially incurred;
    d. The amount of the original obligation;
    e. The purpose or consideration for which the obligation was incurred;
    f. A description of any security connected with the obligation;
    g. The rate of interest on the obligation;
    h. The present unpaid balance of the obligation;
    i. The date and amounts of installment payments; and
    j. The date of maturity of the obligation.
13. Are you owed any money or property? If so, state:
    a. The name and address of the debtor;
    b. The form of the obligation;
    c. The date the obligation was initially incurred;
    d. The amount of the original obligation;
    e. The purpose or consideration for which the obligation was incurred;
    f. The description of any security connected with the obligation;
    g. The rate of interest on the obligation;
    h. The present unpaid balance of the obligation;
    i. The dates and amounts of installment payments; and
    j. The date of maturity of the obligation.
14. State the year, make and model of each motor or motorized vehicle, motor or mobile home and farm machinery or equipment in which you have an ownership, estate, interest or claim of interest, whether

individually or with another, and with regard to each item state:

    a.   The date the item was acquired;

    b.   The consideration paid for the item;

    c.   The name and address of each other person who has a right, title, claim or interest in or to the item;

    d.   The approximate fair market value of the item; and

    e.   The amount of any indebtedness on the item and the name and address of the creditor.

15. *Have you purchased or contributed towards the payment for or provided other consideration or improvement with regard to any real estate, motorized vehicle, financial account or securities or other property, real or personal, on behalf of another person or entity other than your spouse during the preceding three years? If so, with regard to each transaction state:*

    a.   The name and address of the person or entity to whom you contributed;

    b.   The type of contribution made by you;

    c.   The type of property to which the contribution was made;

    d.   The location of the property to which the contribution was made;

    e.   Whether or not there is written evidence of the existence of a loan; and

    f.   A description of the written evidence.

16. *During the preceding three years have you made any gift of cash or property, real or personal, to any person or entity not your spouse? If so, with regard to each such transaction state:*

    a.   A description of the gift;

    b.   The value of the gift;

    c.   The date of the gift;

    d.   The name and address of the person or entity receiving the gift;

    e.   Whether or not there is written evidence of the existence of the gift; and

    f.   A description of the written evidence.

17. *During the preceding three years have you made any loans to any person or entity not your spouse and, if so, with regard to each such loan state:*

    a.   A description of the loan;

    b.   A value of the loan;

       c.   The date of the loan;
       d.   The name and address of the person or entity receiving the loan;
       e.   Whether or not there is written evidence of the existence of a loan; and
       f.   A description of the written evidence.

18. During the preceding three years, have you sold, transferred, conveyed, encumbered, concealed, damaged or otherwise disposed of any property owned by you and/or your spouse individually or collectively? If so, with regard to each item of property state:
       a.   A description of the property;
       b.   The current location of the property;
       c.   The purpose or reason for the action taken by you with regard to the property;
       d.   The approximate fair market value of the property;
       e.   Whether or not there is written evidence of any such transaction; and
       f.   A description of the written evidence.

19. During the immediately preceding three years have any appraisals been made with regard to any property listed by you under your answers to these interrogatories? If so, state:
       a.   The name and address of the person conducting each such appraisal;
       b.   A description of the property appraised;
       c.   The date of the appraisal; and
       d.   The location of any copies of each such appraisal.

20. During the preceding three years have you prepared or has anyone prepared for you any financial statements, net worth statements or lists of assets and liabilities pertaining to your property or financial affairs? If so, with regard to each such document state:
       a.   The name and address of the person preparing each such document;
       b.   The type of document prepared;
       c.   The date the document was prepared;
       d.   The location of all copies of each such document.

21. State the name and address of any accountant, tax preparer, bookkeeper and other person, firm, or entity who has kept or prepared books, documents and records with regard to your income, property, business or financial affairs during the course of this marriage.

22. List the non-marital property claimed by you, identifying each item of property as to:
    a. The type of property;
    b. The date received;
    c. The basis on which you claim it is non-marital property;
    d. Its location; and
    e. The present value of the property.
23. List all marital property of this marriage, identifying each item of property as to:
    a. The type of property;
    b. The basis on which you claim it to be marital property;
    c. Its location; and
    d. The present value of the property.
24. What contribution of dissipation has your spouse made to the marital estate, including but not limited to each of the items or property identified in the response to interrogatories No. 22 and No. 23 above, citing specifics, if any, for each item of property?
25. Pursuant to Illinois Supreme Court Rule 213(f), provide the name and address of each witness who will testify at trial and state the subject of each witness' testimony.
26. Pursuant to Illinois Supreme Court Rule 213(g), provide the name and address of each opinion witness who will offer testimony, and state:
    a. The subject matter on which the opinion witness is expected to testify;
    b. The conclusions and/or opinions of the opinion witness and the basis therefore, including reports of the witness, if any;
    c. The qualifications of each opinion witness, including the curriculum vitae and/or resume, if any; and
    d. The identity of any written reports of the opinion witness regarding this occurrence.
27. Are you in any manner incapacitated or limited in your ability to earn income at the present time? If so, define and describe such incapacity or limitation, and state when such incapacity or limitation commenced and when it is expected to end.
28. Identify any statements, information and/or any documents known to you and requested by any of the foregoing interrogatories which you claim to be work product or subject to any common law or statutory privilege, and with respect to each interrogatory,

specify the legal basis for the claim as required by Illinois Supreme Court Rule 201(n).

Ill. Sup. Ct. R. 213(j).

Post-decree Interrogatories

If you are already divorced, you may be served with post-decree interrogatories. Post-Decree refers to any litigation that follows the original final orders in a case and the subject is generally requesting modification or enforcement of the previous orders. Orders regarding spousal support, property division, child custody, and child support may be subject to future modification after the parties' divorce goes into effect.

The Post-Decree Interrogatories will be somewhat the same as the Matrimonial Interrogatories except for use of the word "spouse", and the questions are not standard like in pre-decree matters. Depending on the case, the questions could ask for information from the past 2 years, or from the date the Judgment of Dissolution of Marriage was entered to present. This all depends on what information the attorney is looking for from you.

Parenting Interrogatories

Custody or Parenting Interrogatories are different then Matrimonial Interrogatories and Post-Decree Interrogatories as they do not ask about financials. The questions specifically ask about the party's living arrangements, school districts, parenting time, education, religion, etc. This gives both parties and both counsels a good idea as to how to handle the case going forward knowing what each party's intentions are with regard to specific issues.

The following represents standard Custody/Parenting Interrogatories:

1. *What is your full name, date of birth, address and social security number?*
2. *What is the condition of your health at the present time?*
3. *Do you have any infirmities or chronic ailments? If so, explain in detail the extent of these infirmities or ailments.*
4. *If you are presently employed, state your work days and hours and whether you are required to work overtime.*
5. *If you are seeking custody of your child:*
    a. *Would you be able to devote your full time to the child's care and upbringing?*
    b. *If not, who would be able to devote full time care when you are not available? Please name each person/institution that you will rely on to care for the child.*

6. *Do you drink alcoholic beverages? If so, state:*
   a. *What type of alcoholic beverages you drink;*
   b. *When do you drink alcoholic beverages;*
   c. *The amount of alcoholic beverages you drink per week.*
7. *Does anyone in your household and/or any caretaker of the minor child drink alcoholic beverages and/or smoke tobacco products? If so, state:*
   a. *The name of each person who drinks alcoholic beverages;*
   b. *What type of alcoholic beverages each person drinks;*
   c. *When each person drinks alcoholic beverages;*
   d. *The amount of alcoholic beverages each person drinks per week.*
   e. *The name of each person who smokes tobacco products;*
   f. *What type of tobacco products each person smokes;*
   g. *When each person smokes tobacco products;*
   h. *The amount of tobacco products each person smokes per day;*
   i. *Whether each person smokes tobacco products in the presence of the minor child.*
8. *If this Court allows removal of the minor child from the State of Illinois, what type of visitation schedule would you want?*
9. *How much time per day would you be able to spend with the minor child?*
10. *Would anyone else take care of your minor child when you were not able to? If so, state:*
    a. *Who would take care of the child;*
    b. *When they would take care of the child.*
11. *If you receive custody of your minor child, where do you intend to reside?*
12. *If you are not granted sole physical custody, state with specificity the visitation time that would be appropriate, including overnights, holidays and school vacation.*
13. *If you are granted sole physical custody, state with specificity the visitation time that would be appropriate for the other parent.*
14. *When you move from your present residence, state:*
    a. *Where you intend to move to;*
    b. *Whether your new residence will be owned or rented by you;*

        c.   A description (including how many rooms and the use of each room and whether there is a yard for child to play in) of the residence you intend to move to;
        d.   The anticipated monthly expense of the new residence.

15. *Please list the names and addresses of any and all schools the child may attend should you obtain custody.*
16. *Please list the school in which you intend to enroll the child should you obtain custody.*
17. *Please describe in detail any investigation you have done into the possible schools the child may attend.*
18. *Please list any and all teachers/school administrators with whom you have met regarding the child's possible schooling.*
19. *Please list the method by which the child will get to and from school.*
20. *Do you participate in any recreational activities with your minor child on a regular, daily, weekly or monthly basis? If so, for each activity, state:*
    a.   The activity;
    b.   The length of time you have participated in said activity;
    c.   How often you participate;
    d.   Briefly describe the nature and extent of your participation.
21. *Does your spouse or significant other participate in any recreational activities with your minor child on a regular (daily, weekly or monthly) basis? If so, for each activity, state:*
    a.   The activity;
    b.   The length of time they have participated in said activity;
    c.   How often they participate;
    d.   Briefly describe the nature and extent of their participation.
22. *Are you and/or the child involved with a particular religion? If so, please describe.*
23. *For the 24 months preceding your separation, who primarily performed the following duties for the child? If both, what percentage of each did you perform:*

DESCRIPTION OF DUTY	PETITIONER	RESPONDENT
Prepared meals.		

Took the child to the doctor.		
Administered medication.		
Got the child up in the morning.		
Put the child to bed.		
Attended parent/teacher conferences.		
Arranged for child care.		
Enrolled child in extracurricular activities.		
Transported child to activities.		
Attended child's activities and events.		
Helped with homework.		
If applicable, took the child to a place to worship.		
Arranged for child's haircut.		
Purchased the child's clothing.		
Arranged play dates with other children.		

24. If you claim to have been the child's primary caretaker, please describe in detail your basis for such belief.
25. If you deny that your spouse has been the child's primary caretaker, please describe in detail the basis for such belief.
26. State whether you are aware of disagreement(s) with the other parent concerning the child's education, religious upbringing, health care needs, discipline, other (identify) and/or extracurricular activities and, if so, complete the following:

Type of Disagreement	Explain Differences

Education	
Religious upbringing	
Health Care	
Extracurricular activities	
Discipline	

27. What are your strengths and weaknesses as a parent?
28. What are the strengths and weaknesses of the other parent?
29. Disclose the name of each person that has pertinent information pertaining to custody/visitation of the child. In addition, disclose which, if any, such persons who you will call as witnesses.
30. Disclose with particularity the action, inaction or conduct, that you intend to place into evidence at the time of trial or hearing supporting your petition or claim. The description should include dates, places and persons present.

Ill. Sup. Ct. R. 213(j).

Witness Interrogatories

213(f) and (g) Interrogatories, also known as Witness Interrogatories, is a form for the client to list witnesses who will testify on her/his behalf, and the subject matter the witnesses will be testifying to if the case should go to Trial. Ill. Sup. Ct. R. 213(f), (g). The Illinois Supreme Court Rule regarding this is stated above in the Matrimonial Interrogatories.

Below is an example of the questions you may be required to answer:

INTERROGATORY NO. 1-LAY WITNESSES: For each lay witness (a "lay witness" is a person giving only fact or lay opinion testimony) that may be called to offer any testimony at trial, please provide the following information:
   a. The full name and address of the lay witness.
   b. The subject matter on which the lay witness is expected to testify.

INTERROGATORY NO. 2-INDEPENDENT EXPERT WITNESSES: For each independent expert witness (an "independent expert witness" is a person giving expert testimony who is not the party, the party's current employee or the party's retained expert) that may be called to offer any testimony at trial, please provide the following information:

> a. The name and address of the independent expert witness.
> b. The subject matter on which the independent expert witness is expected to testify.
> c. The opinions the party expects to elicit from the independent expert witness.
>
> INTERROGATORY NO. 3-CONTROLLED EXPERT WITNESSES: For each controlled expert witness (a "controlled expert witness" is a person giving expert testimony who is the party, the party's current employee, or the party's retained expert) that may be called to offer any testimony at trial, please provide the following information:
> a. The name and address of the controlled expert witness.
> b. The subject matter on which the controlled expert witness is expected to testify.
> c. The conclusions and opinions of the controlled expert witness is expected to testify.
> d. The qualifications of the controlled expert witness, including a curriculum vitae and/or resume if any; and
> e. The contents of all reports of the controlled expert witness. It shall be sufficient in answers to this section e. to attach copies of all written reports of the controlled expert witness, as well as a summary of any oral reports of the controlled expert witness.

Ill. Sup. Ct. R. 213(f).

As additional information becomes known to you, your attorneys and/or any witness named in your answer to Supreme Court Rule 213(f) and (g) Interrogatories which supplements, modifies or updates your answer(s) to any of the foregoing Interrogatories, provide additional or supplemental answers to these Interrogatories.

214 NOTICE TO PRODUCE

Pre-Decree / Notice to Produce

For the Notice to Produce, to the extent the documents are in your possession and control, they should be gathered together and provided to your attorney per his/her instructions. The litigant is required to produce documents from the past three (3) years from the date the request was issued to present date.

If opposing counsel requests bank records or credit card statements or the like, and the copies no longer exist, it is incumbent on the litigant to attempt to locate duplicates from the entities, however, in the event that they want to charge you per page or per statement, unless otherwise directed, you are not generally required to pay for the copies.

Additionally, a practice pointer for completing the Notice to Produce is to answer every question. Sample answers include: 1) already produced, 2) documents exist, but in the opposing party's possession, 3) documents are attached, 4) documents are forthcoming or 5) not applicable/none, as this will help with the drafting of same.

Parties are usually required to tender an Affidavit of Compliance, along with their documents, which is a form signed by the litigant which states that he/she has produced all discovery documents to the best of his/her ability in accordance with the 214 Notice to Produce, that he/she has no other documents in his/her possession that have not already been tendered to opposing counsel, and that the he/she states that the documents contained herein are true and accurate.

Illinois Supreme Court Rule 214 states as follows:

Rule 214. Discovery of Documents, Objects, and Tangible Things-Inspection of Real Estate: (a) Any party may by written request direct any other party to produce for inspection, copying, reproduction photographing, testing or sampling specified documents, including electronically stored information as defined under 201 (b)(4), objects or tangible things, or to permit access to real estate for the purpose of making surface or subsurface inspections or surveys or photographs, or tests or taking samples, or to disclose information calculated to lead to the discovery of the whereabouts of any of these items, whenever the nature, contents, or condition of such documents, objects, tangible things, or real estate is relevant to the subject matter of the action. The request shall specify a reasonable time, which shall not be less than 28 days after service of the request except by agreement or by order of court, and the place and manner of making the inspection and performing the related acts; (b) With regard to electronically stored information as defined in Rule 201 (b)(4), if a request does not specify a form for producing electronically stored information, a party must produce it in a form or forms in which it is ordinarily maintained or in a reasonably usable form or forms; (c) One copy of the request shall be served on all other parties entitled to notice. A party served with the written request shall (1) identify all materials in the party's possession responsive to the request and copy or provide reasonable opportunity for copying or inspections. Production of documents shall be as they are kept in the usual course of business or organized and labeled to correspond with the categories in the request, or (2) serve upon the party so requesting written objections on the ground that the request is improper in whole or in part. If written objections to a part of the request are made, the remainder of the request shall be complied with. A party may object to a request on the basis that the burden or expense of producing the requested materials would be disproportionate to the likely benefit, in light of the factors set out in Rule 201 (c)(3). Any objection to the request or the refusal to respond shall be heard by the court upon prompt notice and motion of the party submitting the request. If the party claims that the item is not in his or her possession or control or that he or she does not have information calculated to lead to the discovery of its whereabouts, the party may be ordered to submit to examination in open court or by deposition regarding such claim. The producing party shall furnish an affidavit stating whether the production is complete in accordance with the request. Copies of identifications, objections and affidavits of completeness shall be served on all parties entitled to notice; (d) A party has a duty to seasonably supplement any prior response to the extent of documents, objects or tangible things which subsequently come into that party's possession or control or become known to that party; (e) This rule does not preclude an independent action against a person not a party for production of documents and things and permission to enter upon real estate.

Ill. Sup. Ct. R. 214.

Below is an example of some requests you may be required to answer:

1. Your Principal Business or Income Producing Activity. If you are an officer and/or principal stockholder in a corporation, sole proprietorship, partnership or any other business entity, or if you derive income from any business activity, please provide the following documents for the last three years: federal and state tax returns, business partnership agreements, Articles of Incorporation; buy/sell agreements; corporate minute book; promissory notes outstanding; general ledger and journal documents evidencing your capital or other monetary contributions thereto; documents evidencing your receipts of funds therefrom, whether by way of salary, bonus, draw, dividend, allocation of profits or otherwise, including contributions to profit sharing or retirement plans; appraisals of your interest in each said entity, including profit and loss statements, balance sheets, statements of net worth and retained earnings; written offers by any person or entity to purchase said business; cash receipts journals, accounts payable, and all other accounts and/or records kept or maintained in connection with any

business in which you have any interest; and any leases or property in which the business has an interest.

2. Salary or Regular Monthly Compensation. To the extent not covered in the preceding request, for the past three years to date, please provide copies of your pay check stubs, all complete personal federal and state tax returns including all attachments, W-2 statements, K-1 statements, 1099 statements or other schedules, all records pertaining to draws, dividends, bonuses, sick pay, reimbursed expenses, gratuities, gifts, loan proceeds or other money received. Also provide copies of contracts executed relative to your employment, together with all amendments thereto, and copies of all contracts and amendments being negotiated currently, but not yet executed; and all evidence as to all compensation which has been earned by you but not as yet paid to you or that you are holding but have not yet cashed.

3. Disability Income, Other Benefits or Compensation. Any and all documentation relating to any and all disability income and/or other related forms of benefits or compensation paid out to you or that you may be entitled to past present or future; including but not limited to worker's compensation pay, pension, disability pay or benefits, and the like.

4. Personal Financial Statements. All personal or joint financial statements, loan applications, credit applications, or net worth statements prepared by or for you in the last three (3) calendar years, whether or not submitted to any bank, savings and loan, or any other financial institution.

5. Resume and Employment/Job Search. All resumes prepared by you during the last three (3) years for employment purposes and all documents in your possession pertaining to your efforts to seek employment at any time within the last three years including all correspondence to and from prospective employers.

6. Social Security Administration. Any and all documents regarding applications, determination of benefits, denial letters and supporting documents for same from Social Security Administration, including any and all documents pertaining to the appeal for benefits to Social Security Administration for the past three (3) years.

7. Retirement Plan Interest. All records pertaining to any interest in all annuity, retirement, individual retirement accounts, Keogh plans, and pension and profit-sharing plans, including, but not limited to, the governing documents by which the interests were created and defined, all amendments thereto, certificates or other evidence of participation, the contributions made to the account therein, the date full vesting of and date payable to you and your total interest as of the date of production and the value thereof for a period of three (3) years. Furnish all documentation regarding any loans made from such plans and all writings reflecting your current interest therein and the value thereof.

8. Stocks and Bonds. For each account maintained by you and/or your spouse with a brokerage or securities firm or otherwise, within the last three (3) years, please furnish monthly account statements from the last three (3) years to date, and copies of all stock certificates or other documents evidencing ownership and all documents reflecting the value of the stock.

9. Certificates of Deposit and Similar Instruments. For each certificate of deposit, money market account, and similar instruments, owned by you and/or your spouse, please provide a copy of each document evidencing your interest in said instrument, the amount invested, maturity date, and rate of interest.

10. Checking and Savings Accounts. For each checking or savings account currently maintained by you and/or your spouse, or in which you and/or your spouse have (or have had) an interest in the last three (3) years, please provide the following: monthly bank statements, canceled checks, check registers and duplicate deposit slips, passbooks and all other documents reflecting deposits or withdrawals, into or from said account.

11. Authorized User/Signator. Any and all statements and records for any account in which you are listed as an authorized user or signator within the last three (3) years to date, including but not limited to, bank accounts, investment accounts, credit card accounts, loan accounts, etc.

12. Safe Deposit Boxes. For each safe deposit box in which you and/or your spouse have or had an interest in the last three (3) years, please provide all writings, correspondence or other documents evidencing your

ownership or interest in each said box, and the contents therein.

13. Household Furniture and Furnishings. Please provide all documents relating to all household furniture, furnishings, works of art, silver, jewelry, furs, collections and antiques owned by you individually or jointly with any other person or entity; such documents and lists to include the purchase price of each item, the source of the funds used to purchase each item, and the current fair market value of each item. Also provide documents regarding insurance or third-party appraisals of any of the above; copies of insurance policies listing the above for which coverage was provided.

14. Real Property. For each parcel of real property, whether improved or unimproved, which is owned fully or in part by you and/or your spouse or, which you and/or your spouse have an option or other interest, or which you and/or your spouse have a lease interest, please provide the following: deeds; leases; promissory notes; escrow documents; purchase documents; financing documents; closing documents; closing disclosures; real estate consummation documents; tax bills for the last three (3) years to date; documents listing improvements (or value of same), from date of purchase to present date; appraisals of value made at any time within the last three (3) years to date; any documents relating to any contributions made by you toward the acquisition of said property and all documents regarding liens, mortgages, loan estimates or other encumbrances on any of the above property.

15. Automobile and other Vehicles. For each automobile or vehicle owned or regularly operated by you and/or your spouse, please provide the following: current Department of Motor Vehicle registration cards; purchase documents; financing documents; payments; appraisals; proof of insurance and any other applicable documents for the past three (3) years.

16. Country Club or Social Club Memberships. For each membership, in any club or social organization or business association that you are a member or have been a member for the last three (3) years, please provide the following: documents evidencing membership, purchase price of membership, transfer price, appraisal of membership interest.

17. Life Insurance. For each policy of life insurance in which you and/or your spouse is the named owner or beneficiary, or in which you or your spouse pay all or part of the premium, please provide a copy of each said policy and any other documents pertaining to said policies including, but not limited to: money received in connection with canceled policies, loans on the policies, and face value of the policies.
18. Medical Insurance. For each policy of medical insurance that you have, please provide a copy of the policy and the persons covered under said policy as well as any other documents you have in your possession or control relative to that policy.
19. Other Insurance. Please provide copies of all policies and other documents of any insurance you have, including, but not limited to, disability, liability, accident and automobile. The foregoing shall include policies maintained at any time within the past three (3) years.
20. Wills, Trusts, Codicils. Please provide copies of each will, trust and codicils executed by you within the last three (3) years. Please further provide a copy of any will or trust agreement in which you are a beneficiary or ultimate beneficiary, including codicils thereto. For each trust in which you are a beneficiary, please provide all statements of condition or statement of trust corpus, together with all trust documents covering any such trust from its inception to the present.
21. Unsecured Debts and Obligations. For each debt or obligation (unsecured by real property) which is owed by you and/or your spouse to any third person or entity, please provide all promissory notes, writings, correspondence, billings, notices or other documents evidencing said debt or obligation, the date incurred, date due and payable, nature of said debt or obligation, any payment made therein, defense as to payment or liability thereon, and any lawsuits now pending in any court of any kind or nature.
22. Charge/Credit Card Accounts. For each charge card, gasoline card, department store card or credit card account maintained by you and/or your spouse, please provide a current account statements evidencing the debt balance of each said account, and number of each account, and all bills and credit card statements and all backup receipts for any and all charges made in the past three (3) years.

23. Written Agreements Affecting Property. If you and your spouse entered into any written pre-marriage agreement or agreement entered into during the marriage; or if such was drafted but not signed, please provide: a copy of such document; correspondence between you and your spouse concerning same or any other writings referring to same, made at any time and all other documents you rely upon to claim to give you ownership to non-marital property.
24. Gifts or Loans. All records pertaining to gifts or loans made by you to another or others having a value in excess of $50 including the evidences of security for each such loan, for the past three (3) years.
25. Contracts. For each contract entered into between you or anyone representing you or in which you have any interest, please provide a copy of that contract and any statement of account or payments due on these contracts.
26. Legal Fees. All documents, including but not limited to the source of all payments, statements, invoices, notices, contracts regarding legal fees incurred or paid by you or on your behalf by others for the past three (3) years.
27. Monthly Expenses. All documentation including but not limited to: paid bills, receipts evidencing payments, records of outstanding debts, canceled checks and contracts relative to all monthly expenses incurred by you on behalf of yourself or your children relating to rent, mortgage payments, real estate taxes, homeowner's insurance, telephone charges, electricity charges, heating or other utility gas charges, automobile expenses, clothing expenses, medical, dental, legal and accountant expenses and bills, educational expenses, private investigator expenses, appraisal fees, water, refuse, child care, maid, laundry, dry cleaning and any other living expenses within the past three years.
28. Medical Reports. All medical reports supporting your contention, if any, that you presently are having or have had in the past, a medical problem, evidence of medication taken and evidence of physical limitations, disabilities or serious illness as result thereof.
29. Inheritance. All documentation evidencing your receipt of inheritance at any time during or prior to the marriage, and disposition of said inheritance.

30. Other Claims. All documents regarding any accident which you have been involved in, including all documents reflecting any monies received as a result of any claim or settlement, whether or not an actual law suit was instituted.
31. Other Items.
    a. Any diaries, logs, notes, video tapes, cassette tapes or any other tapes, computer discs and hard drive information, memoranda or other documents or recording items that refer to, relate to, evidence or reflect any conversations or agreements between the parties at any time within the last two years.
    b. All other documents that relate to this proceeding or that you intend to use in this Dissolution of Marriage action or that reflect, refer to or pertain to or have as their subject matter, the assets or debts of you or your spouse.
    c. Any and all videotapes and photographs which depict the minor children, the parties or the families of the parties at any time during the marriage.
32. Subpoena Responses. Copies of any and all documents received in response to Subpoenas for Depositions-Records Only and/or Subpoenas for Deposition-Personal Appearance issued not already produced.
33. Social Security Statement. A true and correct copy of your most recent Social Security Statement, obtainable at www.ssa.gov.
34. Military Benefits. All military benefits received as a result of disability and/or provided for disabled or military veterans, including but not limited to Form DD 214, insurance benefits (health, life and the like), housing benefits, tax credits or deductions, disability income, and the like.
35. Financial Affidavit. A completed and signed Financial Affidavit as required by Local Court Rules.
36. Affidavit. An Affidavit of compliance in accordance with Supreme Court Rule 214.

Post-Decree Notice to Produce

The same holds true for Post-Decree cases. The requests are a bit different than in Pre-Decree requests, and usually the start date is from the date of the divorce forward (depending how long ago the divorce was) or depending on what information is relevant.

Below is an example of some requests you may be required to answer for Post Decree Matters:

1. YOUR PRINCIPAL BUSINESS OR INCOME-PRODUCING ACTIVITIES. If you are an officer and/or principal stockholder in a closely held corporation, or if you own or operate a business as sole proprietor, a partner or joint venture, or if you derive a significant part of your earned income from a single business activity, please provide the following, where applicable; partnership agreements, articles of incorporation; buy-sell agreements; corporate minute book; fictitious name statement; general ledger and journals; documents evidencing your receipt of funds therefrom in the last three (3) years to date whether by way salary, bonus, draw, dividend, allocation of profits, or otherwise, including contributions to profit sharing or retirement plans; appraisals of the value of said entity, made any time in the last three (3) years to date; all financial statements prepared by or for each said entity in the last three (3) years, including profit and loss statements, balance sheets, statements of net worth and retained earnings; annual reports to stockholders, investors or partners; written offers by any person or entity to purchase all or a part of said business, made within the last three (3) years.

2. SALARY OR REGULAR MONTHLY COMPENSATION. To the extent not covered in the preceding request, please provide copies of your weekly paycheck stubs, indicating gross monthly pay, deductions and net pay, for the last three years.

3. DISABILITY INCOME, OTHER BENEFITS OR COMPENSATION. Any and all documentation relating to any and all disability income and/or other related forms of benefits or compensation paid out to you or that you may be entitled to past present or future; including but not limited to worker's compensation pay, pension, disability pay or benefits, and the like.

4. PERSONAL TAX RETURNS. Please provide complete copies of the last three (3) years of federal

and state personal income tax returns filed by you, including W-2 forms and all schedules.

5. BUSINESS TAX RETURNS. Please provide complete copies of the last three (3) years of federal and state tax returns filed by any business in which you are an officer or hold 5% or more of the outstanding share of stock.

6. PERSONAL FINANCIAL STATEMENTS. Please provide copies of each personal financial statement prepared by or for you for the last three years, whether or not submitted to any bank, savings and loan, or any other financial institutions.

7. RETIREMENT PLAN INTEREST. Please provide copies of the following:
   A. Retirement plan "Summary Plan Descriptions";
   B. Participant's annual retirement plan statements, provided to you for the last three years;
   C. Actual evaluation of your retirement plan interests, calculated at any time for the last three years;
   D. Profit sharing plan "Summary Plan Description";
   E. Participant's annual profit-sharing plan statements, provided to you for the last three years;
   F. Actuarial or accountant's evaluation of your profit-sharing plan interest, calculated at any time for the last three years;
   G. All other deferred income plans, including but not limited to Keogh, IRA, 401(k) etc., showing plan description and documents showing amount in plans.

8. INTEREST IN PARTNERSHIPS. For each interest you have in a partnership, please provide the following: partnership agreement; amendments, revisions or additions thereto; last three partnership income tax returns filed; last three K-2 income tax forms filed; promissory notes; appraisals of value of your interest in said partnership as a whole or of its underlying assets, made within the last three (3) years to date; written offers by any person or entity offering to purchase your interest therein, made within the last three (3) years to date; any correspondence or other writings evidencing the value of the partnership, its underlying assets, or of your interest therein at any time within the last three (3) years and any insurance carried on your life by the partnership.

9. CORPORATE STOCK. For each interest you have in stock in a closely-held corporation, or for any stock which is not traded over the counter or on an exchange, please provide the following: copies of all such stock certificates, or other documents regarding your interest in same, correspondence from any person or entity which places a value on shares of said stock, or which contain information which could lead to a valuation of said shares; any insurance carrier on your life by said corporation.

10. STOCKS AND BONDS. For each account maintained by you and others with a brokerage or securities firm within the last three (3) years, please furnish monthly account statements from the last three (3) years to date, and copies of all stock certificates or other documents evidencing ownership which contain your name as an owner of securities.

11. CERTIFICATE OF DEPOSIT AND SIMILAR INSTRUMENTS. For each certificate of deposit, time deposit, and similar instrument owned by you and/or others or in which you and/or others have an interest in during the last three (3) years, please provide a copy of each document evidencing your interest in said instrument, the amount vested, maturity date, and rate of interest.

12. CHECKING ACCOUNTS. For each checking account currently maintained by you and/or others, or in which you and/or others have (or have had) an interest, direct or indirect in the last three (3) years, please provide the following: monthly bank statements, canceled checks, check registers and duplicate deposit slips, from the last three (3) years to date.

13. SAVINGS ACCOUNTS. For each savings account you and/or others, at your direction, have deposited money in the last three (3) years to date, please furnish bank statements and the passbook for each said account.

14. AUTHORIZED USER/SIGNATOR. Any and all statements and records for any account in which you are listed as an authorized user or signator within the last three (3) years to date, including but not limited to, bank accounts, investment accounts, credit card accounts, loan accounts, etc.

15. SAFETY DEPOSIT BOXES. For each safety deposit box in which you have had an interest in the last three (3) years, please provide all writings, correspondence

or other documents evidencing your ownership, rental or interest in each said box, and the contents therein.

16. LIFE INSURANCE. For each policy of life insurance or annuity in which you and/or others is/are the named owner or beneficiary, or in which you and/or others pay all or part of the premium, please provide a copy or each said policy, and the current cash value.

17. UNSECURED DEBTS AND OBLIGATIONS. For each debt or obligation (unsecured by real property) which is owed by you to any third person or entity, please provide all writings, correspondence, bills, notice or other documents evidencing said debt or obligation, the date incurred, date due and payable, nature of said debt or obligation, defenses to payment or liability thereon and financial statements prepared for banks or other financial institutions, including but not limited to those prepared to secure loans or credit for the last three (3) years.

18. CHARGE CARD ACCOUNTS. For each charge card, gasoline card, department store, or major credit card account maintained by you, please provide a correct account statement evidencing the debt balance in each said account, and the number of each account for the last three (3) years to date.

19. CONTRACTS. For each contract entered into between you and anyone representing you or in which you have any interest, please provide a copy of that contract and any statement of accounts or payments due on these contracts.

20. LEGAL FEES. All documents, including but not limited to the source of all payments, statements, invoices, notices, contracts regarding legal fees incurred or paid by you or on your behalf by others for the past three (3) years.

21. TRUSTS. Any and all trusts of which you are the grantor or beneficiary.

22. INVESTMENTS. All documents relating to any investment or other asset owned wholly, directly or indirectly, or jointly with others by you.

23. RESUME AND EMPLOYMENT/JOB SEARCH. All resumes prepared by you during the last three (3) years for employment purposes and all documents in your possession pertaining to your efforts to seek employment at any time within the last three years including all correspondence to and from prospective employers.

24. SUBPOENA RESPONSES. Copies of any and all documents received in response to Subpoena for Depositions-Records Only and/or Subpoenas for Deposition-Personal Appearance issued on behalf of your client not already produced.
25. SOCIAL SECURITY STATEMENT. A true and correct copy of your most recent Social Security Statement, obtainable at www.ssa.gov.
26. MILITARY BENEFITS. All military benefits received as a result of disability and/or provided for disabled or military veterans, including but not limited to Form DD 214, insurance benefits (health, life and the like), housing benefits, tax credits or deductions, disability income, and the like.
27. FINANCIAL AFFIDAVIT. A completed Financial Affidavit as required by Local Court Rules.
28. AFFIDAVIT. An Affidavit of compliance in accordance with Supreme Court Rule 214.

It is true that many of the same documents were requested in the pre decree matter, but if same remain relevant, the same documents can be requested for your post decree matter.

Parentage Case Notice to Produce

Even though the Custody/Parenting Interrogatories do not ask about financials, the Notice to Produce requests financial documents (tax returns, pay stubs, bank account statements, investment account statements, etc.). This is important when determining the child support calculations in cases where parentage is the issue.

REDACTING OF DOCUMENTS

Mainly in Post-Decree and Parentage matters, it is customary to redact (black out) personal information from their documents to protect identities and usually redact up to the last 4 digits. Ill. Sup. Ct. R. 137(b)-(c). Examples of this are social security numbers, driver's license numbers, bank account numbers, retirement/investment account numbers and credit card numbers. Ill. Sup. Ct. R. 137(b)(1)-(4). There are special circumstances in divorce cases when items might be redacted, but this is not the norm. The reason for leaving the last 4 digits in account numbers is so that we can identify the different accounts the litigants possess.

The basis for redacting is Illinois Supreme Court Rule 138 states as follows:

> *(a) Applicability; (1) In civil cases, personal identity information shall not be included in documents or exhibits filed with the court except as provided in paragraph (c). This rule applies to paper and electronic filings; (2) This rule does not*

apply to cases filed confidentially and not available for public inspection; (b) Personal identity information, for purposes of this rule, is defined as follows; (1) Social Security and individual taxpayer-identification numbers; (2) driver's license numbers; (3) financial account numbers; and; (4) debit and credit card numbers. A court may order other types of information redacted or filed confidentially, consistent with the purpose and procedures of this rule; (c) A redacted filing of personal identity information for the public record is permissible and shall only include:(1) the last four digits of the Social Security or individual taxpayer-identification number; (2) the last four digits of the driver's license number;(3) the last four digits of the financial account number; and (4) the last four digits of the debit and credit card number. When the filing of personal identity information is required by law, ordered by the court, or otherwise necessary to effect disposition of a matter, the party shall file a form in substantial compliance with the appended "Notice of Confidential Information Within Court Filing," prepared by utilizing, or substantially adopting the appearance and content of, the form provided in the Article II Forms Appendix. This document shall contain the personal identity information in issue and shall be impounded by the clerk immediately upon filing. Thereafter, the document and any attachments thereto shall remain impounded and be maintained as confidential, except as provided in paragraph (d) or as the court may order. After the initial impounded filing of the personal identity information, subsequent documents filed in the case shall include only redacted personal identity information with appropriate reference to the impounded document containing the personal identity information. If any of the impounded personal identity information in the initial filing subsequently requires amendment or updating, the responsible party shall file the amended or additional information by filing a separate "Notice of Confidential Information Within Court Filing" form; (d) The information provided with the "Notice of Confidential Information Within Court Filing" shall be available to the parties, to the court, and to the clerk in performance of any requirement provided by law, including the transfer of such information to appropriate justice partners, such as the sheriff, guardian ad litem, and the State Disbursement Unit (SDU), the Secretary of State or other governmental agencies, and legal aid agencies or bar association pro bono groups. In addition, the clerk, the parties, and the parties' attorneys may prepare and provide copies of documents without redaction to financial institutions and other entities or persons which require such documents; (e) Neither

the court nor the clerk is required to review documents or exhibits for compliance with this rule. If the clerk becomes aware of any noncompliance, the clerk may call it to the court's attention. The court, however, shall not require the clerk to review documents or exhibits for compliance with this rule; (f)(1) If a document or exhibit is filed containing personal identity information, a party or any other person whose information has been filed may move that the court order redaction and confidential filing as provided in paragraph (b). The motion shall be impounded, and the clerk shall remove the document or exhibit containing the personal identity information from public access pending the court's ruling on the substance of the motion. A motion requesting redaction of a document in the court file shall have attached a copy of the redacted version of the document. If the court allows the motion, the clerk shall retain the unredacted copy under impoundment and the redacted copy shall become part of the court record; (2) If the court finds the inclusion of personal identity information in violation of this rule was willful, the court may award the prevailing party reasonable expenses, including attorney fees and court costs; (g) This rule does not require any clerk or judicial officer to redact personal identity information from the court record except as provided in this rule.
Ill. Sup. Ct. R. 138.

It is important to keep the non-redacted copies of this discovery as well to be able to prove if there is a controversy that only protected information was redacted. In some instances, the Courts will require the production of non-redacted documents.

237 Notice to Produce

A 237 Notice to Produce is only issued when there are evidentiary hearings and for Trials. Ill. Sup. Ct. R. 237(b). This is issued for either Appearance Only of the opposing party which requires the party to appear in court only or "to appear and produce," meaning that the opposing party is required to appear and produced the requested documents. *Id.* The purpose of these requests are to receive any and all updated documents if the opposing party had previously produced anything in response to the 214 Notice to Produce, and to produce any and all documents that may not have been previously produced. *Id.* A Notice to Produce must be issued before a 237 Notice to Produce unless it is an expedited hearing or is for appearance only. Ill. Sup. Ct. R. 237(b), (c). The requests in the 237 Notice to Produce cannot request documents that were not previously requested in other discovery methods or it is possible that the responding party will object to the request. Ill. Sup. Ct. R. 237(b).

Illinois Supreme Court Rule 237 states as follows:

> *Compelling Appearances of Witnesses at Trial: (a) Service of Subpoenas. Any witness shall respond to any lawful subpoena of which he or she has actual knowledge, if payment of the fee and mileage has been tendered. Service of a subpoena by mail may be proved prima facie by a return receipt showing delivery to the witness or his or her authorized agent by certified or registered mail at least seven days before the date on which appearance is required and an affidavit showing that the mailing was prepaid and was addressed to the witness, restricted delivery, with a check or money order for the fee and mileage enclosed; (b) Notice of Parties et al. at Trial or Other Evidentiary Hearings. The appearance at the trial or other evidentiary hearing of a party or a person who at the time of trial or other evidentiary hearing is an officer, director, or employee of a party may be required by serving the party with a notice designating the person who is required to appear. The notice also may require the production at the trial or other evidentiary hearing of the originals of those documents or tangible things previously produced during discovery. If the party or person is a nonresident of the county, the court may order any terms and conditions in connection with his or her appearance at the trial or other evidentiary hearing that are just, including payment of his or her reasonable expenses. Upon a failure to comply with the notice, the court may enter any order that is just, including any order sanction or remedy provided for in Rule 219(c) that may be appropriate; (c) Notice of Parties at Expedited Hearings in Domestic Relations Cases. In a domestic relations case, the appearance at an expedited hearing of a party who has been served with process or appeared may be required by serving the party with a notice designating the party who is required to appear. The notice may also require the production at the hearing of the original documents or tangible things relevant to the issues to be addressed at the hearing. If the party is a nonresident of the county, the court may order any terms and conditions in connection with his or her appearance at the hearing that are just, including payment of his or her reasonable expenses. Upon a failure to comply with the notice, the court may enter any order that is just, including any sanction or remedy provided for in Rule 219(c) that may be appropriate.*

Ill. Sup. Ct. R. 237.

Responding to discovery requests can be cumbersome; however, discovery can be the key to obtaining a favorable outcome in the case. If the litigant is feeling overwhelmed with the requests, they should certainly contact their attorney to work through the requests together. One key to remember is that the attorney should also be reviewing what the litigant has provided in order to ensure accuracy and, during this review, can provide the litigant with pointers if additional items might be needed.

Subpoenas

What is a Subpoena? Is it a court document? Do I really need to appear? Do I really need to produce everything the subpoena asks for?

A subpoena is a request for documents/evidence, or a request to appear in court or other proceeding. It is a court-ordered demand that basically requires you to do something, such as testify or produce records that may help support the facts that are at issue in a pending case. Ill. Sup. Ct. R. 204(a). A person/entity who receives a subpoena but does not comply may be subject to civil or criminal penalties, such as fines, jail time, or whatever the Court may deem equitable and just. Ill. Sup. Ct. R. 205(d)(2).

There are a couple different types of Subpoenas. A subpoena can require a person/entity to appear before the court, require a personal appearance for deposition, including bringing documents or not to the deposition, or a request for the production of documents, materials or other tangible evidence only. A subpoena can either ask for one of these or all three within the same form. Generally, most counties have a basic Subpoena form on the clerk's office website. When issuing any kind of Subpoena, you must pay a witness fee and travel costs; the clerk of the circuit court usually can help you figure out the appropriate amount if help is needed. Ill. Sup. Ct. R. 204(a)(2).

The purpose of a subpoena is to help attorneys/ unrepresented litigants obtain information to help prove or disprove their point in a case. Most of the time, subpoenas are not the first choice for obtaining certain information, such as employment information, bank account statements, credit card statements, etc. The first step is to try to request this type of information from the opposing party during discovery requests; however, this route doesn't always work. Whether the opposing side is non-compliant, not producing everything requested, or simply doesn't have any or all the documentation needed, it might be decided to pursue a subpoena. Sometimes, certain records are needed within a timeframe and waiting for the 'discovery process' isn't always the best approach. Additionally, sometimes attorneys make the decision to issue a subpoena for evidentiary purposes; records received via a subpoena are often fast tracked into evidence via a Certificate of Authenticity, often making this a streamlined evidentiary process.

When Can a Subpoena be Issued

Each county has their own rules for when discovery/subpoenas can be issued in a case. For our purposes, three counties will be examined, however, look at the local court rules for your circuit court for guidance.
- For Will County at this time, a subpoena can be issued at any time during the litigation. There is no local court rule with respect to the same. If the

case has an Order setting its own due dates or restrictions, you will need to comply with those.
- For DuPage County, pursuant to Local Court Rule 15.05(3)(d), a party shall not make any discovery request until they have tendered to the opposing party a completed Financial Affidavit. DuPage Cty. Local Ct. R. 15.05(3)(d). A Subpoena is considered a discovery request.
- For Cook County, pursuant to Local Court Rule 13.3.1(c), in both pre-judgment and post-judgment cases, a completed Financial Affidavit shall be served to the opposing party before seeking discovery. Cook Cty. Local Ct. R. 13.3.1(c).

This is why it is crucial for litigants to complete the Financial Affidavit during the beginning phase of their case so there are no hold ups for issuing further discovery down the road. Once a Subpoena is properly filled out and issued, it will need to be served on the individual/ entity. The following are ways to serve same:
- Hand delivery by way of a special process server. Once service is completed, the process server will execute an Affidavit of Service which then would be filed with the court, so all parties involved in the case as well as the Judge are aware personal service has been completed. Normally, personal service is not necessary and can increase the costs for the litigant. If a Subpoena needs to be issued on an immediate basis or personal service is required in the specific instance, this would be the best route to go.
- Certified mail with a return receipt requested. This is the most common means of service. If using this method, make sure you provide the Return Receipt Number on your Subpoena form so anyone could look up the status of same being delivered to the recipient. Ill. Sup. Ct. R. 204(a)(2).
- E-mail/fax to last known e-mail address or fax number. This method is typically used if this information is readily available but also issue by certified mail since proof of receipt for email/fax is complicated and not as easily proved in court. If an individual is your witness and is willing to accept service by email or fax, this will work as well. One pointer might be to have the individual respond to the email with confirmation of receipt in case an issue is raised in court.

Once the Subpoena is properly issued and served, you will need to provide notice to the opposing side with a Notice of Filing. Simply serve the Notice of Filing and copy of your Subpoena to the opposing party if they are an unrepresented litigant or their attorney if they are represented. If no notice is served, there could be complications such as a request that the subpoena be 'quashed'. Since a Subpoena is subject to limits, one can file a Motion to Quash the Subpoena. Some limits could be anywhere from: how far someone is required to travel to comply, the person receiving the Subpoena is out of state, how much notice was given, cannot be too much of a burden, etc. While we know a Subpoena should not be ignored, if one has an issue with the issuance of said Subpoena, a Motion to Quash should be filed with the court which puts the production of documents/appearance in court 'on hold' until the Court rules on said Motion. The Motion shall be filed before the subpoena due date and served to all parties involved on the matter.

When filling out a Subpoena form, make sure you gather all the requested information needed to complete the same- for example, case caption, address for person/entity you are issuing Subpoena to. If you are issuing a subpoena to a witness for a court appearance only, you will need to provide all information for the court date: address of courthouse, courtroom, date and time. When preparing a subpoena to an entity, such as a bank, please check with your state's Secretary of State website to see if an entity has a registered agent, meaning an address where you should be sending your subpoena. Sometimes a telephone call to the entity will go a long way as well.

If you are requesting for production of documents with your Subpoena and the form itself doesn't have enough room to include everything you are looking for, create a Rider which will be a detailed explanation of any and all records you are looking for and can be attached to your Subpoena. Having your Rider as detailed as possible is the best option so there are no questions on what documentation you are looking for. Make sure your Subpoena gives a due date for production of documents. Depending on your county's rules, 7 days' notice from receipt of the Subpoena is proper. Typically, most entities may request for additional time to respond to your subpoena and usually that is not an issue. For instance, most banks have a standard letter they send out when a Subpoena is issued and ask for about 60 days to comply with same. Lastly, another document to include with your Subpoenas that requests records to be produced, is a Certificate of Authenticity of Records. A Certificate of Authenticity of Records is a simple form you can create that the entity is required to execute and return to your office. Additionally, a practice tip is to include said Certificate in your Rider so that said entity knows this is required to be sent back in their response. This Certificate is important to have because it is ultimately certifying that the records produced are original records or true copies. If your case were to go to Trial, you will need this Certificate at Trial. Some entities and bank institutions have their own Certificate which can certainly be used; however, supplying your own in case they do not have a standard is good practice. This Certificate of Authenticity of Records goes towards authenticating the subpoena response received under Illinois Rules of Evidence.

When a response is received pursuant to a subpoena you issued, it is your duty to ensure all parties/attorneys involved in the pending litigation are served with a complete copy of same. Pursuant to Illinois Supreme Court Rule 204(a)(4), this rule requires disclosure to all parties with prompt and complete production of all materials received, regardless of whether material in addition to those specified are furnished by the deponent. Ill. Sup. Ct. R. 204(a)(4). You CANNOT PICK AND CHOOSE which documents you want to tender to the other side. Sometimes this rule needs to be explained to litigants so they are aware that everything received will be supplied to the opposing side. Sometimes when a Subpoena Response is received, some entities may have an Invoice that needs to be paid that your original check did not cover. This cost will need to be paid for by whoever issued the Subpoena. If you are issuing a Subpoena, but don't want to exceed a certain amount of monies towards same, it might be a good idea to mention somewhere on your Subpoena and/or Rider that if more monies are needed in order to complete such request, that they reach out to you prior to completion of same. This is not necessarily binding; however, at least you made an official note of same.

After all is said and done, and the implications that one can get into if a Subpoena is not complied with, some still choose not to follow through and respond to same. Making attempts on your end to receive cooperation is the first step, whether it's contacting the individual/ entity by phone or sending a demand letter for cooperation. If this does not work, you may have no other choice but to file a Motion with the court, which you will need to provide notice of same to the entity/person you are compelling to produce records or their appearance.

Out of State Subpoenas

When issuing a Subpoena, there may be some extra steps you have to accomplish to get the subpoena answered. This is particularly true for an out of state Subpoena. Pursuant to 735 ILCS 35/3, you will need to request issuance of a Subpoena in the state you are looking to conduct discovery in. 735 Ill. Comp. Stat. Ann. 35/3(a) (LexisNexis through P.A. 101-631). You or your attorney will need to submit a foreign subpoena to the clerk of the court for the county you are looking for documents in. *Id.* It will be the clerk's responsibility to promptly issue a subpoena for service upon the person/entity the subpoena is directed to. 735 Ill. Comp. Stat. Ann. 35/3(b).

Under the Uniform Interstate Depositions and Discovery Act, parties or their attorneys may issue subpoenas within foreign states. In order to properly do so, there is a process that must be followed before a foreign state may properly issue a subpoena to a citizen who is domiciled in another state. You should first make sure that the state in which you are trying to serve your out-of-state subpoena has enacted some version of the Uniform Interstate Depositions and Discovery Act, and review the terms of the Act as it is enacted in the other state. Currently, there are 42 states which have enacted their own version of the Uniform Interstate Depositions and Discovery Act, as well as the District of Columbia and U.S. Virgin Islands. *Interstate Depositions and Discovery Act*, UNIFORM LAW COMMISSION, https://www.uniformlaws.org/committees/community-home?CommunityKey=181202a2-172d-46a1-8dcc-cdb495621d35 (last visited Jul. 7, 2020). As of May 15, 2020, the Missouri legislature had introduced a bill to establish the Uniform Interstate Depositions and Discovery Act, but no further action had been taken except for referring the bill to a committee. *Id.* The following states have not enacted the Uniform Interstate Depositions and Discovery Act: Wyoming, Nebraska, Oklahoma, Texas, Connecticut, Massachusetts, and New Hampshire. *Id.*

In that instance, there will be two subpoenas that must be issued. First, one will have to issue a foreign subpoena in the county in which the case is currently pending in. 735 Ill. Comp. Stat. Ann. 35/3(a) (LexisNexis through P.A. 101-631). Then, one will need to send a foreign subpoena to the county where the person/entity is domiciled in, along with a pre-completed subpoena form. *Id.* Upon receiving the foreign subpoena, the other county's Circuit Clerk is to issue a subpoena in their county containing the information in the foreign subpoena. 735 Ill. Comp. Stat. Ann. 35/3(b) (LexisNexis through P.A. 101-631). Once a party submits a foreign subpoena to the clerk of court in which the citizen/entity is domiciled in, the clerk shall promptly issue a subpoena for service upon the person/entity to which the foreign subpoena is directed to. *Id.* This subpoena issued by the clerk of court shall incorporate the terms used in the foreign subpoena and contain or be accompanied by the names, address, and telephone numbers of all counsel of record in the proceedings to which the subpoena relates and of any party not represented by counsel. 735 Ill. Comp. Stat. Ann. 35/3(c)(A)-(B) (LexisNexis through P.A. 101-631). If a subpoena is issued by a clerk of court, it shall be served in compliance with that state's Rules of Civil Procedure relative to service of process. The issuing party needs to properly provide notice to the opposing side by sending a copy of both the subpoena in your county and the foreign subpoena. Please note that it is your responsibility to make sure you are reviewing the Interstate Depositions and Discovery Act for both your state and the state to which you are issuing the out of state subpoena.

Depositions

What is a deposition? A deposition is the opportunity to understand the case better by taking the testimony of a witness under oath before a court reporter. Depositions don't take place in courtrooms and are generally taken at an attorney's office. All parties involved in the case, along with their attorneys, may attend the deposition. The attorney will ask the deponent a series of questions regarding the case, with the entire deposition being recorded by the hired court reporter. A transcript of the deposition can be made available upon request and payment is received for same. The purpose of a deposition is to find out what the witness knows and preserve the witness' testimony. Ill. Sup. Ct. R. 202. This is the time to allow both parties to learn all the facts of the case before the Trial date so no one is surprised. Depending on the case and the pending issues, a deposition may not be needed. Each case is unique and has different circumstances. At times, one may issue a subpoena for deposition to the opposing side to get the case moving along or push to try to settle the case. What usually happens is once one side issues a deposition to the other, the opposing side will issue one right back.

There are two kinds of depositions, a discovery deposition and an evidence deposition. Pursuant to Illinois Supreme Court Rule 202, if the notice, order or stipulation to take a deposition doesn't say otherwise, then the deposition is a discovery deposition only. *Id.* If someone wants to take an evidence deposition, then the notice, order, or stipulation to take a deposition must specify that it is to be an evidence deposition. *Id.* A discovery deposition can be used for the following purposes, under Illinois Supreme Court Rule 212: to impeach the testimony of the deponent as a witness for inconsistent statements; as a former statement, for Rule of Evidence 801(d)(2); if it is otherwise admissible as an exception to the hearsay rule; for any purpose that an affidavit may be used; or as evidence at trial against a party that appeared at the deposition or was given notice of same, if the court finds the deponent is not a controlled expert witness, the deponent's evidence deposition has not been taken, and the deponent can't attend or testify because of death or infirmity, and if the court finds such evidence at trial or hearing will do substantial justice between or among the parties. Ill. Sup. Ct. R. 212(a)(1)-(5). Evidence depositions of physicians or surgeons may be introduced into evidence at trial on the motion of either party, whether or not the deponent is available, and without barring the right of either party to subpoena or otherwise call the physician or surgeon for attendance at trial. Ill. Sup. Ct. R. 212(b). For all other evidence depositions, they may be used the same as discovery depositions, and may be used by any party for any purpose if the court finds the following at the time of trial: the deponent is dead or otherwise unable to attend because of age, sickness, infirmity, or imprisonment; the deponent is out of the country, unless the absence was caused by the party offering the evidence deposition into evidence; or that the party offering the deposition into evidence has exercised reasonable diligence but has been unable to procure the attendance of the deponent by subpoena, or upon notice and motion before trial that exceptional circumstances exist which make it desirable to allow the deposition to be used. Ill. Sup. Ct. R. 212(b)(1)-(3).

Depositions may also be taken by video, and generally the same rules for depositions will apply to video depositions as well. If a video deposition is being conducted, then it must begin with the operator of the equipment stating on camera the following information: his or her name and address; the time and place of the deposition; the caption of the case; the name of the witness; the party on whose behalf the deposition is being taken; and the party at whose instance the deposition is being recorded on an audio-visual recording device. Ill. Sup. Ct. R. 206(g)(1). Additionally, after the deposition, the operator will go through the recording of the deposition to determine how long it is, then sign an affidavit that states the length of the deposition. Ill. Sup. Ct. R. 206(g)(2). The recording will not be filed with the court. Ill. Sup. Ct. R. 206(g)(3). If it is a discovery deposition, the recording will only be filed with the court if there has been good cause shown. *Id.*

A discovery deposition can last anywhere from 15 minutes to 3 hours maximum, unless all parties stipulate otherwise or the court enters an order after a showing that good cause warrants a lengthier deposition. Ill. Sup. Ct. R. 206(d). A deposition should be taken seriously. Listening carefully to each question is key to ensure you are properly answering the question. Since the deponent is under oath, no false statements should be made or there could be possible penalties.

As previously mentioned in the Subpoena section, some counties in Illinois require a Financial Affidavit to be tendered before any issuance of discovery, which includes a deposition. When one is ready to issue a deposition, who are you issuing a deposition to? Third-party or the opposing side. This makes a difference because a third party will require a Subpoena for Deposition, however a party to the case only requires a Notice of Deposition. Usually when a deposition is needed to be taken, you are also looking for a production of documents to be supplied before or during the deposition. It's not required but can be helpful to your case and also want the back-up documentation to support their testimony. If documents are produced, it is your duty to supply a copy of said response to all parties involved in the case.

When clients are required to appear for their deposition, it is important to prepare for same and know what to expect. A practice pointer for attorneys is to review potential questions with your clients prior to the deposition so the client feels comfortable as possible. No one can tell a deponent how to answer a specific question; however, reviewing specific topics and ways to answer a question will be beneficial. If you have an attorney, they should be present the day of your deposition and object to any questions that are overly broad, simply do not pertain to the pending issues, or just seems to be more of a harassment issue by the opposing side. Part of the preparation for the deposition will likely include a review of the procedure for objections during the deposition, because the approach to objections differ during a deposition than during a court hearing or trial. However, the deponent is required to answer all proper questions in a truthful manner. Remember you are under oath.

Overall, the discovery is a long but necessary process in your case. Remember knowledge is power and irrespective of your agreement, you want to make sure you know the ins and outs of your case facts before you settle. Further, if the case goes to trial, it is imperative that the evidence be located and proven. This journey will be costly but you only have one opportunity to gather the information and these items are critical to your case.

FAMILY SUPPORT BASICS

Part of a financial settlement in a divorce case can be support—whether it is maintenance and/or child support. Not every case will have these components, but many have one, if not both. In a parentage case, only child support will be involved. It's important to spend some time getting familiar with both forms of support.

Maintenance

The first form of support is called maintenance, formerly known in Illinois as "alimony". Maintenance is spousal support that is paid from one spouse to the other for support for his or her expenses, and as such cannot be awarded in parentage cases. The purpose of maintenance is to help a spouse maintain the standard of living they were accustomed to during the marriage if they are not able to support themselves in that manner. More often, maintenance is meant to "rehabilitate" a spouse who gave up a career or was out of the workforce for some time to take care of the home and family while the other spouse worked and was the breadwinner.

Prior to January 1, 2019, maintenance was considered taxable to the party receiving maintenance, and deductible to the party making maintenance payments. So long as a maintenance order was entered on or before December 31, 2018, the maintenance payments are still includable in the income of the recipient for tax reporting purposes, and deductible from income for the payer for tax reporting purposes. *Divorced or Separated Individuals*, I.R.S. Pub. No. 504, Cat. No. 15006I (Jan. 10, 2020). However, as of January 1, 2019, the Federal Government changed the taxability of maintenance thereby stating that maintenance payments are not taxable to the party receiving maintenance, nor are they deductible to the party making maintenance payments, unless it is a modification of a prior order and the parties agree to keep the same taxable effects. *Id.* As such, the Illinois legislature has had to adjust the formula for calculating maintenance, which will be discussed below. The Illinois legislature has also made changes to how we calculate the duration of maintenance, which will also be discussed below.

Entitlement to Maintenance

A spouse is not automatically entitled to receive maintenance. There are a number of factors that a court will consider in order to determine if an award of maintenance is proper. 750 Ill. Comp. Stat. Ann. 5/504(a) (LexisNexis through P.A. 101-631). The Court will look at the following factors to determine whether an award of maintenance is appropriate:

1. *The income and property of each spouse, including marital property apportioned and non-marital property assigned to the party seeking maintenance, as well as all financial obligations imposed on the parties as a result of the divorce;*
2. *The needs of each party;*
3. *The realistic present and future earning capacity of each party;*
4. *Any impairment of the present and future earning capacity of the party seeking maintenance as due to that spouse devoting time to domestic duties or having forgone or delayed education, training, employment, or career opportunities due to the marriage;*
5. *Any impairment of the realistic present or future earning capacity of the party against whom maintenance is sought;*
6. *The time necessary to enable the party seeking maintenance to acquire appropriate education, training, and employment, and whether that party is able to support himself or herself through appropriate employment;*
7. *The effect of any parental responsibility arrangements and its effect on a party's ability to seek or maintain employment;*
8. *The standard of living established during the marriage;*
9. *The duration of the marriage;*
10. *The age, health, station, occupation, amount and sources of income, vocational skills, employability, estate, liabilities, and the needs of each of the parties;*
11. *All sources of public and private income including, without limitation, disability and retirement income;*
12. *The tax consequences to each party;*

> 13. *Contributions and services by the party seeking maintenance to the education, training, career or career potential, or license of the other spouse;*
> 14. *Any valid agreement of the parties; and*
> 15. *Any other factor the court expressly finds to be just and equitable.*

750 Ill. Comp. Stat. Ann. 5/504(a)(1)-(14) (LexisNexis through P.A. 101-631).

No one factor is more important than the other, and the Court must consider each and every factor. If the Court determines a maintenance award is appropriate, you move onto the calculations for the duration and amount of maintenance. If not, then maintenance is not appropriate and you do not calculate duration or amount.

Length of Maintenance Award

If, after considering all of the above factors, the Court finds that maintenance is appropriate, then the duration of the maintenance award will need to be determined. The duration of a maintenance award is determined based on the length of the marriage at the time the divorce action was filed. Pursuant to the statute, utilize the below chart to determine the multiplier for duration:

Number of Years	Duration Multiplier
Less than 5 years	.20
5 years or more, but less than 6 years	.24
6 years or more, but less than 7 years	.28
7 years or more, but less than 8 years	.32
8 years or more, but less than 9 years	.36
9 years or more, but less than 10 years	.40
10 years or more, but less than 11 years	.44
11 years or more, but less than 12 years	.48
12 years or more, but less than 13 years	.52
13 years or more, but less than 14 years	.56
14 years or more, but less than 15 years	.60
15 years or more, but less than 16 years	.64
16 years or more, but less than 17 years	.68

17 years or more, but less than 18 years	.72
18 years or more, but less than 19 years	.76
19 years or more, but less than 20 years	.80
20 years or more	Length of marriage or indefinite

750 Ill. Comp. Stat. Ann. 5/504(b-1)(1)(B) (LexisNexis through P.A. 101-631).

The easiest way to calculate the duration is to determine the number of months of the marriage (for example, if the parties were parried for 12 years and 6 months when the divorce action was filed, then they were married for 150 months). After you have converted the length of the marriage into months, you will multiply the number of months by the multiplier in the right column. For example, when using the parties who have been married for 12 years and 6 months, you would multiple 150 months by .52, for a total of 78 months.

If the Court orders maintenance payable as a temporary support order during the pendency of the divorce proceedings, the time frame temporary maintenance was paid may be a credit towards the total duration. 750 Ill. Comp. Stat. Ann. 5/504(b-1)(1.5) (LexisNexis through P.A. 101-631). This means if the paying spouse was ordered to pay maintenance for the amount of 78 months, and they paid temporary maintenance for 8 months during the divorce proceedings, the final judgment dissolving the marriage may only order the paying spouse to pay maintenance for an additional 70 months after entry of judgment. Additionally, there may be termination events which also may shorten the duration of maintenance, which are discussed below.

If the Court awards maintenance for a fixed time frame, then a termination date will be set by the court. 750 Ill. Comp. Stat. Ann. 5/504(b-4.5)(1) (LexisNexis through P.A. 101-631). At the end of this period, maintenance is then barred. *Id.* However, if the court grants indefinite maintenance for a marriage 20 years or longer, then maintenance will continue until modification, or termination under one of the situations discussed below. 750 Ill. Comp. Stat. An. 5/504(b-4.5)(2) (LexisNexis through P.A. 101-631). Lastly, if the Court grants reviewable maintenance, then a specific time frame for review shall be outlined. 750 Ill. Comp. Stat. Ann. 5/504(b-4.5)(3) (LexisNexis through P.A. 101-631). When a Court is asked to review maintenance, it may make any of the following decisions: extend maintenance for further review; extend maintenance for a fixed non-modifiable term; extend maintenance for an indefinite term; or permanently terminate. 750 Ill. Comp. Stat. Ann. 5/504(b-8) (LexisNexis through P.A. 101-631).

Amount of Maintenance Award

Once the Court has determined that a maintenance award is proper, you will also need to determine what the "proper" amount of support is according to the statute (this is called "guideline" support). Under the statute, if a maintenance obligation is being determined on January 1, 2019 or later, it will no longer be taxable maintenance (i.e., it is no longer includable in the recipient's taxable income). *Divorced or Separated Individuals*,

I.R.S. Pub. No. 504, Cat. No. 15006I (Jan. 10, 2020). The formula below follows the statute to calculate non-taxable maintenance.

In order to account for maintenance no longer being taxable, maintenance is calculated using net income, which is how child support is also calculated. 750 Ill. Comp. Stat. Ann. 5/504(b-1)(1)(A) (LexisNexis through P.A. 101-631). The court will look at each party's gross income. Gross income is income from all sources, except for means-tested public assistance, or income received for another child in the household not shared between the parties. 750 Ill. Comp. Stat. Ann. 5/505(a)(3)(A) (LexisNexis through P.A. 101-631). After gross income is included, a deduction for taxes will be applied to calculate net income. 750 Ill. Comp. Stat. Ann. 5/505(a)(3)(B) (LexisNexis through P.A. 101-631). In order to ensure accuracy, this should be done as if taxes are properly calculated with neither party receiving a refund or owing a liability at the end of the year.

Once the parties' net incomes have been determined, both incomes are added together. Under the maintenance statute, a recipient of maintenance can only receive 40% of the total net income between their earned income and a maintenance award. 750 Ill. Comp. Stat. Ann. 5/504(b-1)(1)(A) (LexisNexis through P.A. 101-631). Because of this, you will need to multiply total net income by 40% to determine the maximum amount of income that the recipient may be allotted. If the recipient's net income is more than 40% of the total net income, then the recipient is barred from receiving maintenance and maintenance will not be awarded. If the recipient's net income is less than 40% of the total net income, then move forward to calculate the maintenance award. If the recipient is not barred by the 40% of total income rule, guideline maintenance will be applied.

First, multiply the net income of the party who earns more by 33 1/3% ("Number 1"). *Id.* Then, multiply the income of the party who earns less by 25% ("Number 2"). *Id.* Thereafter, subtract Number 2 from Number 1. *Id.* This resulting number is the maximum maintenance amount allowable. Add this resulting number to the lower earning party's net income. *Id.* If this number is less than 40% of the monthly net income, then maintenance is not reduced and the recipient party will receive the full amount as maintenance. *Id.* If the proposed maintenance plus the lower earner's net income is more than the 40% cap, then the maintenance award will need to be further reduced to meet the 40% cap. *Id.* When doing these calculations, it is easiest to utilize annual numbers, but remember that any resulting number will need to be divided by 12 in order to determine the monthly amount of maintenance.

Modification of Maintenance

Modification of a maintenance award is governed by Section 510 of the Illinois Marriage and Dissolution of Marriage Act. An order for maintenance may be terminated or modified upon a showing of a substantial change in circumstance. 750 Ill. Comp. Stat. Ann. 5/510(a-5) (LexisNexis through P.A. 101-631). The updates to the maintenance statute, effective January 1, 2019, are not a change in circumstance which warrants a modification. *Id.* In proceedings for modification, or termination, of maintenance, the court will look at all the factors outlined above, to determine whether an award of maintenance is appropriate as listed above, as well as the following additional factors:

1. Any change in employment status of either party and whether the change was in good faith;
2. The efforts, if any, made by the party receiving maintenance to become self-supporting, and the reasonableness of the efforts where they are appropriate;
3. Any impairment of the present and future earning capacity of either party;
4. The tax consequences of the maintenance payments upon the respective economic circumstances of the parties;
5. The duration of the maintenance payments previously paid (and remaining to be paid) relative to the length of the marriage;
6. The property, including retirement benefits, awarded to each party under the judgment of dissolution of marriage, judgment of legal separation, or judgment of declaration of invalidity of marriage and the present status of that property;
7. The increase or decrease in each party's income since the prior judgment or order from which the review, modification, or termination is being sought;
8. The property acquired and currently owned by each party after entry of the judgment of dissolution of marriage, judgment of legal separation, or judgment of declaration of invalidity of marriage; and
9. Any other factor that the court expressly finds to be just and equitable.

750 Ill. Comp. Stat. Ann. 5/510(a-5)(1)-(9) (LexisNexis through P.A. 101-631).

In any case where a Court adjudicates modification, or termination, of maintenance, the Court is required to make specific factual findings. 750 Ill. Comp. Stat. Ann. 5/510(c-5) (LexisNexis through P.A. 101-631). These factual findings must be concerning the reason for the modification, as well as the amount, nature, and duration of the modified maintenance award. *Id.*

Termination of Maintenance

A Court may also terminate maintenance prior to the expiration of a maintenance award. There are certain situations in which maintenance may terminate. The first is the death of either party. 750 Ill. Comp. Stat. Ann. 5/510(c) (LexisNexis through P.A. 101-631). The next situation in which maintenance will terminate is if the recipient spouse remarries. *Id.* The last situation is when the party receiving maintenance cohabits with another person on a resident, continuing conjugal basis. *Id.* What this means is very case specific and the facts of the case may determine if this was the case. The real issue is one of public policy in that if a new family type structure is established, maintenance will terminate. As a matter of law, the obligor's obligation to pay maintenance may terminate on the date the recipient spouse remarries, or the date the Court finds that cohabitation began. *Id.* If an obligor overpaid support after a recipient spouse remarried or cohabited, then the obligor is entitled to a reimbursement for all maintenance paid from the date of remarriage or cohabitation forward. *Id.* The Obligor is the person paying and the Obligee is the person receiving the support.

Child Support

The next form of support is called child support. Child support is money paid by one parent to the other parent as and for their "share" of the cost of raising a child. Child support does not include child care, out-of-pocket medical expenses, school expenses, or extracurricular expenses and the same are treated differently. Child support is payable in divorce cases as well as parentage cases.

The Illinois legislature has also made changes to the child support laws recently. Previously, child support was calculated as a percentage of the net income of the non-custodial parent, based on the number of children support was being paid for. The custodial parent's income was not considered at all in the calculation of support. However, as of July 1, 2017, Illinois has shifted with the majority of the states in the United States, and now utilizes an "income shares" model for calculation of child support. *Child Support Guideline Models by State*, NATIONAL CONFERENCE OF STATE LEGISLATURES (February 20, 2019), https://www.ncsl.org/research/human-services/guideline-models-by-state.aspx. As of February 29, 2019, a total of forty states in the United States utilize some form of income shares for calculation of child support. *Id.* The formula for calculation of child support will be discussed below. The theory behind utilizing an income shares model for calculating child support is that both parents are responsible for supporting and raising the child, so both parents' incomes are relevant when determining how much "should" be paid in support from one parent to the other. An income shares model looks at the amount of money that would be available for raising a child had the relationship not broken down.

Calculation of Support

Like maintenance, there is a formula that the Courts follow when determining guideline child support. First, the Court will determine each parent's monthly net income. 750 Ill. Comp. Stat. Ann. 5/505(a)(1.5)(A) (LexisNexis through P.A. 101-631). Next, the Court will add the parents' net incomes together to determine the total combined monthly net income of the parents. 750 Ill. Comp. Stat. Ann. 5/505(a)(1.5)(B) (LexisNexis through P.A. 101-631). After that, the Court will look at the schedule of basic child support obligations released by the Illinois Department of Health and Family Services, and determine the appropriate basic child support obligation based on the combined net income of the parents and the number of minor children the parents share. 750 Ill. Comp. Stat. Ann. 5/505(a)(1.5)(C) (LexisNexis through P.A. 101-631). Lastly, the Court will calculate each parent's percentage share of the basic child support obligation. 750 Ill. Comp. Stat. Ann. 5/505(a)(1.5)(D) (LexisNexis through P.A. 101-631).

The first step is to determine each parent's total net income. 750 Ill. Comp. Stat. Ann. 5/505(a)(1.5)(A) (LexisNexis through P.A. 101-631). First, the Court looks at each parent's gross monthly income. 750 Ill. Comp. Stat. Ann. 5/505(a)(3)(A) (LexisNexis through P.A. 101-631). Under the statute, gross income does not include means-tested public assistance programs (such as TANF, Supplemental Security Income, or SNAP) or benefits or income received by the parent for other children in the household (such as child support, survivor benefits, or foster care payments). *Id.* If there are social security disability or retirement benefits paid for the benefit of a child that will be the subject of the child support order, those benefits must be included in the disabled or retired parent's gross income for purposes of calculating that parent's child support obligation. *Id.* If that is the case, that parent is entitled to a child support credit if the amount of the benefits that are paid to the other party for the minor child. *Id.* Finally, maintenance is included in gross income if it is treated as taxable income for federal income tax purposes, and it is received pursuant to a court order. *Id.* Remember from earlier in this chapter, maintenance is taxable if it was ordered before January 1, 2019, or if it was entered after that date, it was modifying an order entered prior to January 1, 2019, and all parties agree that maintenance should continue to be taxable to the recipient.

However, if a party previously used to earn more money, the Court may "impute" income to a parent. Imputing income means the Court pretends the parent makes more money than they are actually making. According to *In re the Marriage of Gosney*, a Court must find one of the following in order to impute income: the payor is voluntarily unemployed; the payor is attempting to evade a support obligation; or the payor has unreasonably failed to take advantage of an employment opportunity. *In re Marriage of Gosney*, 394 Ill. App. 3d 1073, 1077 (Ill. App. Ct. 3d Dist. 2009). Once each party's gross monthly income is determined, a deduction for taxes will be applied to calculate net income of the parties.

There are two methods to calculate taxes when determining a party's net income: the standardized tax deduction and individualized tax deduction. 750 Ill. Comp. Stat. Ann. 5/505(a)(3)(B) (LexisNexis through P.A. 101-631). Under the statute, "standardized tax amount" is the total of federal and state income taxes for a single person claiming the standard tax deduction, one personal exemption, and the applicable number of dependency exemptions for the minor child (or children) of the parties, and Social Security and Medicare tax calculated at the Federal Insurance Contributions Act (FICA) rate.750 Ill. Comp. Stat. Ann. 5/505(a)(3)(C) (LexisNexis through P.A. 101-631). When determining who gets the applicable exemption(s) for any minor children, the statute says that unless the parties agree otherwise or the Court determines otherwise, whichever parent has majority parenting time shall be entitled to claim the dependency exemption. 750 Ill. Comp. Stat. Ann. 5/505(a)(3)(C)(I) (LexisNexis through P.A. 101-631). When utilizing the "standardized tax amount" when determining net income, you will utilize the most up-to-date standardized net income conversation table set out by the Illinois Department of Healthcare and Family Services. 750 Ill. Comp. Stat. Ann. 5/505(a)(3)(C)(II) (LexisNexis through P.A. 101-631). Utilizing the conversion table provides the "standardized tax amount" for net income based on his or her gross income.

You may also utilize the individualized tax amount, in certain situations. If the individualized tax amount is utilized, then it will include federal income tax, the state income tax, social security tax or self-employment tax (or, if social security taxes or self-employment taxes are not taken out, then mandatory retirement contributions required by law or as a condition or employment), and Medicare tax calculated at the FICA rate. 750

Ill. Comp. Stat. Ann. 5/505(a)(3)(D)(I)-(III) (LexisNexis through P.A. 101-631). For state and federal taxes, "properly calculated" means properly calculated withholding or estimated payments (i.e., the party will not owe taxes with the filing of their tax return and will not receive a refund with the filing of their tax return).

After determining the net income, the Court will then look at adjustments to the party's incomes. The first adjustment to income that the Court will look at is the "multi-family adjustment." 750 Ill. Comp. Stat. Ann. 5/505(a)(3)(F)(I) (LexisNexis through P.A. 101-631). This will apply if a parent is also legally responsible for support of a child not shared with the other parent and not subject to the proceeding at hand. *Id.* An important distinction to note here is that the parent receiving the adjustment to their income must be legally obligated to support that other child. *Id.* If dad is paying for expenses for his girlfriend's child that he is not the father of or has not legally adopted, he does not get the deduction to his net income for support calculation purposes. The child must be a parent's biological child or legally adopted child. If there is a court order for support of the other child, then the court will deduct from that parent's net income the amount actually paid pursuant to court order. 750 Ill. Comp. Stat. Ann. 5/505(a)(3)(F)(I)(i) (LexisNexis through P.A. 101-631) If there is a support order on another child that is not being paid, then it will not be counted as an adjustment to net income for that parent.

If there is not a child support order, then the multi-family adjustment is calculated in a different manner. The child still must be a child that parent is legally responsible for (a presumed, acknowledged, or adjudicated child of that parent). 750 Ill. Comp. Stat. Ann. 5/505(a)(3)(F)(I)(ii) (LexisNexis through P.A. 101-631). The court will take the lesser of two numbers for the adjustment: the amount of financial support actually paid for that child, or 75% of the support that parent should pay under the child support guidelines for that child. When determining the second number, the Court will only utilize that parent's income when calculating support for the other child. *Id.*

The last adjustment to income is for payment of spousal maintenance. 750 Ill. Comp. Stat. Ann. 5/505(a)(3)(F)(II) (LexisNexis through P.A. 101-631). This adjustment comes into play in two situations. The first situation is when there is a court order for maintenance obligation paid or payable to the parent to whom child support is going to be paid to. *Id.* The other situation is when there is maintenance actually paid to a former spouse pursuant to a court order. *Id.* If the maintenance obligation is not tax deductible to the paying spouse, then it will be adjusted after taxes have been deducted from gross income. *Id.* If the maintenance obligation is tax deductible to the paying spouse, then it will be deducted from gross income prior to taxes being deducted from same. *Id.*

After a determination of the net of the parties is calculated, add the parties' net incomes together to determine the parties' combined net income. 750 Ill. Comp. Stat. Ann. 5/505(a)(1.5)(B) (LexisNexis through P.A. 101-631). After the parties' net incomes are combined, the current Income Shares Schedule based on net income released by the Illinois Department of Health and Family Services will need to be analyzed. This table is simple to use. The rows on the right correspond with the total net income of both of the parties. Find the range that the total calculated net income of the parties. That table, based on the total combined net income of the parties, will provide the basic support obligation by locating the correct column for the number of children shared between the parties (i.e., one, two, three, four, five, or six or more). The number in that pinpointed cell will be the total base child support obligation for the parties.

Once the total base child support obligation has been determined, each parent's share of the total base child support obligation will need to be determined. 750 Ill. Comp. Stat. Ann. 5/505(a)(1.5)(D) (LexisNexis through P.A. 101-631). In order to do this, the Court will look at what percentage of the total net income each parent has. For each parent, you will determine this by dividing the amount each parent earns by the total income. For example, if Parent 1's monthly net income is $2,000.00 and Parent 2's monthly net income is $3,000.00, then for Parent 1 you would divide $2,000.00 by $5,000.00 for 40%. For Parent 2, you would divide $3,000.00 by $5,000.00 for 60%. After you have determined the percentage of the total net monthly income each parent has, you will multiply each parent's percentage of the total net income by the total base child support obligation for the parties. If Parent 1 has 40% of the income and the total base child support obligation from the chart is $1,000.00, then $400.00 is Parent 1's share, which is presumed to be spent on the minor child. If Parent 2 has 60% of the total income and the total base child support obligation is $1,000.00, then Parent 2 will pay $600.00 per month to Parent 1 as their base child support.

As you may have heard, this new method of calculating child support also takes the non-residential (formerly known as "non-custodial") parent's overnights exercised with the children into consideration. What happens if the non-residential parent has 40% or more of the overnights? This means that the non-residential parent has 146 or more overnights in one year. Once that threshold of 146 overnights has been met, the calculation will change. 750 Ill. Comp. Stat. Ann. 5/505(a)(3.8) (LexisNexis through P.A. 101-631). All of the above steps will still apply except for multiplying the percentage of income by the basic child support obligation. Prior to multiplying the percentage of income by the basic child support obligation, the basic child support obligation should be multiplied by 1.5. *Id.* Thereafter, a determination of the percentage of time each parent shares with the child must be determined.

First, the number of overnights per year each parent will share with the minor child must be calculated. The easiest way to do this is to outline each parent's parenting time with the child or children on a printed calendar. After the determination of the number of overnights each parent shares with the child, that number will be divided by 365, the total number of overnights in the year. For example, if Parent 2 has 164 overnights with the child, and Parent 1 has 201 overnights with the child, then Parent 2 will divide 164 by 365 to get 0.449. This is 44.9%. Parent 1 will divide 201 by 365 for 0.551. This is 55.1%.

After a determination of the percentage of overnights each parent has with the child and each parent's share of the increased basic child support obligation has been calculated, the next step is to multiple each parent's share of the increased basic child support obligation by the percentage of the other parent's overnights with the child. *Id.* This means for Parent 1, you will multiply their share of the increased basic support obligation by the percentage of time Parent 2 is exercising with the minor child. Likewise, for Parent 2, multiply their share of the increased basic support obligation by the percentage of time Parent 1 is exercising with the minor child. Once these two amounts are determined, deduct the smaller number from the larger number. *Id.* Whichever parent had the larger basic support obligation would then pay the remainder leftover after this offset. *Id.*

What about cases where the parents split the children? Mom has one child, and Dad has the other? The calculation will change again. In the below explanation, we will assume that Parent 1 has one child, and Parent 2 has one child in their care. You will need to perform a different child support calculation for each parent. 750 Ill. Comp. Stat. Ann. 5/505(a)(3.9) (LexisNexis through P.A. 101-631). For Parent 1, complete a child support calculation as if the child that primarily lives with Parent 1 is the only child of the parties. 750 Ill. Comp. Stat. Ann. 5/505(a)(3.9)(A) (LexisNexis through P.A. 101-631). For Parent 2, complete a child support calculation as if the child that primarily lives with Parent 2 is the only child of the parties. 750 Ill. Comp. Stat. Ann. 5/505(a)(3.9)(B) (LexisNexis through P.A. 101-631). Once this is done, take those two numbers and offset the larger number by the smaller number. 750 Ill. Comp. Stat. Ann. 5/505(a)(3.9)(C) (LexisNexis through P.A. 101-631). Whichever parent has the larger number will pay as child support the remainder leftover after the offset. *Id.*

Other Support Related Items

In addition to the basic support obligation, the Court may order other kinds of expenses, such as health insurance costs, out of pocket medical expenses, child care expenses, school and extracurricular expenses, and contribution to post-high school education expenses.

With regard to health insurance costs, if one parent is not already providing health insurance for the minor child, the Court may order one or both parents to provide health insurance coverage for the minor child. 750 Ill. Comp. Stat. Ann. 5/505(a)(4)(A) (LexisNexis through P.A. 101-631). If either party is covering the minor child on his or her insurance plan, then a portion of those costs may be added to or deducted from a party's basic child support obligation. 750 Ill. Comp. Stat. Ann. 5/505(a)(4)(E) (LexisNexis through P.A. 101-631). First, the Court will look at what the cost is for the insurance to cover the child only. 750 Ill. Comp. Stat. Ann. 5/505(a)(4)(D) (LexisNexis through P.A. 101-631). The benefit summary will often tell you the costs for covering an employee, employee plus spouse, employee plus child(ren), or employee plus family. In order to determine which portion of the monthly premiums is for the child, you will subtract the amount for the employee only from either employee plus child(ren) or employee plus family costs, whichever is applicable for the plan the providing parent has chosen. Then, divide that number by the number of people covered (so if it is employee plus family, and there is a spouse AND the child covered, you would divide the difference by 2 to determine the portion for the child). *Id.* This amount will be the monthly premium apportioned for the child. *Id.* After the determination of the monthly premium for the child's portion of the health insurance premiums has been established, multiply that by each parent's percentage of net income. *Id.* This resulting number is each parent's portion of the insurance costs. *Id.* If the person paying child support provides the health insurance, then the amount of the child's health insurance cost that is apportioned to the parent receiving child support will be subtracted from the basic support obligation. 750 Ill. Comp. Stat. Ann. 5/505(a)(4)(E) (LexisNexis through P.A. 101-631). If the parent receiving child support is providing health insurance for the minor child, then the paying parent's portion of the health insurance premiums can be added to their basic child support obligation. *Id.*

Additionally, the Court may order that the parties split medical expenses that are not covered by insurance. 750 Ill. Comp. Stat. Ann. 5/505(a)(4)(B) (LexisNexis through P.A. 101-631). These expenses may include unreimbursed medical, dental, orthodontic, or vision expenses and prescriptions not covered by insurance. *Id.* These expenses may be split equally, or the Court may order the parties to contribute in a percentage equal to their percentage of the total net income of the parties. The Court may also order parents to contribute to the "reasonable" school and extracurricular activity expenses incurred. 750 Ill. Comp. Stat. Ann. 5/505(a)(3.6) (LexisNexis through P.A. 101-631). The statute does not provide what "reasonable" school expenses are, but generally school expenses will cover any registration fees, monthly tuition fees, and fees charged by the school to the family (such as activity fees, book or material fees). "Extracurricular activity expenses" are labeled as those which are intended to enhance the educational, athletic, social, or cultural development of the child. *Id.*

Parents may also be ordered to split child care expenses for their minor children. 750 Ill. Comp. Stat. Ann. 5/505(a)(3.7) (LexisNexis through P.A. 101-631). Under the statute, "childcare expenses are expenses reasonably necessary to enable a parent custodian to be employed, to attend educational or vocational training programs to improve employment opportunities, and to search for employment." 750 Ill. Comp. Stat. Ann. 5/505(a)(3.7)(A) (LexisNexis through P.A. 101-631). They may also include deposits to secure placement in a childcare program, the cost of before and after school care, and camps when school is not in session. *Id.* If a child has special needs, that will also be taken into consideration when determining reasonable child care expenses. *Id.* Child Care expenses are prorated in proportion to each parent's percentage of the total net income. 750 Ill. Comp. Stat. Ann. 5/505(a)(3.7)(B) (LexisNexis through P.A. 101-631). The Court may add these expenses to the basic child support obligation if the parents do not directly pay the provider of said child care services. *Id.* Otherwise, they are payable directly to a party or to the child care provider at the time of services. *Id.*

Modification of Child Support

Once a child support order is set, it can be subject to modification. Child Support is not a non-modifiable order, and Illinois public policy does not allow you to make child support non-modifiable. The statute governing the modification is Section 510 of the Illinois Marriage and Dissolution of Marriage Act.

What happens if an obligor has a percentage-of-income order and they want to modify their support obligation? The Court still must look to a substantial change in circumstances. 750 Ill. Comp. Stat. Ann. 5/510(a)(1) (LexisNexis through P.A. 101-631). The Second District Court of Appeals stated that if a child support order was entered prior to July 1, 2017, then the amended guidelines will be applied only if the obligor can establish a substantial change in circumstances that were not contemplated at the time support was calculated under prior guidelines. *In re Marriage of Salvatore*, 2019 IL App (2d) 180425, 33. If events alleged as a substantial change in circumstances were contemplated and expected at the time of entry of the child support order, then the Second District Court of Appeals warns that courts should be reluctant to find a change in circumstances. *Id.* The problem for obligors who have a strict percentage-of-income order in trying to modify support is that a percentage of income order covers any range of income he or she may have.

In Illinois, there are a few ways to request modification of child support. The first is on a showing of "a substantial change in circumstances." 750 Ill. Comp. Stat. Ann.

5510(a)(1) (LexisNexis through P.A. 101-631). This change must be a change from the last time a child support order was entered. Examples of a substantial change in circumstances may include the loss of a job, a change in the parenting time schedule, or retirement. Generally, the loss of a job must be more than just voluntarily resigning or quitting.

The next way to request a modification of a child support obligation will only apply if the Department of Healthcare and Family Services is providing child support enforcement services. 750 Ill. Comp. Stat. Ann. 5/510(a)(2)(A) (LexisNexis through P.A. 101-631). If that is the case, then a substantial change in circumstances does not need to be shown. *Id.* A party may request a modification of a child support order if they can show an inconsistency of at least 20% between the existing child support order, and the guideline child support that results from application of the child support statute. *Id.* However, this inconsistency cannot be less than $10 per month, and this request cannot be made until at least 36 months have passed since the child support order was entered or last modified. 750 Ill. Comp. Stat. Ann. 5/510(a)(2)(B) (LexisNexis through P.A. 101-631).

Additionally, a child support order may be modified without a change in circumstances by showing there is a need to provide for the health care needs of the child through health insurance or other means. 750 Ill. Comp. Stat. Ann. 5/510(a)(2)(B) (LexisNexis through P.A. 101-631). Under the statute, the child being eligible for or receiving medical assistance is not considered to meet the need to provide for the child's healthcare needs. *Id.*

Termination of Child Support

Child support does not go on and on for eternity. Child support is automatically terminated by the emancipation of the child. 750 Ill. Comp. Stat. Ann. 5/510(d) (LexisNexis through P.A. 101-631). In some cases, this may be the child's 18th birthday. *Id.* However, if the child is still attending high school when they turn 18, then child support will not terminate until the child either graduates from high school or turns 19. *Id.* Child support terminates on the earlier of those two events occurring. *Id.* Although child support is "generally" terminated upon these events, it is good practice to file a motion with the Court to ensure a corrected Order for Support is entered to reflect the emancipation of a child.

What may surprise you to learn is that child support is not terminated by the death of either parent in Illinois. *Id.* If a parent who is obligated to pay support or educational expenses (discussed below) unfortunately passes away, the amount of support or educational expenses may still be enforced. *Id.* A petition may be filed before or after a parent's death, requesting that the court award sums of money from the late parent's estate for child support, educational expenses, or both. 750 Ill. Comp. Stat. Ann. 5/510(e) (LexisNexis through P.A. 101-631). The time frame for which this claim may be filed against the estate of a late parent is governed by the Probate Act as a bearable, non-contingent claim. *Id.* In some instances, the Court orders life insurance which can result in a waiver of the claim against the estate.

Support for a Non-Minor Child

Under Illinois law, a parent may also be ordered to provide support for a disabled, non-minor child. This kind of support is governed by Section 513.5 of the Illinois Marriage and Dissolution of Marriage Act. See the chapter on Special Needs for further discussion of support for a non-minor child.

College Contribution

If a child has reached age 18 and graduated from high school, a parent may still be required to provide support for the child, pursuant to Section 513. Under that section, a court may award sums of money (from property or income of either parent, or the estate of a deceased parent) for the educational expenses of any child of the parties. 750 Ill. Comp. Stat. Ann. 5/513(a) (LexisNexis through P.A. 101-631). The educational expenses should be incurred no later than the child' 23rd birthday, except for good cause shown, then no later than the child's 25th birthday. *Id.* Section 513 provides authority for college education, vocational or professional or other training after graduation from high school, and also while the child is still attending high school after attaining age 19. 750 Ill. Comp. Stat. Ann. 5/513(c) (LexisNexis through P.A. 101-631).

In addition to ordering the payment of educational expenses, Section 513 may also allow a Court to require both parties and the child to complete the Free Application for Federal Student Aid and other financial forms. 750 Ill. Comp. Stat. Ann. 5/513(b) (LexisNexis through P.A. 101-631). In addition to completing the FAFSA, parents can also be ordered by a Court to pay for the cost of the following: up to five college applications; the cost of 2 standardized college entrance exams; and the cost of one standardized college entrance examination prep course. *Id.*

Section 513 provides a non-exhaustive list of what should be included in "educational expenses." Educational expenses may include the following:

1. *The actual cost of the child's post-secondary expenses, including tuition and fees, so long as it does not exceed the amount of in-state tuition and fees paid by a student at the University of Illinois at Urbana-Champaign for that same academic year;*
2. *The actual costs of the child's housing expenses (on-campus or off-campus), so long as the housing expenses do not exceed for the cost for the same academic year for a double-occupancy student room with a standard meal plan, in a residence hall operated by the University of Illinois at Urbana-Champaign;*
3. *Actual costs of the child's medical expenses, including medical insurance and dental expenses;*
4. *The reasonable living expenses of the child during the academic year and periods of recess:*
    a. *If the child is living on campus while attending a post-high school education program; or*

> b. *If the child is living with one of the parents while attending a post-high school education program, then the living expenses include an amount that pays for the reasonable cost of the child's food, utilities, and transportation; and*
> 5. *The cost of books or other supplies necessary to attend college.*

750 Ill. Comp. Stat. Ann. 5/513(d)(1)-(5) (LexisNexis through P.A. 101-631).

If the court makes an order under Section 513, the amounts ordered may be payable to any of the following: the child, either parent, or directly to the school. 750 Ill. Comp. Stat. Ann. 5/513(e) (LexisNexis through P.A. 101-631). Additionally, if Section 513 support is ordered, then both parties and the child must sign any consent documents necessary for the educational institution to provide supporting parties with access to the child's academic transcripts, records, and grade reports, but this consent shall not apply to non-academic records. 750 Ill. Comp. Stat. Ann. 5/513(f) (LexisNexis through P.A. 101-631). If the consent is not signed, and therefore a supporting parent does not have access to academic records, transcripts, and grade reports, then the failure to execute the consent may be grounds for modification or termination of a Section 513 Order. *Id.*

There are certain conditions that will terminate the Court's authority to make provisions for educational expenses, which include the following:

> 1. *The child fails to maintain a cumulative "C" grade point average, except in the event of illness or other good cause show;*
> 2. *The child attains the age of 23;*
> 3. *The child receives a bachelor's degree; or*
> 4. *The child marries.*

750 Ill. Comp. Stat. Ann. 5/513(g) (LexisNexis through P.A. 101-631).

A child's enlistment in the armed forces, incarceration, or pregnancy does not terminate the Court's authority to make provisions for educational expenses of a child. *Id.*

What if a 529 Plan exists? If the plan was in existence at the time of entry of a Judgment for Dissolution of Marriage or a Financial Order in a parentage case, then the funds in the 529 plan are considered the resources of the child. 750 Ill. Comp. Stat. Ann. 5/513(h) (LexisNexis through P.A. 101-631). However, if a parent makes a contribution to a 529 plan after entry of a Judgment in a divorce or parentage case, then the amount of said contributions will be considered contributions from that parent. *Id.*

What kinds of factors does the Court look at when making an order under Section 513? The first factor the court looks at is the present and future financial resources of both parties to meet their needs, including savings for retirement. 750 Ill. Comp. Stat. Ann. 5/513(j)(1) (LexisNexis through P.A. 101-631). The next factor is the standard of living the child would have enjoyed had the marriage (or relationship) not been dissolved. 750 Ill. Comp. Stat. Ann. 5/513(j)(2) (LexisNexis through P.A. 101-631). The third factor is the financial resources of the child. 750 Ill. Comp. Stat. Ann. 5/513(j)(3) (LexisNexis through P.A. 101-631). Remember from above, that includes amounts in a 529 account before entry of a judgment in a divorce or parentage case. 750 Ill. Comp. Stat. Ann. 5/513(h) (LexisNexis through P.A. 101-631). The last factor the court looks at when making an order under Section 513 is the child's academic performance. 750 Ill. Comp. Stat. Ann. 5/513(j)(4) (LexisNexis through P.A. 101-631).

A Court can only establish an order for educational expenses for a child retroactive to the date of filing of a Petition, pursuant to the statute. 750 Ill. Comp. Stat. Ann. 5/513(k) (LexisNexis through P.A. 101-631). However, if there is a prior obligation, either parent has the right to enforce a prior obligation to pay before or after the obligation is incurred. *Id.* If the final judgment in your parentage or divorce case does not specifically state a payment schedule, it would not be a bad idea to ensure you are watching closely and take action with plenty of time so your child's post-high school education is not delayed due to payment issues.

Conclusion

In conclusion, there are many considerations that go into calculating child support and maintenance. It is also important to note that there have been recent changes to the maintenance and child support laws in the past few years. It is important to understand the ways to calculate maintenance and child support in Illinois divorce and parentage cases.

SLICING THE PIE

Spouses acquire many different assets over the course of their marriage. These assets include, but are certainly not limited to, bank accounts, retirement accounts, vehicles, and the home purchased during the marriage. These are just examples of many types of assets that may be acquired during the marriage. In this chapter, we will review the assets acquired during the marriage and explain the division of assets. We will also discuss assets brought into the marriage by one of the spouses, or pre-marital assets. The State of Illinois is an equitable division state, meaning it is the court's discretion whether to divide a marital estate on a 50/50 basis or divide the marital estate equitably to ensure both parties receive a fair share of marital estate. An equitable distribution of the marital estate is considered by many factors, including but not limited to each parties' income and potential of future income. 750 ILCS 5/503 of the Marriage and Dissolution of Marriage Act outlines parameters of the division of marital property and non-marital property during a dissolution of marriage case.

Marital and Non-Marital Assets

Assets that are acquired after a wedding, when the marriage begins, are considered marital assets. 750 Ill. Comp. Stat. Ann. 5/503(a) (LexisNexis through P.A. 101-631). This includes everything from bank accounts, retirement accounts, stocks and bonds, or companies that are established during the marriage, whether the company is established by only one spouse or not.

Non-marital assets are any assets acquired by a spouse before the marriage. Non-marital assets can include property purchased by one spouse before the marriage, retirement accounts accumulated before the marriage, any other type of property acquired prior to the marriage, gifts and inheritances received, whether during the marriage or not. 750 Ill. Comp. Stat. Ann. 5/503(a)(1)-(8) (LexisNexis through P.A. 101-631). Most pre-marital assets will be the sole property of the spouse who acquired the asset before the marriage. There are, however, certain instances in which pre-marital property could be considered partial marital property. For instance, if one spouse receives a pension through his or her employment prior to the marriage and continues to contribute to the pension after the marriage, part of this pension is considered a marital asset. This situation will be discussed further throughout this book.

Commingled Assets

Most people in a divorce action would like to keep their non-marital assets as their sole property after the divorce is finalized. For the most part, the parties are able to see clear distinctions in the classification of non-marital property and have no issues with each party keeping their respective non-marital assets. However, where a non-marital asset has been commingled with marital assets, there is often litigation surrounding the commingled assets and whether the non-marital asset should be considered as a marital asset.

Commingling of assets often occurs when a marital asset contributes or is included in a party's non-marital asset, or vice versa. Illinois statute provides that if the contributed property loses its identity, meaning that you are unable to distinguish between marital and non-marital property, then the contributed property becomes a part of the estate receiving the contribution. 750 Ill. Comp. Stat. Ann. 5/503(c)(1)(A)(i) (LexisNexis through P.A. 101-631). An example of an asset that becomes commingled and in which you may be unable to distinguish between marital and non-marital identities is a bank in which one party contributed non-marital funds into a joint account and then eventually both parties made several deposits and withdrawals. Although you have proof of how much was deposited, the fact the several other deposits and withdrawals were made by the parties makes it hard to trace whether the parties used non-marital property only.

If the non-marital and marital property are combined to acquire new property and the identity of the non-marital property is lost, the non-marital property can be considered to be commingled. 750 Ill. Comp. Stat. Ann. 5/503(c)(1)(B) (LexisNexis through P.A. 101-631). In this case, the non-marital property may be deemed to have converted to marital property. It doesn't sound fair, right? In the following section, we will look at a reimbursement of the contribution. If the contributed property does not lose its identity and you are able to distinguish between the two properties, then the contributed property remains the property of the contributing estate. 750 Ill. Comp. Stat. Ann. 5/503(c)(1)(A)(ii) (LexisNexis through P.A. 101-631). In other words, the identity of the contributed property does not change.

The divorce process can get ugly and it may be devastating to hear that the innocent decision to make a contribution has caused your non-marital property to now be considered as marital property. It is best to keep your non-marital property separate and not to deposit or contribute to the purchase of new property if you have a concern about keeping your non-marital property separate.

Right of Reimbursement from One Estate to the Other Estate

You do not have to feel that all hope is lost for you to be made whole and recover your contributions to another asset. In Illinois, the statute provides that when one estate makes a contribution into another estate, the contributing estate can be reimbursed from the estate receiving the contribution. 750 Ill. Comp. Stat. Ann. 5/503(c)(2)(A) (LexisNexis through P.A. 101-631). There are a few requirements to consider in order to obtain reimbursement. First, you must be able to trace the contribution by clear and convincing evidence. You should consider saving all of your receipts in paper and electronic form as proof of contribution so that the amount for reimbursement can be easily traced. Also, the receipts will be clear and convincing evidence of the transfer. The second requirement is for you to be able to prove that the contribution was not a gift.

If the contribution is deemed to be a gift to the marriage, then you could possibly miss out on the opportunity to be reimbursed. Save all written forms of communication that identify the reasons and conditions of the contribution.

If you put in personal time and efforts to increase the value or preserve a non-marital asset, you can also receive a form of reimbursement. In Illinois, in order to be reimbursed for your personal efforts, the efforts must be significant and result in a substantial appreciation and increase in value to the non-marital estate. 750 Ill. Comp. Stat. Ann. 5/503(c)(2)(B) (LexisNexis through P.A. 101-631). The key to being reimbursed for personal effort is that the personal effort was to increase the value of non-marital property. The use of personal efforts to increase the value of a marital asset will not result in reimbursement. This is because the increase in the value of the marital asset will result in an increase in value of the overall marital estate which will directly benefit the contributing party.

If the Court finds that there is a right to reimbursement, then you will likely be reimbursed from the marital property to be divided during the divorce. Some courts may even put a lien on the property receiving the contribution for the amount of reimbursement. Keep all of your receipts, deposit slips, transfer documents, and signed documents in a safe and secure location. You never know if you will need them later down the road to prove the right for reimbursement.

Types of Assets to be Divided

All assets accumulated during the marriage are subject to division. The same is true of debts. Some types of assets are unique or titled in a manner that require further investigation. Before we discuss the types of assets to be divided, a discussion regarding the overall division is necessary. Many times, people are concerned about the taxability of the division of assets. In general, the division of marital assets subject to a Court Order or a Judgment for Dissolution of Marriage, are not taxable transactions. 29 U.S.C.S. §1041(a)(2) (LexisNexis through P.L. 116-145). This is just a general rule of thumb and if there are unique issues, it is best to consult with a tax specialist as attorneys are not able to provide specific tax advice. However, an example of this principle is that if the parties are required to sell a marital residence, the proceeds from the sale are not taxable in the same manner that they would be in the event that the house was sold outside divorce proceedings.

Bank and Investment Accounts

Married couples generally open a joint bank account during the marriage, typically right after their wedding day or shortly before their wedding. Joint bank accounts list both individuals as an owner and operator of the account, and both parties contribute to this account by depositing paychecks, bonuses, retirement funds, tax refunds, and the like. If only one spouse is working outside the home, the joint account continues to be the property of both spouses. If each spouse opens their own checking account, it can still be considered property of the marriage.

The funds on deposit in joint savings accounts are also jointly owned by the spouses. As with the joint bank accounts, joint savings accounts continue to be the property of both spouses, regardless if one spouse does not work outside the home. Each spouse may open a savings account in their respective names and deposit marital funds into the account. These individual savings accounts are considered marital property. In essence, regardless if it is a checking or savings account, all money earned during the marriage, by either party, is considered to be marital money.

Certificates of deposit and money market accounts would also be considered marital assets if opened and funded during the marriage. This is true even if only one spouse's name is attached to the account. However, if these accounts were opened prior to the marriage, the only marital asset with regard to certificates of deposit and money market accounts could be the interest accrued on these accounts during the marriage.

Any bank accounts that a spouse may have opened and funded prior to the marriage are considered non-marital property. If a spouse has such an account and does not contribute marital funds to his or her pre-marital bank account, it is considered a pre-marital asset. Should marital funds be deposited into a premarital bank account, that account could be considered a marital asset and any balance of the account may be split on a fifty-fifty basis.

In most cases, each spouse will retain his or her non-marital bank accounts at the conclusion of the divorce. As for the marital joint accounts, typically those accounts are split between the spouses on a fifty-fifty basis or however the Judge feels is equitable. Every situation is different, so there may be times when certain situations require the uneven distribution of joint bank accounts.

Marital Residence and other Real Property

When married couples purchase their home together, it is referred to as the marital residence. Young married couples work together to save money for a down payment on their first home. When the home is purchased after the marriage, it is considered marital property. If only one spouse is working outside of the home and contributing his or her paycheck to the payment of the mortgage and household expenses, the marital home is still considered marital property.

During divorce proceedings, the parties can agree to either sell the marital home or for one spouse to buy the other spouse's equity in the home through a refinance of the home. Should the marital home be listed for sale, the proceeds from the sale of the marital home may be split between the parties after the costs of sale and the payoff of the existing mortgages. If one party wants to keep the home, the equity of the marital residence will need to be established prior to one spouse refinancing the marital residence to remove the other spouse's name from the property. Once the equity of the marital residence is established and upon the refinance of the marital residence, the spouse refinancing the marital residence may pay a share of the equity in the home to his or her spouse.

If the marital residence is not sold or refinanced during the marriage, specific language may be included in the Judgment for Dissolution of Marriage explaining how the sale or refinance of the marital home will proceed after the entry of the Judgment for Dissolution of Marriage. The language may include a time frame within which one spouse attempts to refinance the marital residence into his or her own name, and, should the marital residence be listed for sale, provisions for a reduction in price should the home not sell in a specific time frame will often be included as well.

If the couple is living in a home purchased by one spouse prior to the marriage, there is no claim the other spouse has on the property. For instance, if the wife purchases a home prior to her wedding, her husband has no claim to the home, and the home will be considered the property of the wife during a divorce proceeding. However, if the couple decide to update or renovate the wife's home, the husband may have a claim to the increase in the value of the home, or he may have a claim to be reimbursed for his share of the funds used for updates or renovations to his wife's house. Same is true if marital monies (marital income) were used to pay down the mortgage, or real estate taxes on the property. Any marital monies used toward the residence, could turn the non-marital asset into a marital asset by way of commingling the asset, not being able to show evidence of what is marital or non-marital. This can be a contentious negotiation tactic during divorce proceedings.

Summer cottages, investment properties, and time shares are additional types of properties acquired during the marriage. The division of these properties are handled in a similar manner to the way the marital residence is handled. One party will buy out the other party's equity interest in any other property purchased during the marriage by either spouse, and purchased together during the marriage. Again, the equity in real property will be split between the parties during the marriage or after the entry of the Judgment for Dissolution of Marriage. In order to accomplish this, you can offset assets and assign equity to one party and make up the value in the division of other assets.

Vehicles

Vehicles are property of the marriage, even if the title or lien is solely in the name of the other spouse, as long as it was purchased during the marriage. In most cases, each spouse keeps the car he or she is driving at the time of the entry of the Judgment for Dissolution of Marriage. If the vehicle is lien-free and the vehicles are titled in both spouses' names, both spouses may cooperate in signing over the title to the rightful spouse. If there is a lien on a vehicle in both spouses' names, the spouse keeping the vehicle may refinance the automobile loan to remove the other spouse's name from the lien and the parties may cooperate in signing over the title to the spouse who is awarded the vehicle.

This is also true for other motorized vehicles purchased during the marriage. Snow mobiles, jet skis, boats, motorcycles, and four-wheelers are some examples. These are also marital assets if purchased during the marriage, even if the motorized vehicles are purchased by and titled in the name of one spouse. The disposition of these other motorized vehicles is the same as the disposition of a vehicle.

A "fair market value" is assigned to each motorized vehicle in order to obtain a total of all vehicles purchased during the marriage. The fair market value is the price that a reasonable buyer would pay for the item in its current condition. This aids in the equal distribution of all marital assets at the time of the dissolution of the marriage to ensure each party is receiving an equitable share of the marital estate as a whole. For example, if one spouse desires to keep the marital boat, he or she may pay to the other spouse the equity in the boat, or apply an offset to other marital assets to the other spouse.

Household Furniture and Furnishings

Furniture, furnishings, kitchenware, televisions, paintings, and lamps are a small list of household furniture and furnishings acquired during the marriage. The division of household furniture and other household items is typically negotiated between the spouses without the need for attorney interference. Each spouse makes a list of the household furniture and furnishings he or she desires to retain after the dissolution of marriage. Some negotiation may be needed between the spouses or the attorneys. It is best for the spouses to reach an agreement as to the distribution of the marital furniture and furnishings to save on legal costs and the Court's time. The Courts rarely want to get involved in dividing the household furniture and furnishings, and may just order the property to be sold, if the parties cannot reach an agreement on their own. The distribution of marital furniture and furnishings is addressed in the Judgment for Dissolution of Marriage.

Tools and Other Garage Items

As with the household furniture and furnishings, tools and garage items are also marital property. Tools include hand tools, such as screwdrivers and hammers, and power tools, such as drills and electric saws. Garage items include, but are not limited to yard tools, lawn mowers, snow blowers, shovels, and tool boxes. These assets are also distributed between the parties in an equitable fashion. Depending on the amount and value of tools and garage items, there may be an offset of assets due to the spouse who is not receiving these assets or not receiving his or her fair share of these assets.

Collectibles

Some examples of collectibles include signed sports memorabilia, figurines, and toy trains. A fair market value must be established to obtain the value of these marital assets. In most cases, however, spouses are assigned the collectibles he or she has been acquiring during the marriage. If a collectible or collectibles have a high value, this will need to be addressed and satisfied through the equitable distribution of marital assets.

Family Photos and Videos

Over the course of a marriage, many family pictures and videos are taken of the family, family events, and vacations. Each spouse has a claim to the family photo albums and family videos. How are these divided? The parties can agree to divide these assets, or copies of the photo albums and videos can be made, of course at a cost. Who is responsible for the cost of the reproduction of the pictures and videos? Usually, the spouse who is requesting copies will pay the cost of reproduction. Although family pictures and videos hold no monetary value, they are considered an asset of the marriage. These assets are a timeline of the growth of the family and the children and can hold sentimental value of the family history.

Inheritances

A father, mother, grandparent, sibling, aunt or uncle of a spouse may pass away and leave money, property, or valuables to one spouse. For example, a wife's grandmother passes away and leaves her a substantial amount of money in a savings account. Is this considered marital property because the husband and wife were married when the wife's aunt passed away? No, it is not marital property, but the sole property of the wife, if she so chooses to keep that money as her own. 750 Ill. Comp. Stat. Ann. 5/503(a)(1) (LexisNexis through P.A. 101-631).

What happens if the money inherited by the wife is used for marital purposes? For example, what if the couple uses the money inherited by the wife as a down payment for a new home? The wife may receive a credit or the inherited funds back after the sale or refinance of the marital residence. The inheritance from the wife's grandmother may be treated as non-marital property by some judges, and other judges may not award the money back if the transfer is considered a gift to the marriage or co-mingled. It is a case by case situation.

In the example above, if the wife decides to deposit her inheritance money into a joint bank account, she has co-mingled her non-marital funds with marital funds and it would be difficult, if not impossible, to determine her non-marital value of the joint bank account. Commingled funds were discussed early on in this chapter.

What happens if the grandmother leaves a home to the wife? It would also be considered her non-marital property. It does not matter if the couple lives in the house for the duration of the marriage, it is still considered the wife's non-marital property. This is true so long as the wife does not add her husband to the title of the property. If husband's name is added to the title of the inherited home, he is now considered an owner and the property is now considered marital property.

Any proceeds from the sale of the inherited home are also the non-marital property of the wife. 750 Ill. Comp. Stat. Ann. 5/503(a)(1) (LexisNexis through P.A. 101-631). She does not have a responsibility to use these funds for marital purposes. If the wife decides to use the proceeds from the sale of the inherited home for marital purposes, it must be clear that these funds were her non-marital property and that she received these funds upon the entry of the Judgment for Dissolution of Marriage.

Life Insurance

Married couples, with or without children, usually have some type of life insurance plan to protect the other spouse from financial hardship after the death of the other spouse. There are usually three (3) types of life insurance policies purchased for financial protection during a marriage. There is term life insurance, which holds no value other than the death benefit. Universal life insurance policies can hold a cash value and a death benefit. The same goes for whole life insurance policies. These can also carry a cash balance and a death benefit. The cash balances are acquired over a period of time, similar to an annuity. Over time, the whole or universal life insurance policy holds a cash balance. Cash values of these policies are determined by the amount of life insurance (death benefit) purchased, the life insurance company's performance, and the length of time the policy has been in effect. If a whole or universal life insurance policy is purchased at the beginning of a twenty-year marriage, there should be a cash value balance.

Who is the owner of the cash balance of a whole or universal life insurance policy? Is it the insured? The beneficiary? Neither. The cash balance of any whole or universal life insurance policy is a marital asset and divided between the spouses at the entry of the Judgment for Dissolution of Marriage, if the policy was acquired during the marriage.

Personal Injury/Workman's Compensation Lawsuits

What happens if a spouse files a claim or lawsuit for injuries sustained in an accident or work-related accident? Is the settlement from these claims marital or non-marital property? This is a good question and these lawsuits should be considered during a divorce proceeding.

Personal injury lawsuits and workmen's compensation lawsuits are filed on behalf of an injured party. The claims alleged in these lawsuits are centered around injuries sustained by the injured spouse. Therefore, if an injured spouse receives compensation from injuries from a car accident, for example, or from work-related activities, any monies received by settlement or verdict of a trial may be the sole property of the injured spouse. Settlements and verdicts are not marital property on their own merit. However, if monies from the lawsuit are for lost wages, then a portion of those monies could be determined "marital".

Many times, an injured spouse who receives a settlement or verdict in his or her favor, co-mingles these funds into marital accounts. If this happens, all non-marital claims the injured spouse has on any settlement or verdict are out the window. If the spouse deposits lawsuit settlements or verdicts into a joint account or accounts, these funds are now considered marital, and it will be difficult, if not impossible to trace those funds to effectively prove the source of the funds.

Unused Sick Time/Vacation Time

Some employers, especially government employers, allow employees to accrue unpaid time off during the course of employment. For example, a husband works for the Metropolitan Water Reclamation District and has accrued 10 weeks of unused sick time during the course of the marriage. If this time is unused at the time of his retirement or termination of employment, he will receive payment for the unused sick time. Should this unused sick time be considered an asset of the marital estate? According to the statute, 750 ILCS 5/503(a), yes, it should. The time off that the husband has accrued during the marriage is earned income not yet paid. His wife should have a claim to half of the unpaid, accrued time off banked by the husband during the marriage. In some cases, the amount of income could be substantial and should be considered during a divorce proceeding. But, not so fast. In 2010, the Illinois Supreme Court ruled in *Marriage of Abrell* that while accrued vacation and sick days are marital property, they have no present value, and their future value is speculative, so days cannot be divided as a marital asset. *Marriage of Abrell*, 923 NE 2d 791, 800 (Ill. 2000).

529 College Plans for Children of the Marriage

It is customary, nowadays, that parents build a college fund for their minor child. College funds are typically funded by the parents, and sometimes they are funded by grandparents. These accounts, no matter what depository company is used, are in the name of one parent and the child, or both parents and the child. Marital funds, by one or both spouse's income during the marriage, are typically used to fund college accounts. What happens if the child does not go to college, but instead joins the military and receives an education through the G.I. Bill, for example. Any funds deposited into a college fund using marital funds will be returned to the marital estate. These funds would then be distributed as a marital asset and divided between the parties. Special provisions must be in place in any Judgment for Dissolution of Marriage outlining the distribution of funds deposited into a college fund that are not eligible to be used to fund a child's college education. Additionally, the funds that are remaining after the payment of a child's college education, including tuition, books, dormitory fees (or apartment rental), lab fees, supplies, and the like should be returned to the marital estate and distributed equally, unless otherwise agreed by the spouses.

There are several ways to save for your child's college education and it is important for you to understand the type of account that you are setting up for your child. Two of the most commonly created accounts for children is a 529 account or a Uniform Gift to Minor account (hereinafter UGMA). There are a few distinctions to consider when you are looking at setting either of the two aforementioned accounts for your child. It is important to know the type of account you are setting up for your child(ren) in order to understand taxability and control of the account.

The gift to the child under UGMA is irrevocable and once the child turns 18 or 21, it becomes their sole account. For the 529 account, you are able to change beneficiaries to someone else and you can maintain control over the account. The 529 account is a tax-free account and as stated above, it would be considered a marital asset and not an asset of the child. However, a UGMA is taxed at the child's tax rate. This tax rate is lower than the parent's tax rate and the UGMA is considered an asset of the child.

The UGMA can affect the Financial Aid of a student because it is considered as an asset of the child, whereas a 529 is not considered as an asset of the child. Another distinction between a 529 account and a UGMA is that the 529 can only be used for qualifying expenses, while a UGMA has no restrictions for spending. The qualifying expenses for the 529 are the specific expenses related to education. You cannot purchase a car from the funds in a 529 account and avoid tax consequences.

For most parents, the decision as to which type of account to create comes down to the ways in which the account will be used, who will have control of the account, and what are the tax ramifications for the account. Consider these questions when you are making the decision as to which account to set up for the benefit of your child.

Stocks

It is becoming more and more accessible for people to purchase and sell stock on their own through websites or mobile apps like ETrade, Robinhood, or TD Ameritrade. For some, this is an exciting, although risky, way of building wealth. There are some instances where one spouse is buying and selling stock online using marital funds, or non-marital funds, without the knowledge of the other spouse. What happens with these stocks when couples are in the midst of a divorce? What is considered marital property when it comes to buying and selling stock online? Stocks are considered an asset of the marriage, if purchased with marital funds. Since stocks are assets of the marital estate, they can be sold and the proceeds split between the parties. In some cases, the value of the stock can be used to negotiate an offset of other marital assets.

Some employers offer company stock as a benefit or bonus to their employees. What happens when one spouse receives company stock as part of his or her benefit package or as a bonus? Any stock gifted by an employer, during the marriage, is considered a marital asset. If one spouse received stock from his or her employer before and during the marriage, the only claim the other spouse has is the value of the stock gifted during the marriage. This situation is complex and should be evaluated by a competent accountant or other financial expert.

Some companies will grant a certain number of stock options for the employee to purchase while they are employed with the company. The purchase of stock options does not require a certain period of employment before they can be purchased. The amount in which the stock is purchased may be less than the market value offered to the general public. With stock options, the employees give bonuses equal to the differences between the stock value and the price paid.

Unlike stock options, stock grants are given to employees only after a certain period of employment. The employer sets the time in which a client must be employed with the company in order to receive a certain amount of stock. The stock grant retains its equitable value even when the market is volatile.

In Illinois, stock options, restricted stock, and other similar forms of benefits may be subject to division in a divorce action. Stock options and stock grants could be considered as property to be divided in the divorce process. Before the division of any stock options or grants, the court will look at when the stock was acquired. If the stock was acquired during the course of the marriage, then there is a presumption that the stock option or grant is marital property. However, this presumption can be overcome by showing that the stock option, stock grant, or other restricted stock benefit was acquired by gift, inheritance, or other means that would identify the stock as non-marital. 750 Ill. Comp. Stat. Ann. 5/203 (a)(8)(b)(3) (LexisNexis through P.A. 101-631).

At the time of the entry of the Judgment for Dissolution of Marriage, the Court can allocate stock options and restricted stock regardless as to whether the interest in the stock is vested or non-vested, or whether the value is ascertainable at the time of Judgment. The Court recognizes that the stock options and restricted stock or similar form of benefit may not be determinable and that the actual division of the option may not occur until a future date. The issue regarding the value can present some difficulty.

The difficulty with allocating stock options and similar benefits is that their value is almost always uncertain at the time that the Judgment for Dissolution of Marriage is entered. The courts in Illinois may either delay dividing the asset but order how it will be divided when it is exercised, or the court can determine the method of apportionment when the asset is received. *In re Marriage of Peters*, 760 N.E.2d 586, 592 (Ill. App. 2d Dist. 2001). Once the stock option has been divided, it is at the sole discretion of the party holding the option if and when to exercise it. *See In re Marriage of Frederick*, 578 N.E.2d 612, 618 (Ill. App. 2d Dist. 1991).

One thing to consider is that the person who owns the stock has the ability to determine when to exercise the stock option. In other words, all though the stock is divided, the court will not enter a specific timeline for the stock to be exercised. This matters because only when the stock is exercised does the option have value. This is something to consider when you are looking to divide marital assets and there is a desire to get an immediate value for the asset.

Business Interests

Jack and Jill were married in 2005, and in 2008, Jack was laid off from his construction job, and decided to start his own construction business. He marketed his business and, over the years, became the owner of a successful construction business. During the time Jack's business was getting off the ground, Jill worked outside the home in an effort to financially support the household and Jack's business venture.

In 2016, Jack decided to file for divorce. Jack's business was started and flourished during the marriage. His name is on all accounts and he filed tax returns for his business separately from the parties' joint tax returns. Does this mean the business is his sole property, or is it the property of the marriage? Actually, it is the property of the marriage and considered a marital asset. Further discussion of the effect of divorce on marital or non-marital businesses will be further discussed in this book.

Companion Animals

Some couples adopt or purchase pets during the marriage. Both the husband and wife can become very attached to these pets. If the parties also have children, the children become attached to the pets. What will happen to the pets acquired by the parties during the marriage? Are they considered marital property?

Companion animals are considered marital property if acquired during the marriage. 750 Ill. Comp. Stat. Ann. 5/503(n) (LexisNexis through P.A. 101-631). How is the ownership of companion animals dealt with after a divorce? There are a few scenarios for which the ownership and companionship of marital pets can be addressed. A married couple with no children or no minor children may develop a visitation schedule for the marital companion animals similar to a parenting time schedule for minor children. Each spouse would have scheduled time with the pet or pets.

Although the law is not specific with regard to visitation schedules for marital companion animals, it is in the best interest of these pets to live in a stable home with the person who can best take care of the animal. If one spouse travels a majority of the week, it is obvious that the pet should live primarily with the other spouse. Another alternative is that one spouse relinquishes ownership of the marital pet to the other spouse. In the situation described above, this could be the best scenario for the pet.

Taking care of a companion animal involves more than time with the pet. Responsible pet owners take their furry loved ones to the vet on a regular basis for check-ups and required shots. Who is responsible for vet costs when a divorced couple decided to retain co-ownership of the marital companion animal? Veterinarian bills should be divided between the parties, and each spouse should supply the pet's food, toys, and treats while the pet is staying at their home. If the couple has minor children, one parent typically keeps the pets at their home, or the pet can be included in the parenting time schedule outlined in an Allocation Judgment, so that the companion animal travels with the child between homes.

Retirement Accounts

Many people have some sort of retirement savings through various employer-sponsored retirement accounts or individual retirement accounts funded by the individual themselves. Unions, and other corporations, still provide a pension (also known as a Defined Benefit Plan) as a retirement benefit to employees. These assets are subject to division in the marital estate. See the Next Chapter, "You Mean I have to Share My Retirement" for details. It should also be noted that so long as the proper procedures for dividing retirement accounts is followed, these divisions are tax and penalty free. *Divorced or Separated Individuals*, I.R.S. Pub. No. 504, Cat. No. 15006I (Jan. 10, 2020), https://www.irs.gov/pub/irs-pdf/p504.pdf. In the event that a party chooses to withdraw funds from the retirement account, other tax/penalty rules may apply and specific tax specialists should be consulted.

Conclusion

No matter what assets or debts that exist the Court and/or your settlement agreement must address same. Take the time to ensure your final document deals with everything in your estate. Failure to not include everything only leaves you open to further problems when your case was to be done.

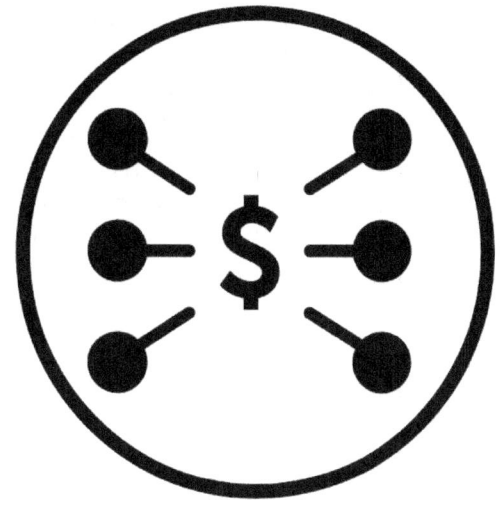

YOU MEAN I HAVE TO SHARE MY RETIREMENT?

The idea for some that their retirement benefits are subject to division in the event of divorce is devastating. In fact, the accumulation of these funds may have been your motivation to get to work each day. These issues can be complex and tricky. It is imperative that you pay attention to details to navigate through the division of these types of assets.

Defined Benefit Plans

Defined benefit plans are qualified employer-sponsored retirement plans (commonly known as Pension Plans). It is a 'defined' or guaranteed amount of money, also known as benefit, which you will receive when you retire. The amount of your benefit depends on a number of factors, including but not limited to your salary, age, gender, years of service, to name a few.

Most plans require that you work for a specific number of years before you are entitled to receive a benefit under the plan. This term is generally referred to as "vesting". If you leave a company before you were fully vested into the plan, you may not receive your full benefits from the plan. Some plans allow for a buyout of your interest, while other plans offer reciprocal service, where you can combine years of service from different organizations. Reciprocal service is generally offered in State Retirement Plans.

There are many options for tax incentives to defined benefit plans for both employers and participating employees. Most Defined Benefit Plans are funded by the employer; however, some plans provide for voluntary, or in some instances, mandatory, contributions from the participants. Most plans do not tax the contributions being made to the plan, thereby making the contribution a pre-tax contribution; however, you will owe taxes on those contributions once you start to receive distributions from the plan.

All the rules regarding the taxation (pre-tax and post-tax), fall under the Employee Retirement Income Security Act of 1974 (ERISA) and the Internal Revenue Code.

Benefits distributed in a defined benefit plan are based on a formula. This formula can provide for a set dollar amount for each year you work for the employer, or it can provide for a specified percentage of earnings. Many plans calculate an employee's retirement benefit by averaging the employee's earnings during the last few years of employment (or, alternatively, averaging an employee's earnings for his or her entire career), taking a specified percentage of the average, and then multiplying it by the employee's number of years of service. Actuaries are utilized by the employer to calculate the projected benefits utilizing the plans formula and determine what amounts need to be contributed into the plan to pay projected benefits.

Many defined benefit plans allow you to choose how you want your benefits to be paid. Payment options generally offered include:

- A single life annuity: You receive a fixed monthly benefit until you die; after you die, no further payments are made to your survivors.
- A qualified joint and survivor annuity: You receive a fixed monthly benefit until you die; after you die, your surviving spouse will continue to receive benefits (in an amount equal to at least 50 percent of your benefit) until his or her death.
- A lump-sum payment: You receive the entire value of your plan in a lump sum; no further payments will be made to you or your survivors.

It is important that you choose the payment option that will work best for your financial situation, as the option you choose is, in most cases, irrevocable; meaning you cannot reverse your decision. Considering all your options carefully to ensure that you are making the best decision for your personal financial situation is key. Perhaps discussing your options with a financial advisor, tax advisor or even a legal representative, is always something to consider as well.

Defined benefit plans do not center their projected payouts on underlying investments, as opposed to defined contribution plans, which will be addressed later in this chapter. Employers who provide defined benefit plans to their employees as a benefit, basically promise to pay the employee, upon retirement, a certain dollar amount based upon their specific formula described in the plan, despite if the market and/or investments didn't perform at the highest level. It is the employee's obligation to pay into the plan, to ensure you receive your defined benefit, despite the ebbs and flows of the market. This will ensure that you can plan on a specific dollar amount each month upon your retirement. Some plans offer cost of living adjustments, also known as COLA benefits, which provides for an annual increase in your monthly benefits. Much of the benefits held in defined benefit plans are covered and protected by the federal government through the Pension Benefit Guaranty Corporation (PBGC), which provides extra security for your retirement.

Some employers offer hybrid plans. Hybrid plans include defined benefit plans that have many of the characteristics of defined contribution plans. Defined contributions plans are discussed later in this chapter. One of the most popular forms of a hybrid plan is the cash balance plan.

Cash Balance Plans

Cash balance plans are defined benefit plans that in many ways resemble defined contribution plans. Like defined benefit plans, they are obligated to pay you a specified amount at retirement and are insured by the federal government. But they also offer one of the most familiar features of a defined contribution plan: Retirement funds accumulate in an individual account. This allows the participant to easily track how much retirement benefit has accrued during their participation in the plan. The plan is also portable, meaning that if you leave your employer, in most cases, opt to receive a lump-sum distribution of the vested account balance. So long as these funds are rolled into an IRA (individual retirement account), or to another qualified retirement plan, are not taxable. However, be sure to check with a tax professional for all concerns regarding distributions from retirement plans.

QDROS for Defined Benefit Plans

A QDRO (Qualified Domestic Relations Order) is a judgment, decree or order for a retirement plan to pay child support, alimony or marital property rights to a spouse, former spouse, child or other dependent of a participant. The QDRO is generally based on a prior Order or Judgment, which specifically designates the spouse, former spouse, child or other dependent of a participant (known as the Alternate Payee), with a specific award from the participant's retirement plan. Technically, a "QDRO" is not considered to be a "QDRO", until the Plan Administrator for the retirement plan approves the QDRO, thereby "qualifying" the order, making it a QDRO. Otherwise, it is simply a DRO or Domestic Relations Orders.

Federal law, specifically requirements under ERISA, Employee Retirement Income Security Act of 1974, states that a retirement benefit can only be divided by way of a QDRO. This means that an underlying Order of Judgment is not sufficient to divide a retirement plan, despite the Order, or Judgment, clearly stating that the retirement benefits are to be divided and awarded to the Alternate Payee. Although a QDRO can be processed long after the underlying Order awarded the benefits to the Alternate Payee, it is recommended that a QDRO is entered as soon as administratively possible after the underlying Order is issued by the Court. This is recommended, due to the fact that if the retirement plan is not provided with notice of the division of the retirement benefits, 100% of benefits could be paid to the Participant, despite a portion of those benefits being the Alternate Payees benefit. If the QDRO is processed after payments to the retiree or participant has commenced, then the Alternate Payee would only receive future payments, and not receive retroactive benefits from the date the retiree or participant started receiving the benefits under the plan.

There are strict guidelines that must be followed when drafting a QDRO. Generally, the Summary Plan Description provides detailed information about the plan, the requirements, and contact information for the plan administrator of the plan. Due to the specific requirements under the retirement plan, many plan administrators for the plan may have sample QDRO forms or language that they specifically require in a QDRO. Although every plan is different with its own specifications of what must be included in a

QDRO, per ERISA, Employee Retirement Income Security Act of 1974, a QDRO must, at a minimum, contain certain specific information, including:

- the name of the Plan;
- the participant and each alternate payee's name and last known mailing address;
- the dollar amount or percentage of the participant's benefits to be paid to each alternate payee (or the method of determining the amount of percentage);
- the order must specify that the order is issued pursuant to state domestic relations law and create or recognize the rights of an individual who is an alternate payee (spouse, former spouse, child, or other dependent of a participant); and
- The number of payments or time period to which the order applies (for example, from date of marriage to date of divorce).

Even still, rules imposed by the U.S. Department of Labor specify restrictions that cannot be included in a QDRO; meaning that a QDRO cannot include provisions that are against the individual plan rules. Those restrictions are as follows:

- The court order cannot force a retirement plan to disburse any benefit or option that is not provided through the plan.
- The QDRO cannot require increased benefits from the retirement plan.
- Benefits cannot be required from a plan for an alternate payee when those benefits are already required to be covered by another alternate payee who is under the decree of another QDRO.
- The order must not require a plan to pay benefits to an alternate payee in the form of a qualified joint and survivor annuity for the lives of the alternate payee and his or her subsequent spouse.

Under Federal law, the administrator of the retirement plan that provides the benefits affected by an order is the individual (or entity) initially responsible for determining whether a domestic relations order is a QDRO. Plan administrators have specific responsibilities and duties with respect to determining whether a domestic relations order is a QDRO. A plan must establish reasonable procedures to determine the qualified status of domestic relations orders and to administer distributions pursuant to qualified orders. Administrators are required to follow the plan's procedures for making QDRO determinations, as well as required to furnish notice to participants and alternate payees of the receipt of a domestic relations order and to furnish a copy of the plan's procedures for determining the qualified status of such orders. The administrator of an employee benefit plan is the individual or entity specifically designated in the plan documents as the administrator. If the plan documents do not designate an administrator, the administrator is the employer maintaining the plan, or, in the case of a plan maintained by more than one employer, the association, committee, joint board of trustees, or similar group representing the parties maintaining the plan. The name, address, and phone number of the plan administrator is required to be included in the plan's summary plan description. The summary plan description is a document that the administrator is required to furnish to each participant and to each beneficiary receiving benefits which summarizes the rights and benefits of participants and beneficiaries and the obligations of the plan.

A spouse or former spouse who receives QDRO benefits from a retirement plan reports the payments received as if he or she were a plan participant.

Determining Marital Portion.

Determining the marital portion of a Defined Benefit Plan is generally calculated utilizing the HUNT formula. *In re Marriage of Hunt*, 78 Ill. App. 3d 653, 664 (Ill. App. Ct. 1st Dist. 1979). The HUNT formula method is commonly used as it is the fairest method to determine the marital portion of a Defined Benefit Plan. In essence, the HUNT formula determines the marital portion using a fraction the numerator of which represents the number of pension credits accrued by the participant during the period of the marriage; and the denominator represents the number of total pension credits accrued by the participant as of the earliest of the participant's retirement or the alternate payee's benefit commencement dates. *Id.*

Separate vs. Shared Interest QDROs.

When dividing a Defined Benefit Plan, the retirement benefits can be divided by way of a QDRO using two different methods; Separate Interest Approach and Shared Interest Approach. Each approach will be explained herein.

Separate Interest Approach allows the Alternate Payee to be paid for his or her life, regardless of the longevity of the Participant. Basically, the benefit paid to the Alternate Payee is adjusted based upon the Alternate Payee's lifetime, through an actuarial assessment of the benefits. This approach, in most cases, allows the Alternate Payee to elect to commence his or her benefits any time after the Participant reaches his or her earliest retirement age, regardless if the Participant actually retires at that time. However, keep in mind that every plan is different and there may be some specific plan provisions that may reduce the benefit if the Alternate Payee chooses to elect to receive the benefit prior to the actual Participant retiring. It is best to consult with an attorney to know what is in your best interest. Furthermore, benefits paid to the Alternate Payee are paid even after the death of the Participant. However, there are some qualified preretirement survivorship options that may be available to the Alternate Payee, if the Participant is not yet retired. It is important that a QDRO is entered, to award the Alternate Payee these benefits, in the event of the Participant's death prior to retirement.

Generally, the separate interest approach can only be applied when the participant has not actually retired, or what is known as "not pay status". If the Alternate Payee should die before receiving their benefits, the benefits may be paid to their estate, or revert back to the Participant or potentially be absorbed back into the plan. The plan rules in the Summary Plan Description of the particular plan will provide the specific rules as to the Alternate Payee's benefits upon death.

Whereas, a shared interest approach is to be used when the Participant is already in pay status or retired. In this approach, the Alternate Payee, in essence, shares in the participant's pension when the participant collects it. This approach is not as flexible with the benefits assigned to the Alternate Payee. In that this approach does not actuarially adjust the benefits over the Alternate Payee's lifetime. Therefore, the benefits assigned to the Alternate Payee will cease upon the Participant's death. However, the Alternate Payee may have rights under a survivor annuity election. These elections are made prior to the Participant's death and can range from 50% Joint and Survivor Annuity, up to 100% Joint and Survivor Annuity. This basically means that the Participant would take a reduction in their benefit, to secure a benefit for the survivor after the Participant's death. This election is mandatory prior to the Participant's retirement, and if the Participant is currently married, the spouse of the Participant must also consent to the election. This election is irrevocable; meaning that once the Participant elects, that election cannot be changed. In that this election can reduce the Participant's actual benefit, the Participant may want to choose an election that gives them the largest benefit now, versus choosing a reduced benefit to secure a benefit to the surviving spouse. It is essential that the spouse or Alternate Payee review any documentation provided to them, by the Plan, with an attorney, to ensure that they are not irrevocably, electing to a payment option that does not provide a survivor annuity option. Additionally, in most instances, this election must take place within a specific time frame. If no response is received by the Alternate Payee, the election is irrevocably waived, meaning the Alternate Payee will have no right into the future to change the waiver.

Under the Shared Interest Approach, if the Alternate Payee should predecease the Participant, the benefits may be paid to the Alternate Payee's estate, or revert back to the Participant, depending on the Plan Rules. Once again, working with an attorney to ensure the best options for your particular situation is the best way to protect your benefits now and into the future.

Benefit & Payment Options Under a Defined Benefit Plan

Many defined benefit plans allow options for how you want to receive your benefits and payments. Most payment options offered include:

- Single Life Annuity: This option allows the participant to receive a fixed monthly benefit until the participant dies; after the death of the participant, no further payments are made to the estate of the participant or its survivors;
- Qualified Joint and Survivor Annuity: This option also provides for a fixed monthly benefit until the participant dies; however, after the participant deceases, the designated surviving spouse will continue to receive benefits in an amount equal to at least 50% of the participant's benefit through the lifetime of the surviving spouse, or Alternate Payee. Some plans further allow you to elect 75% joint and survivor annuity or 100% joint and survivor annuity. Any of these options elected would reduce the payment that would be received in the single life annuity set forth above;
- Lump Sum Payment: This option allows for the Participant to receive the entire value of the plan in a lump sum; no further payments would then be available to the participant or the survivors.

As stated previously, it is important to carefully consider and choose the best option for you as there is so much that may hinge on the decision and especially if the decision is irrevocable. Discussing your options with your attorney is your best course of action.

Accounting for Subsidies including Cost of Living Increases

Defined Benefit Plans have additional benefits that must also be considered when dividing the plan by way of a QDRO. These additional benefits, sometimes known as subsidies, provide for potential future increases in benefits due to increases in the participant's compensation, additional years of service, or changes in the plan's provisions. These benefits can only be divided prior to the participant's retirement in a Separate Interest Approach. For example, a defined benefit plan may offer an "early retirement subsidy" to employees who retire before the plan's normal retirement age but after having worked for a specific number of years for the employer maintaining the plan. In some cases, this subsidized benefit provides payments in the form of an annuity that pays the same annual amount as would be paid if the payments commenced instead at the normal retirement age. The subsidy may be available only for certain forms of benefit. A QDRO can also address the disposition of any subsidy to which the participant may become entitled after the QDRO has been entered.

A participant's basic retirement benefits may increase due to circumstances that occur after a QDRO has been entered, such as increases in salary, crediting of additional years of service, or amendments to the plan's provisions, including amendments to provide cost of living adjustments. The treatment of such benefit increases should be considered when drafting a QDRO using the separate interest approach.

Disability Benefits

Defined Benefit Plans may also offer disability benefits to its participants, which may be attributable to the benefits under the plan prior to retirement. Ensuring that any QDRO that is entered includes language for a division of these possible disability benefits will protect the Alternate Payee and potentially provide for the Alternate Payee to receive a portion of such benefits. If this language is not included in a QDRO, the Plan Administrator has no right to award any such benefits to the Alternate Payee.

Defined Contribution Plans

A defined contribution plan is a type of retirement plan that provides for an individual account for each participant. The participant's benefits are based solely on the amount contributed to the participant's account and any income, expenses, gains or losses, and any forfeitures of accounts of other participants that may be allocated to such participant's account. Examples of defined contribution plans include 401(k) plans (26 U.S.C.S. § 401 et al (LexisNexis through Pub. L. 116-145)), 403(b) plans, (26 U.S.C.S. § 403 et al (LexisNexis through Pub. L. 116-145)), 457 Plans, (26 U.S.C.S. § 457 et al (LexisNexis through Pub. L. 115-145)), profit-sharing plans, and other governmental plans. In these plans, the employee or the employer (or both) contribute to the employee's individual account under the plan, sometimes at a set rate, such as specified percent of earnings annually. These contributions generally are invested on the employee's behalf. The employee will ultimately receive the balance in their account, which is based on contributions plus or minus investment gains or losses. The value of the account will fluctuate due to the changes in the value of the investments.

The name, 'Defined Contribution Plan', essentially means that the Participant contributes a "defined" amount of money into his or her Plan, to save for their retirement. This defined amount (either dollar amount or percentage of income) can be changed by the Participant throughout their participation in the plan and withheld from the participant's income. A participant's basic retirement benefit in a defined contribution plan is the amount in his or her account at any given time. This is generally known as the participant's "account balance." Defined contribution plans commonly provide for retirement benefits to be paid in the form of a lump sum payment of the participant's entire account balance. Defined contribution plans by their nature do not offer subsidies. It should be noted, however, that some defined benefit plans provide for lump sum payments, and some defined contribution plans provide for annuities.

401(k) Plan.

A 401k Plan, (26 U.S.C.S. § 401 et al (LexisNexis through Pub. L. 116-145)) is a defined contribution plan that is a cash or deferred arrangement. Employees can elect to defer receiving a portion of their salary which is instead contributed on their behalf, before taxes, to the 401(k) plan. *Id.* Sometimes the employer may match these contributions. There is a dollar limit on the amount an employee may elect to defer each year per the IRS rules which change year to year. An employer must advise employees of any limits that may apply.

Withdrawals and distributions from 401(k) plans.

All monies withdrawn or distributed from the 401(k) after age 59 ½ are penalty-free. *Id.* The Participant will be required to pay ordinary income tax on the distributions. The thought process on this is that when you become retirement age and begin taking distributions from your Plan, it is presumed that you will be in a lower tax bracket than you were in while you were working and receiving a regular salary. The tax savings comes from the money you are contributing while you are working, presuming you are in a higher tax bracket as opposed to when you retire.

Early Withdrawal from 401k

Early withdrawals are considered any withdrawals taken from a 401k before age 59 ½. *Id.* The withdrawals are taxed as ordinary income, and additionally, subject to an additional 10% penalty as a result of the early withdrawal. However, in some instances, there are exemptions to the penalty, including but not limited to total and permanent disability, loss of employment when you're at least age 55, and distribution of the account pursuant to a QDRO (Qualified Domestic Relations Order) in a divorce. However, in this situation, the penalty-free withdrawal only applies to the non-participant. For example, if the Wife is the participant in the plan, and the Husband was awarded a percentage of the plan, the Husband could take a distribution from his portion of the plan that he was awarded without penalty. The wife, in that instance, since she is the Participant in the plan, is not allowed to take a distribution penalty free.

Some plans allow for hardship distributions, but there are very strict guidelines which must be met in order to qualify for the distribution, including proving the use of the funds, the immediate financial need and most times, no more than the specific amount of money required is allowed. All plan rules differ with their own specific plan rules and requirements relative to withdrawals and distributions and it is best to review your Summary Plan Description to determine what qualifies as a hardship distribution with your specific plan.

401(k) Loan

A 401(k) loan may be a more advantageous option rather than a distribution, presuming that your employer or plan allows for loans. *Id.* Although the monies must be paid back to yourself with interest, the interest rate is generally lower than most banks. The monies must be paid back within five years or in some instances, when you leave that employment. Allowing for loans is not a requirement under the plan, and every employer has their own specific rules and requirements relative thereto.

Some disadvantages to a 401(k) loan is that you lose the main tax benefits of the 401(k), because you are paying back the loan with after-tax money; thereby losing the tax incentives of contributing to said plan with pre-tax dollars. Also, the monies taken out of the plan will miss the investment returns on the monies taken out. If you leave or are terminated from the employment and are unable to pay back the loan, you may be required to take the remaining monies as a distribution, whereby treating the monies as taxable ordinary income and potentially an early withdrawal penalty as well.

403(b) Plan

A 403(b) plan, or a tax-sheltered annuity plan, is a retirement plan for certain employees of public schools, employees of certain tax-exempt organizations and certain ministers. 26 U.S.C.S. § 403 et al (LexisNexis through Pub. L. 116-145). A 403(b) plan allows employees to contribute some of their salary to the plan. *Id.* The employer may also contribute to the plan for employees. *Id.* A 403(b) Plan is very similar to a 401(k) Plan in that the only major difference is the organization who is sponsoring the plan. 403(b) plans are usually sponsored by a public school, or nonprofit organization, whereas 401(k) plans are usually sponsored by private or for-profit organizations. 26 U.S.C.S. §§ 401 et al, 403 et al (LexisNexis through Pub. L. 116-145). The same basic rules apply with both plans, where the employee or the employer or both may contribute to an individual retirement account which is tax-sheltered until time of distribution.

457(b) Plan

A 457(b) plan is also an employer-sponsored, tax savings retirement account. 26 U.S.C.S. § 457 et al (LexisNexis through Pub. L. 116-145). These plans are also called deferred compensation plans. *Id.* They are generally offered to state and local government employees such as police officers, firefighters, or other civil servants. *Id.* Some high-paid executives at certain nonprofits like hospitals, charities, and unions are also able to use 457(b) plans. *Id.* 457(b) plans are similar to a 401(k) plan or 403(b) plan, but there one unique difference with a 457(b) plan as compared with a 401(k) or 403(b) plan, is that if you leave a job or retire before the age of 59 ½, and decide to take a withdrawal from the plan, the participant does not pay a 10% penalty fee.

QDROs for Defined Contribution Plans

As stated above, a QDRO (Qualified Domestic Relations Order) is a judgment, decree or order for a retirement plan to pay child support, alimony or marital property rights to a spouse, former spouse, child or other dependent of a participant. The QDRO is generally based on a prior Order or Judgment, which specifically designates the spouse, former spouse, child or other dependent of a participant (known as the Alternate Payee), with a specific award from the participant's retirement plan. Technically, a "QDRO" is not considered to be a "QDRO", until the Plan Administrator for the retirement plan approves the QDRO, thereby "qualifying" the order, making it a QDRO. Otherwise, it is simply a DRO or Domestic Relations Order.

In that federal law, specifically ERISA, Employee Retirement Income Security Act of 1974, dictates that a retirement benefit can only be divided by way of a QDRO, the underlying Order or Judgment is not sufficient to divide a retirement plan. As previously discussed above, QDROs for Defined Benefit Plans specifically identify certain benefits that are divided. Same is true for Defined Contribution Plans.

For most Defined Contribution Plans, similar with Defined Benefit Plans, the QDRO must identify certain key information, specifically:

- the name of the Plan;
- the participant and each alternate payee's name and last known mailing address;
- the dollar amount or percentage of the participant's benefits to be paid to each alternate payee;
- the order must specify that the order is issued pursuant to state domestic relations law and create or recognize the rights of an individual who is an alternate payee (spouse, former spouse, child, or other dependent of a participant); and
- The date in which the account is being valued for purposes of dividing the benefit (in many instances this is known as the Valuation Date and tends to coincide with the date of the divorce);

Similar to Defined Benefit Plans, rules imposed by the U.S. Department of Labor specify restrictions that cannot be included in a QDRO for Defined Contribution Plans as well; meaning that a QDRO cannot include provisions that are against the individual plan rules. Those restrictions are as follows:

- The court order cannot force a retirement plan to disburse any benefit or option that is not provided through the plan.
- The QDRO cannot require increased benefits from the retirement plan.

- Benefits cannot be required from a plan for an alternate payee when those benefits are already required to be covered by another payee who is under the decree of another QDRO.
- The order must not require a plan to pay benefits to an alternate payee in the form of a qualified joint and survivor annuity for the lives of the alternate payee and his or her subsequent spouse.

Income and Losses

In addition to the above, when drafting a QDRO for a Defined Contribution Plan, the parties should consider how to allocate any income or losses attributable to the participant's account that may accrue during the determination period. Essentially, there will be a period of time from the entry of QDRO, and final implementation of the QDRO, in which the account balance will continue to be subject to income and/or losses. It is important to ensure that the QDRO identifies this, so that each party is awarded their share of the interest and/or losses during such time. If the QDRO fails to identify this, the Alternate Payee may lose any interest on his or her share of the monies awarded under the QDRO.

Percentage or dollar amount.

If an order allocates a specific dollar amount rather than a percentage to an alternate payee as a shared payment, the order should address the possibility that the participant's account balance or individual payments might be less than the specified dollar amount when actually paid out, if, say the market were to experience a loss during the determination period. By including language "subject to income and losses to the date of segregation" in a QDRO, will provide protections to both the Participant and the Alternate Payee of any risks or fluctuations in the market. Both parties would be at the same level of risk during the determination period.

Loan Balances

A QDRO for a Defined Contribution Plan should also address whether or not any loan balances shall be included or excluded in dividing the retirement plan. This is important due to the fact that if the QDRO is left silent, plan rules may automatically assign the loan to the Participant, leaving the Alternate Payee with a larger share of the account. To prevent the Plan from making assumptions as a result of the QDRO not addressing the provision, it is best to simply include language about any loan balance. Including the loan balance means that the Participant would be solely responsible for the loan. Excluding the loan balance means that both parties would equally share the loan balance.

Segregation

Once the account is segregated by the Plan Administrator, the Alternate Payee will receive notice from the Plan Administrator and is treated like a Participant in the Plan. In many cases, the Alternate Payee may be allowed to transfer the monies, as a tax-free transfer to another retirement account, such as a Traditional/Rollover IRA. If the Alternate Payee chooses to take a distribution from the plan, assuming the plan allows for such distribution, the Alternate Payee is allowed to take such distribution without having to pay the normal penalty associated with taking a distribution from the plan before age 59 ½. Despite not having a 10% penalty on the distribution, the distribution is taxable at the Alternate Payee's current tax bracket.

Child or Other Dependent of the Participant

In other situations, a QDRO may be issued as a result of past due child support for a child or other dependent of the Participant. If this is the case, the Participant will be apportioned the tax consequence as a result of the distribution.

Accounting for pre-marital values.

Dividing a Defined Benefit Plan can be complicated when trying to account for a pre-marital value in the account. For instance, if a spouse contributed into his employer provided retirement account for five years prior the parties' marriage, and continued to contribute into the plan after the parties' marriage, the non-marital portion of the plan has now been commingled with the marital portion of the plan. It is a very common mistake to look at the account balance as of the date of the marriage and state that this is the non-marital portion, when that balance would have continued to fluctuate based on the market. In order to provide evidence as to the non-marital portion of the account, based upon market fluctuation, the account owner should provide all statements for the account, to evidence the rate of return on the non-marital balance of the account. By simply using the straight dollar amount of the non-marital portion, the owner is not receiving the income and losses associated with their original balance. In some cases, actuaries are retained in order to calculate the marital vs. non-marital portion of the plan. However, account statements are required in order for the actuary to determine the value of the marital vs. non-marital portion. It is best to save all account statements, as many financial institutions will only allow a look back for a certain amount of years. If the account statements cannot be obtained going back to the date of marriage, it is difficult to provide evidence as to the market fluctuations and the actual balance of the non-marital portion.

Once the marital and non-marital portion of the account is determined, a QDRO can be drafted with assigning the owner a set dollar amount of the plan first, as their non-marital portion. Thereafter, the account would be divided in accordance with the parties' agreement. For example, the owner would be assigned the first $75,000.00 of the plan. Thereafter, the remaining account balance would be divided 50/50. It is important for the account owner to save their statements, so that the evidence on the market fluctuation can be presented. If no evidence is provided, the Court could simply state that the entire account balance is marital and order the account be divided equally by and between the parties, without taking into consideration the balance of the account prior to the marriage.

IRA – Individual Retirement Accounts

An IRA is an Individual Retirement Account, which is held in an individual name (not held jointly). 26 U.S.C.S. § 408 et al (LexisNexis through Pub. L. 116-145). There are several different types of IRAs, identified as a Traditional IRA (26 U.S.C.S. § 408 et al (LexisNexis through Pub. L. 115-145)) vs. a ROTH IRA, (26 U.S.C.S. § 408A et al (LexisNexis through Pub. L. 115-145)), specifically as it relates to the tax consequences of each.

Traditional (or Rollover) IRA

A traditional individual retirement account, or IRA, is a retirement savings account that allows an individual to contribute to a retirement account using pretax dollars, similar to a 401k or other Defined Contribution Plan. 26 U.S.C.S. § 408 et al (LexisNexis through Pub. L. 116-145). In essence, the individual can take a dollar for dollar tax deduction for the contribution into a Traditional IRA Account. *Id.* The individual is deferring the taxes until the time of withdrawal. *Id.* A Traditional IRA is appealing in that it is assumed that while you are working and earning an income, you will be in a higher tax bracket than when you retire. Therefore, the monies withdrawn from the account will more than likely be taxed at a lower rate.

There are further limitations to Traditional IRAs, which can change year to year, based upon the IRS rules, but generally, individuals are unable to withdraw from their Traditional IRA account until age 59 ½; otherwise, the individual will incur a 10 percent penalty, unless the money is used for certain eligible qualified expenses per the IRS rules. *Id.* Furthermore, pursuant to the IRS Rules in 2020, an individual cannot contribute more than $6,000.00 per year (if you are under the age of 50); and not more than $7,000.00 per year if you are over the age of 50, as of 2020. The IRS may change these limits year to year.

An individual should be mindful of making contributions to a Traditional IRA when they, or their spouse, are a participant in an employer provided retirement plan, as there are further limits to contributions to a Traditional IRA. *Id.* The IRS provides a table for tax payers to determine the deduction allowed for a Traditional IRA if an individual, or spouse, is a participant in another employer provided retirement plan. *Id.* If the tax payer is over a certain income level, then there is no allowable tax deduction when contributing to a Traditional IRA. *Id.*

When an individual contributed to a 401k Plan or other Defined Contribution Plan while they were working and leaves said employment, they may have the ability to transfer the monies into another qualified retirement plan or a Rollover IRA, which is treated the same as a Traditional IRA in that the monies used to contribute to the employer provided 401k Plan were pre- tax dollars. *Id.* The monies held in a Rollover IRA, would only be taxed upon withdrawal of said funds at the age of 59 ½. *Id.* Unlike a Traditional IRA there is no limit when rolling over monies from a qualified retirement account into a Rollover IRA. *Id.*

Additionally, just like other retirement accounts, you cannot keep the money in the Traditional IRA indefinitely. *Id.* The IRS Rules require individuals to take minimum withdrawals from the Traditional IRA Accounts. *Id.* Although these rules may change from year to year, as of 2020, you may be required to take minimum distributions from your account by April 1 of the year after you reach age 70½ (age 72 if born after June 30, 1949), even if you have not retired. *Id.* These required minimum distributions are known as RMDs. The IRS has created a table to calculate the RMD, which is based on the account balance as of the end of the year and divided by a specific formula provided by the IRS.

Not all IRAs are the same. Although many of the rules that apply to Traditional IRAs, (26 U.S.C.S. § 408 et al (LexisNexis through Pub. L. 115-145)), apply to ROTH IRAs, (26 U.S.C.S. § 408A et al (LexisNexis through Pub. L. 115-145)), there are some differences with a ROTH IRA, as compared with a Traditional IRA.

ROTH IRA

A Roth IRA is an IRA and is subject to the rules that apply to a traditional IRA, however, there are some exceptions. 26 U.S.C.S. § 408A et al (LexisNexis through Pub. L. 116-145). First, ROTH IRA contributions cannot be deducted from your income, as opposed to a Traditional IRA; hence you are using post-tax dollars to fund the retirement account. *Id.* Although there is no up-front tax break to contributing to a ROTH IRA, the tax incentives are at the time you take distributions. Qualified distributions may be taken tax-free, so long as the distributions are pursuant to the requirements provided by the IRS. *Id.* Additionally, unlike a Traditional IRA, you are not required to take Minimum Required Distributions from the ROTH IRA. *Id.* Basically, you can leave the money in the account for as long as you choose. Even still, a ROTH IRA allows an individual to withdraw 'contributions' from their account, penalty-free at any time for any reason. However, if any monies are withdrawn on the 'investment earnings' on the contributions, prior to age 59 1/2 (unless for a qualifying reason), an individual will have to pay a 10% penalty on the investment earnings withdrawn. *Id.* After age 59 ½, an individual is allowed to take distributions at any time, tax-free and penalty-free; or keep the money in the account. *Id.*

A Simplified Employee Pension Plan (SEP) IRA.

A SEP IRA is another form of a retirement savings account. 26 U.S.C.S. § 408K et al (LexisNexis through Pub. L. 116-145) A SEP IRA allows employees to make contributions on a tax-favored basis using pre-tax dollars to individual retirement accounts (IRAs) owned by the employees. *Id.* SEPs are subject to minimal reporting and disclosure requirements. *Id.* Under a SEP, an employee must set up an IRA to accept the employer's contributions. *Id.* SEP IRAs are customarily utilized for businesses that would otherwise not set up employer-sponsored plans. Sole proprietors, partnerships, and corporations, including self-employed people, can establish SEPs. *Id.* Employers then can make tax-deductible contributions on behalf of their eligible employees into their SEP IRAs. *Id.*

SEPS are advantageous, especially for the small business, as they have low administrative costs and allow an employer to determine how much to contribute each year. SEP IRAs also have higher annual contribution limits as compared with standard IRAS. *Id.* SEP IRAs are similar to Traditional IRAs, however, employers, not employees, make contributions to SEP IRAs , and the decision as to whether to contribute and how much can vary. *Id.*

SEP IRA accounts are treated like traditional IRAs for tax purposes and allow the same investment options. *Id.* The same rules apply for all transfer and rollover options, as to a Traditional IRA. When an employer makes contributions to SEP IRA accounts, it receives a tax deduction for the amount contributed. *Id.* Additionally, the business is not locked into an annual contribution—decisions about whether to contribute and how much can change each year. Although the contribution limits are much higher with SEP IRAs as opposed to a Traditional IRA. These limits change from year to year, but generally are significantly higher than a Traditional IRA.

How to Divide in the Event of Divorce

Dividing IRAs in the event of divorce is somewhat tricky, as every financial institution has their own set of rules that must be followed in order to divide the account. Unlike dividing employer sponsored retirement plans by way of a QDRO, as defined previously, an IRA should be divided per the financial institution's requirements, commonly known as "transfer incident to divorce". In that an IRA is held solely by one individual, a transfer of a designated amount or percentage to the other spouse must be effectuated through the financial institution. In general, the financial institution has a specific form that the owner must complete to request a transfer to the non-owner. In most cases, the non-owner must establish their own individual account with that financial institution in order for the funds to be transferred into their own name. Once the funds are transferred, then, if the spouse chooses to move the funds into a different financial institution, then a separate transfer can occur thereafter. Generally, most financial institutions prefer to do an in-house transfer from one spouse to another, to guarantee the fund transfer goes smoothly.

In dividing, or instances of IRAs, transferring, a portion of an IRA account from one spouse to another, is different than dividing an employer provided retirement account, in that the IRA is transferred on the date the actual segregation or division of the account occurs. Hence, a valuation date is not permitted when dividing an IRA, unlike an employer provided retirement account. The value of the IRA will be divided as of the date of the actual segregation, without being able to go back to a certain date in time for a value. Therefore, the account is automatically subject to income and losses until the actual date of segregation, so long as the parties are dividing the account by way of a percentage.

If the IRA is being divided by way of providing the non-owner spouse with a specific dollar amount, the parties risk market fluctuation on the account balance. Therefore, if the market takes a dip, the owner of the account may lose more than what was originally anticipated in the division and the non-owner spouse, may end up with more of the account balance than was what originally anticipated. As a result, it is best to divide the IRA by way of a percentage, to account for market fluctuation. Alternatively, if a dollar amount is agreed upon, the parties can agree to convert the dollar amount into a percentage based upon a specific date (i.e. date of divorce), to ensure that both parties are subject to the income and losses of the account during the segregation process.

The segregation process can be time consuming depending on the financial institution and their specific requirements. Most institutions require all forms to be completed by both the owner and the non-owner spouse, executed by both parties in the presence of a Medallion Signature Guarantee, which is different from a Notary. A Medallion Signature Guarantee is a guarantee by the transferring financial institution that the signature of the owner is genuine and the financial institution accepts liability for any forgery. These forms, along with a Certified Copy of the Divorce Decree or Judgment for Dissolution of Marriage are usually required by the financial institution to transfer the funds. It is best practice to prepare these forms in advance of the divorce, to prevent any unnecessary delay in transferring the funds, especially when market fluctuations can potentially vary the ultimate distribution of the funds.

Also, a common mistake in dividing IRAs is combining Traditional IRAs, with ROTH IRAs and then dividing the total amount of the accounts. In that there are different tax incentives and consequences with Traditional IRAs versus ROTH IRAs, the two different accounts cannot be combined, as they represent pre-tax and post-tax dollars. This often occurs when parties are trying to off-set one asset for another, to equally divide the total amount of the account balances and provide an off-set to one spouse or the other. To ensure that the parties take advantage of the tax incentives with both Traditional IRAs and ROTH IRAs do not combine the values before dividing. If the parties choose to do an offset, the parties must keep all Traditional IRAs, and Rollover IRAs, as well as any Defined Contribution Plan in one category, while keeping all ROTH IRAs with other post-tax dollar assets, such as a residence, vehicle, or bank account.

State and Public Retirement Systems of Illinois

State and Public Retirement Systems of Illinois, Illinois Pension Code 40 ILCS 5/ et al., include workers from many different sectors, including government and municipal workers, county workers, state workers, police, fire teachers, judges and Illinois lawmakers. Specifically, in Illinois, including Cook County and the City of Chicago, there are approximately 667 government-worker pension funds that are supposed to provide retirement security for more than 1 million government workers and retirees. Those funds include:
- Five state-run funds that cover downstate and suburban teachers, state employees, state-university employees, judges, and Illinois lawmakers
- 355 suburban and downstate police pension funds, 296 suburban and downstate firefighter pension funds, and a pension fund for suburban and downstate municipal workers
- Seven pension funds in Chicago and three pension funds in Cook County

Some of the retirement plans are as follows:
- Chicago Teachers' Pension Fund;
    - County Employees' Annuity & Benefit Fund of Cook County;
    - Forest Preserve District Employees' Annuity & Benefit Fund of Cook County;
    - Illinois Municipal Retirement Fund;
    - Judges' & General Assembly Retirement Systems;
    - Laborers' Annuity & Benefit Fund of Chicago;
    - Metropolitan Water Reclamation District Retirement Fund;

- Municipal Employees' Annuity & Benefit Fund of Chicago;
- Park Employees' Annuity & Benefit Fund of Chicago;
- State Employees' Retirement System of Illinois;
- State Universities Retirement System; and
- Teachers' Retirement System.

These plans are considered Defined Benefit Plans that provide benefits to its members including but not limited to, retirement, survivor, disability, and death benefits. Generally, employees are required to participate in these plans as part of their employment agreement and are automatically enrolled when employment commences. The Illinois Pension Code 40 ILCS 5/ et al., determines how these retirement plans operate and how they are administered. Workers earn their pension by contributing a portion of each paycheck toward their retirement. These contributions are then combined with their employer's contributions and invested. The member will then receive a guaranteed monthly benefit that could last for the rest of their life.

Generally, pensions use an employee's years of service and average salary to calculate the monthly pension benefit in retirement. The longer an employee has worked and the higher their salary was, the larger their pension benefit will be because they paid into the system longer. Although each plan is different, they all encompass the majority of the same benefits to its members, including but not limited to a guaranteed monthly benefit upon retirement, annual cost of living increases, disability benefits, death benefits and refunds.

Dividing State and Public Pensions By Way of a QILDRO.

In most marriages today, retirement assets tend to be the parties' largest asset and must be considered when dividing the assets between the parties. Public pension funds are no different than any other retirement asset, with the exception that they are controlled by the Illinois Pension Code 40 ILCS 5/ et al., and specific documents must be prepared in order to divide the state pension funds. These forms are known as QILDROs or Qualified Illinois Domestic Relations Orders. Each public pension fund has its own QILDRO form, but the information contained therein must include:
- The name and address of the Member and Alternate Payee;
- The method of payment (dollar amount, percentage of marital portion or percentage of the gross amount) of the member's benefits to the Alternate Payee;
- When the benefits to the Alternate Payee shall commence;
- Termination of the Alternate Payee's benefits;
- If the Alternate Payee's benefits are subject to post-retirement increases;
- The method of payment (dollar amount, percentage of marital portion or percentage of the gross amount) of any refund (or partial refund) upon termination or any lump-sum retirement benefit that may become payable to the member;
- The method of payment (dollar amount, percentage of marital portion or percentage of the gross amount) of any death benefits that become payable to the member's death benefit beneficiaries or estate; and

- Determination of marital portion and if same shall include permissive service, upgrades and benefit formula enhancements.

After the QILDRO is entered by the Court and processed to the Plan, the QILDRO, if determined to be found "qualified", will be placed in the member's record and will remain dormant until the member begins receiving retirement benefits, a refund or lump sum death benefit subject to when the QILDRO becomes payable. Generally, when the member applies for retirement benefits under the plan rules, the plan will provide notice to the alternate payee of the member's intent to retire. It is also important to note that it is the alternate payee's responsibility to ensure that the plan has up to date contact information for the alternate payee, so that any notices issued by the plan relative to the benefits are received by the alternate payee.

Determining Marital Portion

As stated previously, determining the marital portion of a Defined Benefit Plan, including public pension plans, is generally calculated utilizing the HUNT formula. The HUNT formula determines the marital portion using a fraction the numerator of which represents the number of pension credits accrued by the participant during the period of the marriage; and the denominator represents the number of total pension credits accrued by the participant as of the earliest of the participant's retirement or the alternate payee's benefit commencement dates. *In re Marriage of Hunt*, at 664. The Hunt formula is recognized to be the fairest method for calculating the marital portion of the benefits accumulated in the plan.

Consent to Issuance of QILDRO

A QILDRO will only be valid if the member signs a Consent to Issuance of QILDRO in writing. Each plan has their own specific form which is required when submitting a QILDRO. The Consent form must be signed by the member and the member only. The Consent is required for any employee who is a member of any Illinois public retirement system prior to July 1, 1999. If a member commenced their participation in the plan after July 1, 1999, the Consent is necessarily required and the member accepts the principles of the QILDRO law as a condition of the employment. However, it is good practice to ensure that the Consent is executed by the member and submitted to the plan at the time the QILDRO is processed to the plan, as it is not always known when the member commenced their participation in the plan.

QILDRO Calculation Order

A QILDRO Calculation Court Order is a separate court order issued by the Illinois Court that instructs the plan how much to pay the alternate payee. It is only necessary if the QILDRO indicates that the alternate payee is to receive a percentage of the benefit. The Calculation Order must be completed and entered by the Court, in order for the plan to establish payments to the alternate payee. Generally, a QILDRO is issued at the time of the divorce, and the parties would return to the court to obtain the Calculation Order at the time of the member's retirement, when the amount of the retirement benefit becomes known. In that the HUNT (*In re Marriage of Hunt*, 78 Ill. App. 3d 653 (1st Dist. 1979)) formula considers the member's entire length of service in the plan, the amount of the member's benefit is not known until a date of retirement is established.

Federal Retirement Plans in Divorce

Civil Service Retirement System ("CSRS"), or the Federal Employees Retirement System ("FERS").

Most federal government employees accrue retirement benefits under the Civil Service Retirement System ("CSRS"), or the Federal Employees Retirement System ("FERS"), 10 U.S. Code § 12732 et al., which are similar to Defined Benefit Plans. These Plans do not accept QDROs in that these Plans are not governed by ERISA. These plans have their own set of statutes and regulations establishing their existence and regulating their operation. In most instances, a division order is entered by the Court and sent to the Office of Personnel Management (OPM) to administer the Order; however, in that these plans have their own unique mechanisms and features for the division of the underlying retirement benefits, it is best to seek the advice of an attorney to ensure that the rules and requirements of dividing such federal retirement benefits.

Thrift Savings Plan & Divorce Issues.

A Thrift Savings Plan (TSP) 5 U.S. Code § 84 et al., is a retirement savings and investment plan for Federal employees and members of the uniformed services. It offers the same types of savings and tax benefits that many private corporations offer their employees under 401(k) plans. The TSP, 5 U.S. Code § 84 et al., is a defined contribution plan, meaning that the retirement income you receive from your TSP account will depend on how much you (and your agency, if you are eligible to receive agency contributions) put into your account during your working years and the earnings accumulated over that time.

In that the TSP, 5 U.S. Code § 84 et al., is provided by the Federal Government, it is not subject to ERISA, Employee Retirement Income Security Act of 1974, and therefore, a QDRO is not required. In order to divide the TSP Account, a retirement benefits court order will be required. The Court Order will require a specified dollar amount or percentage of the account, as of a specific date, to be awarded to the alternate payee. Said Court Order must be processed by the Office of Personnel Management.

Military Retired Pay

The United States Armed Forces, 10 U.S. Code § 12732 et al., offer retirement benefits to the members of their various branches. The Defense Finance and Accounting Service (DFAS) administers the military retirement system for all branches. DFAS is primarily a payroll office that establishes and maintains military retired pay, annuity accounts and issues monthly payments to military retirees and their eligible survivors. In that military retired pay is a complicated and unique area of the law, it is best to seek the advice of an attorney when dividing any military retired pay. DFAS maintains a website that contains useful information and guides.

Railroad Retirement Plans

As a railroad employee, certain retirement and disability benefits may be available to its employees and spouses and former spouses and dependents. Railroad Retirement, 45 USC 231 et al., provides retirement benefits and comprehensive survivor benefits. Railroad Retirement is administered by the Railroad Retirement Board (RRB), an independent agency in the executive branch of the Federal Government and RRB also has administrative responsibilities under the Social Security Act for certain benefit payments and railroad workers' Medicare coverage.

Railroad retirement, 45 USC 231 et al., is a highly complex and unique retirement plan and has numerous levels of benefits provided to its members. The eligibility criteria are strict, and the formulas for calculating benefits are exacting, especially if you have also worked for a non-railroad employer and accrued Social Security benefits. When attempting to divide such benefits, it is best to seek the advice of an attorney to ensure that all benefits are calculated properly and handled to the exact specifications of the Railroad Retirement Board.

Conclusion

As set forth above retirement assets are critical assets in divorces. The division is quite complicated and it is important that you get your assets divided formally. Your divorce decree is not enough in that each plan has specific rules governing when a retirement asset is divided. Make sure you follow through to ensure that the assets awarded in your Judgment for Dissolution of Marriage will truly be yours when the time comes.

WHOSE BUSINESS IS THIS?

In cases where there is a business involved that was owned during the marriage, the finances and assets of the business will also need to be considered when dividing the marital estate. Sometimes, when attempting to account for business funds and assets, it is discovered that there have been business assets that may have been dissipated by one party. In relation to a business, said dissipation could include, but is certainly not limited to:

- Creating a new business and transferring assets and claiming that the previous business has no value;
- Paying personal expenses from the business that were previously paid using marital funds;
- Disposing of assets held in the name of the business;
- Disposing of a party's interest in a business.

As stated above, the Court will make the final determination as to whether or not the actions of a party constitute dissipation and whether or not the other party is entitled to reimbursement related to the same. If the Court determines that business funds or assets have been dissipated by one spouse, they may award a higher percent of the business and/or marital estate to the other spouse in an attempt to make them whole again.

Setting aside the issue of dissipation, in cases involving a marital business, it is important to have the business valued, in order to accurately consider the value of the same when dividing the marital estate. In some cases, this is fairly simple, while in other cases it can be pretty daunting. However, even where the situation is amicable and agreed upon, it is important to recognize the different kinds of businesses and what implications the same may have during the process of divorce.

In some cases, couples have an interest in a family business, a business of one or both spouses, or an entity set up for investment purposes (such as an entity holding real estate). No matter how the marital interest may be held, certain aspects of the business itself will need to be reviewed, depending on the specific type of business. Here are several types of businesses that are commonly divided in divorces:

C Corporations

C corps are what most people think of as a standard corporation. They are separate taxable entities. 26 U.S.C.S. § 11(a) (LexisNexis current through P.L. 116-145). They file a corporate tax return. In addition, corporate income may be distributed to business owners as dividends, which is then considered personal income - which would be taxable as income and includable as income for the purposes of determining support obligations.

S Corporations

S corps are pass-through, and not separate tax entities. 26 U.S.C.S. § 1366 (LexisNexis through P.L. 116-145). They file a federal tax return for informational purposes, but no income tax is actually paid at the corporate level. The profits/losses of the business are instead "passed-through" the business and reported on the owner's' personal tax returns. 26 U.S.C.S. § 1366(a)(1) (LexisNexis through P.L. 116-145). Any tax due is paid at the individual level by the owners.

Limited Liability Corporations

A limited liability company (LLC) is a business structure that protects the owners, generally called members, from personal liability for the company's debts and liabilities. 805 Ill. Comp. Stat. Ann. 180/10-10 (LexisNexis through P.A. 101-631). This structure allows the business owner to combine the characteristics of a corporation, with the characteristics of a partnership or sole proprietorship. The regulations for LLCs vary from state to state. Most states do not have restrictions on ownership of an LLC, which means that its members aren't limited to individuals, but can also include corporations, foreigners, foreign entities, or even other LLCs. This structure allows more flexibility and protection and is much easier to set up than a corporation. However, there are some entities that are unable to form LLCs, such as banks and insurance companies.

There are several types of LLCs:

- Domestic LLC: Conducts business in the state in which it was formed and incorporated;
- Foreign LLC: When an existing LLC opens an office or has any physical presence in another state, it must register in that state as a foreign LLC;
- Professional LLC: When an LLC is formed to perform a professional service (i.e., medical or legal practice), certain members must have the necessary state licenses and professional qualifications and in this type of LLC, the protection from personal liability does not extend to professional malpractice claims (805 Ill. Comp. Stat. Ann. 185/13 (LexisNexis through P.A. 101-631));

- Series LLC: A unique type of LLC, that has what's referred to as a "parent" LLC, which provides limited liability protection to a series of "child" LLCs, and the "child" LLCs are protected from the liabilities of the other businesses under the Series LLC;

In order to incorporate an LLC, the articles of organization for the business must be filed with the state. 805 Comp. Stat. Ann. 180/5-1 (LexisNexis through P.A. 101-631). LLCs do not pay taxes directly, as their profits and losses are passed through to members, who then claim same on their tax returns, also known as pass-through taxation. However, if it is more beneficial, LLCs can elect to be taxes as a C-Corporation or S-Corporation. Additionally, there are state-level taxes that vary from state to state, that may apply to the LLC. This structure does not require the company to assign formal officer roles, unlike C-Corporations and S-Corporations.

The way the members of the LLC are paid depends on the method of taxation that the LLC uses, how many members exist and any formal agreements entered into by the members with regards to profit sharing and equity. The methods used to pay members include distributions that pass through the member's individual tax return or paying members a reasonable salary and a distribution as an S-Corp.

Partnerships

A business structured as a partnership is formed by an agreement between two or more individuals that share in the profits or losses. 805 Ill. Comp. Stat. Ann. 201/101 (LexisNexis through P.A. 101-631). Although there is no federal statute defining partnerships, the Internal Revenue Code includes detailed rules on their federal tax treatment. 26 U.S.C.S. § 701 (LexisNexis through P.L. 116-145). Partnerships do not pay income tax, as the tax responsibility passes through to the partners and they are not considered employees for tax purposes. *Id.*

There are three main types of partnerships:

- General Partnership: All partners share legal and financial liability equally, as well as the profits, and the partners are personally responsible for the debts of the partnership; Usually the details regarding the profit sharing are set out in the partnership agreement;

- Limited Liability Partnership: An arrangement that limits partners' personal liability so that the assets of the other partners are not at risk as a result of the actions of another partner;

- Limited Partnership: This structure is almost a combination of general and limited liability partnerships and require at least one general partner whom has full liability for the company's debts; There is at least one "silent" partner that generally does not participate in day-to-day operations and whose liability is limited to the amount they invested in the partnership;

Partnerships generally are formed under a Partnership Agreement, which should address the purpose of the business, as well as the authority and duties that each partner is responsible for. 805 Ill. Comp. Stat. Ann. 206/103 (LexisNexis through P.A. 101-631). These agreements also should contain some sort of language that addresses how disputes will be resolved between partners and how to handle a buyout of a partner. *Id.*

Marital vs. Non-Marital Business Interests

Whether the corporation is a C or S Corp, both the individual and corporate tax returns will be vital in a divorce proceeding. Any corporation, whether marital or non-marital, will have to be valued in order for the parties to make an informed decision about the division of either that asset, or their other assets. Under Illinois law, the size of a spouse's non-marital estate can inform the court's decision on things such as the property settlement, maintenance obligation, or child support obligation. So, even if a spouse does not have an interest in the corporation, it will still impact divorce proceedings.

Also, the status of the corporation as marital or non-marital property should be carefully evaluated. In a long-term marriage, it is common that money may have gone in or out of the corporation from home equity or other marital property. The co-mingling of funds in this way may bolster a claim that a small business is actually marital property. When a corporation is marital property, the valuation is even more crucial, because the non-participant spouse will generally be bought out of the business.

Some spouses may want to remain business partners even after going through a divorce. However, it is important to fairly evaluate the long-term implications of retaining an interest in a formerly marital corporation. Inevitably, one former spouse will have more control over the day-to-day operations of the business and may be able to make decisions that create a liability for the other former spouse. In addition, relationships that may be amicable at one point may be difficult in the future. These and other risks should be carefully considered before former spouses remain in business partnership together.

Additionally, individuals may receive income from a business in the form of a salary or in terms of dividends. However, in a divorce, a party may have the motivation to reduce their income in the hopes of a court establishing a lower amount for maintenance or child support. This can be done by leaving money in the business in the form of retained earnings. However, in Illinois, retained earnings may be marital property even if the corporation itself is a spouse's non-marital property, when the spouse is in control of the decision whether or not to leave the money in the business.

In addition, a spouse may try to do other things such as payout dividends or salaries to third parties fraudulently. A recent case involved a spouse who hired his new live-in girlfriend at an artificially inflated salary. He was attempting to circumvent support obligations by reducing his income, while maintaining his standard of living with the income being paid to his girlfriend. When a spouse intentionally and wrongfully reduces his income, the total income into the business may be imputed to the individual for the purposes of calculating support obligations. These issues are only some of the many challenges presented when a divorce involves a corporation, no matter the size or scale.

In most cases involving a marital business, a value will need to be assigned to the business, whether the value is decided by agreement of the parties or by an outside business evaluator. Once the value of the business has been accurately determined, the parties will have a more realistic idea of what they may be entitled to in the division of their assets. In all cases, this value and the division thereof is at the discretion of the Court, which may not be a 50/50 split of the value. Furthermore, parties may find that litigation only leads to issues that could endanger their business. For that reason, it is highly recommended that the parties attempt to reach an agreement regarding the same that both parties can live with. Obviously, the options change on a case by case basis; however, a few examples of options the parties could agree to, or the Court could Order in the absence of an agreement, may include:

- The spouse who intends to keep the business can "buy-out" the other spouse, which may result in depleting liquid assets, but could allow them to retain the business.
- The parties could remain co-owners of the marital business, but this is not often a recommended solution as stated above, given that it could create a contentious post-decree situation;
- The parties could sell the business and its assets and split the proceeds, which obviously dissolves the business, but could provide both parties with more liquid assets.

Overall, when dividing the marital estate, it is important to keep in mind all of the aspects of your financials and the recent history of what was spent, sold, transferred or otherwise disposed of. When contemplating divorce, remember to track expenses, inventory property and begin gathering documents relative to the assets contained in your estate, including business assets. The more information and documentation you can obtain, the easier it will be to determine if there needs to be further investigation of any possible dissipation on behalf of your spouse.

Business Valuations and Forensic Accounting

In most divorces involving a business that operated during the marriage, the business will need to be valued in order to determine the portion of equity each party is entitled to. In these cases, there is generally a business valuation done, which even under normal circumstances can be complex. There are several methods that can be used to determine the economic worth of a business, but each method generally involves a full assessment of every piece of the company, such as equipment, inventory, property, liquid assets, etc. Several other factors that can come into play include the management structure, projected earning, retained earnings, share price, revenue, etc.

However, often times it is also necessary to obtain a forensic accounting, as the business valuation is only as accurate as the records on which it is based, which will not be accurate if the information in the records is not accurate. Forensic accounting is similar to an audit, and is used in divorce cases to determine income of one or both spouses, and to evaluate the lifestyle or analyze the marital spending during the marriage, and sometimes during the divorce litigation. Due to the freedom that comes with owning a business, it is easy for a party to a divorce to intermingle business and personal funds, without revealing that business funds are being spent on personal expenses, which is considered income.

As part of the business valuation and/or forensic accounting, there must be attention placed on the income from the business versus the value of the business, to ensure there is no "double-dipping." The concept of double-dipping refers to the double counting of marital assets, once in the division of assets and then again in any support that is awarded. *In re Marriage of Eberhardt*, 387 Ill. App. 3d 226, 232 (Ill. App. Ct. 1st Dist. 2008). This error occurs when a stream of income is used to determine the value of the business to be divided and then that same stream of income is used to determine the amount of support to be paid on said income. *In re Marriage of Zells*, 143 Ill. 2d 251, 256 (1991). This is one of the main reasons that it could be absolutely necessary to obtain a business valuation or forensic accounting, or sometimes both, in divorces where a business is subject to division between the spouses.

Retained Earnings and Triple AAA Accounts

One question that often gets raised is what about the retained earnings of a business which operates as a S Corporation. These can also be known as AAAs or Accumulated Adjustment Accounts and can generally be found on the last page of Form 1120S. The AAA measures the amount of previously taxed but undistributed earnings of a corporation. The account is adjusted each year to reflect business activity such as current income and distributions.

In general, retained earnings in a marital business will be part of the valuation of the business and subject to division. *In re Marriage of Schmitt*, 391 Ill. App. 3d 1010, 1020 (Ill. App. Ct. 2d Dist. 2009). Retained earnings are corporate net income which would be available for distribution as dividends, for payment of wages, or the like, but instead remain in the possession and control of the business for other corporate purposes, like reinvestment into the business. Another matter to determine is whether the retained earnings are controlled by a party to a divorce. That is to say, are the earnings left in the business because of the necessity of having funds to operate or does a primary majority owner simply leave the funds in the business to not increase his or her income.

In the case of a non-marital business, the retained earnings may have accumulated during the marriage and might be attributable to the efforts of the owning spouse. In 2016, Illinois revised the statute regarding division to clarify the law. Specifically, in 750 ILCS 5/503(c)(2)(B), it states, "when a spouse contributes personal effort to non-marital property, it shall receive reimbursement for the efforts if the efforts are significant and result in substantial appreciate to the non-marital property except that if the marital estate reasonably has been compensated for his or her efforts, it shall not be deemed a contribution to the marital estate and there shall be no reimbursement to the marital estate. 750 Ill. Comp. Stat. Ann. 5/503(c)(2)(B) (LexisNexis through P.A. 101-631). The court may provide reimbursement out of the marital property to be divided or by imposing a lien against the non-marital property which received the contribution." *Id.*

In this case the argument is essentially that a spouse's personal efforts into the non-marital business increased the value of the business and therefore the marriage should be entitled to compensation for those efforts. The statute has attempted to correct that argument by stating that so long as the individual was compensated for efforts, the retained earnings would not become marital property.

The issues relating to retained earnings can be very fact specific and might vary industry to industry. Therefore, it is something that should be addressed early in the case to determine if the retained earnings are something that might become a bigger issue. Retained earnings are a complex issue that you must address with your attorney.

Conclusion

The ownership of a business interest during a divorce adds an entirely new set of circumstances to navigate. You need to work closely with your attorney to understand navigating these issues. Careful attention to the nature and scope of authority related to the ownership interest can have a real impact on your case.

YOU SPENT WHAT? FOLLOW THE MONEY

Although Illinois is a "no-fault divorce" state, meaning the Court will not consider either party's arguments regarding their spouse's alleged misconduct or indiscretions that led to the divorce, the Court may consider a party's dissipation of marital assets when determining an equitable division of the marital estate. 750 Ill. Comp. Stat. Ann. 5/503(d)(2) (LexisNexis through P.A. 101-631). In other words, when deciding the issues of maintenance and the division of the remaining marital assets, the Court will take into account any marital property or funds that one spouse spent, transferred, converted or otherwise disposed of for non-marital purposes. *Id.* Some of the most common forms of dissipation include, but are certainly not limited to, the following examples:

- Spending marital funds on extramarital relationships and/or other non-marital purposes;
- Extraordinary cash withdrawals that cannot be accounted for;
- Excessive gambling or drinking;
- Cashing out investments;
- Transferring assets or property to a family member or third party;
- Purposely diminishing value in a marital business or marital property;
- Sale or destruction of marital property;
- Expensive vacations and hobbies;
- Large "gifts" to friends or family
- Transactions that are for undetermined purposes and began occurring after the breakdown of the marriage and/or during the proceedings.

When contemplating filing for divorce, it is crucial to determine the assets that currently exist in the marital estate in order to determine what the division of those assets will actually look like for you and your spouse, and in some cases, whether or not any marital property has been dissipated by your spouse. If possible, it can be beneficial to gather the relevant documents, such as bank statements, tax returns, property titles and deeds, and the like, prior to consulting with attorneys so they can offer the most accurate advice possible. However, there are scenarios in which a party may not have access to the documents related to their assets, or in some situations, may not have any idea what assets even exist. Sometimes this is due to the fact that one party is secretive or controlling when it comes to the parties' finances, or it could simply be that one party has handled all of the finances throughout the marriage and the spouse just wasn't involved in managing any of the bills or financials.

Obviously in any scenario where a party feels as though they have no knowledge of their financial circumstances, it can create feelings of anxiety and uneasiness when considering divorce, as there are a lot of unknowns regarding what will happen after they file; however, it is important to remember that regardless of which party has historically managed or controlled the marital funds and assets, it does not mean that party will have the upper hand or get all of the assets, nor does it mean it is impossible to claim dissipation because the assets are currently unknown. As part of the divorce process, all of the marital assets and the documents related thereto will be produced by the party in possession of the same, pursuant to discovery requests that are issued by the other party, which are discussed in detail in another chapter. However, as many of you are probably thinking, what if the other party refuses to produce the documents? There are several remedies available in the event that a party refuses to produce relevant discovery during a divorce. The other party can file a Motion to Compel and request that the Court intervene to require a party to produce the requested documents or information, and if they continue to refuse the Court can bar certain evidence or issue certain sanctions. Alternatively, or in addition, the documents can be subpoenaed directly from the entity or person that possesses the same (i.e., banks, credit card companies, casinos, tax preparers, closing companies, airlines, etc.). Even further, either party can issue a Notice of Deposition to any party of the divorce, as well as to third parties, which would require the Deponent to sit down and answer questions on the record, in addition to producing documents, if requested.

Dissipation

The Illinois statute that addresses the division of the marital estate, as well as dissipation, specifically 750 ILCS 5/503(d), states in pertinent part as follows:

> *(d) In a proceeding for dissolution of marriage or declaration of invalidity of marriage, or in a proceeding for disposition of property following dissolution of marriage by a court that lacked personal jurisdiction over the absent spouse or lacked jurisdiction to dispose of the property, the court shall assign each spouse's non-marital property to that spouse. It also shall divide the marital property without regard to marital misconduct in just proportions considering all relevant factors, including:*
>
> *…*

> *(2) the dissipation by each party of the marital property, provided that a party's claim of dissipation is subject to the following conditions:*
> *(i) a notice of intent to claim dissipation shall be given no later than 60 days before trial or 30 days after discovery closes, whichever is later;*
> *(ii) the notice of intent to claim dissipation shall contain, at a minimum, a date or period of time during which the marriage began undergoing an irretrievable breakdown, an identification of the property dissipated, and a date or period of time during which the dissipation occurred;*
> *(iii) a certificate or service of the notice of intent to claim dissipation shall be filed with the clerk of the court and be served pursuant to applicable rules;*
> *(iv) no dissipation shall be deemed to have occurred prior to 3 years after the party claiming dissipation knew or should have known of the dissipation, but in no event prior to 5 years before the filing of the petition for dissolution of marriage;*

750 Ill. Comp. Stat. Ann. 5/503(d) (LexisNexis through P.A. 101-631).

Pursuant to the language included in the statute as set forth above, the Court must consider numerous factors when determining whether one spouse has dissipated a portion of the marital estate. In Illinois, the most commonly used definition for dissipation emanates from the Supreme Court's decision *In re Marriage of O'Neill*, where the term "dissipation" is defined as the "use of marital property for the sole benefit of one of the spouses for a purpose unrelated to the marriage at a time the marriage is undergoing an irretrievable breakdown." *In re Marriage of O'Neill*, 138 Ill. 2d 487, 497 (1990). In the event that the Court rules that one spouse has dissipated assets belonging to the marital estate, the value and/or amount of said assets essentially gets "put back into the pot" and the other spouse is entitled to an equitable portion of the value of the same, at the Court's discretion.

Proving Dissipation

In order to prove dissipation, a spouse must show that marital funds and/or assets were spent and/or disposed of for non-marital purposes, or unknown purposes, during a time when the marriage was undergoing an irretrievable breakdown. 750 Ill. Comp. Stat. Ann. 5/503(d)(2)(ii) (LexisNexis through P.A. 101-631). Once a party makes a "prima facie" showing that the other party has dissipated marital assets, the burden shifts to the other spouse to prove that the assets were not dissipated. The spouse charged with dissipation must establish by clear and specific evidence how the marital funds were expended. *In re Marriage of Partyka*, 158 Ill. App. 3d 545, 549 (Ill. App. Ct. 1st Dist. 1987); *In re Marriage of Hubbs*, 363 Ill. App. 3d 696, 700 (Ill. App. Ct. 5th Dist. 2006). Basic statements that funds were spent on marital or living expenses will not suffice to defeat a dissipation claim. Therefore, it is very important to make sure you are properly tracking your finances and documenting expenditures while contemplating or going through the process of divorce.

Once a dissipation claim has been established, the Court may consider this when dividing the remaining marital estate and debts. 750 Ill. Comp. Stat. Ann. 5/503(d)(2) (LexisNexis through P.A. 101-631). The Court has discretion to reimburse the other party for said dissipation or to offset other debts and/or assets to make the other spouse whole again.

Case Law Regarding Dissipation

To explain further, here are some cases in which the Court found that one party's actions related to the marital estate did in fact constitute dissipation:

- Money transferred to one party's mother. *In re Marriage of Vehlein*, 265 Ill. App. 3d 1080, 1089 (Ill. App. Ct. 1st Dist. 1994);
- Intentional failure to make mortgage payments on marital residence. *In re Marriage of Siegel*, 123 Ill. App. 3d 710, 719 (Ill. App. Ct. 1st Dist. 1984); *In re Marriage of Cook*, 117 Ill. App. 3d 844, 854 (Ill. App. Ct. 1st Dist. 1983); *In re Marriage of Aslaksen*, 148 Ill. App. 3d 784, 789 (Ill. App. Ct. 2nd Dist. 1986);
- Intentionally or carelessly causing a family business to be less profitable. *In re Marriage of Thomas*, 239 Ill. App. 3d 992, 995 (Ill. App. Ct. 3rd Dist. 1993);
- Intentional destruction of photographs. *In re Marriage of Ferkel*, 260 Ill. App. 3d 33, 39-40 (Ill. App. Ct. 5th Dist. 1994);
- Transfer of large sums of money to children shortly before separation and inconsistent with prior transfers. *In re Marriage of Lee*, 246 Ill. App. 3d 628, 635 (Ill. App. Ct. 4th Dist. 1993);
- Purchase of truck for son without wife's consent. *In re Marriage of Frey*, 258 Ill. App. 3d 442, 448-49 (Ill. App. Ct. 5th Dist. 1994);
- Withdrawal of funds from a marital account used to pay child support to an ex-wife. *In re Marriage of Klingberg*, 68 Ill. App. 3d 513, 517-18 (Ill. App. Ct. 1st Dist. 1979);
- Taking of European vacation with a minor child against the wishes of another spouse when marriage was breaking down. *In re Marriage of Ryman*, 172 Ill. App. 3d 599, 608 (Ill. App. Ct. 2nd Dist. 1988);
- Expenditures of marital funds by husband on vacations taken with another woman. *In re Marriage of Osborn*, 206 Ill. App. 3d 588, 601 (Ill. App. Ct. 5th Dist. 1990);
- Expenditures for gambling. *In re Marriage of Hagshenas*, 234 Ill. App. 3d 178, 196 (Ill. App. Ct. 2nd Dist. 1992);

- A failure to pay income tax on time and substantial penalties in that regard. *In re Marriage of Charles*, 284 Ill. App. 3d 339, 346 (Ill. App. Ct. 4th Dist. 1996);
- Contribution made to a church after the marital breakdown not consistent with prior contributions. *In re Marriage of Cerven*, 317 Ill. App. 3d 895, 901-02 (Ill. App. Ct. 2nd Dist. 2000);
- Cost of defending false abuse allegations in a family law court proceeding. *In re Marriage of Patel*, 2013 IL App (1st) 112571, 74;
- The use of an insurance settlement to purchase a new truck and tools. *In re Marriage of Uehlein*, 265 Ill. App. 3d 1080, 1089 (Ill. App. Ct. 1st Dist. 1994);
- Money transferred to a girlfriend to pay living expenses of the girlfriend and her family. *In re Marriage of Vehlein*, 265 Ill. App. 3d 1080, 1088-89 (Ill. App. Ct. 1st Dist. 1994);
- Money given to the girlfriend, including down payment and mortgage payments on the girlfriend's house, and support for the child he had with the girlfriend. *In re Marriage of Charles*, 284 Ill. App. 3d 339, 343-44 (Ill. App. Ct. 4th Dist. 1996);
- Payment for expensive trips, jewelry, rings, music equipment for a girlfriend and for payment of girlfriend's debts. *In re Marriage of Dunseth*, 260 Ill. App. 3d 816, 831 (Ill. App. Ct. 4th Dist. 1994); *In re Marriage of Meadow*, 256 Ill. App. 3d 115, 118 (Ill. App. Ct. 1st Dist. 1993); *In re Marriage of Frey*, 258 Ill. App. 3d 442, 448-49 (Ill. App. Ct. 5th Dist. 1994);
- Purchase of a car for a girlfriend along with excessive amounts of checks written for cash and unexplained use of a tax refund. *In re Marriage of Awan*, 388 Ill. App. 3d 204, 216-17 (Ill. App. Ct. 3rd Dist. 2009);
- Creation of a trust for the education of the children without wife's knowledge when marriage began to break down. *Head v. Head*, 168 Ill. App. 3d 697, 702-03 (Ill. App. Ct. 1st Dist. 1988);
- The payment of income tax on non-marital income. *In re Marriage of Toole*, 273 Ill. App. 3d 607, 618 (Ill. App. Ct. 5th Dist. 1995).

On the other hand, here are some cases in which the Court found that a spouse's actions did NOT constitute dissipation:

- Spending of marital funds during the period of separation for necessary, appropriate and legitimate living expenses. *In re Marriage of Murphy*, 259 Ill. App. 3d 336, 340-41 (Ill. App. Ct. 4th Dist. 1994); *In re Marriage of Hagshemas*, 234 Ill. App. 3d 178, 198 (Ill. App. Ct. 3rd Dist. 1992); *In re Marriage of Severson* 228 Ill. App. 3d 820, 827 (Ill. App. Ct. 1st Dist. 1992);
- A lawyer paying his paralegal $225.00 per week for her services and expenses for a social club originating many years prior to the dissolution. *In re Marriage of Calisoff*, 176 Ill. App. 3d 721, 727 (Ill. App. Ct. 1st Dist. 1988);
- Expenditures for the husband's mother similar to what he spent before the marriage breakdown with no objection by wife. *In re Marriage of Ard*, 142 Ill. App. 3d 320, 331 (Ill. App. Ct. 5th Dist. 1986);

- Expenditure of funds used to pay a tax against a jointly owned business. *In re Marriage of Randall,* 157 Ill. App. 3d 892, 897 (Ill. App. Ct. 1st Dist. 1987);
- Expenses for vacation trips with parties' children similar to those taken before the marital breakdown. *In re Marriage of David*, 215 Ill. App. 3d 763, 777-78 (Ill. App. Ct. 1st. Dist. 1991);
- A continuation of spending patterns enjoyed prior to the breakdown of the marriage. *In re Marriage of Aud*, 142 Ill. App. 3d 320, 331-32 (Ill. App. Ct. 5th Dist. 1986); *In re Marriage of Adams*, 183 Ill. App. 3d 296, 303 (Ill. App. Ct. 4th Dist. 1989);
- Most recent cases have held that ordinary living expenses after the breakdown of the marriage are not dissipation. *In re Marriage of Seversen*, 228 Ill .App. 3d 820, 827 (Ill. App. Ct. 1st Dist. 1992); *In re Marriage of Hagshenas*, 234 Ill. App. 3d 178, 198 (Ill. App. Ct. 2nd Dist. 1992); *In re Marriage of Phillips*, 229 Ill. App. 3d 809, 25-26 (Ill. App. Ct. 2nd Dist. 1992); *In re Marriage of Toole*, 273 Ill. App. 3d 607, 615-16 (Ill. App. Ct. 2nd Dist. 1995);
- Payment for a reasonable apartment for a required business assignment for a period of time in another state, even though his girlfriend stayed in the apartment with him. *In re Marriage of Toole*, 273 Ill. App. 3d 607, 616 (Ill. App. Ct. 2nd Dist. 1995);
- Purchase of a mobile home by husband with the agreement of his wife. *In re Marriage of Frey*, 258 Ill. App. 3d 442, 448 (Ill. App. Ct. 5th Dist. 1994);
- Withdrawal by wife of funds from a joint account and her IRA to pay reasonable expenses for her and her daughter after separation, especially since the wife received no child support for the first 7 months after separation. *In re Marriage of Schmidt*, 242 Ill. App. 3d 961, 972 (Ill. App. Ct. 4th Dist. 1993);
- Payment of family expenses from a joint checking account similar to what the other party expended from a similar account. *In re Marriage of Schinelli*, 406 Ill. App. 3d 991, 1000 (Ill. App. Ct. 2nd Dist. 2011);
- Vacations by husband similar to those taken by the parties prior to the breakdown of the marriage. *In re Marriage of Beibaret*, 2012 IL App (4th) 110749, ¶57;
- Losses incurred by wife on ESOP with her company when the setting up of the plan was in good faith. *In re Marriage of Isaacs*, 260 Ill. App. 3d 423, 430 (Ill. App. Ct. 1st Dist. 1994);
- Losses incurred on rehabbing house similar to transactions prior to the marriage breakdown. *In re Marriage of Phillips*, 229 Ill. App. 3d 809, 825-26 (Ill. App. Ct. 2nd Dist. 1992);
- Failure to make mortgage payments leading to foreclosure after wife had lost her job. *In re Marriage of Parker*, 252 Ill. App. 3d 1015, 1019 (Ill. App. Ct. 1st Dist. 1993);
- Expenses not objected to while the parties were living together. *In re Marriage of Davis*, 215 Ill. App. 3d 763, 777 (Ill. App. Ct. 1st Dist. 1991); *In re Marriage of Adams*, 183 Ill. App. 3d 296, 303 (Ill. App. Ct. 4th Dist. 1989); *In re Marriage of Ard*, 142 Ill. App. 3d 320, 331 (Ill. App. Ct. 5th Dist. 1986).

Overall, dissipation can result in returning the assets to the marital pie before it is divided. If dissipation is proven, the spouse who engaged in dissipation gets the value assigned to their share of the assets even though the asset no longer exists. In general, dissipation can be highly contested and very fact specific. You have to get very granular to prove to the court the money is missing and not spent on a legitimate family expense. However, the remedy does exist and should be pursued if necessary, to divide the estate in a fair manner.

MAKE SURE YOU'RE COVERED

Figuring out health insurance coverage for you and your children following a divorce is absolutely critical. Especially when your spouse has been the one providing health insurance for the family during the marriage. While it doesn't get as much attention as some of the other high-profile hot button issues in a divorce, the impending loss of insurance coverage, (and the looming prospect of getting new coverage) can quietly become one of the most unsettling things a spouse may have to face in the divorce process.

New coverage will probably mean some degree of disruption unless existing healthcare coverage is part of a divorce settlement. However, when a divorcing spouse is responsible to secure individual or family coverage post-divorce, there are several options available to consider.

Here are 6 of the more common options:

- COBRA
- Illinois Continuation Coverage
- Obamacare, Affordable Care Act, Marketplace
- New Group Coverage
- Temporary Plan
- Concierge services with a high deductible

COBRA

Here are several things you should know about the Consolidated Omnibus Budget Reconciliation Act (COBRA).

In all cases following a divorce, an employer will no longer cover a spouse under an employee's healthcare policy. Federal law dictates that health insurance coverage ends as soon as you are divorced. However, a spouse does have rights under COBRA to continue coverage. A spouse will have 60 days to notify the employee's health plan administrator that they would like to continue coverage. 29 U.S.C.S. § 1166(a)(1) (LexisNexis through P.L. 116-145). They will be able to do so, as long as they pay the healthcare plan premium.

Most insurance plans allow an ex-spouse to get health insurance through COBRA for up to 36 months following a divorce. 29 U.S.C.S. § 1162(2)(A)(iv) (LexisNexis through P.L. 116-145). To qualify, a spouse's company must employ at least 20 people, and insurance must already be offered as a benefit through the employer. 29 U.S.C.S. § 1161(b) (LexisNexis through P.L. 116-145). The primary drawback of COBRA insurance is that the premiums can be expensive, and it may be wise to look elsewhere for coverage. You will want to compare costs, because you may find that other options are much more affordable than COBRA coverage. The other limitation with COBRA is that coverage ends in 36 months. You will need to have new coverage in place within three years if you go with a COBRA option.

Illinois Spousal Continuation Coverage

Illinois law provides for Spousal Continuation coverage for an employee's spouse and dependent children who lose group health insurance coverage due to death or retirement of the employee or divorce from the employee. This coverage is provided to employees whose employers offer fully insured group health plans, and HMO coverage, regardless of group size.

Spousal continuation coverage is triggered when one of the following qualifying events occurs: divorce from the employee, death of the employee or retirement of the employee as follows: The divorced or widowed spouse (any age) and dependent children of the employee who were covered under the group plan on the day before the qualifying event; or specifically in the event of a divorce, the spouse of an employee (or retired employee still receiving insurance benefits), who is age 55 or older, who was covered under the group plan on the day before the qualifying event. 215 Ill. Comp. Stat. Ann. 5/367.2(A) (LexisNexis through P.A. 101-631).

The eligible spouse must notify the employer and insurance company in writing of the dissolution of marriage or the death or retirement of the employee within 30 days of the qualifying event. 215 Ill. Comp. Stat. Ann. 5/367.2(B) (LexisNexis through P.A. 101-631). The employer must notify the insurance company within 15 days after receiving your request for spousal continuation. *Id.* The insurance company must notify you of the right to continuation by certified mail, return receipt requested, within 30 days after receipt of the notice from the employer. 215 Ill. Comp. Stat. Ann. 5/367.2(C) (LexisNexis through P.A. 101-631).

Coverage for the eligible spouse must be the same as what was offered under the group plan, and the maximum period of continued coverage is until the qualified spouse is eligible for Medicare. Illinois Spousal Continuation Coverage will terminate if the employee (former spouse) separates from his or her employer; the non-employee qualifying former spouse becomes an insured employee under any other group health plan or remarries.

Current Employer Healthcare Plan

If you are employed and your employer offers healthcare coverage as a benefit, then you should explore this as a possibility as well. Most companies offer open enrollment periods at one time or another throughout the year. However, divorce is considered a significant life event, and enrollment in healthcare can generally take place at any time of the year under these circumstances.

Affordable Care Act (Obamacare)

If you do not have access to employer healthcare coverage through either your spouse or your employer, you are eligible for coverage under the ACA (Obamacare).

In that divorce is considered a qualifying life event, you will have 60 days after your divorce to get coverage during a special enrollment period. If the 60 days lapses, you will have to wait until the regular open enrollment period takes place to sign up for a healthcare plan. Open enrollment typically takes place in November and December each year. You can shop for various plans on your state exchange, the federal marketplace, or in the private marketplace.

However, given so many choices and options to consider, shopping for healthcare insurance under the Affordable Care Act (aka Obamacare) may seem a bit overwhelming at first. But, if you consider things logically, and apply your circumstances to the process of deciding what is best for you, it's possible to come up with the healthcare plan that is optimal for your needs.

Here are some things to consider as you work through the Obamacare process.

Metal Tiers. One of the first things you'll encounter when shopping for an ACA plan is that Metal Levels sort offerings.
Bronze, Silver, Gold, and Platinum tiers help you to decide what the cost split is between you and your insurer.
Typically, the greater the insurer's split is, the more the plan will cost.
- **Bronze Tier.** These are the most inexpensive but have the highest out-of-pocket premiums, deductibles, coinsurance, and copayments. If you have this coverage but don't use it, then you will pay less until such time you have a medical expense. Bronze plans typically pay 60% of your healthcare bills, and you pay the remaining 40%.
- **Silver Tier.** Silver tier plans pay 70% of healthcare costs, and the insured pays the remaining 30% of out-of-pocket expenses.
- **Gold Tier.** Gold tier plans pay 80% of healthcare costs, and the insured pays the remaining 20% of out-of-pocket expenses.

- **Platinum Tier.** Platinum tier plans pay 90% of healthcare costs and the insured pays the remaining 10% of out-of-pocket expenses.

When comparing plans and tiers, you need to consider if you have an ongoing medical condition that will require more frequent care or if you will only use a plan sporadically. For more ongoing care, it may make sense to buy a plan with a lower deductible and lower copayments. If you only use healthcare coverage from time to time, a plan with cheaper monthly premiums could be the preferred way to go.

Budget and Price. You will need to decide how much of your budget can be allotted to health insurance costs and then make sure you can afford to make those payments. You may need to adjust the level of your plan either up or down so that it can accommodate your health care needs as well as your spending allotment for health insurance.

Short-Term Health Insurance

If you need health insurance to bridge a short lapse in coverage because you will either get coverage through an employer or Obamacare, then a short-term policy may be the best way to go. Coverage can start in as little as 24 hours and can last for up to 6 to 12 months, depending on the state where you live. Because coverage takes place so quickly, you cannot have certain pre-existing conditions. Also, you will have the option of seeing the doctor of your choice, or you can save money by choosing to go to doctors who participate in discount networks.

Concierge Insurance Plans

Concierge medicine (also known as retainer medicine) is a relationship between a patient and a primary care physician in which the patient pays an annual fee or retainer. This may or may not be in addition to other charges. In exchange for the retainer, doctors agree to provide enhanced care, including principally a commitment to limit patient loads to ensure adequate time and availability for each patient.

The practice has been referred to as concierge medicine, retainer medicine, membership medicine, cash-only practice, and direct care. While all "concierge" medicine practices share similarities, they vary widely in their structure, payment requirements, and form of operation. In particular, they differ in the level of service provided and the fee charged. Estimates of U.S. doctors practicing concierge medicine range from fewer than 800 to 5,000.

Most concierge models usually fall into one of the following categories:

- **The Fee for Care ('FFC');** which is an annual retainer model, where the patient pays a monthly, quarterly, or annual retainer fee to the physician. The retainer fee covers most services provided by the physician in his/her office. Often, vaccinations, lab work, x-rays, and other services are excluded and charged for separately on a cash basis.
- **The Fee for Extra Care ('FFEC')** is similar to the FFC model, however, the additional services are charged to Medicare or the patient's insurance plan. Some of the benefits and services typically included in these two retainer

models are: same day access to your doctor; immediate cell phone and text messaging to your doctor; unlimited office visits with no co-pay; little or no waiting time in the office; focus on preventive care; unhurried atmosphere; cell phone, text message, and online consultations; prescription refills; and convenient appointment scheduling.

FFC or retainer plans may typically not be purchased with pre-tax dollars utilizing HSA and/or FSA accounts because it is not a fee incurred for a service. Instead, it functions more as an insurance policy where fees are paid in anticipation of an expense.

Some concierge practices are cash-only or 'direct' primary care practices and do not accept insurance of any kind. In doing so, these practices can keep overhead and administrative costs low, thereby, in theory, providing more affordable healthcare to patients under this particular model.

Typically, concierge physicians' care for fewer patients than those in a conventional practice, ranging from 50 patients per doctor to 1,000, compared to 3,000 to 4,000 patients that the average traditional physician now sees every year. All generally claim to be accessible via telephone or email at any time of day or night or offer some other service above and beyond the customary care. The annual fees vary widely, ranging anywhere from $195.00 to $5,000.00 per year for an individual. The higher priced plans generally include most "covered" services where the client is not charged additional fees for most services (labs, x-rays, etc.).

Some of the other benefits of concierge healthcare are: in-home visits, worldwide access to doctors, and expedited emergency room care. The take-away here is that there are affordable options healthcare coverage options out there for you, post-divorce. Go to HealthCare.gov to explore what is available given your individual situation, or you can contact a trusted Insurance agent familiar with the Affordable Care Act's marketplace options, Short Term and Concierge Options to help you understand all the plans and associated costs. Healthcare coverage is vital, and even in uncertain times, it is important to make sure you make securing individual (or family coverage) a priority as you navigate through your "new normal" post – divorce.

Overall, making sure you obtain coverage is important. This is a costly future expense that needs to be considered seriously in your overall plan to move forward with your life.

GET OUT OF MY HEAD: MENTAL HEALTH PROTECTION

Mental illnesses can affect persons of any age, race, religion or income. Mental illnesses are not the result of personal weakness, lack of character or poor upbringing. Mental illnesses are treatable. Most people diagnosed with a serious mental illness can experience relief from their symptoms by actively participating in an individual treatment plan. Dealing with mental illnesses has become a part of our everyday lives when we associate with family, clients, and colleagues who suffer from various mental medical conditions.

According to the National Alliance on Mental Illness (NAMI), a mental illness is a medical condition that interrupts a person's mood, behavior, ability to relate to others, ability to complete daily functions and mental processing. *About Mental Illness*, NATIONAL ALLIANCE ON MENTAL HEALTH ILLINOIS, https://namiillinois.org/about-mental-illness/ (last visited Jun. 22, 2020). Millions of Americans are affected by mental ILLNESS and the following shed light on this sobering reality:

- 1 in 5 U.S. adults experience mental illness each year
- 1 in 25 U.S. adults experience serious mental illness each year
- 1 in 6 U.S. youth aged 6-17 experience a mental health disorder each Year
- 50% of all lifetime mental illness begins by age 14, and 75% by age 24

Mental Health Conditions, NATIONAL ALLIANCE OF MENTAL ILLNESS, https://www.nami.org/Learn-More/Mental-Health-Conditions (last visited June 22, 2020).

Serious mental illnesses include major depression, schizophrenia, bipolar disorder, obsessive compulsive disorder (OCD), panic disorder, posttraumatic stress disorder (PTSD) and borderline personality disorder can be challenging for most families. Some may find that their partner's aggression, narcissism, and self-centered behavior led to the breakdown of the marriage.

Divorce is difficult enough for a family to deal with and process the new family dynamic post-divorce. Adding to mental health issues with court proceedings can make for difficulty in maneuvering through the court system. Marriages in which one party suffers from a mental illness disorder may have periods of high conflict and explosive situations. It is imperative that mental illnesses are diagnosed and properly treated. There are several mental health professionals and organizations that offer a bevy of resources to treat nearly every known mental illness. Ultimately, the inability to cope with mental Illness can result in divorce and the breakdown of relationships.

In some divorce and parenting cases, a person's mental disorder could lead to violent or dangerous behaviors that would require immediate and protective action. If there is a fear of a threat to the safety of yourself, your child(ren) or other household member(s) Illinois provides protection by way of the order of protection. Review the chapter on domestic violence and Orders of Protection within this book for further information.

In some family law cases, it is not uncommon for another party to feel that the other is "psychotic" or has mental health issues. This notion can be used to attach a person's ability to be a parent or to facility parental responsibilities. Before a party puts another party's mental health at issue, there are a few things to consider. What is the purpose? Is it to get a leg up or is it to truly protect the best interest of the child(ren)? It would seem obvious that once a party has been treated for a mental illness, then treatments should automatically be a part of the divorce and parentage proceedings, right? Wrong. There are certain provisions in place to prevent the breach of confidentiality and disclosure of medical and mental health records. Even when it seems obvious that there are mental health issues, attorneys and litigants must be sure to comply with current laws in order to be sure not to risk sanctions or inappropriate dissemination of mental health issues. The reasons for protecting mental health records were described in *Laurent v. Brelji*, 74 Ill. App. 3d 214, 217 (Ill. App. Ct. 4th Dist. 1979):

> *Presumably, the patient in psychotherapeutic treatment reveals the most private and secret aspects of his mind and soul. To casually allow public disclosure of such would desecrate any notion of an individual's right to privacy. At the same time, confidentiality is essential to the treatment process itself, which can be truly effective only when there is complete candor and revelation by the patient. Finally, confidentiality provides proper assurances and inducement for persons who need treatment to seek it.*

The Illinois Mental Health and Developmental Disabilities Confidentiality Act (740 ILCS 110) provides guidance for the confidentiality and restricted disclosure of records and communications kept in connection with individuals receiving mental health services. The Illinois legislature enacted the Illinois Mental Health and Developmental Disabilities Confidentiality Act in an effort to add a layer of protection and confidentiality for individuals, as it relates to records and communications kept in connection with receiving mental health or developmental disabilities services, for the sole purpose of allowing individuals to receive necessary treatment while remaining confident that their privacy would remain protected at all times. In doing so, the legislature intended to encourage individuals to seek proper treatment by ensuring that their privacy and confidentiality was protected by law as it relates to records and communications being kept during their treatment. 740 ILCS 110/3(a) provides in pertinent part as follows:

> *...records and communications made or created in the course of providing mental health or developmental disabilities services shall be protected from disclosure regardless of whether the records and communications are made or created in the course of a therapeutic relationship." [emphasis added]*

740 Ill. Comp. Stat. Ann. 110/3(a) (LexisNexis through P.A. 101-631).

This specific language broadens the protection under this Act, with the purpose of ensuring that individuals seeking mental health or developmental disabilities services are afforded the same protection when communicating with any provider that is rendering a service in connection with providing mental health or developmental disabilities services. *Id.* The specific language set forth in this provision extends the confidentiality requirement to those individuals that are assisting in rendering said services, regardless of whether or not the assistance is therapeutic in nature, including but not limited to first responders, police officers, social workers, and the like. *Id.*

According to Illinoislegalaid.org, the term "records of mental health or developmental disabilities services includes all documents about you and the services provided to you." *Confidentiality for Mental and Developmental Disabilities,* ILLINOIS LEGAL AID ONLINE, https://www.illinoislegalaid.org/legal-information/confidentiality-mental-and-developmental-disabilities (last visited June 22, 2020). The definition goes on to state:

> *This includes documents related to: physical or mental examinations, diagnosis, treatment or training, evaluations, medications, aftercare, habilitation and rehabilitation, notes about services provided, letters, and other documents found in your file.*

Id.

Additionally, under 740 ILCS 110/10(a)(1), the legislature implemented a provision concerning the introduction of mental health records and communications in any civil, criminal or administrative proceeding, granting recipients of mental health services the privilege to refuse to disclose and to prevent the disclosure of all records and communications kept in connection with receiving mental health services. 740 Ill. Comp. Stat. Ann. 110/10(a)(1) (LexisNexis through P.A. 101-631). This privilege was also extended to the provider of said mental health services, granting the same privilege on behalf of and in the best interest of the recipient, to refuse and prevent the disclosure of the records and communications kept in connection with rendering the mental health services. *Id.* Under this provision, a party's mental condition or any aspect of services received for said condition, cannot be introduced by any party unless the recipient of said services has introduced their mental condition or the services rendered for said condition, as an element of his or her claim or defense. *Id.* Even then, the records and communications may only be disclosed to the extent the court in which the proceedings have been brought finds after an in camera examination that it is "relevant, probative, not unduly prejudicial or inflammatory, and otherwise clearly admissible." *Id.*

As it relates to the disclosure of mental health records, as set forth in 740 ILCS 110/10 (c) of the Confidentiality Act, any disclosure shall not occur in any public proceeding and any personally identifiable data of the recipient and provider shall be removed from the records and communications prior to disclosure. 740 Ill. Comp. Stat. Ann. 110/10(c) (LexisNexis through P.A. 101-631).

Even further, under the same provision, the legislature incorporated specific language related to the introduction of a party's mental condition in any action brought or defended under the Illinois Marriage and Dissolution of Marriage Act (IMDMA). The provision related to the IMDMA, states in pertinent part as follows:

> *...in any action brought or defended under the Illinois Marriage and Dissolution of Marriage Act, or in any action in which pain and suffering is an element of the claim, mental condition shall not be deemed to be introduced merely by making such a claim and shall be deemed to be introduced only if the recipient or a witness on his behalf first testifies concerning the record or communication. [emphasis added]*

740 ILCS 110/10 (a)(1) (LexisNexis through P.A. 101-631).

Lastly, as part of the Confidentiality Act, the legislature set forth a provision for individuals to seek relief in the event that their records and/or communications that are protected under this Act are disclosed in violation of the rights afforded under the Act, by granting individuals the right to sue for damages, an injunction, or other appropriate relief, as well as attorneys' fees and costs if they are successful in proving their rights were in fact violated. 740 ILCS 110/15 states as follows:

> *Any person aggrieved by a violation of this Act may sue for damages, an injunction, or other appropriate relief. Reasonable attorneys' fees and costs may be awarded to the successful plaintiff in any action under this Act.*

740 Ill. Comp. Stat. Ann. 110/15 (LexisNexis through P.A. 101-631).

An article published by the Loyola University Chicago Law Journal, citing REPORT: GOVERNOR'S COMMISSION FOR REVISION OF THE MENTAL HEALTH CODE OF ILLINOIS as published by the Mental Disability Law Reporter, vol. 1, no. 4, 1977, pp. 278–287, the enactment of the MHDDCA was widely supported, stating in pertinent part as follows:

> *the entire psychotherapist community, including psychologists, psychiatrists, and law enforcement, was involved in the drafting of the MHDDCA and the members of this community fully supported the MHDDCA.*

See Elinor L. Hart, *The Illinois Mental Health and Developmental Disabilities Confidentiality Act: Lest We Forget the Search for the Truth*, 41 Loy. L. J. 885, 899 (2010).

As noted in the Commission Report, the protection afforded under the Act was fully supported by not only the members of the community, but also the entire psychotherapist community, including law enforcement officers, who have increasingly become the first responders to calls involving mental health concerns, making them an essential part of providing mental health services.

Absent the added protection under the provisions of this Act, the effects of disclosure of mental health records would be detrimental to the success of any mental health services rendered to an individual, as the possibility of records being disclosed outside of treatment would more than likely cause the recipient hesitation when discussing such sensitive, private, and sometimes embarrassing information. The necessity of this Act lies in the fact that private information relevant to mental health will likely be withheld by the recipient of any mental health service, if they feel that the information may be released outside of their treatment. In turn, the withholding of information by a recipient when receiving mental health services undoubtedly delays the provider's ability to successfully and effectively treat that individual, as the information withheld by the individual could likely impact the services that are rendered during treatment.

Application of 740 ILCS 110

As is the case with all statutes, the language set forth in the Confidentiality Act is subject to interpretation by the Courts. However, the controlling case law related to 740 ILCS 110, predominantly holds that the confidentiality and privacy of a recipient of mental health services is of utmost importance. The Courts have set a precedence that the recipient of mental health services is entitled to protection from disclosure, as the Courts have recognized that the purpose of this Act is to ensure that all individuals receiving these services are afforded an opportunity to effectively and successfully treat their condition, without fear that their records could be subject to review by the public or by the court system.

In *People v. Kaiser*, the Second District Appellate Court of Illinois, held that the Act applies to all communications and records generated in connection with providing mental health services, which is broader than the physician-patient privilege. *People v. Kaiser*, 239 Ill. App. 3d 295, 301 (Ill. App. Ct. 2d Dist. 1992). The Appellate Court stated specifically as follows:

> *The protection of the Confidentiality Act is broader than the physician-patient privilege, and all communications and records generated in connection with providing mental health services to a recipient are protected unless excepted by law. [emphasis added].*

Id.

In *Johnston v. Weil*, the Supreme Court of Illinois set a precedent related to disclosure and introduction of mental health records in litigation, pursuant to the Confidentiality Act. Specifically, The Supreme Court held in pertinent part as follows:

> *The records made confidential under the Confidentiality Act refer to "any record kept by a therapist or by an agency in the course of providing mental health or developmental disabilities service to a "recipient concerning the recipient and the services provided"; the communications made confidential under the Act refer to "any communication made by a recipient or other person to a therapist or to or in the presence of other persons during or in connection with providing mental health or developmental disability services to a recipient.) Communication includes information which indicates that a person is a recipient." 740 ILCS 110/2 (West 2006). Further, the term "recipient" means "a person who is receiving or has received mental health or developmental disabilities services"; ...and the term "mental health or developmental disabilities services" "includes but is not limited to examination, diagnosis, evaluation, treatment, training, pharmaceuticals, after-care, habilitation or rehabilitation." 740 ILCS 110/2 (West 2006)." [emphasis added].*

Johnston v. Weil, 241 Ill. 2d 169, 181-82 (2011).

The Illinois Supreme Court in *Johnston v. Weil* goes on to state:

> *This court has repeatedly recognized that the Confidentiality Act constitutes "a strong statement" by the legislature about the importance of keeping mental health records confidential. Reda, 199 Ill. 2d at 60; Norskog, 197 Ill. 2d at 71-72. We expressly reaffirm this unmistakable legislative intent. [emphasis added].*

Johnston, at 187.

In *Mandziara v. Canulli*, the First District Appellate Court of Illinois affirmed the Trial Court's decision regarding the disclosure of mental health records, stating in pertinent part as follows:

> *We held section 10 grants the recipient of services a privilege to refuse or prevent disclosure, Renzi, 249 Ill. App. 3d at 8. Any common law right to witness immunity that might exist "must give way" to that statutory privilege. Renzi, 249 Ill. App. 3d at 8....The Act, we said, provides safeguards to balance a patient's privacy with the trial court's truth-seeking function. Renzi, 249 Ill. App. 3d at 8. [emphasis added].*

Mandziara v. Canulli, 299 Ill. App. 3d 593, 598 (Ill. App. Ct. 1st Dist. 1998).

Further, the First District Appellate Court in *Mandziara v. Canulli* proceeds to address the introduction of mental health records and the waiver of a recipient's confidentiality, stating in pertinent part as follows:

> *Section 10(a)(1) allows disclosure of confidential mental health records only when the patient introduces her mental health as an element of her claim or defense. 740 ILCS 110/10(a)(1) (West 1994)."A recipient [of mental health services] waives the confidentiality of her records only if she affirmatively places her own mental condition at issue." Sassali, 296 Ill. App. 3d at 83...Mandziara did not introduce the issue of her mental health. Her husband, through his lawyer, did. Because section 10(a)(1) was not satisfied, there could be no waiver. Disclosure under either section 10(b) or section 10(d) was not authorized by the statute. [emphasis added].*

Mandziara, at 599-600.

An example of affirmatively placing your own mental health at issue can include your mental condition in a pleading or response filed with the court. Oftentimes we feel that we need to tell the story in our pleadings and responses so that the Judge can know the background. Sometimes too much is not necessary.

The Court's Interpretation of 740 ILCS 110

The sole purpose of the Confidentiality Act, as affirmed by the Appellate and Supreme Courts, is to encourage individuals to seek mental health treatment by ensuring that the recipient of said treatment is confident that the records and communications generated in connection with these services will remain private and confidential, absent their own desire and consent to release the records. As the Courts have held on multiple levels, mental health records cannot be introduced during any court proceedings, unless and until the party receiving mental health services introduces the mental health records his or herself, as provided for in the language specifically contained in 740 ILCS 110 *et seq*.

The only exception to this provision as stated above, would be a court-ordered mental evaluation or examination, in which the recipient submitting to the exam was adequately informed prior to the exam taking place that all records obtained during the exam would not be confidential and would be subject to disclosure. The provision granting individuals the power to seek remedies in connection with any violation of this Act and unlawful disclosure of their records, is in furtherance of the intent of the Act, to allow the recipient to be comfortable fully disclosing any and all private and sensitive information relevant to their mental health; which in turn, allows the provider to effectively treat the individual.

The IMDMA and Mental Health

The protection against the introduction of mental conditions in any action or defense brought under IMDMA, requires that parties attempting to introduce testimony or evidence related to mental conditions of the other party seek alternative means to do so, specifically as set forth in 750 ILCS 5/604.10. Appointing an expert under section 604.10 is the only avenue available to introduce the opposing party's mental health in cases being litigated pursuant to IMDMA, unless the opposing party has already put their mental condition at issue. Even in the event that a mental evaluation is ordered by the court under 604.10, prior to records and communications being disclosed, the Court must first find that the recipient was properly informed before submitting to an examination, that the records generated as a result of same will not be considered confidential or private. Pursuant to 750 ILCS 5/604.10(b):

> *The Court may seek the advice of any professional, whether or not regularly employed by the court, to assist the court in determining the child's best interests. The advice to the court shall be in writing and sent by the professional to counsel for the parties and to the court, under seal. The writing may be admitted into evidence without testimony from its author, unless a party objects. A professional consulted by the court shall testify as the court's witness and be subject to cross-examination. The court shall order all costs and fees of the professional to be paid by one or more of the parties, subject to reallocation....*

750 Ill. Comp. Stat. Ann. 5/604.10(b) (LexisNexis through P.A. 101-631).

Pursuant to 740 ILCS 110/10(a)(1), the mental health history of an individual may only be disclosed where:

> *Recipient introduces his mental condition or any aspect of his services received for such condition as an element of his claim or defense, if and only to the extent the court in which the proceedings have been brought or in the case of an administrative proceeding, the court to which an appeal or other action for review of an administrative determination may be taken, finds after in camera examination of testimony or other evidence, that it is relevant, probative, no unduly prejudicial or inflammatory, and otherwise clearly admissible; that the other satisfactory evidence is demonstrably unsatisfactory as evidence; and that disclosure is more important to the interest of substantial justice than protection from injury to the therapist recipient relationship or to the recipient or other whom disclosure is likely to harm.*

740 Ill. Comp. Stat. Ann. 110/10(a)(1) (LexisNexis through P.A. 101-631).

The Statute specifically addressed its intersection with the Illinois Marriage and Dissolution of Marriage Act and its inherent relation to mental health by stating, "in any action brought or defended under the Illinois Marriage and Dissolution of Marriage Act, or in any action in which pain and suffering is an element of the claim, mental condition shall not be deemed to be introduced merely by making such claim and shall be deemed to be introduced only if the recipient or a witness on his behalf first testifies concerning the record or communication," 740 ILCS 110/10(a)(1) (LexisNexis through P.A. 101-631).

A party seeking mental health or medical records must properly seek leave of Court to place a party's mental health at issue as provided by the Illinois Mental Health and Developmental Disability Confidentiality Act. 740 Ill. Comp. Stat. Ann. 110/10(d) (LexisNexis through P.A. 101-631). There is also a requirement that the party seeking the records must provide notice of his request to any and all providers from which he seeks to request records. *Id.*

The Illinois Mental Health Confidentiality Act specifies that, "except as provided herein, in any civil, criminal, administrative, or legislative proceeding, or in any proceeding preliminary thereto, a recipient, and a therapist on behalf and in the interest of a recipient, has the privilege to refuse to disclose and to prevent the disclosure of the recipient's record or communications." 740 ILCS 110/10(a) (LexisNexis through P.A. 101-631).

Before you seek to issue a subpoena for mental health records in Illinois, you should review, 740 ILCS 110/10(d), which states:

> *No party to any proceeding described under paragraphs (1), (2), (3), (4), (7) or (8) of any subsection (a) of this Section, nor his or her attorney, shall serve a subpoena seeking to obtain access to records or communications under this Act unless the Subpoena is accompanied by a written order issued by a judge or by the written consent under Section 5 of this Act of the person whose records are being sought, authorizing the disclosure of the records or the issuance of the subpoena. No such written order shall be issued without written notice of the motion to the recipient and the treatment provider. Prior to issuance of the order, each party or other person entitled to notice shall be permitted an opportunity to be heard pursuant to subsection (b) of this Section.*

740 Ill. Comp. Stat. Ann. 110/10(d) (LexisNexis through P.A. 101-631).

When Mental Health is at Issue

When there is a concern a party may suffer from mental illness or have mental health issues, a party can request that one be done on the other party. Illinois Supreme Court Rules provides a way for a party to request a Mental Health Evaluation. Illinois Supreme Court rule 215(a) provides that if a person's mental or physical condition is in controversy, the court may order that party to submit to a physical or mental examination. Ill. Sup. Ct. R. 215(a). Specifically, the rule states in part:

> *(a) Notice; Motion; Order. In any action in which the physical or mental condition of a party or of a person in the party's custody or legal control is in controversy, the court, upon notice and on motion made within a reasonable time before the trial, may order such party to submit to a physical or mental examination by a licensed professional in a discipline related to the physical or mental condition which is involved.*

Id.

The comments section to this rule state that this rule is intended to provide an orderly procedure for the examination of civil litigants whose physical or mental condition is in controversy.

The purpose of the rule allowing the Court to order a party to submit to a physical or mental examination is not to provide an expert witness for the litigant, but to permit discovery. *Roberts. v. Norfolk and W. Ry. Co.,* 229 Ill.App.3d 706, 721 (Ill. App. Ct. 4th Dist. 1992). The rule was expanded to include other mental health professions, but there is still a requirement for a person's mental condition to be at issue before the examination under 215(a) can proceed. Ill. Sup. Ct. R. 215(a). The Rule remains very clear on this requirement.

The revisions to 215(a) in 1995 allows for physical and mental examinations by "licensed professionals" not merely physicians. Ill. Sup. Ct. R. 215(a) (as revised June 25, 1995). The previous version of the rule authorized examinations pursuant to Rule 215(a) to be conducted only by physicians. The amendment to this rule includes professionals in other health related disciplines. Now sociologists, psychologists, or other licensed professions in juvenile, domestic relations and child custody cases within the scope of the rule.

The person who files the pleading pursuant to 215(a) is required to pay the fee for the examiner and compensate for any loss earnings incurred in the professional's compliance with the order for examination. Ill. Sup. Ct. R. 215(b). The petitioning party must also advance all reasonable expenses incurred by the party/person complying with the order. *Id.*

Now that you have the legal background on mental and physical health evaluations, it may be a good idea to consult with an attorney. You and your attorney can be sanctioned for improperly seeking or obtaining mental health records. The Court has discretion on how to sanction for improper retrieval of mental health records at their discretion pursuant to Illinois Supreme Court Rule 215. 740 Ill. Comp. Stat. Ann. 110/15 (LexisNexis through P.A. 101-631).

An appropriate sanction to protect the physician-patient privilege from defense interviews outside formal discovery is to bar the testimony of the plaintiff's treating physician or enter a finding of contempt. *Id.* Another sanction could be for the Court to order the offending party and/or the attorney advising him/her to pay a portion or all of the expenses of discovery or taxable court costs or both. *Id.* Be careful and fully advised when attempting to put mental health at issue.

ABUSE IS SERIOUS

There is no particular social class, economic class, gender, race, or ethnicity who is exempt from domestic violence.

Domestic violence is not limited to one certain class of individuals who are more prone to violence and there is no particular stereotype. It occurs in affluent families as well as families below the poverty line. Regardless of your background, the law affords the same opportunities for protection to all victims of domestic violence.

Domestic Violence is an epidemic that affects an unknown number of people due to the underreported nature of the issue. This abuse comes in many forms: physical abuse, mental abuse, verbal abuse, spiritual abuse, sexual abuse, and financial abuse. It is estimated that 1.3 million women and 835,000 men are victims of physical violence by an intimate partner each year. *Intimate Partner Violence - Statistics*, EXHALE TO INHALE, https://www.exhaletoinhale.org/dv-statistics (last visited June 23, 2020).

The National Coalition Against Domestic Violence reports that 85% of victims are women and it is believed that one in every four American women will experience or has experienced Domestic Violence in their lifetime. *Id.*

For many, their home is a place of warmth, comfort and stability. It is also the place they feel safe. Most people enjoy time with their families inside their home and have a place to decompress from the hustle of life. For Domestic Violence victims, a home is the opposite of that; it is more like a prison. Because Domestic Violence is a taboo social topic, many people go to great lengths to hide what is happening inside their residence. Instead of disclosing the abuse to family and loved ones, victims become isolated from the people that were close to them in the past.

Domestic Violence has many ripple effects on a victim's life. These effects can be emotional and psychological and can continue long after the abuse has ended. Victims experience fear for their safety, fear for the safety of others, and suffer emotional distress. Many victims alter their daily routines to avoid the persons who are abusing them. Some victims are in such fear that they relocate to another city, town or state. Depending on the connections between the victim and their abuser, the lingering effects of the abuse can evoke many troublesome feelings for the victim.

Due to the commonly reported feelings of shame and guilt, a victim may continue to isolate themselves from loved ones and have issues with poverty and homelessness due to past abusive acts. The connections they may have had in the past may have been eroded or the abuse victim believes the relationships are eroded and they have no one to turn to for help or support. Additionally, survivors of domestic violence have the scars of past abuse significantly influencing their potential for future romantic relationships. Some survivors looking for a loving relationship enter into new relationships which duplicate the same pattern of abuse.

Domestic violence is not a subject to be taken lightly. Domestic violence is a crime. In fact, Section 102 of the Illinois Domestic Violence Act of 1986 (herein IDVA), specifically identifies domestic violence as a serious crime against both the individual as well as society. 750 Ill. Comp. Stat. Ann. 60/102(1) (LexisNexis through P.A. 101-631). The IDVA was enacted to promote the underlying purpose of recognizing domestic violence as a serious crime against the individual and society which produces family disharmony in thousands of Illinois families, promotes a pattern of escalating violence which frequently culminates in intra-family homicide, and creates an emotional atmosphere that is not conducive to healthy childhood development. It also recognizes domestic violence against high risk adults with disabilities, who are particularly vulnerable due to impairments in ability to seek or obtain protection, as a serious problem which takes on many forms, including physical abuse, sexual abuse, neglect, and exploitation. Finally, the IDVA facilitates accessibility of remedies under the Act in order to provide immediate and effective assistance and protection. 750 Ill. Comp. Stat. Ann. 60/102(1)-(2) (LexisNexis through P.A. 101-631).

The IDVA also seeks to support the efforts of victims of domestic violence to avoid further abuse by promptly entering and diligently enforcing court orders which prohibit abuse and, when necessary, reduce the abuser's access to the victim and address any related issues of child custody and economic support, so that victims are not trapped in abusive situations by fear of retaliation, loss of a child, financial dependence, or loss of accessible housing or services. 750 Ill. Comp. Stat. Ann. 60/102(4) (LexisNexis through P.A. 101-631).

The Illinois Domestic Violence Act of 1986 also defines the terms of domestic violence and abuse. Domestic violence is defined as the abuse by a family or household member. The term abuse has been defined as physical abuse, harassment, intimidation of a dependent, interference with the personal liberty, neglect, or willful deprivation. 750 Ill. Comp. Stat. Ann. 60/103(1) (LexisNexis through P.A. 101-631). In recognizing that the legal system was once ineffective when dealing with family violence, the legislators enacted the Illinois Domestic Violence Act of 1986 to avoid the widespread failure to appropriately protect and assist victims of domestic violence.

A recent addition to the Illinois Domestic Violence Act of 1986 is the Victims' Economic Security & Safety Act (VESSA). In previous years, victims of domestic violence found it difficult to seek necessary services for fear of taking too much time off work in order to pursue remedies for domestic violence. As a result of the fear of missing work or losing a job, as of January 1, 2017, employers must allow time off from work for victims of domestic violence in order for the victims to seek medical attention, obtain victim services and/or counseling, seek legal assistance to ensure safety, and to participate in court proceedings related to the violence alleged. 820 Ill. Comp. Stat. Ann. 180/20(a)(1)(A)-(E) (LexisNexis through P.A. 101-631).

VESSA provides for penalties for an employer's failure to implement and follow the procedures as enumerated in VESSA. The Department of Labor is the regulatory agency who will conduct any investigations as to any reported violations of VESSA. 820 Ill. Comp. Stat. Ann. 180/35(a)(1) (LexisNexis through P.A. 101-631). Such penalties include, but are not limited to, paying reasonable attorneys' fees and compensation for lost wages. 820 Ill. Comp. Stat. Ann. 180/35(a)(1)(A)-(C) (LexisNexis through P.A. 101-631).

Illinois has taken measures to include salon professionals in the fight against domestic violence. As of January 1, 2017. Illinois became the first state in the nation to require that hair stylists attend domestic violence training. 225 Ill. Comp. Stat. Ann. 410/3-7 (LexisNexis through P.A. 101-631). This training is to help salon professionals recognize the potential victims of domestic violence and sexual assault. The law does not require salon professionals to become mandatory reporters, but the law urges the professionals to assist and direct their clients to domestic violence resources.

The Illinois Domestic Violence Act ("IDVA") is a law that relates specifically to family and household members. Under the IDVA, a Circuit Court Judge can order and forbid a family or household member from continuous abusive behavior by granting an Order of Protection. Whether you are the person seeking an Order of Protection or the individual who is ordered to comply, it is extremely important to understand the severity and obligations of such an Order.

An Order of Protection is a written Court Order which prohibits abusive behavior by law. The Order is protective by nature and usually requires that the alleged abuser stay away from the victim and cease all contact with him or her. The IDVA considers various behaviors as abusive including physical abuse, harassment, intimidation of a dependent, interference with personal liberty, willful deprivation, exploitation, and stalking. 750 Ill. Comp. Stat. Ann. 60/103(a) (LexisNexis through P.A. 101-631). These types of restraining Orders are only put in place after a Judge deems it necessary. It is imperative to understand the Order and to comply with the restrictions outlined therein. Anyone found to be in violation of an Order of Protection will find themselves in a legal position much worse than that which required the Order in the first place.

Orders of Protection can be entered to protect a spouse, an ex-spouse, a girlfriend/boyfriend who have or have had a dating or engagement relationship, parents, children, stepchildren, significant other/partner, persons who share or allege a blood relationship through a child, persons who live together or formerly lived together and persons with disabilities and their personal assistants.

Illinois Domestic Violence Act, Section 201(a) specifies who is eligible for an Order of Protection. 750 Ill. Comp. Stat. Ann. 60/201(a) (LexisNexis through P.A. 101-631). What you should remember is that eligibility does not mean that you will automatically be granted an Order of Protection by an Illinois court. The provisions of the Act provide that the following persons are eligible for protection by the Act:

    1.   *Any person abused by a family or household member;*

> 2. *Any high-risk adult with disabilities who is abused, neglected, or exploited by a family or household member;*
> 3. *Any minor child or dependent adult in the care of such person; and*
> 4. *Any person residing or employed at a private home or public shelter which is housing an abused family or household member.*

750 Ill. Comp. Stat. Ann. 60/201(a)(i)-(iv) (LexisNexis through P.A. 101-631).

An Order of Protection can protect victims of abuse, minors, or dependent adults in their care, and anyone who lives at or is employed at their place of residence. *Id.* In order to obtain an Order of Protection, allegations of some form of abuse need to be made by the party seeking the Emergency Order of Protection (or the Petitioner). 750 Ill. Comp. Stat. Ann. 60/203(a) (LexisNexis through P.A. 101-631). The allegations can include descriptions of physical abuse, harassment, intimidation of a dependent, interference with personal liberty, or willful deprivation.

Forms of Abuse

Physical abuse can be defined as any act using physical force, confinement, or restraint against another person. 750 Ill. Comp. Stat. Ann. 60/103(14)(i) (LexisNexis through P.A. 101-631). Physical abuse also includes sexual abuse, sleep deprivation, and creating an immediate risk of physical harm. 750 Ill. Comp. Stat. Ann. 60/103(14)(ii)-(iii) (LexisNexis through P.A. 101-631). The evidence of physical abuse shows up in bruises, broken bones, cuts, scars, blackened eyes, and open wounds. The court can visibly see some signs of physical abuse. Be sure to document the evidence of physical abuse. Take pictures and video upon the first appearance of any signs of physical abuse. Document the attack and the areas attacked with a physician.

Harassment means knowing, unnecessary, and unreasonable conduct that is causing emotional distress. 750 Ill. Comp. Stat. Ann. 60/103(7) (LexisNexis through P.A. 101-631). Some examples of harassing behavior include but are not limited to making a disturbance at work or school, repeated calls or texts, threatening suicide, or threatening physical violence, confinement, or restraint. 750 Ill. Comp. Stat. Ann. 60/103(7)(i), (ii), and (vi) (LexisNexis through P.A. 101-631).

Also, snatching a child or repeatedly threatening to do so is a harassing behavior. 750 Ill. Comp. Stat. Ann. 60/103(7)(v) (LexisNexis through P.A. 101-631). The key to understanding harassment is to evaluate whether the conduct is unreasonable and whether the conduct causes emotional distress.

There have been cases where an abuser calls a victim more than 100 times every day just to get the victim to "talk" to them and work things out. Granted, the reason for the call may have seemed innocent enough to the abuser, but the excessive calling is unreasonable conduct. Repeated and excessive calls can lead to emotional distress and the feeling that the calls will never end unless you do something about it.

Stalking occurs when a person knowingly engages in two or more acts of surveillance and monitoring of a specific person, and he or she knows or should know that this course of conduct would cause a reasonable person to fear for his or her safety or the safety of a third person; or suffer other emotional distress. 720 Ill. Comp. Stat. Ann. 5/12-7.3(a-3)(1)-(2) (LexisNexis through P.A. 101-631).

Stalking generally refers to a course of conduct, not a single act. 720 Ill. Comp. Stat. Ann. 6/12-7.3(c)(1) (LexisNexis through P.A. 101-631). The course of action could be direct, indirect, or through third parties. *Id.* Stalking actions may include a method, device, or other means in order to follow, monitor, observe, surveil, threaten, or communicate to or about who the abuser is stalking. *Id.* If a person engages in other non-consensual contact or interferes with or damages a person's property or pet, the action could be stalking if the same is under surveillance. *Id.*

Stalking behavior includes following a person, conducting surveillance of the person, appearing at the person's home, work or school, making unwanted phone calls, sending unwanted emails, unwanted messages via social media, or text messages, leaving objects for the person, vandalizing the person's property, or injuring a pet. 740 ILCS 21/5 (LexisNexis through P.A. 101-631).

While estimates suggest that 70% of victims know the individuals stalking them, only 30% of victims have dated or been in intimate relationships with their stalkers. *Id.* All stalking victims should be able to seek a civil remedy requiring the offenders stay away from the victims and third parties. Illinois statute has expanded protections to include Cyberstalking as a form of abuse, and the use of electronic communication as a way to follow and surveil a victim. *Id.*

Be careful before you go out and hire that private investigator to surveille your significant other or household member. You may believe that you are gathering information in order to get back at your cheating spouse. But, by the above definition, you could be stalking.

Interference with personal liberty includes forcing someone to do things that they would not normally do through actual (or the threat of) physical force, abuse, harassment, intimidation or willful deprivation. 750 Ill. Comp. Stat. Ann. 60/103(9) (LexisNexis through P.A. 101-631).

Intimidation of a dependent means involving or engaging in physical abuse of another in front of a dependent. 750 Ill. Comp. Stat. Ann. 60/103(10) (LexisNexis through P.A. 101-631). Willful deprivation is defined as willfully denying someone the care they need due to their disability, age, or health. 750 Ill. Comp. Stat. Ann. 60/103(15) (LexisNexis through P.A. 101-631).

Examples of such deprivation include depriving the abused of food, shelter, medical care, and physical help. *Id.*

Neglect is defined as the failure to exercise a reasonable person's degree of care towards a high-risk adult with disabilities and includes: failure to take appropriate measures to protect against abuse; failure to provide food, shelter, clothing, and personal hygiene; failure to provide appropriate medical intervention; and failure to protect for health and safety hazards. 750 Ill. Comp. Stat. Ann. 60/103(11)(A)(i), (iii), (iv), and (v) (LexisNexis through P.A. 101-631). Neglect can also include repeated careless imposition of unreasonable confinement. 750 Ill. Comp. Stat. Ann. 60/103(11)(A)(ii) (LexisNexis through P.A. 101-631).

Exploitation includes but is not limited to, the misappropriation of assets or resources of a high-risk adult with disabilities by undue influence, by breach of a fiduciary relationship, by fraud, deception, or extortion, or the use of such assets or resources in a manner contrary to law. 750 Ill. Comp. Stat. Ann. 60/103(5) (LexisNexis through P.A. 101-631).

The Process

Under the Illinois Domestic Violence Act, there are three types of Orders of Protection. The Orders of Protection include: Emergency Order of Protection, Interim Order of Protection, and Plenary Order of Protection. Each of the aforementioned Orders of Protection have special conditions and vary as to the length of time the order of protection is in place after entry.

An Emergency Order of Protection (EOP) is an ex parte order that can be granted for a period of 14 to 21 days without notice to the abuser (Respondent). 750 Ill. Comp. Stat. Ann. 60/220(a)(1) (LexisNexis through P.A. 101-631). This order may include a provision requiring the Respondent to stay away and have no contact with the Petitioner (the abused party). 750 Ill. Comp. Stat. Ann. 60/217(a)(3)(i) (LexisNexis through P.A. 101-631). Other provisions may also be included at the discretion of the Judge. In order to obtain an EOP, a Petitioner must be able to demonstrate specific abusive conduct by a Respondent. 750 Ill. Comp. Stat. Ann. 60/217(a)(2) (LexisNexis through P.A. 101-631). The EOP will likely list specific allegations of abusive conduct. These allegations will be the "facts" which will be presented at the hearing for an EOP.

An Interim Order of Protection is an order that can be granted and remain in place for a period of up to 30 days. 750 Ill. Comp. Stat. Ann. 60/220(a)(2) (LexisNexis through P.A. 101-631). Typically, this is used to extend the EOP to give parties time to get ready for a full hearing to determine the need for a Plenary Order of Protection. A Plenary Order of Protection can be granted for up to a two-year period only after a hearing or agreement of the parties. 750 Ill. Comp. Stat. Ann. 60/220(b)(0.05) (LexisNexis through P.A. 101-631). A hearing must be held with both parties having been afforded the opportunity to either obtain legal counsel and/or present evidence and witnesses in court. 750 Ill. Comp. Stat. Ann. 60/219 (LexisNexis through P.A. 101-631).

The process for obtaining an Order of Protection begins with the filing of a Petition for Order of Protection. 750 Ill. Comp. Stat. Ann. 60/202(a)(1) (LexisNexis through P.A. 101-631). The process can be initiated online in Will and DuPage County but must be verified and signed prior to appearing before a Judge. In other counties in Illinois, you will need to appear in person or research local rules for filing.

The Petition must include past and current proceedings between the parties as well as a detailed timeline of abuse that occurred by the abuser. 750 Ill. Comp. Stat. Ann. 60/203(a) (LexisNexis through P.A. 101-631). It is important to remember when preparing the Petition, the victim will be expected to testify about the allegations plead in their Petition for Order of Protection; and therefore, the allegations must be true, accurate and complete, otherwise issues may arise at the hearing.

Untrue statements, allegations and denials, made without reasonable cause and found to be untrue, shall subject the party pleading them to the payment of reasonable expenses actually incurred by the other party by reason of the untrue pleading, together with reasonable attorney's fees to be summarily taxed by the court upon motion made within 30 days of the judgment or dismissal, as provided in Supreme Court Rule 137. 750

Ill. Comp. Stat. Ann. 60/226 (LexisNexis through P.A. 101-631). The court may direct that a copy of an order entered under this Section be provided to the State's Attorney so that he or she may determine whether to prosecute for perjury. *Id.* This Section shall not apply to proceedings heard in Criminal Court or to criminal contempt of court proceedings, whether heard in Civil or Criminal Court. *Id.*

Filing for an Order of Protection (OP) is typically a very stressful process. Someone in a position to file for an OP should consider a variety of things based on their specific situation and the domestic abuse that occurred. First, it is important to realize that the period immediately following the filing of an OP is the most dangerous because it signifies to an abuser that the victim is taking steps to leave the relationship. Therefore, remembering that filing (and obtaining) an OP is the first important step in the process of getting away from an abuser, but preparing for what comes next is just as important.

When filing an OP, it is important to remember each county is different. The county where you choose to file the OP must meet one of four criterion; (1) the victim lives in that county, (2) the abuser lives in that county, (3) the abuse took place in the county, or (4) the OP is filed in the county the victim fled to for their protection. 750 Ill. Comp. Stat. Ann. 60/209(a) (LexisNexis through P.A. 101-631). One option to start the process of obtaining an OP is to complete certain forms online (such as the "Petition for Order of Protection"); i.e. the document wherein the specifics of the alleged abuse are outlined.

The Petition may exclude the petitioner's address if there is fear that the disclosure may further risk the safety of the petitioner or any family member. 750 Ill. Comp. Stat. Ann. 60/203(b) (LexisNexis through P.A. 101-631). However, an alternate address must be provided. *Id.* An address for the Respondent (abuser) is vital to the process. The county sheriff department is responsible for serving the Respondent with a summons and without a viable address service cannot be performed.

A plenary no contact or order of protection could be entered by default for the remedy sought in the petition, if the abuser has been served or given notice in accordance with service requirements and if the abuser then fails to appear as directed or fails to appear on any subsequent appearance or hearing date agreed to by the parties or set by the court. 750 Ill. Comp. Stat. Ann. 60/219(3)-(4) (LexisNexis through P.A. 101-631). It is imperative for the victim to be sure to appear on the necessary court dates in order to move forward with the EOP. If the petitioner/victim fails to appear, it would likely result in the dismissal of the Petition for order of Protection/No Contact Order.

To determine what counties in Illinois offer online access log onto http://www.illinoisprotectionorder.org/OOP/. (Note, this option may not be available in all counties). If available, completing any or all of the initial filing forms online before traveling to the courthouse can save a significant amount of waiting time. Thereafter, the victim will still need to go to the local county courthouse to begin the OP filing process with the Courthouse Clerk. At that time the victim will sign their "Petition for Order of Protection" to attest to its content, and soon thereafter appear in front of a Judge for an Emergency hearing to determine if their Petition for Order of Protection will be granted. If online access to initial OP forms is not available, the victim should travel to the appropriate courthouse to prepare the Petition for Order of Protection and file the OP.

Depending on the county, there are generally court advocates who can assist the victim with the completion of the necessary paperwork. The Court advocates are available to discuss the incidents that caused a victim to seek an OP, as well as discuss what remedies are available for a victim to request from the Judge that may be put in place for the duration of the Emergency OP (14-21 days). 750 Ill. Comp. Stat. Ann. 60/205(b) (LexisNexis through P.A. 101-631). Some of these "remedies" would include, but not be limited to, no physical contact between the victim of the abuser, no contact between the abuser and children of the parties or other family members; no phone or email contact; and exclusive possession of the shared home, if applicable. 750 Ill. Comp. Stat. Ann. 60/214(b)(1), (2), (3) (LexisNexis through P.A. 101-631).

The Remedies in an Order of Protection

There are several remedies afforded to victims of domestic violence. Such remedies include an Order of Protection (Emergency and Plenary), a Sexual Assault No Contact Order, and a Stalking No Contact Order. A variety of additional remedy options are available within the order of protection. These remedies vary depending on the circumstances of each case and the Court's discretion to grant remedies for the safety of the petitioner and other protected individuals. Further IDVA allows for the Judge, at his or her discretion and based on the case facts, to prohibit abuser from continuing threats and abuse (abuse includes physical abuse, harassment, intimidation, interference with personal liberty, or willful deprivation); prohibit abuser from contacting victim through third parties; bar abuser from entering a shared residence, school, work, or other specific location; prohibit the abuser from using drugs or alcohol; and require the abuser to attend certain counseling classes for a period of time. 750 Ill. Comp. Stat. Ann. 60/214(b)(1), (2), (3), and (4) (LexisNexis through P.A. 101-631).

Further remedies in an Order of Protection are to prohibit the concealment or removal of a child out of state, entry of an order returning the child to the Court and setting a restriction or specific visitation rights. 750 Ill. Comp. Stat. Ann. 60/214(b)(5), (6), (7), and (8) (LexisNexis through P.A. 101-631). Especially in cases where abuse occurred to a minor child, the Judge could bar the abuser's access to any of the child's medical and/or school records. 750 Ill. Comp. Stat. Ann. 60/214(b)(15) (LexisNexis through P.A. 101-631). It is not uncommon for the Illinois court to order temporary physical possession of children while the order of protection is pending. 750 Ill. Comp. Stat. Ann. 70/213(b)(5) (LexisNexis through P.A. 101-631).

It is the Court's duty to be sure to maintain the best interest, safety, and care of the child(ren) involved. In considering the restrictions between the abuser parent and the child(ren), the court will consider the facts presented in the Petition for Order of Protection to determine whether the children need to be a protected party and to what extent protections should be put in place.

If you are obtaining an order of protection from the abuser and personal property has been removed or should be protected, the Order can grant you certain personal property and require the abuser to turn over any of your personal property in their possession. 750 Ill. Comp. Stat. Ann. 60/214(10)-(11) (LexisNexis through P.A. 101-631). Additionally, there is a restriction and language in the Order that will bar the abuser from damaging, destroying, interfering with, or selling certain personal property. 750 Ill. Comp. Stat. Ann. 60/214(11) (LexisNexis through P.A. 101-631). If you have a concern regarding your personal property, please be sure to provide as many details as possible as to the personal property and the reasons why these items need to be protected in the Petition for Order of Protection.

A Judge could order a temporary allocation of parental responsibilities with respect to significant decision-making on behalf of the minor children. 750 Ill. Comp. Stat. Ann. 60/214(6) (LexisNexis through P.A. 101-631). The Petitioner could be awarded temporary decision-making responsibility in accordance with this Section, the Illinois Marriage and Dissolution of Marriage Act, the Illinois Parentage Act of 2015 (IMDMA), and the Illinois State's Uniform Child-Custody Jurisdiction and Enforcement Act with respect to education, medical, extracurricular, and religious decision for the child(ren). Id. If a court finds, after a hearing, that the abuser has committed abuse of a minor child, there is a rebuttable presumption that awarding temporary significant decision-making responsibility to the abuser would not be in the child's best interest. Id.

The court shall restrict or deny an abuser's parenting time with a minor child if the court finds that Respondent (abuser) has done or is likely to do any of the following: (i) abuse or endanger the minor child during parenting time; (ii) use the parenting time as an opportunity to abuse or harass petitioner or petitioner's family or household members; (iii) improperly conceal or detain the minor child; or (iv) otherwise act in a manner that is not in the best interests of the minor child. 750 Ill. Comp. Stat. Ann. 60/214(7) (LexisNexis through P.A. 101-631). The IDVA provides specifically that the court shall not be limited by the standards set forth in Section 603.10 of the Illinois Marriage and Dissolution of Marriage Act. Id. If the court hearing the order of protection grants parenting time for the Respondent, the order must specify dates and times for the parenting time to take place and any other specific parameters or conditions that are appropriate in order for Respondent's parenting time to go forward. Id. The order of protection cannot order for parenting time to occur as "reasonable parenting time". Id. There must be specificity to the order regarding parenting time. Id.

Even while the OP or other protection orders are in place, the abuser can be ordered to pay support for minor child(ren) living with you, for your or your children's shelter or counseling services, and any other expenses that the court deems necessary. 750 Ill. Comp. Stat. Ann. 60/214(12), (16) (LexisNexis through P.A. 101-631). There is a common misconception in Illinois that parenting time is linked to child support. This is a misplaced idea. Whether you are exercising parenting time or not, your obligation to pay child support does not terminate based on how often you get to spend time with your child. Think of it this way, whether your child has parenting time with you or not, the child still needs food, medications, shelter, and clothing.

An Immediate "Stay Away" Order will require the respondent to refrain from both physical and non-physical contact with the petitioner. 750 Ill. Comp. Stat. Ann. 60/214(3) (LexisNexis through P.A. 101-631). This contact can be direct, indirect (including, but not limited to, telephone calls, mail, email, faxes, and written notes), or through third parties who may or may not know about the Order of Protection. The Stay Away Order can also prohibit contact with the minor child/children. If a "Stay Away" Order is not implemented, the Court can enter an order for no offensive contact.

If you have a house or rental property in common with the respondent, the court can order the respondent to leave the residence. 750 Ill. Comp. Stat. Ann. 60/214(2) (LexisNexis through P.A. 101-631). The petitioner can be granted exclusive possession of the residence. Id. The respondent will also be prohibited from entering or remaining anywhere while petitioner and/or protected person(s) is/are present. 750 Ill. Comp. Stat. Ann. 60/214(3) (LexisNexis through P.A. 101-631). This measure is to ensure that the abuser will not be present in the same home with the victim to increase the potential of repeat acts of violence.

Within the Order of Protection, the Court has the authority to prohibit the respondent from possessing firearms. 750 Ill. Comp. Stat. Ann. 60/214(14.5)(a) (LexisNexis through P.A. 101-631). Prohibition of firearms possession, pursuant to Section 60/214(14.5), requires that the respondent has received certain due process rights before the respondent is stripped of access to firearms. 750 Ill. Comp. Stat. Ann. 60/214(14.5)(a)(1)-(3) (LexisNexis through P.A. 101-631). The order of protection must have been issued after a hearing was conducted and the respondent received actual notice and the opportunity to participate. 750 Ill. Comp. Stat. Ann. 60/214(14.5)(a)(1) (LexisNexis through P.A. 101-631). The order of protection must also prohibit and restrain the Respondent from harassing, stalking, threatening and intimidating a partner or child, or engaging in conduct that would place the protected party in reasonable fear of bodily harm to the protected party or child. 750 Ill. Comp. Stat. Ann. 60/214(14.5)(a)(2) (LexisNexis through P.A. 101-631). Finally, the order of protection must include a finding that the respondent is a credible threat to the physical safety of the protected parties/party. 750 Ill. Comp. Stat. Ann. 60/214(14.5)(a)(3)(i) (LexisNexis through P.A. 101-631).

Once the above criteria have been met, then the Respondent will be ordered to turnover firearms and will be prohibited from possessing firearms as long as the order of protection remains in place. 750 Ill. Comp. Stat. Ann. 60/214(a) (LexisNexis through P.A. 101-631). The Court will issue a warrant for the firearms in possession of the Respondent and the firearms will be held in safekeeping for the duration of the order of protection. 750 Ill. Comp. Stat. Ann. 60/214(14.5)(a)(3)(i) (LexisNexis through P.A. 101-631). The Respondent's Firearm Owner's Identification Card ("FOID Card") will also be turned over to the local law enforcement agency. *Id.* The respondent cannot buy new firearms. Federal law further prohibits a person who is the subject of an order of protection from possessing a firearm or ammunition that has gone through interstate or foreign commerce. 18 U.S.C.S. § 922(g)(8) (LexisNexis through P.L. 116-145).

In reviewing the matter and deciding the remedies to outline in an EOP, the Judge must balance the hardships of the abuser if the court were to enter a certain remedy. 750 Ill. Comp. Stat. Ann. 60/214(d) (LexisNexis through P.A. 101-631). For example, what will be the hardship on the abuser if he/she was ordered to stay away from their employment and you both work for the same employer? If the abuser is ordered to pay support and to make financial contributions, interference with either parties' ability to work for an extended period of time could result in a hardship. The IDVA states that if the court finds that the balance of hardships does not support the granting of certain remedies, which may require such balancing, the court's findings shall so indicate and shall include a finding as to whether granting the remedy will result in hardship to respondent that would substantially outweigh the hardship to petitioner from denial of the remedy. *Id.* The findings shall be an official recording or in writing. *Id.*

A Stalking No Contact Order will order one or more of the following remedies: prohibit the respondent from threatening to commit or committing stalking; order the respondent not to have any contact with the petitioner or a third person specifically named by the court; prohibit the respondent from knowingly coming within, or knowingly remaining within a specified distance of the petitioner or the petitioner's residence, school, daycare, or place of employment, or any specified place frequented by the petitioner; however, the court may order the respondent to stay away from the respondent's own residence, school, or place of employment only if the respondent has been provided actual notice of the opportunity to appear and be heard on the petition; prohibit the respondent from possessing a Firearm Owners Identification Card, or possessing or buying firearms; and order other injunctive relief the court determines to be necessary to protect the petitioner or third party specifically named by the court. 750 Ill. Comp. Stat. Ann. 21/80(b)(1)-(5) (LexisNexis through P.A. 101-631).

Enforcement of the Order of Protection

Once an Order of Protection is entered, questions may arise regarding the enforcement of the order. What happens if the abuser violates the order? Violation of an order of protection can lead to criminal or civil sanctions. If the accuser is in violation, call the police or the sheriff. Even if you think it is a minor violation, call the police to help enforce the order and to make sure you are safe. An Order of Protection is only a piece of paper unless the petitioner enforces the order.

The Illinois Domestic Violence Act requires the police to take all reasonable steps in preventing further abuse. 750 Ill. Comp. Stat. Ann. 60/304(a) (LexisNexis through P.A. 101-631). If police are called, be sure to write down the name(s) of the responding officers and their badge number(s) just in case you may need to follow up at a later date. Insist that a police report is filed, even if no arrest is made. Have a copy of the order of protection ready to show the police. You should keep a copy of the order of protection at home, at your office, and on your person at all times. If the police do not arrest the Respondent or file a criminal complaint, there is still the option to file for civil contempt for a violation of the order. 750 Ill. Comp. Stat. Ann. 60/223(b) (LexisNexis through P.A. 101-631). It is a crime and contempt of court if the abuser knowingly violates the order in any way.

Once a respondent receives service of an Emergency Order of Protection (EOP), he/she must abide by it. Even if the order was obtained by false testimony, resist the urge to correct the wrong by confronting the accuser. Do not use third parties to communicate for you while the EOP or any order of protection is in place. Violating the EOP or any order of protection may result in prosecution for contempt of court or violation of an Order of Protection. The violation would be a Class A Misdemeanor, which is punishable by 364 days incarceration sentence and or up to $2,500.00 in fines. 720 Ill. Comp. Stat. Ann. 5/12-3.4(d) (LexisNexis through P.A. 101-631); 730 Ill. Comp. Stat. Ann. 5/5-4.5-55(a), (e) (LexisNexis through P.A. 101-631). The violation will likely result in a Plenary Order of Protection being granted or extended.

If an Order of Protection has been filed against you, you will need to prepare your defense. One method is to dispute the allegations with presentation of evidence to refute the claims against you. Be prepared to present witnesses that were present when the alleged incident(s) took place and find someone who could testify that no threatening conduct occurred.

Physical evidence, such as pictures, receipts or phone records or logs may also help contradict the plaintiff's assertion that there was threatening behavior. You may subpoena any records you deem necessary and compel the attendance of any necessary or material witnesses. Typically, a hearing for a Plenary Order of Protection will be assigned to a large court docket that can take a few hours to get through. Contact your witnesses prior to the court date and be sure that they will be present in court on the day of the hearing.

Bring any physical evidence with you to court. Some counties may prohibit camera phones from entering the building. If you have evidence on your camera phone, you may ask the clerk when checking in to grant an order allowing you to bring the cell phone into the building. If an order of protection is filed and there are impending divorce proceedings, then it is likely that your divorce matter and order of protection will be combined or heard by the same Judge.

Seeking help for victims of Domestic Violence is essential to the victim's survival and the process of regaining a sense of self. The longer abuse continues there is more potential long term physical and psychological damage the victim possibly will experience. There are many avenues for victims to seek help, and some are provided below:

- If you are hurt or in impending danger, please call **911** immediately and do what you can to get in a safer situation.
- Consider seeking an Order of Protection.
- Contact an attorney for support within the judicial system and to understand your legal rights in a Domestic Violence situation.
- Contact the **National Domestic Violence Hotline at 800-799-SAFE (7233) or 800-787-3224 (TDD**). The national hotline can guide you to local shelters in your community and/or to vital services.
- Seek local therapists and counselors to provide support through the healing process.

Help does exist for Victims who experience Domestic Violence; and an understanding of the options available is a key component to providing the victim with the specific help that they need.

I'M TOO OLD FOR THIS

If you are a person over 50 years old, contemplating divorce, you may be overwhelmed. You may be trying to care for your aging parents, while trying to care for your adult children, while trying to maintain access to your grandchildren, while trying to take care of yourself, your career, your physical health, your sanity!

All while getting divorced. You can't go through your divorce alone, and your family members may not be the experts you need. Consider calling on attorneys who practice family law exclusively, so that you can confidentially share your unique difficulties with attorneys who help people every day who may be in the same position you face now.

The Issue of Emotions

The issue of emotions is so important during the divorce process. As hard as it is, keeping your emotions under control is critical to making good decisions during your divorce. If you cannot perform this task on your own, seek help. Speaking with a therapist, joining a support group, or simply discussing your financial concerns with a good family law attorney can help you overcome these problems.

When family law attorneys work with clients, we seek to be the voice of reason amid the chaos. Having someone who can think rationally on your behalf can have a tremendous and positive impact on your outcome. Look at your divorce as a business transaction because this is really the business of your life!

You have questions wrapped in emotions: anger, fear, anxiety, helplessness, sorrow, guilt, hate, revenge. These emotions are toxic and will cost you both your money and your sanity. Far better to discuss the situation with a family law attorney who will guide you through the divorce process and help you conserve your mental energy and your finances.

You want to move on in life with your fair share. Sometimes, because of emotional issues, the smallest things become areas of contention. There have been cases where couples have spent much more money in legal fees fighting for an item, than the item could ever be worth. That does not make financial sense. Bring common sense back into the moment: when you consult with your attorney, be as clear as possible on your goals. Ask your family law attorney to develop and implement a plan that works for you.

The biggest mistake you can make is the one we hear most often: I'm willing to let my spouse have whatever, so that we can be done. This statement is made from emotion. Making decisions based on emotion will likely cost you money in the long run. Use your family law attorney to guide you to make choices that are sensible and calculated. Emotion does not serve you well here, but your family law attorney will.

Be smart from the start. Understand that you have options. Divorce is a foreign place that you could never have imagined on your wedding day, and you may not want this divorce, but it is happening and you must protect yourself moving forward. You can find answers to your questions and make it through this turbulent time with your mind and your money intact, if you arm yourself with the skills that are available. The scariest part is trying to figure out what to do. You are not aware of what you don't know. There are financial pitfalls. To be educated is to be empowered.

You want to have a clear mind to make wise decisions during this process. You don't need to take a crash course in law or finance, but don't settle without proper legal and financial advice. When you have a family law attorney with extensive financial experience, you will start thinking of your divorce as a business transaction and conduct yourself accordingly. Tangled money issues may call for a divorce financial planner. Much of the drama and trauma of divorce can be avoided if you know that you can be protected for tomorrow while being done with it today.

Your family law attorney can help you create a settlement that is fair, equitable and reasonable. With the specialized financial advice available at a family law firm, you can make the best decisions for the overall outcome. You have the choice to make wise decisions in your divorce from the start and avoid the mistake of making decisions based upon emotion. No matter what your finances look like, or especially if you have no knowledge of your finances, it is vitally important that you have a legal and financial advisor, so that you may gain a clear understanding of your situation.

A divorce can be devastating in more ways than one. Your living arrangements may be uprooted. Your spouse has changed his or her mind about beneficiaries of his or her life insurance. Property or investments are bought or sold. You may have a fear of losing your independence or alternatively your dependence. Sources of income may dry up. Tax law for you will change. There is a substantial increase or decrease in your estate. There is a mysterious change to a business. A charity wants your spouse's support. Your spouse is giving money away to scam artists or other friends or making questionable purchases on a limited income.

Get organized. Dealing with the emotions of divorce on top of everyday life can be an exhausting and draining experience. Knowing where to begin can be just as difficult because the entire process feels so overwhelming. But getting organized can be the first step toward empowerment. It is one of the best things you can do for yourself mentally, emotionally, and especially financially. It may be that you have no clue what income and expenses you have as a couple, because your spouse was the one who handled all the money during your marriage. Here is a word to the wise person you are becoming: going forward in life, you must have an understanding and a plan for where your money is and where it goes. Otherwise, you may always find yourself at the mercy of whoever is handling your money for you.

Taking Care of Yourself

Now is the time to seek advice on nutrition and exercise. In case you hadn't noticed, no one is going to take care of you, everyone is busy taking care of themselves, and your mental power depends upon your physical health.

Your best critical thinking and powerful decisions are dependent upon a healthy body. Each day, plan to be frustrated, upset, lonely, bored, angry, hurt, and emotionally overwrought. When you plan for these emotions to attack, have your weapons ready: healthy food and regular exercise.

Nutrition and exercise are perhaps the least costly, and most effective, weapons we have against the forces of fatigue and despair. You can empower your mind by improving the health of your body. Ask your family law attorney to recommend a nutritionist or life coach so that you can learn the art, and science, of caring for yourself. Develop a routine and implement your self-care as the foundation of your divorce strategy. The divorce process is exhausting and bewildering, and maybe more so for persons over 50, but you can't help yourself if you are not at the top of your game right now.

You may have spent the entirety of your marriage taking care of other people, sometimes at the expense of your health. Now that you are facing divorce, those old learned behaviors won't work anymore, and you need to learn new behaviors that will serve to advance your situation. Harness the knowledge and skill of experts who can help you survive your divorce at less cost to your mental and physical health. You have options, and you have the power to exercise those options.

Making the Tough Plans

If you are a person over 50 years of age, and contemplating divorce, you are in a unique position of doubt. Seek a family law attorney with a concentration in elder law, and conversant with Federal, State, local Court rules, and the rules governing trusts, Medicare, Powers of Attorney, Advance Directives, Living Wills, and all other aspects of your situation.

Plan now for your future. You can determine who will make decisions for you in the event you cannot – and you can help to avoid conflict between family members.

As we progress in years, in order to make a common-sense plan for your future, and set forth your personal plan for how you want to turn over legal control of your finances or healthcare, you must act while you are competent to sign on your own behalf. With the help of an elder law attorney, you can ensure that your wishes are met even if you can't make your preferences known. Start the discussion early, because it is more comfortable to talk about these topics when it is a hypothetical future issue rather than a current, looming one.

Your Powers of Attorney

As we age, we need to identify who will make decisions for us when we can't. When you create your Power of Attorney for Property, the document will give another individual the ability to handle your financial affairs. This power can be durable (starts immediately) or springing (starts upon the occurrence of a given event, such as a determination of incapacity by two physicians). The power can be very broad or limited in scope, depending on your wishes and needs. You can only name one Power of Attorney at a time, but you can name multiple successors.

When you create your Power of Attorney for Health Care, the document will give a designated agent the right to make medical decisions on your behalf. The power can also be durable but is generally only invoked if you are unable to make decisions for yourself. The POA for healthcare also has a section where you can direct that the person who has the power should be appointed guardian if one is to be appointed by the court, which helps to add further protection against someone taking advantage of you. There is also a shortened version of a living will included in the statutory POA, which allows you to state that you do not want to be kept alive artificially if it is determined by your physician that you will not recover.

Your Advance Directives

When you create your Living Will or Advance Directive, the document will explain whether or not you want to be kept on life support if you become terminally ill and will die shortly without life support, or fall into a persistent vegetative state. Having this in place eases the burden on loved ones and on the power of attorney should the decision to terminate life support become necessary. Including a HIPAA release, your attorney will distribute copies to regular healthcare providers, the hospital, and close family members.

You can see that it is not a simple matter to consider the end of your life or the end of your livelihood. No one else can do this task for you – only you can determine your healthcare choices for end of life, create powers of attorney so that major decisions can be made by a trusted person in the event your capacity to make decisions is diminished. Let your loved ones know and relieve some of the burden of making hard choices about medical care, and help avoid conflict between family members by turning over legal control of healthcare, so that your caregivers will understand how you would have chosen for yourself.

Beware of Scams

Divorce after 50 can be more difficult than divorce when we were younger. A younger person's financial mistakes can be corrected with a couple of decades of prudent money management, but after 50 we must guard our savings. Poverty in our old age may be caused by our own inattention.

Awareness is power! Stay informed to prevent fraud, scams, and financial problems. We are living longer, and the number of over-50 divorces is rising. Have you been tempted by scams and frauds, or do you know someone who has? Make sure you know what is going on, especially now that we are conducting not only our business online but also our social gathering online. There are millions of cases of financial abuse toward seniors every year. The financial loss is enormous, but only a small percentage of cases are reported. Seniors often feel guilt or shame when they have been taken advantage of.

There are so many people on the internet, on the phone or even at your doorstep trying to scam or fraud you out of your money. Your divorce is a public record, available to anyone who cares to look. While you are going through your divorce, you are at your most vulnerable, and if you are over 50 you may be more trusting of others.

What is a scam? You are a generous person, and you love the idea of helping people. So, when you get a call from such places as a children's foundation, asking for donations, you pull out your credit card and give. You would give the shirt off your back if someone asked for it, even though you don't have much yourself. You are the perfect target for a scammer. Many seniors don't know when they're being deceived, and if there is no one watching out for them, it can result in huge losses. Someone calls and impersonates a family member, tells the senior that they are in trouble and need some money. The scammers that target seniors do their research; they know who is divorcing, living alone, and they take advantage. Or the senior gets mail in their mailbox; they are excited to see something coming for them. Opening the mail, it says that they have won a prize, all they need to do is send a check to cover this and that. They don't find out until later that their money is lost and they've been scammed.

Living alone makes us more vulnerable to the con artist. The home improvement salesman, who asks for money up front but does not complete the job, takes the senior for a ride. Repair fraud is very common, with scammers showing up at your door saying your roof needs repair and they need the money up front. The fake charity, using a natural disaster to make phone calls to cheat the elderly. The fake grandchild who calls saying they have been in an accident and they need money sent via wire, right away. The email with the link purporting to be a cash payment, just waiting for you to click on it, putting all of their personal information at risk. Many seniors are ashamed of their misplaced trust and don't report the scam.

Trust your intuition. If something seems too good to be true, it is. Practice protection skills: say you will call them back. Check out their story. Do not be fooled by a person who knows details about your life, because this is just a way of getting more information and money out of you.

Divorce after 50 can make a person lonely and eager for human contact. But be suspicious of phone calls from people wanting your banking information. The person may say they are from an official agency but check it out. If they are really calling from your bank, why do they need you to tell them your banking information?

When you are going through a divorce, it is harder to make impartial decisions. A divorce brings with it a certain sort of grief. You need better business sense at this time, because you make poor decisions when you are grieving.

Fraud Warning: legitimate lotteries and sweepstakes will never ask you to wire money. If you have a doubt about whether you should send money, check with the Better Business Bureau. The BBB is a good place to start any time you begin a financial relationship with a company.

Some seniors have fallen for the bereavement scam. Just a few days after a loved one's death, the senior is contacted. The caller says that the lost loved one owes money and they have to pay up to have things corrected. To protect yourself from this scam, simply tell the caller you will call them back after you verify. Then hang up. You can call the BBB. You can call the police. Both the BBB and the police are interested in scammers out there in the community.

Some seniors have fallen for the medical scam. Legitimate medical groups will never call asking for your medical information, or social security number. If someone calls saying they will help you with your meds, tell them you will call back after you verify. Then hang up. Check with the BBB, or the police.

Making a decision, especially a financial one, is hard enough when you are at your best. But when you are going through a divorce, you may be at your worst. No legitimate organization will ever call and need you to make a financial decision right away. You will never be forced by a legitimate company to make a decision on the phone, right now. You may be interested in investing in the company, but you need to take the time to read their information before doing so. If you think you may have been scammed, call the police. Maybe you won't get your money back, but you can surely help it from happening again. Are you receiving two telemarketing calls each day, and at least one scam-type letter or email? Be sure to share your experience with others in your neighborhood who may not be as savvy as you are.

The Love Scam

Divorce after 50 often involves people who have been married all of their adult lives. When their spouse is gone, it is like a part of them is gone too. And financial decisions, even seemingly small ones, are hard to make alone when you have been making them together for decades. There are scammers out there who pretend to be love advisors, and some seniors have turned to them, and been burned by them. These love advisors just take your money and run. In order to get your money, they will urge you to act right now, do not wait because you will miss out, and you will be alone and lonely. They can't give you any details – because they don't have any. They just want to get your credit card number and run. They will say that this is a once-in-a-lifetime opportunity.

They will say that this investment is only available through them and no one else. You can trap the scammer by asking, how do you earn your money? How many clients do you have right now? Are you registered with the Better Business Bureau? Would it be OK for me to talk to my personal advisor about this first, before I make a decision? Does your company have any complaints against it? Do not be afraid to ask questions. It is your money to do with as you wish. If you have an intuition that someone is trying to scam or defraud you, speak up. Do not be as willing to trust those who claim to be a financial expert, they might not be looking out for your best interests.

Educate yourself.

Have you ever opened an email from someone who is looking to help you with viruses on your computer? All you need to do is enter your credit card number online, pay them some money, and you will be protected against viruses that are attacking your computer. By now you are suspicious that someone has collected your email address and has sent you a scamming message to steal your money.

Have you ever received an email that looks and sounds like it is from your friend or family member, but the person is saying they need help because their daughter is very ill and needs surgery, and they have lots of expenses that they cannot afford? Don't send money through emails. The message was not from your friend or family member, it was from a thief. Once you have become internet/phone/mail savvy, talk to your local police community resource person, and offer to share your experience.

Your Money

As you make your plans for divorce, gather any documents you think might be useful to your attorney. You will need some resources to start over after your divorce, so pre-planning is essential.

First off, start thinking of your divorce as a business transaction, and conduct yourself accordingly. To get the best results, tell your attorney you want to get educated, get organized and become a proactive partner with the members of your divorce team. Consider choosing a divorce team that works with a divorce financial planner, to analyze and work out the money issues and potentially save you significant amounts of money. Your attorney can also eliminate the need for much of the drama and trauma of divorce, by potentially brokering an agreement on divorce financial issues.

If you want to be done with your divorce today, but also be protected for tomorrow, especially if you have a contentious divorce ahead of you, your divorce team will help you with both legal and financial advice.

Gather necessary data to assist in the documenting process. Be as clear as possible on your goals. Prepare for a good settlement by gathering every possible financial statement or document pertaining to you and your spouse's financial life, whether held individually or jointly. You will aid your divorce team in identifying assets, such as cash and financial accounts; bank statements for checking, savings, and money market accounts; investment statements, such as stocks and stock options, bonds, mutual funds, annuities, exchange traded funds; life insurance policies, trust funds; real estate property records, whether residential or commercial properties, timeshares, or land, mortgage applications and home equity line of credit (HELOC) applications, refinance documents, and property tax records; tax returns, pay stubs, retirement account statements, IRA plans, 401(k) plans, 26 U.S.C.S. § 401 et al (LexisNexis through Pub. L. 116-145), 403(b) plans, pension plans, profit sharing plans, government pension plans, and social security statements.

Maybe you have no idea what your spouse's gross monthly income from all sources is, including salary, wages, bonus, commissions, fees, tips, self-employment, small business, independent contracting, rental income, overtime, severance pay, interest and dividends, income from royalties, capital gains, disability benefits, or recurring income from pensions or retirement plans. Maybe your spouse has voluntarily left their employment, in order to artificially reduce their income. An imputed amount may be applied, regardless of whether the person is actually working or being paid any money. Once your attorney has this information, they can help you to move forward, you will feel empowered to craft the savvy settlement that works best for you.

Understanding where you are financially can help ease some of the financial strain and pain of divorce, and help you create a brighter future. Much of what we fear in life comes from the unknown. Getting to know your money and grasping the full financial picture can ease some of that fear as you step into your new reality. Armed with an accurate accounting of your financials, combined with your attorney's assessment of your particular situation, you will gain greater options in the process. In your divorce, property division is contingent upon an accurate calculation of all assets and debts, and your eligibility for spousal support (also known as alimony or maintenance) is also contingent upon this calculation. The manner in which the marital assets are distributed is flexible, and this is where you and your attorney work together to craft the settlement that works best for you.

Figuring out this information is crucial if you came into the marriage with assets of your own and have kept them titled solely in your name. If you commingled (shared or combined) those separate assets during the marriage, they may no longer be considered separate assets and may be split between you and your spouse as marital assets. Generally, separate assets are considered apart from marital property (those things acquired while married). However, the value that those separate assets have grown into during the marriage may be considered marital property and may be divided accordingly. You will benefit from your divorce attorney's experience here, as adding the power of a divorce legal team may dramatically increase your financial outcome. What about growth or appreciation of separate property during your marriage? This can be a huge issue in divorce.

Do you suspect that you will need to uncover hidden assets? Divorce can unfortunately bring out the worst in people. Mistrust and thoughts of hidden or undisclosed assets, which may or may not exist, can drive a wedge between spouses even deeper. If you suspect hidden assets, talk to your attorney about working with a forensic accountant to determine if there are indeed hidden assets and where they can be uncovered. Assets may be hidden in a variety of ways: your spouse may deny the asset ever existed, or no longer exists; assets may have been transferred to a family member or business partner; or false debt may be created to bring down the value of an asset. You can help your attorney by supplying as many requested documents as possible, especially tax returns, both personal and business.

Having a business in the mix can certainly complicate matters. What to do with it, how to value it, and what may be hidden in it, are all questions to be considered. You may have the option of keeping and operating the business. You may have the option of continuing to jointly own and run the business. You may have the option of selling the business. To maximize the division of business assets in divorce, you must have the emotional maturity to look past what is happening in your personal life and focus on getting the best future plan in place.

Your Retirement Funds

When it comes to the issue of evaluating and splitting retirement plans during a divorce, understand that these are complicated and fraught with many issues. Retirement plans have many complexities and many variations. The vast array of plans can be confusing because of the immense differences from company to company with each setting their own rules, though all qualified plans are subject to ERISA laws and the Internal Revenue Code.

This is a time-consuming area of divorce analysis, but retirement data is critical to getting your fair share in divorce. Next to the marital residence, the retirement funds may be the largest asset to be divided.

Stock Options

Though stock options may or not be qualified funds, they fall under employee benefits. Stock options are another complex asset that must be evaluated by your attorney, who will look at such factors as whether or not the options have vested and do they currently have any value. Even if they are worthless at the moment, that doesn't mean they won't have value in the future. Stock options can change in potential value rapidly and their value can fluctuate daily. Dividing this asset in divorce can be challenging.

As you can see, retirement benefit analysis is complex and should not be taken lightly. Remember that challenges, while unwelcome and uncomfortable, ultimately can lead us to becoming more of whom we really are, if we look beneath the problems for the gifts that lie within. You have strength within you that you may never have imagined, and you can create an awesome new life, if you choose to, no matter the obstacles ahead.

Elder Planning

What does elder law mean?

Elder law encompasses legal concerns that become important as we age, or someone we care for ages. An attorney with a concentration in elder law will assist with decisions and prepare the legal documents that should be in place, as well as decisions regarding financial and health care as health declines.

The landscape of elder law is changing because our population is aging. More and more seniors are planning for a longer and longer future period of unemployment and increasing disability. Litigation is becoming more prevalent due to older adults and their families being more educated and current with trends and policies. As more older adults turn to Medicaid to meet the cost of long-term care, families are requesting assistance from attorneys on denied applications, penalty periods, and spend-down requirements. The elder law attorney provides help in the Medicaid appeal process and advocates for long-term care residents.

As our family members get older, their aging issues are important not only to them but to their employers, landlords, mortgage holders, physicians, and any other people who come into contact with the senior person.

The most important part of elder care is making decisions at a time when you can, for a future version of you. This includes signing documents to appoint others to act on your behalf, if you can't.

Your elder law attorney can help you with Medicaid eligibility, caregivers or nursing homes, disagreements with your spouse, guardianship, special needs planning and Social Security disability, and tax planning for high-net-worth or Medicaid asset protection.

In addition to having a Will or a Living Trust to manage or distribute assets when you die, seniors need to designate an "agent" to make health and other decisions for them, if they no longer can. These legal directives authorize the agent to carry out the senior's healthcare and financial management wishes.

Medicaid for community, home-based services, and long-term care is incredibly complicated, and the rules are often obscure. Your elder law attorney knows what the various programs are, what they cover, where you should go to apply and to appeal, and why or why not you might be eligible. The attorney can offer Medicaid tips on asset valuation, and has a working knowledge of the Department of Healthcare and Family Services Office of the Inspector General's process of reviewing long-term care Medicaid applications and the handling of appeals. Your attorney represents elderly clients with varying degrees of capacity, as well as clients who have been abused or exploited and clients involved in nursing home litigation.

Why plan now? When planning for your old age, the law enables you to put documents in place now, to ensure your intentions and plans are carried out later. What you decide while healthy and well will be honored even if you no longer have your health or wits about you.

It is much easier and cost-effective to empower your loved ones or trusted advisors to make decisions if you no longer can, than to hope things will work out. If the proper documents are not in place, and you can't manage on your own, a court proceeding for guardianship may be needed so someone can take charge of your affairs. The proceeding and the cost of the guardianship are expensive and it's much better to plan ahead.

Planning puts you in the driver's seat. With a plan in place, you can specify what types of medical treatment you do or don't want, who will help you with banking and financial matters, how your assets will pass at your death, and how you'll pay for health care and housing if you need it.

Some hospitals may refuse to honor health care decisions if they conflict with hospital policies. This can happen if the hospital has some religious affiliation that mandates an end of life course of action. Hospitals are obligated to inform you of these restrictive policies before you are admitted, so that you can make an informed decision about your personal health care choices.

Your Living Will, prepared by your attorney and signed by you, covers your end-of-life health decisions only. By way of contrast, an Advance Directive covers any type of treatment. Your Living Will includes your intentions to withdraw or withhold life-prolonging measures. The Advance Directive is broader because it covers all medical conditions and treatments, not just end-of-life measures.

A Living Will "speaks for itself" and its terms will be used to clarify or interpret your medical intentions. With an Advance Directive, your agent "speaks for you" to express your medical intentions. It's best to sign both a Living Will and an Advance Directive, to ensure that your doctors can act as you want them to.

Why should you have an attorney prepare your Powers of Attorney? A series of formalities must be followed in order for the document to be legally valid in the state where you live. These formalities pertain to content, signatures of the principal and agent, notarization and witness requirements. An attorney will make sure it's done right. Additionally, these documents are complicated. While many states have their own statutory forms available online, they are not simple to complete. Some forms have special parts that require additional formalities. Increasingly, banks and other financial institutions only honor a Power of Attorney that is witnessed before its bank officers or executed on a bank-authorized form. These extra procedures are added to protect the bank from liability for honoring a Power of Attorney that was obtained by fraud or no longer valid. Details are important when it comes to a Power of Attorney, and your attorney will ensure that the details are correct.

Health Care Planning for Seniors

Seniors may receive benefits under Social security, Medicare and/or Medicaid and private health care or long-term care insurance policies. Getting the care and coverage you need as you age can be expensive and complicated.

Medicare is health insurance for individuals age sixty-five and over who are entitled to Social Security retirement benefits. Older Americans generally receive Social Security benefits accrued through their own work life, the working life of a spouse or because of disability.

When Medicare was enacted in 1965, the thinking was that working people would "pay in" to Medicare during their earning years, so that illness wouldn't ravage their savings in their later years. And yet now, more than fifty-five years after its enactment, Medicare is not the cure-all many had hoped. Why? Because it doesn't cover the cost of long-term chronic care, which those facing diseases such as Parkinson's, Alzheimer's and dementia will need. Further, it does not cover all pharmaceuticals you may need.

That's where Medicaid may come in. Medicaid provides benefits for home health care, nursing homes and other types of health expenses that are not covered by Medicare. It also provides insurance coverage for those with insufficient resources. Medicaid is a federal government program, funded by you, through your taxes.

Medicaid is administered on the state level, and each state has its own rules as to eligibility and benefits, within the federal mandate. Your elder law attorney can help you learn the benefits available to you.

Paying for Health Care

For many seniors, paying for healthcare entails a patchwork of programs with Medicare as the core coverage. For medical care not covered by Medicare, you may be looking to your own private insurance, a Medigap insurance policy, long-term care insurance and/or Medicaid, for coverage. For those under age sixty-five who are not yet eligible for Medicare, private insurance plans can be obtained through marketplaces. The marketplaces are either run by specific states or the federal government and are intended to offer greater access to health care coverage to those who need it. Even armed with information about emergency services, hospitalization and prescription drugs, the senior will still have important questions about the cost of health care plans and, ultimately, whether they can afford to pay the premiums and deductibles on such policies.

Complex rules apply to Medicare and Medicaid. Your elder law attorney can help you decipher how government regulations and entitlements meet the real world. Plus, each state has its own way of administering these programs on a local level, within federal guidelines. Before you even enroll in Medicare, get informed and make sure you have an understanding of the consequences of the plan you accept.

Medicare

Medicare is a federally sponsored program that provides primary health insurance for Americans age sixty-five and older, and for people younger than sixty-five who have certain disabilities and illnesses, for example Lou Gehrig's Disease (ALS) and kidney failure requiring either dialysis or a kidney transplant. *What's Medicare?*, MEDICARE.GOV, https://www.medicare.gov/what-medicare-covers/your-medicare-coverage-choices/whats-medicare (last visited Jul. 7, 2020) With respect to other disabilities for which Social Security disability benefits are received, recipients are enrolled in Medicare after qualifying for the Social Security disability. Social Security disability benefits are based on Social Security taxes paid on earnings.

Enrollment in Medicare is fairly simple for those nearing age sixty-five. Enrollment is optional and is not necessary for a person age sixty-five whose employer-sponsored health insurance is still in effect. Maintaining employer coverage of health insurance, if possible, on your own or through a spouse's employer, may be the first and most cost-effective way of paying for health care.

If you're age sixty-five or older and you're receiving Social Security benefits, you should be signed up automatically for original Medicare (Parts A and B) and should receive your Medicare card three months before your sixty-fifth birthday. If you're not receiving Social Security benefits, you must enroll in Medicare through the Social Security Administration website.

Supplemental Security Income (SSI) benefits are not the same as Social Security benefits. SSI benefits are paid to disabled persons who have limited income and resources. *Supplemental Social Security Income (SSI) Benefits*, SOCIAL SECURITY, https://www.ssa.gov/benefits/ssi/ (last visited July 7, 2020). Recipients of SSI benefits are eligible for Medicaid in most states.

What is covered by Medicare? Medicare has four parts. Parts A and B are the most commonly known. Part A is hospital services. 42 U.S.C.S. §1395c (current through P.L. 116-145). Under Medicare, there is coverage for up to ninety days for each benefit period, with a sixty-day lifetime reserve. 42 U.S.C.S. §1395d(a)(1) (current through P. 116-145). Part B is medical. Once annual deductibles are met, Medicare generally pays 80% of the approved amounts for covered services such as doctor's visits and outpatient treatments, and you will pay 20%. 42 U.S.C.S. § 1395l(a)(1) (current through P.L. 116-145). Part C is private supplemental insurance, which can include Medicare Advantage. Approved providers offer supplemental coverage for items or expenses that are not covered by Parts A or B, for an additional monthly fee. You must be enrolled in Parts A and B to participate in Part C. Part D is prescription drug coverage. 42 U.S.C.S. § 1395w-101(a) (current through P.L. 116-145). You must voluntarily opt in to Part D and pay a monthly premium to do so. 42 U.S.C.S. § 1395w-101(a)(1) (current through P.L. 116-145). Anyone enrolled in Parts A and B is eligible for Part D coverage. 42 U.S.C.S. § 1395-101w(a)(3)(A) (current through P.L. 116-145).

There are many health care expenses not covered by Medicare, for example co-pays, deductibles, and premiums for Parts A through D, and hospital stays longer than one hundred days per "spell of illness" in a skilled nursing facility. As a result, people who need or expect to need more insurance usually supplement Medicare benefits. This can be done by purchasing an additional Medigap policy to cover the additional out-of-pocket costs, using benefits under a long-term care insurance policy, using personal savings, or applying for Medicaid. If you have additional health insurance coverage from an employer or elsewhere, Medicare is normally the secondary payer after the private health insurance pays.

Medigap Insurance

Medigap insurance is Medicare supplemental insurance sold by private insurance companies to help pay for medical costs that are not covered by Medicare Parts A and B. *What's Medicare Supplement Insurance (Medigap)?*, MEDICARE.GOV, https://www.medicare.gov/supplements-other-insurance/whats-medicare-supplement-insurance-medigap (last visited Jul. 7, 2020). You must be enrolled in Medicare Parts A and B to purchase a Medigap policy. *Id.* Things not covered by Parts A and B include deductibles, co-pays, coinsurance and other extensions of Medicare coverage. *Id.* If you are enrolled in Medicare Advantage (Part C), you should plan to either stay with Part C or switch to Medigap because Medigap will not pay out to Part C participants. *Id.* Medigap insurance plans vary by the coverage they offer, the state where you live, and the insurance company that offers the coverage. In evaluating Medigap coverage, the most important items to look at are those that matter to you most. It may sound obvious, but as you go through these websites and examine what you need, it can be confusing. If you are on several expensive medications, you'll want the plan that provides the most coverage. If you require frequent physical therapy, you'll want to be sure that additional coverage is available. While Medigap policies vary greatly in cost and coverage, nursing home care is only provided as a limited and short-term supplement to Medicare, and NOT on a long-term basis. You should contact an insurance broker servicing these plans to understand the complexities and nuances.

Medicaid

Medicaid was designed to provide health care benefits for low-income and disabled persons. *Medicaid*, MEDICAID.GOV, https://www.medicaid.gov/medicaid/index.html (last visited Jul. 7, 2020). It increasingly provides benefits to seniors who are unable to afford certain health coverage not provided by Medicare. *Id.*

Medicaid covers a vast range of medical services, including long-term nursing home and/or home health aide care. *Benefits*, MEDICAID.GOV, https://www.medicaid.gov/medicaid/benefits/index.html (last visited Jul. 7, 2020). Medicaid is jointly funded by the state and federal governments and administered separately by each state. The key to your Medicaid benefits depends on the eligibility requirements and benefits available under your state's program. *Medicaid*, MEDICAID.GOV, https://www.medicaid.gov/medicaid/index.html (last visited Jul. 7, 2020).

If elderly or disabled persons are receiving Medicare, they can also receive Medicaid (if they qualify) and Medicaid may pay for Medicare premiums, deductibles, co-pays and other services not covered by Medicare. *Get Help Paying Costs - Medicaid*, MEDICARE.GOV, https://www.medicare.gov/your-medicare-costs/get-help-paying-costs/medicaid (last visited Jul. 7, 2020). If those receiving Medicaid have private insurance through an employer, spouse or parent, Medicaid will be billed as secondary insurance. Unlike Medicare, Medicaid DOES cover a portion of the cost of long-term custodial care in a nursing facility and long-term home health care.

To be eligible for Medicaid, you must be a resident of the state in which you apply for Medicaid benefits. Since Medicaid is a program for low-income persons, your assets and income must not exceed certain prescribed amounts, which vary by state, to be eligible. Generally, your monthly income must be below a specified dollar amount, or, in some states, you can "spend down" your monthly income by paying for expenses incurred to meet the income level. *Id.* There are different income requirements for applicants living in the community, at home with or without a caregiver, as opposed to applicants living in a nursing home. Those receiving care at home in the community generally may retain more of their income than those who reside in a nursing home. However, all income levels for eligibility are extremely low.

In addition to a very low-income level, an applicant must also have "resources and assets" below a certain level to be eligible to receive Medicaid. A person's "resources and assets" include all of their property, with certain exceptions. For example, the following items of property are considered exempt and not counted as an applicant's available resources: one home with a limited amount of equity determined by the state of residence, one car, personal effects, clothing, household furniture and appliances, and a burial plot and a prepaid funeral arrangement. To qualify for a homestead exemption, the Medicaid applicant must intend to return to the home to live. *Medicaid Treatment of the Home: Determining Eligibility and Repayment for Long-Term Care*, U.S. DEPT OF HEALTH AND HUMAN SERVICES, (Apr. 1, 2005), https://aspe.hhs.gov/basic-report/medicaid-treatment-home-determining-eligibility-and-repayment-long-term-care. Otherwise, the applicant's spouse must reside in the home. State equity caps range from $500,000 to $800,000 or even $1 million in some states.

In cases where an applicant has resources but a prolonged illness or nursing home stay is anticipated, consider planning for Medicaid in advance. Talk to your elder law attorney about transferring assets to the applicant's family members or into a trust that will benefit them. Special rules apply to these transfers, including penalties and "look-back" periods.

Medicaid has a five-year time period during which it can "look back" to determine if assets should be counted for eligibility purposes. This comes into play for applicants who need nursing home care. Under the look-back rule, Medicaid will review financial records to see if you transferred assets to qualify.

Certain assets do not count as being "transferred" and are known as exempt transfers for purposes of the look-back rule. These include transfers made to a spouse, a child under the age of twenty-one, a disabled child regardless of age, a child who has served as the applicant's caretaker and who has lived in the home for two years prior to the transfer, or a sibling with an equity interest in the home.

If the applicant and a sibling jointly inherit a home that was owned by their parents and lived in the home during the one-year period prior to the transfer, it will be exempt. Transfers which are gifts will cause a period of ineligibility. But if the applicant transfers property and receives something in return, it is considered a transfer for value and not a gift. In short, if you give away your assets, you may not be eligible for Medicaid benefits until the penalty period ends. There is a five-year look-back period for assets you give away if you need nursing home care. It does not apply if you need what's known as "community care" which is care at home or in a daycare center.

If you seek Medicaid benefits for home health care as opposed to nursing home care, you'd be subject to what is known as "community care" eligibility requirements. This term refers to the person's ability to live as a member of the community in a private residence, not a nursing home.

Medicaid Payback Provisions

When a person who has received Medicaid dies, and has assets, special rules may require that those assets be used to repay benefits received. These rules depend on how the Medicaid benefits are offered in your state and each state has its own rules on payback. Be sure to ask your elder law attorney whether any payback provisions in your state will apply.

Medicaid Planning with Trusts

Increasingly, people consider establishing Medicaid trusts so that their assets won't count as "resources" when they apply for Medicaid. These trusts can go by various names such as "asset protection trusts" or "income-only trusts" but the primary goal is to preserve assets for your family if there comes a time when you need to enter a nursing home. With careful planning, it is possible to receive Medicaid benefits and make sure your family savings are not wiped out.

Keep in mind that if you transfer assets to an irrevocable trust more than five years before applying for Medicaid, the amounts you transferred will not affect your eligibility. But if you need benefits during the look-back period, you may want to delay your Medicaid application. Why? Because the assets you transferred out will cause a period of ineligibility. The value of the assets transferred, and the years remaining in the look-back period, get factored in to determine the period of ineligibility. Sometimes it makes sense to pay out of pocket and wait to apply for Medicaid until the five-year look-back period comes to an end. Once the five-year look-back is over, the assets transferred do not create a period of ineligibility.

Medicaid planning to preserve family assets requires an elder law attorney with a concentration in this type of planning. The rules are complex and property must be transferred out of your name, often at a time when you may not know if you'll need Medicaid.

Long–Term Care Insurance

Long –Term Care (LTC) insurance is a popular option for financing long-term care if you have money available to purchase the benefits. The premiums often increase as you age, and often they do not end; it is expensive to get a fully paid policy (as you might with life insurance) in today's marketplace.

Policy provisions must be carefully read and understood because they vary from state to state. LTC insurance policies generally provide coverage for all levels of nursing home care, assisted living, home care (including in-home personal care), adult daycare, respite care, hospice care and Alzheimer's disease/dementia services and facilities. Generally, these services are for health, personal or custodial care over long periods of time, and are either not covered or only partially covered by private health insurance, Medicare and Medicaid.

Coverage under LTC policies typically start when a person is not sick but needs assistance with one or more "activities of daily living" such as dressing, bathing, eating, personal hygiene, toileting, walking and physical mobility. The cost of LTC insurance is determined by the person's age, health, what daily benefit amount will be paid, and the length of time benefits will be paid. LTC policies are often a good option in conjunction with Medicaid planning. Because of the five-year look-back rule, it is often tough to plan that far in advance. Good planning with your elder law attorney is wise. Many of these policies are now incorporated with life insurance benefits.

Elderly Exploitation

Unfortunately, the exploitation of older adults is rampant in today's society. Various local, state, and federal programs aim at preventing and stopping the exploitation of the elderly. Your elder law attorney knows what resources are available to assist in the representation of the aging community, as well as what information is necessary to provide to the family.

The elder law attorney uses the Powers of Attorney Act to avoid and stop financial exploitation. The attorney is sensitive to the potential for financial abuse when drawing up your Powers of Attorney. Additionally, the elder law attorney knows how to use sections of the Powers of Attorney Act to remove an agent that is not acting in the principal's best interests. The attorney knows how to recognize common scams to identify financial exploitation, conduct discovery, and file pleadings to restrain converted assets in Probate Court. The attorney can guide the client when litigating the removal of a trustee who is self-dealing or otherwise not fulfilling their fiduciary duties to the family.

The elder law attorney works with Adult Protective Services and Long-Term Care Ombudsman Programs to implement the range of services offered by these programs that support the rights and benefits of vulnerable older people and persons with disabilities in community and institutional settings. Your attorney knows what these programs do, who they serve, and how they can assist your exploited or abused loved one.

The Family Sandwich and the Aging Parents

Many of an attorney's clients have aging parents. The clients have similar problems and worries about finances, as well as deciding where and how to best care for aging loved ones. Clients wonder what their parents' legal rights are, especially to refuse help. Adult children are overwhelmed with the extensive amount of information on the internet, from legal sites to caregiver sites to questions about how to pay for care. The family sandwich is made of layers of people, from the very young to the very old, and although everyone understands it is best to plan ahead to avoid some of the worst outcomes, no one needs more stress and it is good to know that sound legal decisions can also be made in crisis situations.

It is hard for a person who has siblings and aging loved ones to focus on the family disputes and family conflicts which are the cause of much heartache and pain. The path to peace starts with having the essential conversations with your aging loved ones and your family members. One of the biggest mistakes we adult children make with aging parents is the failure to talk about finances. We don't like to talk about subjects that are uncomfortable. Our parents feel that it's too private, or it's not polite to talk about money.

No one likes the thought of losing independence. But we must prepare for new challenges. We have to address the issue of how our aging parents are going to manage.

Take a look at your loved one's finances and see if there are irregularities or inconsistencies. Talk with family members and determine if your parent is starting to slip in their financial judgment. This can be difficult if your parent does not want to talk about money. They may fear that someone may take advantage of them if they reveal what they have. They may be embarrassed at having so little left. They may feel it's impolite for you to ask. They may fear that you will take their independence from them. No matter the reason behind the resistance, it is important to recognize that finances can be quite an emotional subject.

It does happen that a parent will not give any information, will not sign a Power of Attorney, will not help with estate planning, or will not see a doctor to be evaluated. No one can move forward to protect that parent. The only option is to use the courts. When a parent has failed to appoint anyone as an agent to serve as power of attorney, and then that parent loses their ability to understand or sign a document, you are left with no choice. The court will need to hear evidence and make a decision as to whether a guardianship or conservatorship is needed.

Aging can take a toll on anyone's ability to manage finances safely. Because we have such a widespread problem of elder financial abuse, we all need to be aware that our aging loved ones are at risk. Every family needs to discuss the real possibility that at some time an aging loved one may lose the capacity to make independent financial decisions.

Your aging parent will probably need your help at some point down the road, and you need to talk about it and plan for it. Most adult children whose parents are not wealthy harbor a secret or emerging fear that they are going to have to come up with money every month for their parents. It is a daunting thought, since so many people are struggling with the current recession, have their own financial recovery to do, and are planning for their own retirement.

Most people who have not planned ahead have a belief that if they are older and do not have much money, the government will take care of them. That is only partly true. Benefits offered by the government are very limited and do not cover everything elders need. One of the biggest myths is that Medicare will pay for long-term care at home. It does not pay for care at home, especially the kind of care most aging people need to remain in their homes – help with shopping, bathing, meal preparation, and dressing. It is not skilled nursing, and it is not covered by Medicare.

Assisted living facilities are an option for long-term care for some, but not suitable for everyone. The annual cost of basic assisted living services is quite high. If your loved one needs nursing home care, and is not eligible for Medicaid, a semi-private room in a nursing home can cost more than your annual salary.

Given the high cost of long-term care, it is not surprising that many families have to help their aging loved ones. People are living long enough to run out of money, and this creates a financial burden few have anticipated. The best protection you have if you are concerned that your parents may not have enough to live on as they age is to plan ahead while they are still able to manage on their own for their financial future. Good planning can help your aging parents access every available public benefit for which they may be eligible. If they can qualify for Medicaid, subsidized housing, Veterans' Aid, or any other community resource, they will have a secure future.

Many parents are without the means to provide for themselves, since they live longer than they expected to live. In some cases, the adult children may hire home care workers, either through an agency or directly, and the children become responsible to make sure that the elder is safe and well cared for. Many home care workers are kind, dedicated people who enjoy taking care of elders. They enable your loved one to stay at home, where most elders prefer to be, and to manage the activities of daily living safely. However, not all are honest. A home setting is unsupervised, and it can be very tempting for a dishonest person to take advantage of the elder. Your elder is at risk for financial and other abuse simply because of age, and particularly because of decreased mental ability.

Assisted Living Facilities provide a place for elders to live independently in community settings with some personal care available. Most provide all meals, social activities and services, transportation, and assistance managing the activities of daily living. Typically, an assisted living facility is regulated and licensed by the state and is built on a social model rather than a medical model. Assisted living is not a medical facility with skilled nursing care. Rather, it is a community that strives for a home-like atmosphere.

A nursing home, on the other hand, is licensed by the state to deliver health care. Treatment may include administration of injections, medication, assessment, wound care, administration of oxygen, and delivery of various kinds of therapy.

Where an elder should move when living at home is no longer appropriate or safe is a serious decision. If given a choice, most elders would choose a pretty, well-appointed assisted living facility before a nursing home. An assisted living facility is simply more appealing for many who can manage without skilled nursing care and who can afford the cost. Assisted living facilities can be very expensive, and most are paid for from the elder's own resources, not any kind of insurance.

"Promise you will never put me in a nursing home"

Nursing homes are perceived as places for decrepit people to go to wait to die. But nursing homes provide a level of skilled care that assisted living cannot provide. We may promise that we will never put a parent in a nursing home, thinking that nursing homes must be terrible. We may never think far enough ahead to foresee our parents' health risks. Half of the people who live in nursing homes are age eighty-five or older. Dementia is one of the most common reasons a person needs to live in a nursing home.

People live in nursing homes because their physical or mental condition warrants it or because they have become impoverished by the cost of care at home. Another important factor which causes some people to move into nursing homes is social isolation and lack of family support. While going to a nursing home is no one's first choice, it may become necessary for your loved one at some time.

If you have a loved one in a nursing home, you will need to be the safety police to ensure proper care. You can best prepare for the experience by planning ahead, visiting often, and paying attention to what care your loved one needs and receives. Anyone in a nursing home needs an advocate.

Your elder law attorney can help your family decide which is best at this time: stay-at-home care, assisted living, or nursing home, and also how to plan ahead so that you are ready when needs change.

Nursing Homes and Coronavirus

We know that elders are at higher risk for getting coronavirus. Why? Because many elders have chronic medical conditions, such as heart disease, diabetes, kidney disease, and respiratory illness. These underlying conditions make our elders more susceptible.

Recently there have been many deaths in our nursing homes. You may be concerned that your elder is now at even greater risk of getting coronavirus, and your fears are well-founded. The factors that increase risk at a nursing home are: test shortages; personal protective equipment (PPE) shortages; staff shortages; shared rooms; physical contact with staff and other elders; and transfers of elders between the nursing home and the hospital and back to the nursing home.

So, we know that the risk of getting coronavirus is greater at the nursing home. But it is difficult to accept that best practices require that the nursing home respond to the risk by doing the following: limit visits, yes that means you can't go to visit your elder; no communal dining; no group activities; restrict each elder to their rooms; refuse to transfer your elder during this crisis.

Maybe you were thinking about taking your elder out of the nursing home and caring for your elder in your own home. The sort of "nuclear family" with all members sharing one community, from the babies to the elders, is still practiced in many more agrarian societies, where the adult children are expected to care for their elders until death. But is that even possible now? Is that even allowed by the policy of your nursing home? What is the policy? What is the new law regarding coronavirus? If you are wondering what your legal rights are, and what your elder's legal rights are, give your elder law attorney a call. Anyone in a nursing home needs an advocate.

Granny Pods

You may be searching for a place for your parents to live out their golden years. You are considering a nursing home, or assisted living, or maybe you are considering moving your parents into your own home. Nursing homes are very expensive. Your parent may not be capable of living alone, but not yet in need of skilled nursing care. And your home may not have room in it to furnish a suite for your parent. There is a unique solution called a "granny pod" which is a small dwelling that you place in your own backyard.

A granny pod can be furnished with high-tech medical extras and called a "med cottage" or it can just be a guest house. Granny pods can come to you prefabricated and designed to be installed on your property, according to your local zoning laws.

The granny pod looks like a small bungalow on the outside, and a nice hotel suite on the inside, with room for a bed, living room space, kitchenette and bathroom. Standard safety features include hand railings, defibrillators, first aid supplies, lighted floorboards and a soft floor to minimize damage from falls.

A granny pod can be fitted out with luxury extras like French doors, and it can also accommodate a wheelchair and hospital bed, if needed. A granny pod kit can be assembled by a pro, or you can choose to do the assembly yourself. The small dwelling is hooked up to the main house's existing water, sewer, and electric service. Of course, you must first make sure your local zoning laws, and your homeowners' association rules, allow a granny pod. A granny pod isn't cheap, but it can cost far less than a room in a nursing home, depending on how many years it is in service. And of course, once installed, a granny pod can add value to your property. Your parent may enjoy the privacy of their own space while also seeing the practicality of proximity to their caregiver. It is easy to monitor their safety, and they can stay close to their loved ones. Overall, senior planning is key. Take the time to consider your options. Every case has unique circumstances and should be treated as such.

Overall, seniors face unique issues and considerations when dealing with family law and estate issues. Take the time to educate yourself and ensure that you have your legal documents in order.

NOTHING IS FREE.
WHO FOOTS THE BILL FOR THIS?

If you retained an attorney to assist you in resolving your divorce or parentage matter, it is inevitable that you will incur attorneys' fees, unless your attorney took your case on pro bono, or for free. If there is a balance at the end of a case, there may be different ways that an attorney may collect on these fees.

Who can be ordered to pay attorneys' fees? Either party may be ordered to pay attorney's fees, under different sections of the Illinois Marriage and Dissolution of Marriage Act, however in general the party incurring the fees is responsible.

Under sections 503(j) and 508(a), the opposing party (a.k.a., your ex- or soon-to-be ex-spouse or the parent of your child if you were never married) may be ordered to contribute towards your attorneys' fees.

Additionally, the court may order you to pay your own attorneys' fees under section 508(c), or pursuant to Section 508(e), in a separate civil cause of action for breach of contract or quantum meruit principles. These different Sections will be explained below. When can fees be ordered?

Fees can be ordered during a case, as sanctions (or a penalty or coercive measure that results from failure to comply with a law, rule, or order) to even the playing field, or at the end of a case.

During a case, a court may order attorneys' fees from an opposing party as sanctions under a few different rules: discovery sanctions under Illinois Supreme Court Rule, sanctions under Illinois Supreme Court Rule 137 regarding the signing of pleadings, motions, and other documents, and fee awards under Section 508(b) of the Illinois Marriage and Dissolution of Marriage for a party's failure to abide by the Court Order.

Fees as a Sanction

As stated above, a sanction is defined as a penalty or coercive measure that results from failure to comply with a law, rule, or order. Illinois Supreme Court Rule 219 concerns the consequences of a refusal to comply with rules or orders relating discovery or pretrial conferences. Ill. Sup. Ct. R. 219. If a party unreasonably fails to comply with any provision of the Illinois Supreme Court Rules regarding discovery or an order of the Court regarding discovery, the Court may enter a number of different sanctions, which includes ordering a party or attorney to pay the other party or attorney the amount of reasonable expenses incurred in the paying party's misconduct, which includes attorneys' fees. Ill. Sup. Ct. R. 219(c). In our experience, we have not seen sanctions ordered from an attorney many times, but the statute does allow for it.

Illinois Supreme Court Rule 137 concerns the signing of pleadings, motions, and other documents. Ill. Sup. Ct. R. 137. Pursuant to this rule, every pleading, motion, and other document of a party represented by counsel must be signed by at least one attorney of record in his or her own personal name, and the signature of that attorney is an attestation that the attorney has read the pleading, motion, and other document, and to the best of his or her knowledge, information, and belief formed after reasonable inquiry that it is well grounded in fact, and warranted by existing law or a good-faith argument for the extension, modification, or reversal of existing law, and is not being brought for any improper purpose. Ill. Sup. Ct. R. 137(a). If a pleading, motion, or other document is signed in violation of this rule, the violating party or attorney may be subject to paying an amount of reasonable expenses incurred as the result of the filing of the violating pleading, motion, or other document, which may include reasonable attorneys' fees. *Id.* Essentially, as an attorney if you have not reviewed the document to make sure it is grounded in fact and supported by law (or that there is a good faith basis for extension, modification, or reversal of said law), the attorney runs the risk of being subjected to sanctions, if the Court finds that the same is true. The same applies to self-represented litigants.

Finally, an opposing party may be ordered to pay attorneys' fees pursuant to Section 508(b) of the Illinois Marriage and Dissolution of Marriage Act. Fees are awarded pursuant to Section 508(b) when a party unreasonably fails to comply with a prior order of the court and the other party is forced to bring a proceeding for the enforcement of said court order. 750 Ill. Comp. Stat. Ann. 508(b) (LexisNexis through P.A. 101-631). A proceeding for enforcement of a prior court order may be a Petition for Rule to Show Cause for Indirect Civil Contempt. For example, if a party who owes a child support obligation fails to make the payments for months on end, the party who receives support would file a Petition for Rule, seeking compliance with the Order. After the Petition for Rule has been dealt with, the person who had to bring the Petition for Rule may then file a petition requesting attorney's fees pursuant to Section 508(b). *Id.* Fees awarded pursuant to Section 508(b) must be related to seeking compliance with the prior court order. *Id.* In addition to awarding fees under Section 508(b) for a party's failure to abide by a court order, a Court may also award fees under this section if it finds that a hearing under the Illinois Marriage and Dissolution of Marriage Act was brought for any improper purposes, against the party or attorney found to have acted improperly. *Id.* "Improper purposes" includes harassment, unnecessary delay, or other acts needlessly increasing the cost of litigation. *Id.*

Fees to Level the Playing Field

During the course of litigation, a court may also award fees in order to "level the playing field." When fees are awarded in this capacity, it is called an "interim fee award." Interim fee awards are governed by Section 501(c-1) of the Illinois Marriage and Dissolution of Marriage Act. 750 Ill. Comp. Stat. Ann. 5/501(c-1) (LexisNexis through P.A. 101-631). The purpose of an interim fee award is to even the playing field, and to allow the party petitioning for interim fees to participate adequately in the litigation. An example of leveling the playing field is if Party A has paid his or her attorney $50,000.00, and Party B has paid his or her attorney $10,000.00, a court may order an award of $40,000.00 from Party A (or the marital estate) to Party B if there is sufficient income and assets to ensure the attorneys are being paid similar amounts. A hearing on an interim fee award will be non-evidentiary and summary in nature. 750 Ill. Comp. Stat. Ann. 5/501(c-1)(1) (LexisNexis through P.A. 101-631). This means that the Court will look at the parties' Financial Affidavits, the pleadings, and listen to the arguments of counsel when holding an interim fee hearing. However, if there is good cause shown, the Court may conduct an evidentiary hearing on an interim fee award, meaning the Court would take the testimony of the parties and accept exhibits from the attorneys. *Id.*

When a party files his or her petition requesting interim fees, the petition should be supported by at least one affidavit that lays out the relevant factors, which are discussed below. *Id.* When the other party responds that response must contain the amount of the fees charged to the responding party, and the payments made to the responding party's counsel (whether made by the responding party, or on that party's behalf). *Id.* There are a number of factors that the court will consider when making an interim fee award, which include the following:

1. *The income and property of each party, including alleged marital property in control of one party, as well as alleged non-marital property a party has access to.*
2. *The needs of each party.*
3. *The realistic earning capacity of each party.*
4. *Any impairment to present earning capacity of either party, including age and physical and emotional health.*
5. *The standard of living established during the marriage.*
6. *The degree of complexity of the issues, including allocation of parental responsibility, valuation or division of closely held businesses (or both), and tax planning, as well as reasonable needs for expert investigations or expert witnesses, or both.*
7. *Each party's access to relevant information.*
8. *The amount of the payment or payments made or reasonably expected to be made to the attorney for the other party; and*

> 9. Any other factor that the court expressly finds to be just and equitable.

750 Ill. Comp. Stat. Ann. 5/501(c-1)(1)(A)-(I) (LexisNexis through P.A. 101-631).

If the Court orders an interim fee award, or if the parties agree to one, then the award will be without prejudice to any final allocation of marital property, and without prejudice as to any claim or right of either party or counsel of record at the time of the award. 750 Ill. Comp. Stat. Ann. 5/501(c-1)(2). (LexisNexis through P.A. 101-631). Unless it is ordered otherwise, an interim fee award is considered an advance of that party's portion of the marital estate. *Id.*

Fees at the End of the Case

Attorneys' fees may also be awarded at the end of a case—either from the other party, or against a client in favor of their attorney. Section 508(a) of the Illinois Marriage and Dissolution of Marriage Act provides that the Court, after due notice and hearing, and after considering the financial resources of the parties, may order any party to pay a reasonable amount for his or her own or the other party's attorneys' fees and costs. 750 Ill. Comp. Stat. Ann. 5/508(a) (LexisNexis through P.A. 101-631). Section 508(a) further goes on to state that at the end of any pre-judgment proceeding, contribution to attorney's fees and costs may be awarded from the opposing party in accordance with Section 503(j). *Id.* Additionally, fees and costs may be awarded in any proceeding to counsel from a former client in accordance with Section 508(c). *Id.* Awards may be made in connection with any of the following:

> 1. *The maintenance or defense of any proceeding under the Illinois Marriage and Dissolution of Marriage Act.*
> 2. *The enforcement or modification of any order or judgment under the Illinois Marriage and Dissolution of Marriage Act.*
> 3. *The defense of an appeal of any order or judgment under the Illinois Marriage and Dissolution of Marriage Act, including the defense of appeals of post-judgment orders.*
> 4. *The prosecution of any claim on appeal if the prosecuting party has substantially prevailed.*
> 5. *The maintenance or defense of a petition brought under 735 ILCS 5/2-1401 seeking relief from a final order or judgment under the Illinois Marriage and Dissolution of Marriage Act (only available to the party who substantially prevails.*
> 6. *The costs and legal services of an attorney rendered in preparation of the commencement of the proceeding brought under the Illinois Marriage and Dissolution of Marriage Act.*

> 7. *Ancillary litigation incident to, or reasonably connected with, a proceeding under this Act; and*
> 8. *Costs and attorneys' fees incurred in an action under the Hague Convention on the Civil Aspects of International Child Abduction.*

Id.

In addition to obtaining fees against a former client under Section 508(c), an attorney may file a separate action against his or her former client. Under Section 508(e), an attorney may pursue an award and judgment against a former client in an independent proceeding. 750 Ill. Comp. Stat. Ann. 5/508(e) (LexisNexis through P.A. 101-631).

Section 503(j) Contribution to Fees

The first avenue for obtaining fees from opposing parties is Section 503(j) of the Illinois Marriage and Dissolution of Marriage Act. If the Petition requesting contribution towards attorneys' fees is not filed before the final hearing on the issues between the parties, then it must be filed within 14 days of the closing of proofs in the final order, or within another period ordered by the Court. 750 Ill. Comp. Stat. Ann. 5/503(j)(1) (LexisNexis through P.A. 101-631).

Courts in Illinois have been split on what the standard is for determining a contribution award. Some courts in the past have found that the inability to pay must be proven as a prerequisite to a contribution award. Many appellate courts decisions focus on the inability to pay/ability to pay standard, despite the language not being in the statute. In 2005, the Illinois Supreme Court stated the following, with regard to the "inability to pay,": financial inability exists where requiring payment of fees would strip that party of her means of support or undermine her financial stability. *In re Marriage of Schneider*, 214 Ill. 2d 152, 174 (2005). In 2015, the Third District Appellate Court of Illinois in *In re Marriage of Anderson* explicitly rejected the necessity of proving a spouse's inability to pay a prerequisite to a contribution award. *In re Marriage of Anderson*, 2015 IL App (3d) 140257, ¶20. The Appellate Court further went on to say that the trial court should "consider the parties' relative financial circumstances as directed by the statutory factors in sections 503(d) and 504(a)." *Id.* In 2017, the Illinois Supreme Court in *In re Marriage of Heroy* dealt with the issue of contribution towards attorney's fees. The Illinois Supreme Court further stated that the language in Section 508 of the Illinois Marriage and Dissolution Act is "clear and unambiguous," and that the trial court must consider the financial resources of the parties and make its decision based on Section 503(j). *In re Marriage of Heroy*, 2017 IL 120205, ¶19. The Court also specifically mentioned Schneider in its ruling, and the definition of "inability to pay" and further went on to state it is clear that the "inability to pay" standard was not intended to limit awards of attorney's fees to situations in which a party could show a $0 bank balance. *Id.*

In making the contribution award, the Court will also look at a number of different criteria. Any award of contribution towards attorney's fees shall be based on the criteria for division of marital property under Section 503. 750 Ill. Comp. Stat. Ann. 5/503(j)(2) Those criteria are as follows:

> 1. *Each party's contribution to the acquisition, preservation, or increase or decrease in value of marital or nonmarital property, including:*
>   a. *Any decrease attributable to an advance from the marital estate under 750 ILCS 5/501(c-1)(2).*
>   b. *The contribution of a spouse as a homemaker or to the family unit; and*
>   c. *Whether the contribution is after the commencement of a proceeding for dissolution of marriage or declaration of invalidity of marriage.*
> 2. *The dissipation by each party of the marital property.*
> 3. *The value of the property assigned to each spouse.*
> 4. *The duration of the marriage.*
> 5. *The relevant economic circumstances of each spouse when the division of property is to become effective, including the desirability of awarding the family home, or right to live therein for reasonable periods, to the spouse having primary residence of the children.*
> 6. *Any obligations and rights arising from a prior marriage of either party.*
> 7. *Any prenuptial or postnuptial agreement of the parties.*
> 8. *The age, health, station, occupation, amount and sources of income, vocational skills, employability, estate, liabilities, and needs of each of the parties.*
> 9. *The custodial provisions for any children.*
> 10. *Whether the apportionment is in lieu of or in addition for maintenance.*
> 11. *The reasonable opportunity of each spouse for future acquisition of capital assets and income; and*
> 12. *The tax consequences of the property division upon the respective economic circumstances of the parties.*

750 Ill. Comp. Stat. Ann. 5/503(d)(1)-(12) (LexisNexis through P.A. 101-631).

If maintenance is awarded in a case, then the Court must also consider the criteria for an award of maintenance when making a decision on an award of contributions towards attorneys' fees. 750 Ill. Comp. Stat. Ann. 5/503(j)2((LexisNexis through P.A. 101-631). If an award of maintenance is made in a case where contribution towards attorneys' fees is being decided, then the court will also look at the following:

> 1. *The income and property of each party, including marital and nonmarital property apportioned and assigned to the party seeking maintenance, as well as the financial obligations imposed as a result of the dissolution.*
> 2. *The needs of each party.*

3. *The realistic present and future earning capacity of each party.*
4. *Any impairment of the present and future earning capacity of the party seeking maintenance due to that party devoting time to domestic duties, or delayed or forgone education, training, employment, or career opportunities due to the marriage.*
5. *Any impairment of the realistic present or future earning capacity of the party against whom maintenance is sought.*
6. *The time necessary to enable the party seeking maintenance to acquire appropriate education, training, and employment, and whether that party is able to support himself or herself through appropriate employment.*
7. *Parental responsibility arrangements, and its effect on a party's ability to seek or maintain employment.*
8. *The standard of living established during the marriage.*
9. *The duration of the marriage.*
10. *The age, health, station, occupation, amount and sources of income, vocational skills, employability, estate, liabilities, and needs of each party.*
11. *All sources of public and private income including, without limitation, disability and retirement income.*
12. *The tax consequences to each party.*
13. *Contributions and services by the party seeking maintenance to the education, training, career or career potential, or license of the other spouse.*
14. *Any valid agreement of the parties.*

750 Ill. Comp. Stat. Ann. 5/504(a)(1)-(14) (LexisNexis through P.A. 101-631).

What time frame does the Court look at when considering these factors? Do they look at the circumstances at the time of the filing of the Petition for Contribution, at the time of entry of a final judgment, or at the time of the final hearing? Illinois case law states that when considering a petition for contribution towards attorneys' fees, the Court must look to the circumstances as they exist at the time of the hearing. *In re Marriage of Anderson*, 2015 IL App (3d) 140257, ¶22.

What if an attorney filed a Petition for Contribution towards Attorneys' Fees, but does not represent either party at the time of final hearing? Illinois Courts have ruled that the right to contribution actually lies with the attorney that filed the Petition for Contribution towards Attorneys' Fees, and a waiver of contribution hearing by the parties is not binding as to the attorney who was not a part of that agreement. *Lamar v. Rocca*, 408 Ill. App. 3d 956, 968 (Ill. App. Ct. 2d Dist. 2011).

Section 508(c) Fees Against a Former Client

An attorney may seek an order for attorneys' fees against a former client. 750 Ill. Comp. Stat. Ann. 5/508(c) (LexisNexis through P.A. 101-631). A client may also file a petition against his or her attorney requesting that the Court set the final fees and costs owed to the attorney. 750 Ill. Comp. Stat. Ann. 5/508(c)(1) (LexisNexis through P.A. 101-631). An attorney may not file a petition for final attorneys' fees against a client unless that attorney has been granted leave to withdraw as counsel of record, or if the attorney has filed a motion for leave to withdraw as counsel. Id. However, if an attorney files a petition to set final fees and costs from his or her client, that attorney must file a motion for leave to withdraw as counsel, unless their withdrawal occurs by operation of law. Id.

Once a Petition for Setting Final Fees and Costs has been filed, whether by counsel or a client, a final hearing will not be permitted unless all off the following are met:

1. The counsel and client had entered into a written engagement agreement at the time the client retained the counsel, or reasonably soon thereafter, and the agreement meets the requirements of the statutory provisions.
2. The written engagement agreement is attached to an affidavit of counsel that is filed with the petition or with the counsel's response to a client's petition.
3. Judgment in any contribution hearing on behalf of the client has been entered, or the right to a contribution hearing under Section 503(j) has been waived.
4. The counsel has withdrawn as counsel of record; and
5. The petition seeks adjudication of all unresolved claims for fees and costs between the counsel and client.

750 Ill. Comp. Stat. Ann. 5/508(c)(2) (LexisNexis through P.A. 101-631).

As referenced in the first requirement for setting of a hearing on a Petition for Setting Final Fees and Costs, "subsection (f)" of Section 508 of the Illinois Marriage and Dissolution of Marriage Act is a provision for a "Statement of Client's Rights and Responsibilities" that must be executed by clients, pursuant to the statute. 750 Ill. Comp. Stat. Ann. 5/508(f) (LexisNexis through P.A. 101-631). This subsection provides the verbatim language that should be in this document. Id.

An additional requirement before a hearing on a petition for setting of final fees and costs is that the dispute over fees and costs has been submitted to mediation, arbitration, or any other court approved alternative dispute resolution procedure. 750 Ill. Comp. Stat. Ann. 5/508(c)(4) (LexisNexis through P.A. 101-631). This requirement may be waived in the following situations: in counties with a population in excess of 1,000,000, if both the client and counsel affirmatively opt out of the procedure; or, in any other county if either the client or counsel affirmatively opt out of the procedures. 750 Ill. Comp. Stat. Ann. 5/508(c)(4)(A)-(B) (LexisNexis through P.A. 101-631). For example, in Cook County, both the client and counsel must affirmatively opt out of alternative dispute resolution in order to waive the requirement that the same occur before hearing. This is because Cook

County has a population of over 1,000,000. However, in smaller counties, such as Will County, only one of the parties (client or counsel) is required to affirmatively opt out of alternative dispute resolution in order to waive the requirement that the same occur before a hearing.

When ruling on a petition for setting final fees and costs, any determination made is within the discretion of the trial court. Under the statute, the Court first must look at and consider the written engagement agreement entered into by counsel and former client. 750 Ill. Comp. Stat. Ann. 5/508(c)(5) (LexisNexis through P.A. 101-631). If the court finds that the parties entered into a contract, it will then look to see if there was performance under the contract. *Id.* If the court does make an award on a petition for setting final fees and costs, it must find that the amount awarded to be fair compensation for the services pursuant to the contract, that the court finds were reasonable and necessary. *Id.*

How long does an attorney have to file an action pursuant to Section 508(c)? The statute states that "it shall be filed no later than the end of the period in which it is permissible to file a motion pursuant to Section 2-1203 of the Code of Civil Procedure." 750 Ill. Comp. Stat. Ann. 5/508(c)(5) (LexisNexis through P.A. 101-631). In layman's terms, that is 30 days after entry of judgment, or any further time the court allows within that 30 days or any extensions of that time. 735 Ill. Comp. Stat. Ann. 5/2-1203(a) (LexisNexis through P.A. 101-631).

In connection with a Petition for Setting of Final Fees and Costs, an attorney may also enter into a Consent Judgment with their former client. Consent judgments are governed by Section 508(d) of the Illinois Marriage and Dissolution of Marriage Act. A consent judgment is essentially an agreement between an attorney and their former client, which states that the former client agrees they owe a certain amount and provides a monthly payment plan for the same. This document is signed by both parties and entered with the Court as a valid and enforceable court order. However, there are certain procedures that need to be followed. The first procedure is that a Petition for Setting of Final Fees and Costs under Section 508(c) must be filed. 750 Ill. Comp. Stat. Ann. 5/508(d) (LexisNexis through P.A. 101-631). This document must be a separate document, and cannot be included in a marital settlement agreement, dissolution judgment, or other document that involves the other litigant. *Id.* In order for a consent judgment to be entered, a verified petition for entry of consent judgment must be filed, containing an affidavit of counsel of record and the client. *Id.* The affidavit of the counsel must include the following: the client has been provided an itemization of the billing or billings to the client, detailing hourly costs, time spent, and tasks performed. *Id.* The affidavit of the client must include the following: acknowledging receipt of the documents included in the counsel's affidavit; awareness of the right to a hearing, the right to be represented by counsel (other than the counsel to whom the consent judgment is in favor), and the right to be present at the time of presentation of the petitioner; and agreement to the terms of the judgment. *Id.*

Independent Proceedings Against a Former Client

Under Section 508(e), an attorney may pursue an award and judgment against a former client for legal fees and costs in an independent proceeding, subject to certain rules in the statute. 750 Ill. Comp. Stat. Ann. 5/508(e) (LexisNexis through P.A. 101-631).

While a case under the Illinois Marriage and Dissolution of Marriage Act is still pending, an attorney may seek an award and judgment at any time subsequent to 90 days after entry of the order granting the attorney leave to withdraw. 750 Ill. Comp. Stat. Ann. 5/508(e)(1) (LexisNexis through P.A. 101-631). After the time to file a Petition pursuant to 508(c) has expired, if there is not a petition for setting of final fees and costs pending, any counsel or former counsel may pursue an award in an independent proceeding. 750 Ill. Comp. Stat. Ann. 5/508(e)(2) (LexisNexis through P.A. 101-631). If a former counsel files an independent procedure while a case is still ongoing, the former client may bring his or her spouse in as a third-party defendant with the filing of an appropriate third-party complaint. *Id.* However, this must be done by the final day to file a petition for setting of final fees and costs, as described previously in this chapter. *Id.*

There are a few avenues that an attorney may choose to file an independent action against his or her former client to pursue a judgment. The first is a breach of contract. When an attorney files a complaint for a breach of contract, the attorney is alleging that the former client has not held up their end of the attorney fee contract, where they agreed that they would pay the amounts owed to them. Under Illinois law, the statute of limitations (or time to file an action) for breach of contract is ten years after the cause of action came about.

The next avenue that an attorney may choose to file an independent action against his or her former client is under a principle called quantum meruit. Quantum meruit is a Latin phrase which literally translates to "as much as he has deserved." *Quantum meruit*, BLACK'S LAW DICTIONARY, (5th Pocket Ed. 2016). When an attorney files a suit to be compensated under the principle of quantum meruit, the attorney is asking the Court to compensate the attorney based on the value of legal services actually performed on the client's behalf. *In re Smith*, 168 Ill. 2d 269, 293 (1995). In determining an independent action filed under quantum meruit principles, the Court looks at the value of the services that were provided to the former client.

What Happens After a Fee Award is Entered?

As a matter of law, judgments collect interest after they are entered. Under Section 2-1303 of the Illinois Code of Civil Procedure, judgments recovered in any court shall draw interest until satisfied. 735 Ill. Comp. Stat. Ann. 5/2-1303(a) (LexisNexis through P.A. 101-631). The rate of interest depends on how much is owed, and whether or not the creditor is a governmental entity or private entity.

As of January 1, 2020, if the judgment is less than or equal to $25,000.00, then the interest rate is 5%. 735 Ill. Comp. stat. Ann. 5/2-1303(b)(2) (LexisNexis through P.A. 101-631). This is whether or not the creditor is a governmental entity or not. *Id.* However, if the judgment entered is more than $25,000.00, then the interest rate will change depending on whether or not the creditor is a governmental entity. 735 Ill. Comp. Stat. Ann. 5/2-1303(a) (LexisNexis through P.A. 101-631). If judgment is more than $25,000.00, and the creditor is a governmental entity, then the interest rate is 6% per annum. *Id.* Otherwise, if the judgment is more than $25,000.00, then the interest rate is 9% per annum. *Id.* The only way under the statute to stop the accrual of interest, without the agreement of the creditor, is to tender payment of judgment, costs, and interest accrued to date of the payment. 735 Ill. Comp. Stat. Ann. 5/2-1303(b)(3) (LexisNexis through P.A. 101-631). If a judgment was entered prior to January 1, 2020, then the percentage for interest, no matter the amount of the judgment, is 6% per annum for governmental creditors, and 9% per annum for all other creditors. 750 Ill. Comp. Stat. Ann. 5/2-1303(b)(4) (LexisNexis through P.A. 101-631).

Additionally, there are post-judgment collection remedies that judgment creditors may utilize. A judgment creditor is the person that the judgment is owed to. These include: a non-wage garnishment, a wage garnishment, a citation to discover assets, or a memorandum of judgment. Each of these methods will be discussed below.

The first post-judgment collection remedy attorneys may use to collect on his or her award of fees is called a non-wage garnishment. Non-wage garnishments are governed by Illinois statutory law. These are generally issued against banks, or other entities or individuals that the judgment creditor believes may be indebted to the debtor (other than wages), or that the judgment creditor believes is holding property belonging to the debtor, or which the debtor has an interest in. 735 Ill. Comp. Stat. Ann. 5/212-701 (LexisNexis through P.A. 101-631).

In order to start non-wage garnishment proceedings, the attorney or judgment creditor will file the following: an affidavit that they believe the garnishee is indebted or otherwise holding property that belongs to the debtor or that the debtor has an interest in; a garnishment notice, pursuant to Section 12-705 of the Illinois Code of Civil Procedure; and written interrogatories to be answered by the garnishee with respect the indebtedness or property. *Id.* The attorney, also known as the judgment creditor, will also prepare and file a non-wage garnishment summons for the clerk's office to issue. The summons will require the garnishee to answer the interrogatories in writing under oath. 735 Ill. Comp. Stat. Ann. 5/12-707(b) (LexisNexis through P.A. 101-631). Additionally, the interrogatories must require that the garnishee certify that they have also mailed a copy of their completed interrogatories to the judgment debtor. *Id.*

There are certain things that are exempted from being garnished under a non-wage garnishment. They include the following: benefits and refunds payable by pension or retirement funds or systems; assets of employees held by such funds or systems; and any money an employee is required to pay to such funds or systems. 735 Ill. Comp. Stat. Ann. 5/12-704 (LexisNexis through P.A. 101-631).

A summons for a non-wage garnishment is returnable between 21 and 40 days after issuance of the summons. 735 Ill. Comp. Stat. Ann. 5/12-705(a) (LexisNexis through P.A. 101-631). This means that the answers should be returned and filed in that time frame, and a court date should be set in the time frame as well. If, however, a garnishee is served with the summons less than 10 days prior to the return date, then the court should continue the court date for 14 days after the return date on the summons. *Id.* Additionally, under the statute, service of a non-wage garnishment summons may be made as follows: by an officer or any person over 18 years of age who is not a party to the action; or by prepaid certified or registered mail addressed to the garnishee. 735 Ill. Comp. Stat. Ann. 5/12-705(b) (LexisNexis through P.A. 101-631). If the garnishee is a natural person, then it must be served "restricted delivery." 735 Ill. comp. Stat. ann. 5/12-705(c)(2) (LexisNexis through P.A. 101-631). After service, the garnishee must hold the non-exempt indebtedness or non-exempt property that is in his or her possession that belongs to the judgment debtor or that the debtor has an interest in. 735 Ill. Comp. Stat. Ann. 5/12-707(a) (LexisNexis through P.A. 101-631). The amount held is up to the amount due on the judgment. *Id.* The service of the summons creates a lien on any such non-exempt property. *Id.*

The next avenue for a judgment creditor to collect on a judgment award is a wage garnishment. This may also be called wage deduction. This is when a certain amount is withheld from a debtor's wages, and the employer sends that money to the judgment creditor to go towards the judgment balance.

In order to issue a summons for a wage deduction proceeding, the creditor must file certain documents with a proposed summons. The documents required to be filed include the following: an affidavit of the creditor or its attorney that the affiant (person signing the affidavit) believes that a person is indebted to the judgment debtor for wages; and written interrogatories to be answered by the employer. 735 Ill. Comp. Stat. ann. 5/12-805(a) (LexisNexis through P.A. 101-631). The affidavit should also include the last known address of the judgment debtor known to the affiant, and the name of the judgment debtor, as well as a certification by the creditor or his attorney that, before filing the affidavit, the wage deduction notice was mailed to the judgment debtor by first class mail to his or her last known address. *Id.*

Like the non-wage garnishment, the return date (and court date) should be set 21 to 40 days after the issuance of the wage deduction summons. 735 Ill. Comp. Stat. Ann. 5/12-806 (LexisNexis through P.A. 101-631). In order to serve a wage deduction summons, the same methods for service of a non-wage garnishment summons described above may be used. *Id.* If the wage deduction summons is served on the employer less than 3 days prior to the return date, then the court must continue the case to a new return date at least 21 days after the date the summons was served. *Id.*

Under Illinois law, a certain portion of wages are subject to collection. 735 Ill. Comp. Stat. Ann. 5/12-803 (LexisNexis through P.A. 101-631). The amount of wages, salary, and commission subject to collection under a deduction order for any work week is the lesser of the following: 15% of the gross wages paid for that week; or the amount by which disposable earnings for a week exceed 45 times the Federal Minimum Hourly Wage prescribed by 29 U.S.C. §206(a)(1), as amended, or for summons served after January 1, 2006, the minimum hourly wage prescribed by Section 4 of the Minimum Wage law, whichever is greater, in effect at the time the amounts are payable. *Id.* Under this section, "disposable earnings" means the part of the earnings of any individual remaining after deduction from the earnings amounts required by law to be withheld (for example, taxes or mandatory retirement). *Id.*

As with non-wage garnishments, there are certain exemptions from deduction orders with regard to wage deductions as well. These include benefits and refunds payable by pension or retirement funds or systems and any assets of employees held by such funds or systems, and any money an employee is required to contribute to such funds or systems. 735 Ill. Comp. Stat. Ann. 5/12-804 (LexisNexis through P.A. 101-631).

The third avenue for post-judgment relief for a judgment creditor is a citation to discover assets. The purpose of this is to examine the judgment debtor or any other person to discover assets or income of the debtor not exempt from enforcement of the judgment, a deduction order or garnishment, and compelling the application of non-exempt assets or income discovered towards the payment of the amount due under the judgment. 735 Ill. Comp. Stat. Ann. 5/2-1402(a) (LexisNexis through P.A. 101-631). Every citation served must have a certification by the attorney for the creditor, or the judgment creditor themselves, setting out the amount of the judgment, date of judgment or date of revival of the judgment, the balance due, the name of the court that entered the judgment, the number of the case, and a copy of the citation notice. 735 Ill. Comp. Stat. Ann. 5/2-1402(b) (LexisNexis through P.A. 101-631).

After a citation to discover assets has been served, the person receiving the citation must answer the summons and appear in court on the date specified to be placed under oath. 735 Ill. Comp. Stat. Ann. 5/2-1402(b-10) (LexisNexis through P.A. 101-631). If, after being questioned regarding the assets and income of the debtor, non-exempt income and assets have been discovered, the court may do a number of things. A court may order the following:

1. *Compel the judgment debtor to deliver money, property, or effects in his or her possession or control to be applied towards the judgment. These items must be able to be delivered, and the debtors title or right of possession should not be substantially disputed.*
2. *Compel the judgment debtor to pay the judgment creditor a portion of his or her income, in installments, to be applied towards the judgment. The court may also look to the reasonable income requirements for the debtor and his or her family and other payments made by court order (including other garnishments) to ensure the debtor is not being required to pay exempt wages under the Wage Deduction Statute;*
3. *Compel the person cited, other than the debtor, to deliver assets discovered, to be applied to the judgment, given that the assets are held such that the debtor is able to recover them in kind, or receive a judgment for the proceeds or value of under civil suit for conversion or embezzlement;*
4. *Enter an order or judgment against the person cited that could be entered in a garnishment proceeding;*
5. *Compel any person cited to execute an assignment of a cause of action or conveyance of title to real or personal property, or resign memberships in the same manner and to the same extent a court could do in a proceeding by a judgment creditor to enforce payment of a judgment or aid of the enforcement of a judgment; and*
6. *Authorize the judgment creditor to maintain an action against any person or corporation that is indebted to the judgment debtor for recovery of the debt, forbid the transfer or other disposition of the debt until an action can be commenced and prosecuted to a judgment, direct that the papers or proof in possession and control of the debtor and necessary in the prosecution*

> *of the action be delivered to the creditor or impounded in court, and provide for the disposition of any moneys in excess of the sum required to pay the judgment creditor's judgment and costs allowed by the court.*

735 Ill. Comp. Stat. Ann. 5/2-1402(c)(1)-(6) (LexisNexis through P.A. 101-631).

If after examination upon the citation to discover assets, the Court finds that the judgment debtor does not possess non-exempt income and assets, then a citation will be dismissed. 735 Ill. Comp. Stat. Ann. 5/2-1402(d-5) (LexisNexis through P.A. 101-631)

The last avenue for post-judgment collection is called a memorandum of judgment. This is a lien on real property that is created upon the recording of a document referencing a judgment entered against a person. 735 Ill. Comp. Stat. Ann. 5/12-101 (LexisNexis through P.A. 101-631). Each county should have their own example form for a memorandum of judgment that may be used. *Id.* These will contain information such as: who the judgment creditor is, their address, when and where the judgment was entered, and how much the judgment is for. It will also contain the judgment debtor's name and address. Oftentimes, the address listed for the judgment creditor will be the address for the property in which you are entering the lien against. Once this is properly filed, a Memorandum of Judgment creates a lien on the subject property.

Of the above methods, a non-wage garnishment, wage deduction, or citation to discover assets are likely to be quicker ways to collect on a fee judgment. A memorandum of judgment will not allow you to collect until the subject property is sold. Unless you want to spend the time (and potentially money) to foreclose on a Memorandum of Judgment, it may be some time before you are able to collect on the judgment.

Conclusion

There are many ways in which the Court may order attorney's fees, whether it is during or at the end of the case, as a sanction or to even the playing field, or against the other party or a former client. At the end of a case, settlement of fees does not always have to be contentious. If you are working with an attorney, it is certainly easier to come to an agreement regarding the payment of fees than be at odds over the issue. If you or an attorney are awarded an amount of fees during a case, it is also possible to collect on the same using one of the above-mentioned methods of post-judgment collection.

NEVER MARRIED BUT BONDED BY SHARED CHILDREN

Family Law isn't just Divorce—what is a Parentage suit? The birth of a child is almost always a joyful occurrence, with parents celebrating the new life they have brought into the world. However, this can also be an emotionally and legally confusing time for parents whose relationship isn't traditionally defined. People conceive and have children in many different relational circumstances. It could be a man and woman or a same-sex couple. They might be unmarried, married or divorced. It could be that the child was conceived completely outside of a traditional relationship — when one or both parties were married to another person, or through a one-time encounter. In cases where the parents of a child aren't married, a parentage case may be filed by one of the parents, to establish parental rights and responsibilities of both parents.

First of all, what is paternity? Black's Law Dictionary defines it as being "the quality, state, or condition of being a father, especially a biological one; fatherhood." *Paternity*, BLACK'S LAW DICTIONARY (5th pocket ed. 2016) Essentially, it is establishing that someone is the parent of a specific child. Nowadays, in order to be more inclusive to couples which may not be traditionally a "mother and father" pairing, many courts will refer to these kinds of cases as "parentage" cases. Under the law, there are different ways to determine the parentage of a child, and they are specific to whether or not the statute is talking about mother or father.

A parent-child relationship between a mother and child may be established by the following:

> 1. *The woman having given birth to the child, except as otherwise provided in the Gestational Surrogacy Act;*
> 2. *An adjudication of the woman's parentage;*
> 3. *Adoption of the child by the woman;*

> 4. *A valid gestational surrogacy agreement that complies with the Gestational Surrogacy Act or other law; or*
> 5. *An unrebutted presumption of the woman's parentage under Section 204 of the Illinois Parentage Act.*

750 Ill. Comp. Stat. Ann. 45/201(a)(1)-(5) (LexisNexis through P.A. 101-631).

A parent-child relationship between a father and child may be established by the following:

> 1. *An unrebutted presumption of the man's parentage under Section 204 of the Illinois Parentage Act (see below for presumptions of parentage);*
> 2. *An effective voluntary acknowledgment of paternity by the man, unless the acknowledgment has been rescinded or successfully challenged;*
> 3. *An adjudication of the man's parentage;*
> 4. *Adoption of the child by the man; or*
> 5. *A valid gestational surrogacy agreement that complies with the Gestational Surrogacy Act or other law.*

750 Ill. Comp. Stat. Ann. 46/201(b)(1)-(5) (LexisNexis through P.A. 101-631).

Under Illinois law, there are certain situations in which a person is presumed to be the parent of the child. These situations are located in Section 204 of the Illinois Parentage Act, as referenced above. There are four situations in which a person is presumed to be a parent of the child, which include the following:

> 1. *The person and the mother of the child entered into a marriage, civil union, or substantially similar legal relationship, and the child is born to the mother during the marriage, civil union, or substantially similar legal relationship;*
> 2. *The person and the mother of the child were in a marriage, civil union, or substantially similar legal relationship and the child was born to the mother within 300 days after the marriage, civil union, or substantially similar legal relationship is terminated by death, declaration of invalidity of marriage, judgment for dissolution of marriage, civil union, or substantially similar legal relationship, or after a judgment for legal separation;*
> 3. *Before the birth of the child, the person and the mother of the child enter into a marriage, civil union, or substantially similar legal relationship in apparent compliance with the law, even if the attempted marriage, civil union, or substantially similar legal relationship is or could be declared invalid, and the*

> *child is born during the invalid marriage, civil union, or substantially similar relationship or within 300 days after its termination by death, declaration of invalidity of marriage, judgment for dissolution of marriage, civil union, or substantially similar legal relationship, or after a judgment for legal separation; or*
>
> 4. *After the child's birth, the person and the child's mother have entered into a marriage, civil union, or substantially similar legal relationship, even if the marriage, civil union, or substantially similar legal relationship is or could be declared invalid, and the person is named, with that person's consent, as the child's parent on the child's birth certificate.*

750 Ill. Comp. Stat. Ann. 46/204(a)(1)-(4) (LexisNexis through P.A. 101-631).

Numbers 1, 2, and 3 above are subject to the provisions of the Gestational Surrogacy Act and other laws. *Id.*

Voluntary Acknowledgment of Paternity

In cases in which an unwed man and woman have a child together, many people choose to clarify their parental standings by signing a Voluntary Acknowledgment of Paternity. A Voluntary Acknowledgement of Paternity functions to show that both the woman and man recognize they are the biological parents of the child in question. They accept legal paternity, with the privileges and responsibilities associated with that position. 750 Ill. Comp. Stat. Ann. 46/305(a) (LexisNexis through P.A. 101-631). Substantiating legal paternity is important for a father-child relationship to flourish. It allows the child access to benefits like Social Security, medical insurance, and other state, federal, and inheritance opportunities available. The establishment of legal paternity is the first step in the legal process for every child subject to a Parentage Action to ensure protection and provisions for each child.

A Voluntary Acknowledgment of Paternity (VAP) is the simplest way of establishing legal paternity. More specifically, it serves as a legally binding agreement that acknowledges the father as the biological father of the child. *Id.* It ensures that the child is provided for financially and medically. By signing the VAP, both parents waive their right to obtain genetic testing to determine the father of the child.

It is important to note that a VAP does not establish parental decision making, parenting time rights, or child support; however, it is often used in court proceedings when there is conflict between parents. Signing a VAP could mean an onset of financial obligations; therefore, it is essential that a father is certain of his paternity before signing the VAP. 750 Ill. Comp. Stat. Ann. 46/305(b) (LexisNexis through P.A. 101-631). If a VAP is not rescinded after 60 days, it becomes a final determination of parentage. 750 Ill. Comp. Stat. Ann. 46/307(a) (LexisNexis through P.A. 101-631).

Voluntary Acknowledgment of Paternity forms are typically signed at the hospital when a child is born. The woman and man who sign the Voluntary Acknowledgement of Paternity are then listed on the child's birth certificate as his or her natural parents. From that moment, the man and woman are expected to fulfill their parental duties as dictated by law. Because maternity of a child is rarely in doubt upon birth, Voluntary Acknowledgment of Paternity is mostly relevant to unwed fathers, though mothers also sign the form.

When a child is born to a woman who is married, the State of Illinois law presumes that the woman's spouse is the child's father. 750 Ill. Comp. Stat. Ann. 46/204(a)(2) (LexisNexis through P.A. 101-631). The same applies in the case of same-sex couples who are married. Unless there has been other legal standing filed to establish paternity, the non-birth spouse is presumed to be the other natural parent of the child, regardless of how exactly the child was conceived. *Id.*

Some people choose to sign a Voluntary Acknowledgment of Paternity with knowledge that they are not the child's biological parent, and that is permitted by law. If a non-biological father wants to become a legal parent, it is important that he understands that signing a Voluntary Acknowledgment of Paternity is a serious legal matter not to be entered into lightly and is a legally binding document.

It is not always easy to remove a Voluntary Acknowledgment of Paternity if you should change your mind after it is signed. The State of Illinois allows for the mother or father to withdraw their Voluntary Acknowledgment of Paternity within 60 days of the date of signing. 750 Ill. Comp. Stat. Ann. 46/307(a) (LexisNexis through P.A. 101-631). In case of divorce or death of the mother, the father who signed the Voluntary Acknowledgment of Paternity maintains all the legal responsibilities associated with the child.

After 60 days, withdrawing a Voluntary Acknowledgement of Paternity requires court action to prove that the signer was defrauded, threatened or unduly influenced. 750 Ill. Comp. Stat. Ann. 46/309(a) (LexisNexis through P.A. 101-631). After two years, however, even these reasons may not provide a legal basis for withdrawal. *Id.*

What Does it Mean to Sign a Voluntary Acknowledgment of Paternity?
- Creates a presumption of paternity
- Acknowledges acceptance of paternity and having one's name listed on a birth certificate
- Forfeits the right to having paternity confirmed through a DNA test (except in instances of trying to prove fraud or a serious mistake)
- Makes it possible that the father who signs the VAP could be liable for child support.

What Signing a Voluntary Acknowledgment of Paternity Doesn't Do
- Does not create a claim of or agreement for allocation of parental responsibility.
- Does not create an agreement of child support.

To obtain a copy of a Voluntary Acknowledgment of Paternity, please visit Child Support Services at this link: https://www.illinois.gov/hfs/SiteCollectionDocuments/hfs3416b.pdf (current as of June 25, 2020). Regardless, it is best to consult with a Family Law attorney to recognize all aspects of a parent's rights.

A signed VAP can be challenged by the presumed father or rescinded by either party. Rescinding a signed VAP entails filing out the appropriate form with Health and Family Services, signing the form in front of a notary, and serving it on Health and Family Services within sixty (60) days after the VAP is signed. 750 Ill. Comp. Stat. Ann. 46/307 (LexisNexis through P.A. 101-631). Challenging a VAP is considerably more difficult. Fathers are commonly the parent who will challenge a VAP. The parent challenging the VAP must provide proof that he or she signed the VAP under duress, was a victim of fraud, or there was a material mistake made on the VAP form. 750 Ill. Comp. Stat. Ann. 46/309(a) (LexisNexis through P.A. 101-631). Challenging a VAP is extremely difficult. It is best to consult a family law attorney regarding properly establishing your rights as a father or mother, or properly challenging parentage.

Challenging a Birth Certificate

It is a myth to believe that parentage is established merely by putting a name on a birth certificate. A birth certificate does not establish paternity. In fact, one could place a cartoon character or a historical figure on a birth certificate without any verification process. As a result, there needs to be a means to challenge a birth certificate.

A father has not been deemed the father of a child simply by having his name on the birth certificate. A process is in place to challenge a birth certificate. Adding or removing a parent's name from a birth certificate is called challenging the birth certificate. There are steps that need to be properly followed in order to successfully challenge a birth certificate. The following forms need to be obtained by the Illinois Department of Public Health and filled out completely and correctly: a). Denial of Parentage Form; and b). an Affidavit and Certificate of Correction Request. A Court Order establishing the parentage must be obtained by the Court and included with the Denial of Parentage Form and Affidavit and Certificate of Correction Request. Once all of the forms and the Court Order are completed and obtained, they can be submitted to the Illinois Department of Public Health to determine if the information provided is sufficient to change or add a parent's name to the child's birth certificate. Once the Illinois Department of Public Health determines there is enough evidence to change the birth certificate, the birth certificate will be changed to either add or remove a parent's name. It is highly recommended that any person wishing to add or remove a parent's name from a child's birth certificate consult with an attorney, as each situation is different.

What If There Is No VAP?

What happens if a father is not aware his child was born? He is not at the hospital, so he did not sign a VAP? The mother does not list the father's name on the birth certificate. What recourse does the father have to obtain parentage of the child and receive parenting time and decision making for the child? He must file a complaint with the Court requesting to establish himself as the father of the baby. 750 Ill. Comp. Stat. Ann. 46/601 (LexisNexis through P.A. 101-631). The father and/or mother may request the Court to enter an order requiring a DNA test to establish the parentage of the child. If neither parent makes a request of the Court for a DNA test, in most cases the Judge will order a DNA test without the parent's request. If the DNA test comes back identifying both parties as the parents of the child, the Court will enter an order establishing the parentage of both parties and the process of scheduling parenting time, establishing parental responsibilities, and setting child support will begin. The remaining chapters of this book discuss parenting issues and child support and are the same for paternity cases as with dissolution of marriage cases.

Starting a Paternity Case

How is a child's paternity established? The mother or father can file a complaint with the circuit court in the county he or she resides in. 750 Ill. Comp. Stat. Ann. 46/604(a) (LexisNexis through P.A. 101-631). Such a complaint is called a Petition to Establish Paternity. This is the pleading typically filed by the mother. A Petition to Establish the Father-Child Relationship is filed by the father. Each Petition asks the Court to examine the evidence, and perhaps order a DNA test to prove the paternity of the child in question. Even if a VAP is signed, one or both of the parents may want or need to file a complaint with the Court requesting child support, parenting time, and allocating parenting responsibilities. It is not always required to file a complaint with the Court, the parents may work together in establishing child support, parenting time, or parental responsibilities. Another alternative is to contact the Illinois Department of Health Services requesting help in obtaining child support from the alleged parent.

When filing your complaint for establishing parentage, you must also file a Summons. The other party, or parent, will need to be served with the Summons and Petition to Establish Paternity or Petition to Establish Father-Child Relationship. Once the other party is served, he or she has an opportunity to answer the Petition. The party seeking child support must file a motion requesting child support with the Court. The party seeking parenting time and parenting responsibilities must also file a motion requesting the same. Issues regarding child support matters must follow the same guidelines as divorcing parents, a Financial Affidavit must be filled out and exchanged between the parties to determine the income of each party and the effects of income on child support. See Family Support Basics Chapter above.

Once parentage is established, either by the execution of a VAP or Court order establishing parentage, child support and parenting time and parenting responsibilities will be established usually through the entry of a Parenting Allocation and Financial Judgment. This document outlines each parent's parenting time, parental responsibilities and financial responsibilities for the child. Child support and payment of child expenses are addressed and assigned to the parents as his or her financial obligation regarding the child. Once this is entered with the Court, the matter is presently concluded. The parties may attend mediation to aid in any future disagreements regarding the Parenting Allocation and Financial Judgment. If mediation between the parents fails, either or both parties may file motions relative to unresolved issues with the final Judgment. It is strongly recommended that any parent contact a family law attorney to help navigate and negotiate parenting issues.

Putative Father Registry

In Illinois, under the Adoption Act, there is something called the "Putative Father's Registry." The purpose of this is for the determination of the identity and location of a "putative" father of a minor child who is, or is expected to be, the subject of an adoption proceeding, in order to provide notice to that putative father. 750 Ill. Comp. Stat. Ann. 50/12.1 (LexisNexis through P.A. 101-631). Black's Law Dictionary defines "putative" as reputed; believed or supposed by most people. *Putative*, BLACK'S LAW DICTIONARY (5th pocket ed. 2016). If a man decides to put himself on the Putative Father's Registry, he needs to provide certain personal information about himself and a potential mother, as well as the name, gender, place of birth, and date of birth or anticipated date of birth of the child if it is known to him. 750 Ill. Comp. Stat. Ann. 50/12.1(a)(1)-(3) (LexisNexis through P.A. 101-631). He must provide the following information about himself: his name, including any other names he may be known by; an address at which he can be served with a notice of a petition for adoption, including any change of address; his Social Security Number; his date of birth; and, if applicable, a certified copy of an order by a court of any state adjudicating the putative father as being the father of the child. 750 Ill. Comp. Stat. Ann. 50/12.1(a)(1)(i)-(v) (LexisNexis through P.A. 101-631). A putative father must also provide the following information about the mother of the child: her name, including all other names known to the putative father; her address and if known to the putative father; her Social Security Number; and her date of birth. 750 Ill. Comp. Stat. Ann. 50/12.1(a)(2)(i)-(iv) (LexisNexis through P.A. 101-631). When an individual provides this information, he is added to the Putative Father Registry.

A man has a certain amount of time to register with the Putative Father Registry. He may register any time before the birth of the child to no later than 30 days after the birth of the child. 750 Ill. Comp. Stat. Ann. 50/12.1(b) (LexisNexis through P.A. 101-631). The registration must be signed by the putative father. *Id.* If the father fails to register with the Putative Father Registry within the time frame, it has the legal effect of the following: a waiver and surrender of any right to notice of hearing in any judicial proceeding for adoption of the child, and consent or surrender that person to the adoption of the child is not required; and constitutes an abandonment of the child, and prima facie evidence of sufficient grounds to support termination of such father's parental rights under the Adoption Act. 750 Ill. Comp. Stat. ann. 50/12.1(h) (LexisNexis through P.A. 101-631).

If a man thinks he may be the father of a child born to a woman and would like to be notified in the event of a petition for adoption, he should register on the Putative Father's Registry. This is important in the event he believes that the mother of the child may try to put the child up for adoption before he is able to file a petition with the court to determine his paternity.

Issues to Be Addressed Once Parentage is Established

As discussed above, in a parentage case, just like in a divorce case, discovery will need to be done to determine the incomes of the parties and set child support. Discovery requests in parentage cases will likely not be as in-depth as in divorce cases, however it is still just as important. Make sure you read the discovery chapter in order to understand how the discovery process works. Completing discovery is imperative in a parentage case in order to ensure any child support obligation that is ordered is fair to both parties.

As discussed above, in order to set out parenting time and parenting responsibilities, an Allocation Judgment will need to be entered. This document will lay out each parent's schedule of parenting time, and also lay out the responsibilities of each parent and who has authority to make major decisions regarding the child. There are many things that are contained in an allocation judgment. See the chapter regarding children's issues for an overview of Allocation Judgments, as it will need to be entered in every parentage case.

In addition to an Allocation Judgment, a Court will need to enter some kind of Financial Judgment in order to deal with issues such as child support, post-high school educational costs, the splitting of out of pocket medical costs, and any obligation to carry life insurance to provide for the support of the child. This document will be a legally binding document outlining the financial obligations of each parent to the child. There are many things that should be included to ensure the child is properly provided for. As a parent, you want to make sure you understand each and every provision of the Financial Judgment to ensure you are completely following the Orders, so your co-parent can't allege that you are not following the Judgment.

Conclusion

There are a lot of considerations to take into account with paternity. If you are the father of a child and you are not married to the mother, you have options. You may file a Petition to establish the father-child relationship so you can begin to have court-ordered parenting time. This will also establish some financial obligations you will have for this child. If there is a legal presumption that a child is not yours but you know the child is not biologically yours, you may choose to continue to be that child's father or you may choose to challenge the birth certificate. Whatever your situation, it is best if you consult with a family law attorney to ensure you understand your rights and responsibilities in these situations.

DIVERSE FAMILIES AND UNIQUE ISSUES

Modern society includes various family structures and diverse families which may result in unique family law and estate planning concerns. The following represents only a fraction of these issues. If your situation is not addressed, we urge you to consult with an attorney as the law is constantly evolving to address new issues.

Adoption

The Illinois Adoption Act governs the adoption of an individual and gives direction to the adoption process. In order to initiate the adoption process, a reputable person(s) making application must be of legal age, have no legal disability, and must reside in the state of Illinois for at least six months prior to the beginning of the adoption proceedings. 750 Ill. Comp. Stat. Ann. 50/2(A)(a) (LexisNexis through P.A. 101-631). There are residency exceptions for agency adoptions and foreign adoptions. 750 Ill. Comp. Stat. Ann. 50/2(B)(a)-(b) (LexisNexis through P.A. 101-631). Also, the residency exceptions for members of the armed forces of the United States allow for the filing of adoption as long as the member is domiciled in Illinois for 90 days. 750 Ill. Comp. Stat. Ann. 50/2(A) (LexisNexis through P.A. 101-631).

The adoption process can include a related adoption, non-related adoption, agency adoption, or foreign adoption. Related Adoptions occur in situations in which at least one of the adoptive parties is related by blood, marriage, civil union, or adoption to the child seeking to be adopted. Non-related adoptions that occur outside of agencies, involve parties who have no relation and the biological parents consent to the non-related adoption. An agency adoption refers to an adoption involving the public child welfare agency or a licensed child welfare agency. International and foreign adoptions, although increasingly common, can be very complex. Usually a child adopted in a foreign country is more likely than not arranged through an adoption agency, and the action is commenced in that foreign country.

In Illinois, the process to begin the adoption proceedings for an adult or related child can begin at any time with the filing of a petition for adoption and notice to all parties involved. All other adoptions involve notice and the filing of the petition within 30 days (unless the court allows for a shorter time frame) of when the child becomes available for adoption. Biological parents may consent to terminate their parental rights and consent to the adoption. 750 Ill. Comp. Stat. Ann. 50/5(A) (LexisNexis through P.A. 101-631). Even still, it may be necessary for a background check and an investigation into the home of the person(s) seeking adoption. 750 Ill. Comp. Stat. Ann. 50/6(A) (LexisNexis through P.A. 101-631). Once the Adoption process is completed, the adoptive parent(s) will become the child's legal parent with all of the rights and responsibilities as if the child were born to them.

Same Sex Marriage

Marriage, domestic partnerships, and civil unions between people of the same sex are now treated the same as those between people of the opposite sex. The freedom to marry is a fundamental human right – and with that equality, comes the right to choose what type of legal relationship you deem appropriate under your circumstances. Legal events demonstrate the speed at which things change in the human rights movement for the freedom to marry. Amid the confusion of legal rules and court actions it can be complicated, from a legal standpoint, to be in a same-sex relationship these days.

In June 2013, the U. S. Supreme Court struck down Section 3 of the Defense of Marriage Act (DOMA) which had barred the federal government from recognizing the marriages of same-sex couples. *United States v. Windsor*, 570 U.S. 744, 775 (2013). In 2015, the Court tossed out the remaining state bans against the right of same-sex couples to marry. *Obergefell v. Hodges*, 135 S. Ct. 2584, 2607-08 (2015).

What will a same-sex legal partnership mean to your family? Will it benefit you financially to make a legal commitment, or cause more problems than positives? What does it mean to your plans to have children?

Marital relationships, it is widely accepted, are the basis of significant material benefits and social legitimacy. Marriage provides public legal recognition and the identity of one spouse to the other. But simple cohabitation, or civil union, is also a choice. Each person when they meet Mr. or Ms. Right and want to settle down, is free to ask whether they should simply cohabit, without any formal legal relationship between them, or whether they should "make it legal." There are still inconsistencies regarding parentage and custody rights, problems resulting from disparate tax treatment of same-sex couples, and potential dilemmas for couples who move across state lines. If you're planning to raise children, and you are wondering whether you live in a state that unambiguously protects the rights of same-sex parents, consult with a family law attorney about the parentage laws of that state and how to protect your legal relationship with your child.

Once you elect to get married, the rules of marriage apply, and you are in business together, no matter how you feel about your spouse's level of ambition or financial habits. A married couple is viewed as a single economic unit, a unified economic partnership. It doesn't matter who gets the fatter paycheck, who does the housework, or who indulges in profligate consumer purchases – you are both players on a single financial team. This is why benefits like health insurance are provided to both partners: the employer and the government are treating the couple as a single economic unit.

Have the hard conversations. Talk to your family law attorney about death and property transfers. What are the tax consequences of marriage? Should you draft a premarital agreement? In the event of divorce, the spousal support rules will apply. Same-sex claims for spousal support will begin making their way into the courts.

What are your premarital assets? Consider this, most opposite-sex couples did not acquire much before marriage. Opposite-sex couples have traditionally married before they start acquiring significant property. But same-sex couples weren't able to marry until 2004 or later, so same-sex divorces often involve people with successful careers before the marriage took place.

What are the tax consequences, should your marriage fail? Married couples have the privilege of passing money and property back and forth between them, both during marriage and at divorce, without any tax consequences at all. Now that the federal government recognizes same-sex marriages, federal tax exemptions also apply to same-sex married couples – both during marriage and at divorce.

Before you marry, consult with an attorney and ask some difficult questions: you may be receiving spousal support benefits from a prior marriage, or pension payments from a deceased spouse's former employer, or Social Security survivor benefits, or income under a restrictive trust; will the payments terminate? If you are receiving any payment of this kind, talk with your attorney about the risk of losing this income if you legally partner or marry.

How much do you know about your partner's level of debt? What about their liability for unpaid taxes, or their professional liability if they are in a high-risk profession? Your attorney can help you shield yourself by entering into a premarital agreement. There's no substitute for advice from a lawyer about the state laws and how they apply to your specific situation. However, you must be prepared to show up for a true negotiation. Face the difficult issues. You may want to see a lawyer together to get this education, or you may each want to consult a separate attorney. Then consider the issues you want to address in your "prenup" and see whether you understand what the law would do.

Your family law attorney believes that information bestows power and freedom, by giving everyone the tools to best organize their lives, meet their personal needs, protect their families, and create a sustaining legal framework that fosters their dreams and goals. Same-sex couples are in possession of the same basic knowledge relevant to the formation of their legal lives together.

Surrogacy

Are you considering surrogacy in Illinois? No problem, Illinois is one of the most favorable and accommodating States when it comes to surrogacy.

First of all, what is surrogacy? There is Gestational Surrogacy and Traditional Surrogacy. Gestational Surrogacy is where the surrogate is not related to the child she is carrying and is the most common type of surrogacy today. In traditional surrogacy, the surrogate mother uses her own egg and is artificially inseminated using sperm from the intended father or a donor. The surrogate carries and delivers the baby, and then, because she is the child's biological mother, must relinquish her parental rights so that the child can be raised by the intended parents.

The Illinois Gestational Surrogacy Act under 750 ILCS 47/1 allows for the legality of surrogacy and creates a process in which intended parents are declared the parents of the child without even going to court. "The purpose of this Act is to establish consistent standards and procedural safeguards for the protection of all parties involved in a gestational surrogacy contract in this State and to confirm the legal status of children born as a result of these contracts. These standards and safeguards are meant to facilitate the use of this type of reproductive contract in accord with the public policy of this State." 750 Ill. Comp. Stat. Ann. 47/5 (LexisNexis through P.A. 101-631).

Reproductive Issues

Sometimes, individuals who desperately want to have children are unable to have children the traditional way, whether this is due to fertility issues, or consciously not wanting to carry certain hereditary issues from one or both parents, or a same sex couple wishes to have a child together, but are obviously biologically unable to conceive together. There are some options that they may choose in order to help them conceive.

The first is the use of donor eggs or sperm. In this process, a couple will utilize the sperm or eggs from another individual in order to help them conceive a child. In this process, the donor may be anonymous, or may be someone who is known to the couple. If a couple uses an anonymous donor, sperm banks or facilities which process egg donations will often keep a profile on the donor, which may include their physical characteristics, ethnic and educational backgrounds, career history, and general health. This is important for couples who may want the donor to be of a similar background to them, so the resulting child looks like they fit into the family naturally.

There are a few ways that sperm and egg donors may be used in order to help the couple conceive. The couple may simply try to use donor sperm themselves, or they may work with medical professionals to either transfer the donor sperm directly into the mother's uterus, or to combine a donor sperm or egg with a sperm or egg from the intended parents in a laboratory setting and transplant the resulting embryo into the intended mother. When donor eggs or sperm are used, it is important that you make sure you consult with an attorney, in order to ensure that the intended parents are actually the legal parents of the child, and there are no issues with parental rights remaining with the sperm or egg donors.

Although a couple may not require the use of an egg or sperm donor in order to conceive, some women choose to have their eggs harvested and subsequently frozen in order to preserve fertility. There are a number of reasons for this, which may include the following: chemotherapy, ovarian surgery, or aging. Because a woman's eggs age as they get older, utilizing "younger" eggs is often more desirable. When harvesting and freezing eggs, it is important that you understand the agreement with the entity in which you use in order to store the eggs. Facilities may have rules related to how long they may hold eggs, and there may be laws which dictate this information as well.

Sometimes, a couple will freeze some of their embryos, in order to utilize them at a later date. There are many reasons why they may do this, which may include that a couple wishes to have a child that is biologically theirs, but they are not in a space in their lives to implant the embryo. Perhaps you have seen celebrities in the news having legal battles over the frozen embryos to determine what will happen with them. There are certain legal ramifications that must be considered when a couple who created a frozen embryo will need to determine—when that relationship ends, does either party have a right to those embryos? What if one party wants them destroyed, but the other wishes to transplant some of them in order to try and conceive on their own? If you have frozen embryos, it is important to make sure you talk to an attorney to make sure you understand your rights under your state's law.

All of these things may be very personal to discuss, but it is important to make sure if you are considering any of these things that you talk to an attorney. Make sure you understand your rights in any of the above situations, and that everything is done correctly. The last thing that you want is to go through any of the above processes only to find out that everything you have intended isn't actually going to move forward

Grandparent Rights

Grandparents become an integral part of the lives of children, so what happens when a parent or parent(s) attempt to sever that relationship. Illinois has recognized that this relationship needs to be protected if it serves the best interests of the minor child(ren), however, it is a delicate balance with a parent's United States Constitutional right to raise his/her child as he/she deems fit. As an answer to this balance, Illinois has currently enacted 750 ILCS 5/602.9. At the present this is the controlling statute, however, Illinois has attempted a 'grandparent' statue in the past, only to have that statute overturned by higher courts. Therefore, before any court action is taken on behalf of a grandparent, research should be conducted about the current state of the law.

750 ILCS 5/602.9 provides for visitation by certain 'non-parents.' 750 Ill. Comp. Stat. Ann. 5/602.9 (LexisNexis through P.A. 101-631). The statute then specifically addresses grandparents, great-grandparents, siblings, stepparents, siblings, and certain other individuals who might be eligible to request visitation with the child. 750 Ill. Comp. Stat. Ann. 5/602.9(c) (LexisNexis through P.A. 101-631). For purposes of this statute, visitation is defined as in-person time but may also include electronic communication under conditions and at times determined by the Court. 750 Ill. Comp. Stat. Ann. 5/602.9(a)(4) (LexisNexis through P.A. 101-631).

The first step to establish any kind of visitation under 602.9 is for an appropriate person to file an action in the court by petition or by filing a petition in the pending dissolution proceeding or any other proceeding that involves parental responsibilities or visitation issues regarding the child. 750 Ill. Comp. Stat. Ann. 5/602.9(b)(1) (LexisNexis through P.A. 101-631). It should be noted that the statute specifically provides that there is a rebuttable presumption that a fit parent's actions and decisions regarding third party visitation are not harmful to the child's mental, physical, or emotional health and the burden is on the filing party to prove that the parent's actions and decisions regarding visitation will cause undue harm to the child's mental, physical, or emotional health. 750 Ill. Comp. Stat. Ann. 5/602.9(b)(4) (LexisNexis through P.A. 101-631). A petition may only be filed if there has been an unreasonable denial of visitation by a parent and the denial has caused the child undue mental, physical, or emotional harm. 750 Ill. Comp. Stat. Ann. 5/602.9(b)(3) (LexisNexis through P.A. 101-631). The key thing that the statute repeats is the 'unreasonable denial' and the 'undue harm to the child's mental, physical, or emotional health.' *Id.* This is not a burden to be taken lightly and many grandparents do not qualify to file a Petition under these strict requirements.

Not only does the grandparent or other third party have to demonstrate that there was an unreasonable denial and that denial has caused undue mental, physical, or emotional harm, but also that at least one of the following conditions exist as well:

> (A) The child's other parent is deceased or has been missing for at least 90 days.; or
>
> (B) A parent of the child is incompetent as a matter of law; or
>
> (C) A parent has been incarcerated in jail or prison for a period in excess of 90 days immediately prior to the filing of the petition; or
>
> (D) The child's parents have been granted a dissolution of marriage or have been legally separated from each other and there is pending a dissolution proceeding involving a parent of the child or another court proceeding involving parental responsibilities or visitation of the child and at least one parent does not object to the grandparent or other third party having visitation; or
>
> (E) The child is born to parents who are not married to each other, are not living together, the third-party requesting is a grandparent, great-grandparent or sibling and the parent-child relationship has been legally established.

750 Ill. Comp. Stat. Ann. 5/603.9(c)(1)(A)-(E) (LexisNexis through P.A. 101-631).

The Court shall also consider, whether the child resided with the petitioner for at least 6 consecutive months with or without a parent present, whether the child had frequent and regular contact or visitation with the petitioner for at least 12 consecutive months and whether the petitioner was a primary caretaker of the child for a period of not less than 6 consecutive months within the 24-month period immediately preceding the commencement of the proceeding. 750 Ill. Comp. Stat. Ann. 5/602.9(c)(2)(A)-(C) (LexisNexis through P.A. 101-631). Given these additional factors, it is extremely important to these third parties to take swift action when something has gone awry.

If the grandparent or other third party can demonstrate that it is a proper request, then they must demonstrate that the visitation is in the best interests of the child. The statute has listed the following factors:

> (A) The wishes of the child, taking into account the child's maturity and ability to express reasoned and independent preferences as to visitation;
>
> (B) The mental and physical health of the child;

> (C) The mental and physical health of the grandparent, great-grandparent, sibling, or step-parent;
> (D) The length and quality of the prior relationship between the child and grandparent, great-grandparent, sibling, or step-parent;
> (E) The good faith of the party in filing the petition;
> (F) The good faith in the person denying visitation;
> (G) The quantity of the visitation time requested and the potential adverse impact that visitation would have on the child's customary activities;
> (H) Any other fact that establishes that the loss of the relationship between the petitioner and the child is likely to unduly harm the child's mental, physical, or emotional health; and
> (I) Whether visitation can be structured in a way to minimize the child's exposure to conflicts between the adults.

750 Ill. Comp. Stat. Ann. 5/602.9(b)(5)(A)-(I) (LexisNexis through P.A. 101-631).

While the multiple factors associated with establishing visitation for these select third parties, it certainly provides an opportunity to continue that meaningful relationship with the child even under strenuous circumstances. The cases are very fact specific and require a great amount of detail. Grandparents have an uphill battle in establishing visitation but if the requirements are met, a good schedule can be reached.

PLANNING YOUR LEGACY

There is a lot of confusion out there about exactly what estate planning is. What does estate planning include? What does a plan do? Do I need an estate plan? This section will try to give you a basic understanding of what estate planning is, how a well-drafted plan can benefit and protect you and your loved ones, and how you can utilize estate planning to ensure that you and your loved ones are cared for not only after death, but also during emergencies.

Estate planning is often simply defined as specifying who gets your property when you die. While this statement is true, it is also incomplete. A comprehensive estate plan allows you to give your belongings to your loved ones when you want, in the manner that you want, while retaining control over your property. A complete plan also provides for your own care and the care of your loved ones during emergencies and times of incapacity, and helps to protect your assets from creditors, predators, and taxes. Finally, a comprehensive estate plan accomplishes all of the above without unnecessary cost or delay.

You'll notice that I use the word "comprehensive" above. This is because there are different elements to estate planning, depending on your goals and your specific family and financial situation. There is no "one size fits all" estate plan, and your plan should be tailored to your specific needs. Essentially, your plan should be structured in such a way that it focuses first and foremost on protecting you and your family, then on distribution of your property upon death, and finally on avoiding taxes and unnecessary costs or delays. In the next section we will go over some of the key elements of estate planning and discuss their benefits and shortcomings.

The Basic Elements of a Comprehensive Estate Plan

A comprehensive estate plan consists of several different strategies and documents, depending on your individual situation and goals. Below is a description of some of the core documents utilized in estate planning, a brief description of each document, its main functions, and how each is utilized to help protect you and your loved ones.

Last Will and Testament

Your Last Will and Testament, often simply referred to as your Will, is an attestation of who you want to wrap up your affairs (called your Executor) and who you want to receive your property when you die. One extremely important aspect of a Will is that it allows you to designate your preferred Guardian for underage children under your care. In Illinois, wills are governed by Article IV of the Illinois Probate Act (755 ILCS 5/4-1), which sets forth specific guidelines for the capacity of the person making the will as well as for executing the document in order for it to be considered valid. 755 Ill. Comp. Stat. Ann. 5/4-1 (LexisNexis through P.A. 101-631); 755 Ill. Comp. Stat. Ann. 5/4-3 (LexisNexis through P.A. 101-631). It is very important to ensure that at the time of the drafting of a will, the person executing the document is of sound mind, and is capable of fully understanding the implications of what they are signing. 755 Ill. Comp. Stat. ann. 5/4-1(a) (LexisNexis through P.A. 101-631). As an estate planner, I often get calls regarding planning the estate of an individual with dementia or some other form of cognitive impairment, and it can be difficult to ensure they are of sound mind. This makes it important to ensure you and your loved ones have a will in place prior to any cognitive impairment.

Wills are a specific product of the Probate Act cited above; as such, a will has no legal force or effect unless it is filed with the court and the probate process is followed. The probate process is the process of filing a Will with the court and following the procedures to legally close an estate. This process is discussed in more detail in a later section.

The obvious benefit to having a Will is that you designate what happens to your property when you die and designate your preferred choice as to who will care for and raise your children. Another benefit is that as long as the probate process is properly followed, creditors are barred from making claims against an estate or heirs after the estate is closed.

If you do not have a Will, your estate will be distributed under the Illinois Probate Act, which can often be very different than one would expect!

Wills do have several drawbacks. The first being that, as discussed earlier, they have no legal force or effect unless filed with the court and completing the probate process. This process has many filing and time period requirements, which can cause a delay between a person's death and the time their estate is distributed to their loved ones. Because the process can be lengthy, it can also be expensive, as the Executor will generally need to hire an attorney to ensure all of the court processes are adhered to and the proper filings made. One other potential downside is that because the Will is filed in court, it is generally available to the public, and anyone who wants to know who inherited your property can find this information.

Another drawback is that a Will is generally meant only to designate who will wrap up your affairs and who is to receive your property when you pass away. With limited exceptions that generally require more estate planning, you cannot put specific caveats or leave detailed instructions as to how and when your property will be distributed in a Will.

Living Trust (depending on your circumstances)

A Living Trust, also called a revocable trust, is a very flexible means of estate planning that allows you (the grantor of the trust) to retain complete control over your property while you are alive, and also to designate, very specifically, how that property is to be handled and distributed during your incapacity and upon your death.

Trusts are often seen as complicated or only useful for larger, more complex estates, but that is simply not the case. The way a trust works can be described very simply. When a trust is created, a person assigns their property over to the trust or makes the trust the designated beneficiary of certain accounts. The person creating the trust is appointed as the initial "trustee", which is the person who exercises control over the property. As they are the trustee, the person creating the trust retains complete control over all of the property in the trust and is free to do with it as they please. Upon the initial trustee's death or incapacitation, a successor trustee takes over, following the guidelines set out in the trust. Trusts can be very useful and below are just a few of their main benefits.

First, a trust can completely avoid the probate process. Trusts are governed by the Illinois Trusts and Trustees Act Illinois Trust Code 760 ILCS 3/101) and therefore fall outside the realm of court validation and supervision in most circumstances. Property left to an heir via trust is distributed directly by the successor trustee appointed by the person making the trust, in the manner described in the trust.

As a result of the above, funds and property can be accessed much more quickly by beneficiaries and heirs than if they had to go through the process of probate.

Moreover, trusts allow for much more flexibility and control of assets after your incapacity or death. It is possible to set many restrictions on access to the trust property or funds. For example, you can place age restrictions as to when a beneficiary can access trust funds. This can help limit access to the funds until your heirs reach a certain age, reach a certain milestone, or even restrict what the trust funds or property can be used for. In this way, trusts allow for much more flexibility than a will.

As mentioned briefly above, a trust also allows you to appoint a successor trustee during times when you are incapacitated, which allows for continuous care of your assets. This differs greatly from a will, which only has any effect upon your death and upon filing with the court.

Do trusts have any disadvantages? The short answer is yes. While I do not really consider it a disadvantage, all property that has a registered deed or title must be re-registered in the name of the trust. The process is simple and straightforward, but there are costs involved in doing so. Failing to place such property in the name of the trust will generally exclude it from being considered trust property.

This is not necessarily a disadvantage, but one misconception that I hear often is that a revocable trust will protect someone's assets against creditors. This is not the case. The law views a revocable trust as somewhat of a legal fiction during the grantor's lifetime. As the grantor still retains total control over all of the property in the trust and can do with that property what they wish, a revocable trust does not offer any protection from creditors.

Irrevocable Trusts

Irrevocable trusts are, as the name implies, trusts that cannot be revoked, modified, or amended by the grantor (the person forming and transferring property to the trust). The grantor gives up ownership of property or funds when transferred to the Trust, and generally cannot assert any control over the property or get the property back, so these trusts can offer asset protection, albeit at a price. These trusts are generally used for certain circumstances to fulfill tax or other special planning needs.

Power of Attorney for Property

Simply put, a power of attorney for property is a legal document that allows you to give someone else the ability to handle your financial affairs on your behalf. Such powers of attorney can be "durable" (beginning when signed and terminating on death or revocation), or "springing" (beginning upon a set event, such as a determination of your incapacity and inability to make your own decisions). These powers of attorney can be very broad or they can be limited in scope.

Powers of attorney are very powerful tools to protect yourself and your assets during times of incapacity or in some cases, your absence. They can allow someone else to handle your affairs, make payments, manage investments, etc. if you are unable to do so. 755 Ill. Comp. Stat. Ann. 45/3-4 (LexisNexis through P.A. 101-631). This can help to keep your affairs in order and maintain access funds for your care during emergencies or if you become incapacitated.

As you can imagine, powers of attorney for property do not come without risk. When someone else is given access to your finances and the ability to handle your affairs, it can open the door for fraud. It is therefore very important to take steps to minimize the risks involved, by choosing your power of attorney wisely or putting limits on the powers granted.

One misconception about powers of attorney is that people often look at them as an estate plan in and of themselves; if I give so-and-so power of attorney, they can handle my affairs when I die. I often have folks call me and tell me that they have assisted their father or mother with her financial affairs for years under a power of attorney, only to have the financial institutions tell them they can no longer deal with them once their loved one dies. This is because powers of attorney terminate upon death; they have no force and effect once a person passes away. This helps to illustrate the importance of having a comprehensive plan in place!

Power of Attorney for Healthcare

A Power of Attorney for Healthcare allows you to designate someone to make healthcare decisions on your behalf. These powers can also be "durable" (beginning when signed and terminating on death or revocation), or "springing" (beginning upon a set event, such as a determination of your incapacity and inability to make your own decisions). They can also be limited or very general in scope.

One important aspect of a power of attorney for health care is that the person you appoint should make decisions based upon your wishes, so it is important to choose someone who is aware of your wishes and will follow your guidelines. You should have a very meaningful and detailed discussion with your healthcare power of attorney so they make choices based upon your intent.

The Illinois Statutory Power of Attorney for Healthcare also has a section that acts as an abbreviated Living Will, which is discussed below.

Living Will

A living will is an advance directive whose main purpose is to specify your wishes ahead of time regarding end of life care. A living will can be intricately drafted, but generally a living will states that you do not want life prolonging action taken if you are terminally ill and will not recover.

A living will is an important tool as it allows you to dictate your treatment at the end of your life. 755 Ill. Comp. Stat. Ann. 35/1 (LexisNexis through P.A. 101-631). It also provides clarification if the individual who you have appointed as your healthcare power of attorney does not want to make the decision, or perhaps is making a contradictory decision.

Pay on Death Accounts

Pay on death accounts are those accounts that allow you to designate a death beneficiary, such as life insurance. These accounts generally avoid any probate issues as the company will relinquish the funds or property to the beneficiary when presented with evidence of death. Many institutions allow you to designate a death beneficiary for different types of insurance, banking, investment, or retirement accounts.

When planning your estate, it is important to determine whether your accounts allow for designation of a death beneficiary, whether all of these accounts are up to date and the correct beneficiary is designated, and whether it makes sense to leave the designation as-is or to amend it to better support your wishes and planning goals.

While these accounts often simplify matters at death, they do come with some drawbacks. The main drawback is that YOU are responsible for maintaining and updating your beneficiaries; a life event will generally NOT trigger any automatic changes to your beneficiaries. In other words, if you've listed your spouse as your beneficiary on your life insurance and then get divorced, you want to be sure to update your beneficiary!

Transfer on Death Documents

Transfer on death documents are a bit like the pay on death accounts mentioned above; they designate a transfer of ownership to a named individual upon the death of the individual executing the documents. These documents are filed with the appropriate authority, such as a county's recorder of deeds, and are effective upon the death of the individual providing they still own the property at the time of death.

Other Information And Considerations

What Exactly is Probate and Should I Avoid It?

As mentioned above, Probate is the legal process of administering and closing the estate of a deceased person. This is done by resolving all claims related to the estate and by distributing the deceased person's property under a valid will or under the Intestacy laws of the State of Illinois. The probate process can be relatively simple and straightforward in most matters, but can result in delays and costs in more complicated or contested matters. The Probate Process is governed by Illinois Probate Act (755 ILCS 5/4-1) and local county and court rules of procedure.

Probate cases are opened when a will is filed with the court or, in cases where there is no will, a person petitions the court to open an estate for the deceased. A probate case where a valid will exists and is filed is called a testate estate. If there is no will, the probate case is called intestate, and the deceased's property is distributed pursuant to Illinois laws of intestacy. Depending upon the circumstances and/or the terms of the Will, the Executor may also need to post a surety bond, which is basically a form of insurance that ensures that the wishes of the deceased as expressed in the will are carried out ethically and honestly. The court will then issue letters to the executor or administrator of the estate which will enable them to legally carry out their duties.

The deceased's possible and named heirs must also be notified that a probate case has been opened. The deceased's assets and debts should then be ascertained, and creditors notified. Notice of the estate must also be published, to give any unidentified creditors notice of the estate and therefore the ability to make a claim. Creditors are given six months from the date of first publication to make a claim.
It is the executor's duty to gather and liquidate the deceased's assets, pay creditors, and distribute assets, all while maintaining a complete accounting of the estate. The executor has a fiduciary duty to the estate and to the heirs, which means they have a duty to act in the best interest of the estate and the heirs.

Simply put, probate is a step by step process by which the estate of the deceased is opened, an Executor is appointed, debts are paid, assets are distributed, and the estate is closed. There are some downsides to probate; for example, as a result of the outlined process, notification requirements, and court procedures and delays, the probate process can be time consuming and may delay the distribution of the deceased's assets for a year or more.

As mentioned above, the probate process may result in unnecessary costs to the estate, due to multiple attorney appearances and filings during the process. Additionally, if you own property outside of Illinois.

Estate Planning attorneys often get asked if a person should plan their estate with the intent of avoiding probate entirely, and while this question is situation-specific, the general response is yes. If you can arrange your estate in such a way as to settle your affairs, provide for your loved ones, maintain your affairs in private, and carry out your wishes without court supervision while minimizing potential delays and costs, we truly believe it makes sense to do so.

Planning for Special Circumstances

There are a number of special circumstances that may require additional planning than the circumstances above. For example:

You may be the parent of a child with special needs, and therefore you may want to set up a special needs trust for your child that can allow them to remain qualified for certain government and other benefits while still having supplemental funds available for their well-being.

You may have assets that fall above the current state and federal estate tax exemption limits, so your heirs and your estate may benefit from a plan that emphasizes tax saving strategies.

You may be a member of a blended family, with further estate planning considerations that may want to take into account the estate plan of others to ensure your loved ones are cared for equally.

You may own a business and have specific goals of succession or distribution in mind that require additional estate and business strategies.

These are just a few circumstances that illustrate the importance of speaking with a professional, knowledgeable estate planning attorney who can best guide you on the correct path to accomplish your goals.

When Should I Start Estate Planning?

Many individuals often state that they don't think they have an "estate" large enough to warrant an actual estate plan, but as we have seen above, estate planning is about so much more than your assets. Many folks are surprised by what they own when they sit and take stock of their circumstances and have a frank discussion of what may happen if a plan is not put in place. Regardless of your circumstances, some form of planning can always be done to put wishes in writing and protect the ones you love.

Most often, major life events act as the trigger that bring folks to plan their estate; someone gets married, a child is born, a loved one gets sick, or a loved one passes on. The old cliché has it right, there is no better time than the present to plan your estate. It is important to remember that none of us can predict when an emergency or tragedy may strike and life does not always follow our expectations. This is why planning ahead is so important for your physical and financial health and the well-being of your loved ones. We simply cannot predict what life will throw at us or when, and frankly there is no trigger out there to tell us when it is the perfect time to put a plan in place.

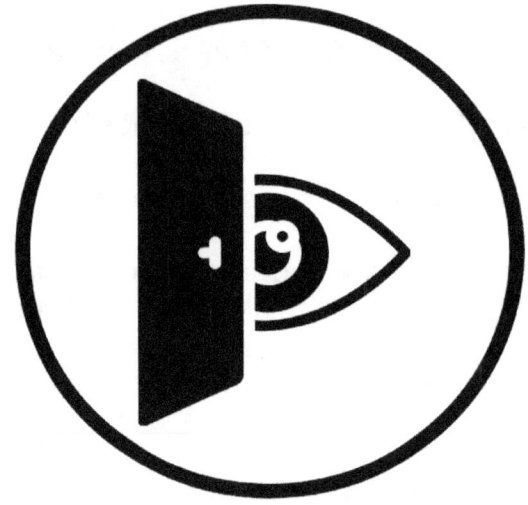

KEEPING A WATCHFUL EYE

Guardianships in Illinois

A guardian manages the affairs of another after being appointed by the Probate Court. The guardian oversees the person called the WARD. The first step to determine if a guardianship action is appropriate is to ask the question WHO needs a guardian followed by who can be a guardian.

Who May Have a Guardian Appointed to Manage His/Her Affairs?

The law presumes that an adult eighteen years of age or older is capable of handling his/her own affairs. A guardian may be appointed to serve as a substitute decision maker if a person is disabled because of the following:
- mental deterioration;
- physical incapacity;
- mental illness; or
- developmental disability.

755 Ill. Comp. Stat. Ann. 5/11a-2 (LexisNexis through P.A. 101-631).

For a guardianship to be necessary, the disability must prevent the person from making or communicating responsible decisions about his/her personal affairs. *Id.*

The law also provides that a guardian may also be appointed if, because of "gambling, idleness, debauchery, or excessive use of intoxicants or drugs", a person spends or wastes their estate so as to put the person or their family in a place of "want or suffering." In either case, guardianship may be necessary to protect the person. *Id.*

Who Can Be a Guardian in Illinois

Illinois law has established the following requirements to be a guardianship in Illinois. To be a guardian, you must be:

1. A person at least 18 years of age;
2. A resident of the US;
3. A person of sound mind;
4. A person not adjudicated disabled under the Probate Act of Illinois; and
5. A person who has not been convicted of a felony unless otherwise approved by the Court. If the felony is not one of harm or threat to a minor or an elderly person or person with a disability, including a felony sexual offense, the court can consider the nature, date, and evidence of the proposed guardian's rehabilitation and waive this requirement.

755 Ill. Comp. Stat. Ann. 5/11a-5(a)(1)-(5) (LexisNexis through P.A. 101-631).

What If There Is a Power of Attorney in Lieu of Guardian

Any agent appointed under a Power of Attorney is entitled to notice under the Probate Act of a Petition to Appoint a Guardian. In general, the power of attorney will supersede the Petition for a Guardianship so long as the agent appointed as power of attorney is not breaching their duties and there are no allegations that the document appointing the agent as power of attorney is not valid. Remember that the person appointing the agent must have had the capacity and understanding to appoint an agent as Power of Attorney at the time the Power of Attorney was executed.

Are Parents Guardians of Their Children

Parents are guardians of their children until the child reaches the age of 18. At that time if a child needs to have a guardian, a guardianship must be established to continue to make decisions for your child. As of July, 2019, Illinois law provides that a court lacks the power to proceed on a petition for the appointment of a guardian or standby guardian of a minor if it finds that the minor has a living parent whose parental rights have not been terminated, unless, among other things, the parent or parents, in the event of an administrative separation, are not presently located in the United States and are unable to consent as evidenced by a sworn affidavit. 755 Ill. Comp. Stat. Ann. 5/11-5.3(c) (LexisNexis through P.A. 101-631). This provision also relates to the appointment of short-terms guardians appointed by a parent or guardian. 755 Ill. Comp. Stat. Ann. 5/11-5.4(b) (LexisNexis through P.A. 101-631).

What Are the Steps of a Guardianship Proceeding in Illinois

If the proposed Guardian meets the qualifications to be appointed, then an action to appoint a guardian can be filed in the Circuit Court where the proposed Ward resides. 755 Ill. Comp. Stat. Ann. 5/11a-7 (LexisNexis through P.A. 101-631); 755 Ill. Comp. Stat. ann. 5/11-6 (LexisNexis through P.A. 101-631). Remember a Ward is the person in need of a guardianship.

In Illinois, the only way someone can be a guardian for a person who is eighteen years old or older is to be appointed by the Circuit Court. Guardianship procedures are set forth in the Illinois Probate Act. Different counties in Illinois may have additional rules that need to be followed.

Step One: Report of Physician

The first step in the process is to obtain a Report of Physician to attach to your Petition seeking to appoint a guardian. 755 Ill. Comp. Stat. Ann. 5/11a-9(a) (LexisNexis through P.A. 101-631). If it is impossible to obtain such a report, then the proposed guardian may petition the court to order "appropriate evaluations to be performed".

The physician's report should provide according to Illinois law the following information:

- a description of the nature and type of the respondent's disability, and an assessment of how the disability impacts on the ability of the respondent to make decisions or to function independently;
- an analysis and results of evaluations of the respondent's mental and physical condition and, where appropriate, educational condition, adaptive behavior and social skills, which have been performed within 3 months of the date of the filing of the petition;
- an opinion as to whether guardianship is needed, and the reasons therefore;
- a recommendation as to the most suitable living arrangement and, where appropriate, treatment or habilitation plan for the respondent and the reasons therefore;
- the signatures of all persons who performed the evaluations upon which the report is based, one of whom shall be a licensed physician and a statement of the certification, license, or other credentials that qualify the evaluators who prepared the report.

Id.

Keep in mind that the report must be dated within 3 months of filing the Petition. *Id.*

Step Two: File The Petition

Court ordered forms must be completed when seeking to be appointed as Guardian. The Petition must state whether a guardianship of an estate or person or both is sought and must contain the value of the personal estate, the value of the real estate and the anticipated gross annual income and other receipts of the alleged disabled adult.

755 Ill. Comp. Stat. Ann. 5/11a-8 (LexisNexis through P.A. 101-631). The Petition must name any agents appointed under the Illinois Power of Attorney Act and all nearest relatives of the proposed Ward. *Id.* The person seeking for the appointment of a guardian does not necessarily have to be the proposed guardian. *Id.*

A Summons for Appointment must also be completed with Notice to the Respondent (proposed Ward) of all of their Rights as Respondent to the action. 755 Ill. Comp. Stat. Ann. 5/11a-10(b), (e) (LexisNexis through P.A. 101-631). All agents and relatives must also be provided notice. An Oath and Bond will need to be presented along with a proposed Order appointing a Guardian. Finally, the proposed Guardian must present personal information in a Verified Statement.

Step Three: Appointment of The Guardian Ad Litem for Alleged Disabled Adult

The Court will appoint a Guardian Ad Litem (GAL) who will interview the proposed Ward and inform the proposed Ward of the Petition and their rights under the Illinois Probate Act. 755 Ill. Comp. Stat. ann. 5/11a-10(a) (LexisNexis through P.A. 101-631). The Guardian Ad Litem's role is to protect the interests of the alleged person with disabilities in the guardianship proceedings. The GAL will attempt to determine the wishes of the alleged disabled person and look at the changes that will result on behalf of the proposed Ward if guardianship is granted. *Id.*

The GAL files a written report and may appear and testify concerning the position of the GAL on the appropriateness of guardianship. *Id.*

Step Four - The Rights of the Alleged Disabled

The proposed Ward has several legal rights during the Hearing as to the appointment of a Guardian. These rights of the alleged disabled include:

- The right to be present at the court hearing;
- The right to be represented by a lawyer, either retained by the proposed Ward or appointed by the Judge;
- The right to ask for a jury of six;
- The right to present evidence to the court and to confront and cross-examine witnesses;
- The right to ask the Judge to appoint an independent expert to examine the proposed Ward and give an opinion about the need for a guardian;
- The right to ask the Court to close the hearing from the public;
- The right to tell the court who the proposed Ward would want as a guardian.

755 Ill. Comp. Stat. Ann. 5/11a-10(e) (LexisNexis through P.A. 101-631).

An individual facing a guardianship adjudication also has the right to request an independent medical evaluation, which must be paid from the funds of the alleged person with disabilities. The proposed Guardian can also present their case to the Court submitting evidence as to the need for the Guardianship

Step Five: Court Grants or Denies the Petition

If the Court grants the Petition for Guardian of the *Person*, then the Guardian must complete the Acceptance of Office of Guardian of the Person of a Disabled Adult. If the Court grants the Petition for Guardian of the *Estate*, then the Guardian must complete the Acceptance of Office of Guardian of Estate of Disabled Adult. The Guardian must then prepare and submit annual reports to the Court consistent with Illinois law.

If the case is presented to a jury, then the Jury will decide whether a guardian is appointed.

Finally, if appointed as Guardian of the Estate, a full Inventory of the Estate Assets must be submitted to the Court.

What Are The Types Of Guardianships

There are many types of Guardianships in Illinois some of which overlap. If you are considering seeking a Guardianship in Illinois, it is important that you understand the terminology in considering what is necessary and in the best interest of the alleged disabled person, also known as the Ward. The following is a summary of the types of guardianships available:

Limited Guardianships

A limited guardianship is an option when a disabled person is able to make some of the disabled adult's financial or personal decisions but not all. The Court will specify the decisions that a limited guardian is empowered to make. One could describe limited guardianship as more personalized to the disabled adult's specific needs. That is to say, the disabled adult with a limited guardian retains as much control over his or her own affairs as is appropriate.

Plenary Guardianships

Total (plenary) guardianship should only be used when the person with disabilities is so incapacitated that the proposed Ward cannot make any decisions themselves. A plenary guardian generally has the power to make all decisions about personal care if appointed guardian of the person and about finances for the disabled person if an appointed guardian of the estate. This type of guardianship is considered to be invasive to the Ward's life.

Emergency Guardianships

In certain situations, an emergency arises which requires the appointment of a temporary guardian. Under the Illinois Probate Act, the Court may make a temporary appointment as follows:

"Upon a showing of the necessity therefore for the immediate welfare and protection of the alleged person with a disability or his or her estate on such notice and subject to such conditions as the court may prescribe." 755 Ill. Comp. Stat. Ann. 5/11a-

4(a) (LexisNexis through P.A. 101-631). A temporary guardianship is valid for up to 60 days. 755 Ill. Comp. Stat. Ann 5/11a-4(b) (LexisNexis through P.A. 101-631).

Guardian of the Person

A guardian of a person can be a limited or plenary guardianship. A guardian of a person deals with the care, comfort, health, education, and anything related to non-financial aspects of the person. 755 Ill. Comp. Stat. ann. 5/11a-17(a) (LexisNexis through P.A. 101-631). The guardian of the person is to use substituted judgment in making the decision. That is to say, the guardian is to try to determine what the disabled adult would have decided if able to decide and make that decision on behalf of the disabled adult. The Guardian of the Person does not have the authority to place the Ward in a residential facility without leave of court. 755 Ill. Comp. Stat. Ann. 5/11a-14.1 (LexisNexis through P.A. 101-631).

Guardian of the Estate

A guardian of the estate can be limited or plenary. This guardian has the authority to manage the ward's property and finances. 755 Ill. Comp. Stat. Ann. 5/11a-18(a) (LexisNexis through P.A. 101-631). This guardian must report to the court and account to the Court all of the assets of the Ward and explain every expenditure made for the benefit of the Ward. This Guardian of the Estate has a fiduciary duty of care and must use the state for the benefit of only the Ward. The Guardian of the Estate may be able to sell assets for the Ward's needs with approval from the Court.

Guardian of a Minor

When a parent is unable or unwilling to care for a minor, a guardian is appointed to care for the child. There are three types of guardian of a minor including plenary guardianship, standby guardianship or short term guardianship. A plenary guardianship of a minor involves court action and an appointment by the Court to provide care until the child reaches age 18. A short-term guardian is responsible for the child for one year or less. 755 Ill. Comp. Stat. Ann. 5/11-13.2(a) (LexisNexis through P.A. 101-631). The parent or guardian picks the short-term guardian. The parent or guardian does not need to go to court, but the agreement must be in writing. A standby guardian automatically has the authority to act as full guardian for up to 60 days. 755 Ill. Comp. Stat. Ann. 11-13.1(b) (LexisNexis through P.A. 101-631). Care must be taken to ensure you have fulfilled the requirements for any of these forms of guardianship for a minor.

Successor Guardianship/Standby Guardian

This a guardian appointed when the initial guardian dies, becomes disabled or resigns. *Id.* A person may name a successor guardian in their estate plan and in that event the Court will give that election deference but is not bound by the appointment. The Court can also preselect the successor guardian by court order often referred to as a

Standby Guardian. The standby guardian has no duties until the death or disability of the permanent guardian. *Id.*

Testamentary Guardianship

This form of guardianship occurs when a person by will designates who will be his or her guardian of their person or estate or who they desire to be their child's guardian in the event of death or disability. In most instances, the designated person must still be appointed by the court before he/she can serve as a guardian. The court will consider the designated person but is not bound by the testamentary designation. It can appoint someone else if the proposed guardian is found to be inappropriate.

Special Issues Relating to Guardians of the Estate

Although the above sets forth the various types of guardianships, the Courts in general grant two types of Guardians, a Guardian of the Person and a Guardian of the Estate. These Guardians can be the same person, but do not have to be. Each are charged with decisions for an individual; however, each has a very different role. The Illinois Probate Act also gives the court flexibility to tailor the guardianship to meet the needs and capabilities of individuals with a disability. The guardianships are also mutually exclusive, meaning that there can be a Guardian over the person but not a Guardian of the Estate and vice versa.

In general, any person 18 years of age or older, who has not been convicted of a serious crime and is of sound mind can serve as guardian, if the court deems that person appropriate. 755 Ill. Comp. Stat. ann. 5/11a-5(a)(1)-(5) (LexisNexis through P.A. 101-631). The proposed Guardian of the Estate must also demonstrate to the Court an ability to provide sufficient protection over the individual's assets. 755 Ill. Comp. Stat. ann. 5/11a-5(a) (LexisNexis through P.A. 101-631). Any agency, public or private, may also serve as a Guardian of the estate, if the court finds that it meets the requirements necessary; however, the court shall not appoint any agency providing residential services to the individual with disabilities in order to protect any potential conflicts of interests. 755 Ill. Comp. Stat. ann. 5/11a-5(b) (LexisNexis through P.A. 101-631). Additionally, if so chosen, a bank institution may serve as the guardian of the estate; however, cannot serve as guardian of the person. 755 Ill. Comp. Stat. Ann. 5/11a-5(c) (LexisNexis through P.A. 101-631).

A Guardian of the Estate is charged primarily with overseeing the financial decision making for the person with a disability. 755 Ill. Comp. Stat. Ann. 5/11a-18(a-5) (LexisNexis through P.A. 101-631). The Guardian of the Estate is tasked with ensuring that no one is taking financial advantage of the person with a disability and ensuring that the funds available are used as economically as possible.

Another issue with Guardians of the Estate is overseeing that the individual's assets are being used to further their care and not for the benefit of others. Subject to court supervision, the Guardian of the Estate will make decisions about the individual's funds and safeguarding these financial assets.

Estate guardians must file inventories on a yearly basis at first, of the ward's assets and periodic accounting of estate expenditures. All expenses are subject to court review and if there is any inappropriate spending, the guardian of the estate may be held accountable for those mismanaged funds.

Substituted Judgment of Guardians of the Person

The Illinois Probate Act states that the guardian of the person with respect to the Ward "shall make provision for their support, care, comfort, health, education and maintenance, and professional services as are appropriate;" 755 Ill. Comp. Stat. Ann. 5/11a-17(a) (LexisNexis through P.A. 101-631). The role of the guardian of the person is to "assist the ward in the development of maximum self-reliance and independence." *Id.* The powers are very open and broad as to non-financial matters and are subject to the Court's ruling on a specific issue if the actions taken are not in the best interest of the ward or not consistent with the Guardians task of using substituted judgment.

In making decisions, the Guardian is to use their "substituted judgment." What this means is when making decisions for the Ward, the Guardian of the Person is to determine what the Ward would have done in a given situation if able to do so. 755 Ill. Comp. Stat. ann. 5/11a-17(e) (LexisNexis through P.A. 101-631). The substituted judgment requirement is superior to what the Guardian believes is in the best interest of the Ward. *Id.* This means not using the will of the Guardian but the will of the ward. It means doing what the ward would want and not what the guardian believes is best. *Id.*

There are several factors the Guardian of the Person should consider including the religious, moral, philosophical or life beliefs as well as the wishes of the disabled adult that were expressed at any time in which the Ward was competent. *Id.* ONLY if these wishes are not available does the guardian of the person make decisions based on what they believe is in the best interest of the disabled adult except for decisions with respect to living arrangements where the living arrangement would cause harm to the disabled adult or their finances.

In making decisions, the law requires that "the guardian shall weigh the reason for and nature of the proposed action, the benefit or necessity of the action, the possible risks and other consequences of the proposed action, and any available alternatives and their risks, consequences and benefits, and shall take into account any other information, including the views of family and friends, that the guardian believes the ward would have considered if able to act for herself or himself." *Id.*

In terms of residential placement, the guardian may not place the ward in a resident facility except by Court Order. 755 Ill. Comp. Stat. ann. 5/11a-14.1 (LexisNexis through P.A. 101-631). Further, the guardian does not have the authority to admit the Ward to a mental health facility for voluntary treatment unless the ward consents to treatment. 755 Ill. Comp. Stat. ann. 5/11a-17(a) (LexisNexis through P.A. 101-631). That is to say, the Illinois Mental Health and Disabilities Code remains in effect as to these decisions. *Id.* This does not preclude the Guardian from filing a Petition with the Court for an involuntary placement subject to the mental health code.

Guardians must avoid removing the disabled adult from his or her home or separating the disabled adult from family and friends unless doing so is necessary to prevent substantial (that is significant harm) to the disabled adult or the disabled adult's estate. A Guardian must also investigate alternative living arrangements and monitor the same to ensure it meets the needs of the Ward.

One of the essential powers of the Guardian of the Person is the ability to make medical decisions on behalf of the Ward. *Id.* This includes consent to treatment but the "Substituted Judgment" standard still applies. *Id.* As for medical records, the Guardian of the Person can both access the records and agree to the release of the same.

Guardians of the person may also file for dissolution of the disabled adult's marriage with permission from the court, consent to an abortion on behalf of the disabled adult, and control who visits the disabled adult. 755 Ill. Comp. Stat. Ann. 5/11a-17(a-5) (LexisNexis through P.A. 101-631). The guardian may even prevent the disabled adult's family from visiting him or her. However, the visitation issue is governed by Court Order. The Guardian must provide notice to the Ward's family of the admission to a hospital or hospice program, the Ward's death and the arrangement for the disposition of the ward's remains. 755 Ill. Comp. Stat. Ann. 5/11a-17(g)(1) (LexisNexis through P.A. 101-631). The Guardian must represent the Ward in all legal proceedings. Other decisions should be viewed in light of the statute and case law.

The Guardian of the Person also has a duty to periodically report to the court and provide the following information:

    *   The mental, physical and social condition of the disabled adult and the disabled adult's dependent children;

- *The disabled adult's current living arrangement;*
- *A summary of the professional services received by the disabled adult;*
- *A summary of the guardian's actions on behalf of the disabled adult;*
- *The guardian's recommendation as to whether the guardianship continues to be necessary; and*
- *Any other information requested by the court.*

755 Ill. Comp. Stat. Ann. 5/11a-17(b) (LexisNexis through P.A. 101-631).

Supported Decision Model

One alternative model that needs to be addressed but it is not currently the law in Illinois is supported decisions. As a general rule, a guardianship strips the Ward of all rights. Limited guardianships, although available, are not the norm. The issue becomes that individuals under a guardianship lose the ability to make their own basic choices including where they live (with limited exceptions requiring court approval), whether or where they may work, the extent to which the ward obtains medical care, what their diet will be, and the location in which they spend the majority of their time. That is to say, their freedoms become very restricted.

An argument can be made that the Ward is treated like a lifelong child. Leaving the ward with little to no individuality. An alternative model, not currently the law in Illinois, is the supported decision model. This alternative allows the individual with disabilities to keep their ability to make decisions for themselves while at the same time having a trusted advisor support the decision. This advisor assists the individual with disabilities understand and make decisions. The advisor also helps the person with the disability communicate or make known the choice. While at this time this alternative is not available in Illinois, where possible it is good practice for the guardian to understand the preference of the Ward and to be flexible if the Ward has a well-reasoned position as to their own care. This allows the ward to the extent possible to be part of decision making. Afterall, if we are not forced to do something, we all generally participate at a better level.

Removal, Transfers And Terminations of Guardians in Illinois

Just because a specific guardian is appointed for a disabled adult over the person or estate, does not mean that the guardian's rights and obligations are forever. Removal, transfer and terminations of guardians of the underlying guardianship itself are available tools. Knowing these are options are important for families, guardians and the wards themselves.

Removal

An Illinois guardian (representative) may be removed pursuant to 755 ILCS 5/23-2 on any of the following grounds:

> (1) *the representative is acting under letters secured by false pretenses;*
> (2) *the representative is adjudged a person subject to involuntary admission under the Mental Health and Developmental Disabilities Code or is adjudged a person with a disability;*
> (3) *the representative is convicted of a felony;*
> (4) *the representative wastes or mismanages the estate;*
> (5) *the representative conducts himself or herself in such a manner as to endanger any co-representative or the surety on the representative's bond;*
> (6) *the representative fails to give sufficient bond or security, counter security or a new bond, after being ordered by the court to do so;*
> (7) *the representative fails to file an inventory or accounting after being ordered by the court to do so;*
> (8) *the representative conceals himself or herself so that process cannot be served upon the representative or notice cannot be given to the representative;*
> (9) *the representative becomes incapable of or unsuitable for the discharge of the representative's duties; or*

(10) there is other good cause.
755 Ill. Comp. Stat. Ann. 5/32-2(a)(1)-(10) (LexisNexis through P.A. 101-631).

The law allows any person to seek the removal of a guardian. The Petition must set forth facts as to the grounds for the removal of the guardian. Once filed, the court will issue a citation directing the guardian to show good cause why he or she should not be removed for the cause stated in the citation. 755 Ill. Comp. Stat. Ann. 5/23-3(a) (LexisNexis through P.A. 101-631). The citation must be properly served in the same manner as a civil summons, at least 10 days prior to the return date shown on the citation. *Id.* The purpose of the Citation is to ensure that property of the guardian has been appropriately accounted for during the proceeding.

After potential discovery to investigate the allegations, a hearing will be held at which both the petitioner and the guardian will have an opportunity to present evidence supporting their cases. The burden is on the petitioner to prove that there are reasonable grounds for removal of the guardian. The Court can order removal and in some cases hold the guardian liable for funds wrongly used and in some cases, Order fees and court costs to be paid by the guardian.

Transfers of Guardianships

This is basically where a guardian is removed because they are no longer to hold the office and the removal is voluntary. In that instance, the Court will transfer a guardianship. A person's Will may provide directions as to the preferred successor guardian. The Court will consider but is not bound to that designation.

Termination

A guardianship in Illinois can be terminated pursuant to 755 ILCS 5/11a-20 which means that the letters of office are revoked. The Ward or any person may file a motion for termination with the Court. 755 Ill. Comp. Stat. ann. 5/11a-20(a) (LexisNexis through P.A. 101-631). A request may be communicated to the court or judge by any means including an informal letter, telephone call or visit. 755 Ill. Comp. Stat. Ann. 5/11a-20(b) (LexisNexis through P.A. 101-631). The Court may appoint a Guardian ad Litem (GAL) to investigate the request. A doctor's report is not a requirement to seek this relief from the court.

The Ward has the right to be represented by counsel, to demand a jury of 6 persons, to present evidence and to confront and cross-examine all witnesses at the hearing. The attorney's fees for the GAL or an attorney for the Ward may be paid from the Ward's estate or if no funds are available from state funds.

At trial, the court has several options including the following:
(1) dismiss the petition;
(2) terminate the adjudication of disability;
(3) revoke the letters of guardianship of the estate or person, or both;
(4) modify the duties of the guardian;
(5) require the guardian to complete a training program; and\

(6) make any other order which the court deems appropriate and in the interests of the ward.

The conclusion of the aforementioned remedies is that a guardianship is not permanent and forever. Same may be terminated, transferred or a guardian may be removed.

Special Needs Guardianship

Having a child with special needs provides so many special circumstances. One such circumstance is when that 'child' turns age 18 (when your child turns age 18, however, because of a disability is unable to make his/her own decisions) you might want to consider obtaining a Guardianship over that 'child.'

According to the law, any person age 18, is of the legal age to make his/her own decisions, including important medical and educational decisions. At age 18, the individual is legally an adult. That adult is then given all rights associated with adulthood. In the case of a child with special needs, it may not be appropriate for that child to make such decisions. Without the proper paperwork in place, it will be automatic that those decisions would be made by the individual with special needs.

For example, once an individual turns age 18, HIPPA protections provide that medical information must remain confidential unless that adult consents to the release. In the case of an individual with special needs, the medical professionals will keep that individual's medical information private and may not even honor a release from the individual because the person lacked the capacity to execute the release. This would then mean that the individual with special needs would not have to discuss any medical issues with his/her care team, leaving the care team at a significant disadvantage in terms of that individual's care.

In order to ensure that as parents with children with special needs, the appropriate decisions are being made, a Guardianship is the legal avenue to provide that protection. A Guardianship is a legal responsibility for the care of someone who is unable to manage their own affairs. This Guardianship ensures that rather than deferring to the individual with special needs to make decisions, the appointed person can make those decisions on the individual's behalf. There are two different types of Guardians. There is a Guardian of the Estate, charged with overseeing the individual's financial wellbeing, and the Guardian of the Person, charged with making decisions regarding the continuing care of the individual. These are mutually exclusive, meaning that a Guardian of the Person can be appointed without a Guardian of the Estate and vice versa. The general focus in probate court, where these cases are heard, is to provide the individual with as much freedom and autonomy as possible, provided his or her ability to make any such decisions.

Simply because the 'child,' turned age 18, does not mean that a Guardianship is automatically necessary. There must be careful consideration as to whether that individual with special needs truly can make his/her own decisions or whether the individual lacks the capacity to do so. Once a Guardianship is in place, the Guardian is tasked with making these important decisions and the individual under the guardianship, or the Ward as is often referred, loses a great deal of independence.

Many critical transitions are occurring as a child with special needs turns age 18. That child might be entering into a transition program at school or applying for Social Security Disability benefits, however, without the proper Guardianship in place, that person with the disability gets to make these decisions on their own. Determining whether a Guardianship is proper prior to the individual turning age 18 is critical. Ideally, a Petition for Guardianship should be filed prior to the individual's 18th birthday with enough time for the Court to make a final determination.

Conclusion

Guardianships are a necessary tool available in Illinois to protect your loved ones. The best way you can prepare for your ongoing care and the needs of your children is for you to create an Estate Plan in which you name your preferred guardians for yourself and your minor children. Further, taking steps to ensure you have appropriate advance directives for power of attorney for property and for health care may alleviate some of the need to address the foregoing through litigation. Other sections of this text address these options. Please read them and understand that these tools may sufficiently address your requirements.

At the same time, if you have a special needs child or if you have an adult relative who needs care personally or financially, you may have no choice but to pursue a guardianship. If you are a grandparent caring for a grandchild and need to obtain healthcare or enroll a child in school, guardianship may be your only option. We urge you to seek legal counsel to determine what steps are necessary. Don't sit back and ignore or delay the inevitable issues that must be addressed. Legal counsel can help you navigate these difficult decisions and seek, on your behalf, the relief you need.

SPECIAL NEEDS AND CIRCUMSTANCES

The population of the United States is expanding; however, the population that is considered 'special needs' is growing at a more rapid rate. The reasons for growth can be attributed to any number of factors, including but not limited to expanded definitions of the necessary delays, change in the methodology for diagnosing conditions, and a better understanding of early indication of developmental delays. In the following chapter, issues that are unique to families with an individual with special needs will be addressed. These issues range from issues which are legal in nature to those that present unique considerations in legal proceedings. In no way is this intended to be an overview of all the possibilities, but as an overview of considerations to be made. One of the running themes for parents with children with special needs is to learn to advocate. To learn to advocate does not mean that a parent will not need legal assistance or an advocate, but rather than a parent with a child with special needs has to become well versed in his/her child's needs and abilities. Parents are given a lot of responsibilities and for parents with children with special needs that is even more so. That parent needs to learn the language of special needs and learn to push, when needed, to ensure that their child receives the benefits they are entitled to. This starts from an early age, even before the child starts Kindergarten.

Early Intervention

As the child begins to learn new skills, there are development markers this child should be hitting. When a child begins to fall behind in these markers, steps might need to be taken to ensure that the child either receives services to catch up or receives those services to reach their best potential. This is where parents first begin their advocacy journey, navigating the Early Intervention system. According to the IDEA, early intervention services has a lengthy definition, but includes the requirements of the developmental delays necessary, what the program must include and who must provide the services. 20 U.S.C.S. §1432(4) (current through P.L. 116-145).

Specifically, the IDEA states that in order to be deemed early intervention services, the services must be "designed to meet the developmental needs of an infant or toddler with a disability, as identified by the individualized family service plan team, in any 1 or more of the following areas: (i) physical development; (ii) cognitive development; (iii) communication development; (iv) social or emotional development; or (v) adaptive development." 20 U.S.C.S. §1432(4)(C)(i)-(v) (current through P.L. 116-145). If the services are designed to meet these needs, the programs must include: family training, counseling and home visits, special instruction, speech language pathology and audiology services, and sign language and cued language services, occupational therapy, physical therapy, psychological services, service coordination services, medical services only for diagnostic or evaluation purposes, early identification, screening, and assessment services, health services necessary to enable the infant or toddler to benefit from other early intervention services, social work services, vision services, assistive technology devices and assistive technology services, and transportation and related costs that are necessary to enable an infant or toddler and the infant's or toddler's family to receive another service provided. 20 U.S.C.S. §1432(4)(D)-(E) (current through P.L. 116-145). These services are to be provided by "qualified personnel," including special education, speech-language pathologists and audiologists, occupational therapists, physical therapists, psychologists, social workers, nurses, registered dieticians, family therapists, vision specialists, including ophthalmologists, and optometrists, orientation and mobility specialists, and pediatricians and other physicians. 20 U.S.C.S. §1432(4)(F)(i)-(xiv) (current through P.L. 116-145).

Early Detection

Pursuant to the IDEA, children who are experiencing developmental delays are entitled to intervention even before they reach traditional school age. These services are critical because vast amounts of research show that identifying children who might have developmental delays and providing assistance can have the greatest influence on the progress that child makes. For example, these services serve as the building blocks for these children's futures. These building blocks can develop the foundation that the child needs and eliminate the need for future interventions or provide the footings to build upon with future services. Early intervention services can begin as early as birth and are often initiated with a referral from a medical professional.

The referral can come from a medical professional for a variety of reasons. First, if as a parent there is a concern with something that has been observed, the parent should speak up. At many well-baby visits, the pediatrician will ask that parents complete questionnaires regarding their child's development. These questionnaires can serve as the basis for follow up questions from the pediatrician. This could lead to a discussion regarding a need for an Early Intervention referral. Additionally, there are various diagnoses that have been identified as having a 'high probability of being associated with a developmental delay.' Children with these diagnoses will likely qualify for Early Intervention Services, without a specific identified need, but because of the future complications that will come. It is important to note, however, that a diagnosis is not required to be evaluated for Early Intervention Services nor to receive such services.

Service Types

Early intervention services can include services by Occupational Therapists, Physical Therapists, Development Therapists, Speech Therapists, and potentially Social Work services. 20 U.S.C.S. §1432(4)(E)-(F) (current through P.L. 116-145). Once a referral has been made and it has been determined that an evaluation is appropriate, the family will be contacted to schedule the various service providers to evaluate the child. This evaluation generally occurs in the child's home but can be at an alternative location where the child is in his/her natural environment, for example a daycare or preschool setting. The parents and/or legal guardians must consent to the evaluation to be completed. As discussed herein, this can become even more complicated with parents who are no longer married or were never married or are contemplating a divorce.

Once that evaluation is completed, a report will be presented to the family containing recommendations from the service providers regarding future services needed. This is generally done in a meeting setting with both parents present in order for the parents to provide consent for the services to begin and to the completion of the evaluation report. In order for services to be recommended, the child must present at least a thirty percent delay in the area recommended. The child must demonstrate the delay in one or more developmental areas. In addition, a child who has a recognized diagnosis does not need to present this percentage delay. This report becomes known as the Service Plan. This family service plan must at a minimum include a description of the appropriate transition services for the infant or toddler, be in writing, and developed by a multidisciplinary team, including the parents. 20 U.S.C.S. §1436(a)(3) (current through P.L. 116-145). This service plan is what guides the services that child will receive and the services are generally provided in terms of how many sessions are necessary in a given time frame. Section "d" of 1436 provides the mandates for the content of the plan. It states as follows:

> *The individualized family service plan shall be in writing and contain (1) a statement of the infant's or toddler's present levels of physical development, cognitive development, communication development, social or emotional development, and adaptive development, based on objective criteria; (2) a statement of the family's resources, priorities, and concerns relating to enhancing the development of the family's infant or toddler with a disability; (3) a statement of the measurable results or outcomes expected to be achieved for the infant or toddler and the family, including pre-literacy and language skills, as developmentally appropriate for the child, and the criteria, procedures, and timelines used to determine the degree to which progress toward achieving the results or outcomes is being made and whether modifications or revisions of the results or outcomes or services are*

> *necessary; (4) a statement of specific early intervention services based on peer-reviewed research, to the extent practicable, necessary to meet the unique needs of the infant or toddler and the family, including the frequency, intensity, and method of delivering services; (5) a statement of the natural environments in which early intervention services will appropriately be provided, including a justification of the extent, if any, to which the services will not be provided in a natural environment; (6) the projected dates for initiation of services and the anticipated length, duration, and frequency of the services; (7) the identification of the service coordinator from the profession most immediately relevant to the infant's or toddler's or family's needs (or who is otherwise qualified to carry out all applicable responsibilities under this subchapter) who will be responsible for the implementation of the plan and coordination with other agencies and persons, including transition services; and (8) the steps to be taken to support the transition of the toddler with a disability to preschool or other appropriate services.*

20 U.S.C.S. §1436(d) (current through P.L. 116-145).

    For example, a child may qualify for physical therapy sessions twice a week and occupational therapy sessions once a month pursuant to the service plan. These ongoing services can be provided in the child's home or in an alternative location that is a child home-like environment. Throughout the participation in the Early Intervention program, there will be update meetings to the service plan and additional evaluations to mark the child's progress and make any necessary adjustments. Specifically, Section 1436 requires that the individualized family service plan shall be evaluated once a year and the family shall be provided a review of the plan at a maximum of six-month intervals. 20 U.S.C.S. §1436(b) (current through P.L. 116-145).

    Because services are protected under the IDEA, the State of Illinois actually runs the Early Intervention program. IDEA provides that children, regardless of income, are entitled to the services. 20 U.S.C.S. §1431(a)(5) (current through P.L. 116-145). Early Intervention Services in Illinois are provided on a sliding scale basis to families, and even at the highest monthly rate on the scale the costs are drastically reduced. Some health insurance plans will cover the co-pays that families are required to pay; however, if the child's health insurance does not cover such services, this should not bar the child from receiving services given the sliding scale fee.

    In the event that after the evaluation services are not recommended, the parents will need to decide whether it is appropriate to engage private services for the child. Private services are generally covered by the child's health insurance; however, co-pays can be costly. Additionally, private services are not generally received within the child's home and more likely at a private facility. This, of course, is a general rule and there are certainly exceptions to that rule.

    One of the other reasons that Early Intervention services is advantageous for parents is that the ongoing review process will also include a transition plan once the child approaches the age of three. Early intervention services end at age three, whether the child continues to need services or not. At the age of three, however, if the need still arises, the child may transition to a preschool program. In order to continue to receive these services free of charge, the child will be evaluated for an IEP/504 Plan. Another possibility would be for the child to receive 'drop-in services.' Drop-in services are where the child's delay is not so severe to require enrollment in preschool, but rather the child comes to the school to receive therapy services of some sort.

IEPs v.504 Plans

An IEP is an Individual Educational Plan. An IEP provides children with special needs to the specified accommodations that are necessary for that child to progress in the school environment. Alternatively, a 504 Plan provides less accommodations for the student and is no longer protected under the IDEA. There are subtle differences between an IEP and a 504 Plan, but the differences are important. Both plans provide students with accommodations; however, an IEP requires that the student needs specialized instruction because of a disability in a school environment.

No matter what the plan is moving forward, Early Intervention Services cease at the age of three and a transition must be made. This is another time that parents need to advocate for their child. Knowing which path is best for your child and their academic future can be tough, but the parents are an integral part in developing this plan.

Parents are faced with multiple decisions during this timeframe, birth to three years old, and navigating these decisions can be tough, but are even more complicated for parents who were never married or are no longer married. Because children receiving Early Intervention Services are within the transition phase, and are young, the parents' communication with each other needs to be strong. Parents must be able to recognize, jointly, their child's delays and agree on the appropriate steps to take. If the parents cannot do so, the first step is likely going to be to attend mediation together. If mediation does not resolve the dispute, then the parties may engage in litigation for the Court to assist in making these decisions for the parties' child.

In the event that an Allocation Judgment, formerly known as a Parenting Agreement or Custody Agreement, has already been entered, this would guide how the parents are to make decisions regarding the child's educational pursuits, including the need for an IEP, Early Intervention Services and the like. If only one parent is empowered to make decisions, this does not preclude the other parent from being involved in the discussions, but they would simply not be permitted to make the underlying decisions.

The parents of children receiving these services must consent to evaluations and ongoing services. In fact, 1436(e) states that, "the contents of the individualized family service plan shall be fully explained to the parents and informed written consent from the parents shall be obtained prior to the provision of early intervention services described in such plan. If the parents do not provide consent with respect to a particular early intervention service, then only the early intervention services to which consent is obtained shall be provided." 20 U.S.C.S. §1436(e) (current through P.L 116-145). Therefore, it is imperative for the parents to be familiar with whatever their Court Orders or final Judgments require regarding these decisions. Many providers will request to review just the paperwork in order to ensure that they are in compliance with the Court's mandates; however, parents should be prepared to offer this paperwork without it being requested.

Another potential complicating factor for parents who are not living together is deciding where services will be provided for Early Intervention. It is a possibility that providers can rotate homes, but it also depends on the distance between homes and the service areas of the providers. This is a consideration that the parties must understand. Additionally, unless specifically addressed by a Court, both parties are generally permitted to attend these service appointments, thereby having the parties going between each other's homes as the services are provided. Again, it is best if the parents can cooperate and communicate, keeping the focus truly on what is best for the child; however, if this is not possible, the Court can become involved to provide the procedures for this as well.

IEP Meetings

Prior to the child reaching the age of three, the child will undergo an evaluation and assessment for continued services. Section 1414 of the IDEA discusses the evaluations, eligibility determinations, individualized education programs, and educational placements. 20 U.S.C.S. §1414 (current through P.L. 116-145). Specifically, Section 1414 (a)(1)(A) provides that, "a State educational agency, other State agency, or local educational agency shall conduct a full and individual initial evaluation in accordance with this paragraph and subsection (b), before the initial provision of special education and related services to a child with a disability under this subchapter." 20 U.S.C.S. §1414(a)(1)(A) (current through P.L. 116-145). Once it has been determined that an evaluation is necessary, the parents of the child must consent to the evaluation. 20 U.S.C.S. §1414(a)(1)(D)(i)(I) (current through P.L. 116-145). The same complication occurs here as in Early Intervention Evaluations when the parties are no longer married or never were married. These complications will be discussed in more detail later in this chapter. However, Section 1414(a)(1)(D) provides specific guidance for the parental consent. 20 U.S.C.S. §1414(a)(1)(D) (current through P.L. 116-145). The institution requesting to conduct the evaluation, generally the school district, must obtain informed consent from the parent of the child before conducting the evaluation; however, this consent is only for the evaluation to occur and shall not be construed as a consent for the placement in special education and related services. 20 U.S.C.S. §1414(a)(1)(D)(i)(I) (current through P.L. 116-145). There are exceptions to the requirement for informed parental consent which are detailed in Section 1415 of the IDEA. 20 U.S.C.S. §1415 (current through P.L. 116-145). As noted, the informed consent only applies to the evaluation and a separate consent is required to place the child in special education and related services.

Once the parental consent is received, the evaluation must occur within 60 days or if the State establishes a separate time frame within that specified timeframe. 20 U.S.C.S. §1414(a)(1)(C)(i)(I) (current through P.L. 116-145). There are many protections that are provided to parents and students during the IEP evaluation and ongoing evaluations that can require parents to use their advocacy skills.

First and foremost, the parents or the parent charged with making educational decisions must first consent to the evaluation being completed. 20 U.S.C.S.

§1414(a)(1)(D) (current through P.L. 116-145). During this evaluation, the Special Education team from the child's public school will be evaluating the child for eligibility for Special Education services. 20 U.S.C.S. §1414(b)(1) (current through P.L. 116-145). Additionally, the educational agency must provide notice to the parents of the child that describes the evaluation procedures and anything that the school proposes to conduct. *Id.* The IDEA also provides rules for the process of conducting the evaluation. For example, the school must...

> *use a variety of assessment tools and strategies to gather relevant functional, development, and academic information, including information provided by the parties that may assist in determining (i) whether the child is a child with a disability; and (ii) the content of the child's individualized education program, including information related to enabling the child to be involved in and progress in the general education curriculum or for preschool children, to participate in appropriate activities; (B) not use any single measure or assessment as the sole criterion for determining whether a child is a child with a disability or determining an appropriate educational program for the child; and (C) use technically sound instruments that may assess the relative contribution of cognitive and behavioral factors, in addition to physical or developmental factors.*

20 U.S.C.S. §1414(b)(2) (current through 116-145).

The IDEA requires public schools to provide special education services for those who qualify. There are thirteen categories that IDEA recognizes are requiring special education services. These categories are:

1.) *Specific Learning Disability (SLD)*
2.) *Other health impairment*
3.) *Autism Spectrum Disorder*
4.) *Emotional Disturbance*
5.) *Speech or language impairment*
6.) *Visual impairment, including blindness*
7.) *Deafness*
8.) *Hearing impairment*
9.) *Deaf-Blindness*
10.) *Orthopedic impairment*
11.) *Intellectual disability*
12.) *Traumatic brain injury*
13.) *Multiple disabilities*

20 U.S.C.S. §1401(3)(A) (current through P.L. 116-145).

More specifically, several of these categories are broad and can cover multiple disabilities. For example, the specific learning disability can cover children with dyslexia, auditory processing disorder, or nonverbal learning disability. 20 U.S.C.S. §1401(30)(B) (current through P.L. 116-145). The 'catch all' category is the other health impairment category. Conditions under this category must limit a child's strength, energy, or alertness. Most often, this category includes children who have been diagnosed with ADHD. One thing to note is that a student who is struggling in school does not automatically qualify for an IEP, but rather must be classified as falling into one of these categories.

During an IEP meeting, the members of the Special education team will assemble with the parents to discuss the progress the child has made and the plan for the coming year. There must be an IEP meeting every year that the child is eligible for IEP services. There are protections for parents under the IDEA, and the school has responsibilities regarding informing the parents of their rights.

Upon the completion of the assessment, the determination will be made whether the child is eligible for special education services. The determination is to be made by a team of professionals and the parent, a copy of the evaluation report and the documentation of determination of eligibility shall be provided to the parent. The IEP team is a group that includes the parents, not less than 1 regular education teacher if the child will be in any regular education classes, not less than 1 special education teacher, a school representative who is qualified to provide or supervise the provision of specifically designed instruction to meet the unique needs, an individual who can interpret the instructional implications of evaluation results, other related services personnel as appropriate, and whenever appropriate the student. 20 U.S.C.S. §1414(d)(1)(B)(i)-(vii) (current through P.L. 116-145).

An IEP is defined under the IDEA as a "written statement for each child with a disability that is developed, reviewed, and revised in accordance with this section," and includes the minimum requirements as described in Section 1414(d) of the IDEA. 20 U.S.C.S. §1414(d)(1)(A)(i) (current through P.L. 116-145). It requires that every IEP include a statement of the student's present levels of academic achievement and functional performance, a statement of measurable annual goals, including academic and functional goals, a description of how the child's progress toward meeting the annual goals described will be measured and when periodic reports on progress will be provided, a statement of the special education and related services and supplementary aids and services to be provided to the child and a statement of the program modifications or supports for school personnel that will be provided for the child, an explanation of the extent to which the child will not participate with nondisabled children in the regular class, a statement of any individual appropriate accommodations that are necessary to measure the academic achievement and functional performance, whether the student will take an alternate assessment on particular Statewide assessments, the projected date for the beginning of the services and modifications, and any transition plans. 20 U.S.C.S. §1414(d)(1)(A)(i)(I)-(VIII) (current through P.L. 116-145). The IEP should be updated annually and each IEP should include all the contents as detailed herein.

In developing an IEP, the IEP teams should consider the strengths of the child, the concerns of the parents for enhancing the education of their child, the results of the most recent evaluation, and the academic, development, and functional needs of the child. 20 U.S.C.S. §1414(d)(3)(A)(i)-(v) (current through P.L. 116-145). The IEP team is also required to consider whether the use of positive behavioral interventions and supports might assist a student whose behavior is impeding the child's learning or that of others.

20 U.S.C.S. §1414(d)(3)(B)(i) (current through P.L. 116-145). There are other enumerated factors contained in Section 1414(d)(3)(B) of the IDEA for those students of limited English proficiency, blind or visually impaired, and deaf or hard of hearing students. 20 U.S.C.S. §1414(d)(3)(B)(ii) (current through P.L. 116-145). Additionally, the IEP shall consider whether the child needs assistive technology devices and services. 20 U.S.C.S. §1414(d)(3)(B)(v) (current through P.L. 116-145).

Once a child reaches the age of 16, the IEP changes slightly, in that transition services are discussed. Once this happens, the IEP should include appropriate measurable postsecondary goals based upon age appropriate transition assessments related to training, education, employment, and where appropriate independent living skills, a detail of transition services needed to assist the student in reaching these goals, and beginning not later than one year before the child reaches the age of majority, a statement that the student has been informed of his/her rights under the IDEA. 20 U.S.C.S. §1414(d)(1)(A)(i)(VIII)(aa)-(cc) (current through P.L. 116-145).

In the event that the child does not qualify under one of these categories, the child might still be eligible for assistance under a 504 Plan. 504 Plans are formal plans developed by schools to give students support that they need, without providing an IEP. These plans in general cover students that have any condition that limits daily school related activities in a major way. 504 Plans are less protected than IEP for families; therefore, parents generally desire to request an IEP if possible.

Once the evaluation is completed and the child is deemed qualified for special education and related services, the parent again must provide informed consent for the child to begin receiving services. 20 U.S.C.S. §1414(a)(1)(D)(i)(II) (current through P.L. 115-145). If the parent refused to provide consent at this point, the educational institution shall not provide special education and related services to the child by following the procedures described in Section 1415 of the IDEA. 20 U.S.C.S. §1414(a)(1)(D)(ii)(II) (current through P.L. 116-145).

An IEP is transferable. This means that once an IEP is provided, the child can transfer school districts within the same academic year, and the new school district should honor that IEP. 20 U.S.C.S. §1414(d)(2)(C)(i)(I) (current through P.L. 116-145). This also applies to students who transfer school districts to a new state. 20 U.S.C.S. §1414(d)(2)(C)(i)(II) (current through P.L. 116-145).

Finding Services

So, you have graduated from Early Intervention, you have your IEP, now what? The next critical step, the PUNS. The area of Special Needs is flooded with acronyms and knowing the lingo can sometimes make a huge difference. The PUNS stands for the Prioritization of Urgency of Need for Services. *Understanding PUNS - DHS 4313*, ILLINOIS DEPARTMENT OF HUMAN SERVICES, https://www.dhs.state.il.us/page.aspx?item=47620 (last visited June 29, 2020). Even knowing what it stands for does not tell you the significant importance of this lingo. This list is a statewide database that records information about individuals who have developmental disabilities who are potentially in need of services. *Id.* The state then uses this information to select individuals for services as funding becomes available. *Id.* Bottom line, if your child is not on the PUNS, they will not receive State funding for services. In Illinois, we run on a significant wait list, and there are strategies with placing your child on the list, being 'pulled' from the waiting list, maybe deferring funding, etc. Those are all discussions that should be had outside of the realm of this Chapter; however, the concept to take away here, Get on the PUNS, end of story. The possible services that PUNS funding can provide includes in-home supports to help the individual live more independently, respite care to provide temporary relief to the caregiver, training programs to teach life and work skills, residential living arrangements to provide security and care needed, adaptive equipment to make independence possible, and other supports to improve quality of life. *PUNS Program Brochure - English Version - DHS 4309*, ILLINOIS DEPARTMENT OF HUMAN SERVICES, https://www.dhs.state.il.us/page.aspx?item=32444 (last visited June 29, 2020). Ensuring that the individual is on the list and will, eventually, qualify is critical.

Another way of locating services for individuals is networking. That sounds incredibly cliché, but providers do not necessarily connect with one another and would rather stay focused on their service area. Finding those other areas that might be needed, for example, a great private speech pathologist and a great summer camp option, might require some networking, some meeting other parents, other providers and asking questions. There are many support groups for families as well. These groups can become a great opportunity to be introduced to not only new providers, but new theories and angles in general. There are support groups through schools, outside of schools, through community centers, private groups and Facebook groups. Finding the right group takes dedication and research as well. Learning the ropes of services can be frustrating but building your own team of professionals to work with your child with special needs is a great accomplishment.

Separated Parents

While discussing decisions in regards to Early Intervention and IEPs, decision making for the child with special needs was briefly discussed; however, these considerations are immensely more complicated if the parents are no longer married or never were married. Not only is this important for Early Intervention and IEP decisions, the considerations for separated parents continues. As discussed elsewhere in this book, parties who are divorcing or were never married, but have a child together, must enter an Allocation Judgment, determining how decisions for the child will be made going forward and what the parenting schedule will look like.

In Illinois, we do not have a presumption of equal parenting time for parents yet. Rather, Section 602.7 of the Illinois Marriage and Dissolution of Marriage Act discusses the allocation of parenting time and lists several factors for the courts to consider. 750 Ill. Comp. Stat. Ann. 5/602.7(b) (LexisNexis through P.A. 101-631). In terms of special considerations for families with children with special needs, there is nothing specific that the Judge can point to, to say, "Yes, I can expressly consider those needs in crafting a parenting schedule." The only option is to apply the enumerated factors differently based upon the child's special needs. Specifically, the statute states that the Judge shall consider the mental and physical health of all individuals involved. This would obviously include the children and their special needs. Between these two factors, there is room for a skilled attorney to address any special needs of a child in regards to parenting time. Lastly, there is a factor that states that the Judge can consider any other factor that the court expressly finds to be relevant. In terms of creating a parenting schedule, the Courts are charged with determining what is in the child's best interest. Therefore, these factors can be used by an attorney to demonstrate to the Court how the child with special needs will be impacted by a suggested parenting schedule and ensure that the parenting schedule that is ultimately Ordered is in that child's best interest.

The other portion of parenting is the decision making. Similar to the factors for parenting time, there is nothing within the applicable statute that says that a child's special needs issues are a specified factor. However, parents with a child with special needs will want to ensure that the allocation of decision-making is very clear. Here, under 602.5 of the Illinois Marriage and Dissolution of Marriage Act, the decision-making allocation should be in the best interest of the child and the child's needs is an enumerated factor. 750 Ill. Comp. Stat. Ann. 5/602.5(c)(8) (LexisNexis through P.A. 101-631). In regards to the decisions for the child, 602.11 also addresses records for the child. Specifically 750 ILCS 602.11 states, "Notwithstanding any other provision of law, access to records and information pertaining to a child including but not limited to medical, dental, child care, and school records shall not be denied to a parent for the reason that such parent has not been allocated parental responsibility; however, no parent shall have access to the school records of a child if the parent is prohibited by an order of protection from inspecting or obtaining such records pursuant to the Domestic Violence Act of 1986 or the Code of Criminal Procedure of 1963." 750 Ill. Comp. Stat. Ann. 5/602.11(a) (LexisNexis through P.A. 101-631). Therefore, for parents with children with special needs, it is not just about decision making, but also about access to records. The access to records would also impact attendance at IEP meetings or other big events that impact the decisions for the child. In general, both parents are permitted to attend IEP meetings, Doctor Appointments; however, if that parent has limited access to records, for a stated reason, it might no longer be in the best interest of the child that the parent be permitted to attend these appointments, including the IEP meetings. Also, as discussed above, parents with children with special needs are faced with multiple decisions regarding the care and future of that child, including the required informed consents for various issues. Given these delicate decisions that need to be made, it should be carefully looked at whether the parents can truly make joint decisions regarding the child moving forward. It is not in the best interest of the child that the parents are faced with a decision that cannot be resolved by agreement, and now they have to wait until they can attempt mediation and then, if no agreement at mediation, file something with the Court and wait for a decision from the Court. This lengthy process can mean that the time for the decision to be made has passed. Another hot topic for parents with children with special needs is medications. These decisions can also cause tension between the parties and cause lengthy delays in the child receiving the necessary care.

Support Issues

Another major factor for parents of children with special needs is financials. As discussed herein, Illinois deploys an income sharing model for calculating child support. There is, generally, very little deviation from that standard calculation, and there is nothing specifically considered for the costs of raising a child with special needs. The only way that an attorney could potentially seek a deviation from the guideline support number is by arguing that the application of the guidelines would be inappropriate based upon the best interests of the child and one of the factors listed in the statute applies. Specifically, 750 ILCS 5/505(a)(2) states: "the Court shall determine child support in each case by applying the child support guidelines unless the court makes a finding that application of the guidelines would be inappropriate, after considering the best interests of the child and evidence which shows relevant factors including but not limited to, one or more of the following (A) the financial resources and needs of the child; (B) the financial resources and needs of the parents; (C) the standard of living the child would have enjoyed had the marriage or civil union not been dissolved; and (D) the physical and emotional condition of the child and his or her educational needs." 750 Ill. Comp. Stat. Ann. 5/513.5(a)(2) (LexisNexis through P.A. 101-631). There are arguments that can be made for a deviation based upon these factors, but this is not commonplace. If a parent feels strongly that raising the child with special needs is going to increase their costs, there are certainly factors to put into place with the Court.

However, usually when parents need the most assistance with financial support is when the child turns age 18 or is otherwise considered emancipated under Illinois law. Illinois in the last decade has taken a larger step toward providing clarity for this type of support in divorced or never married couples. While the statute still leaves much to be desired, it has provided some additional guidance on what to do.

750 ILCS 5/513.5 covers support for a non-minor child with a disability. The statutes states:

> *(a) The court may award sums of money out of the property and income of either or both parties or the estate of a deceased parent, as equity may require, for the support of a child of the parties who has attained majority when the child is mentally or physically disabled and not otherwise emancipated. The sums awarded may be paid to one of the parents, to a trust created by the parties for the benefit of the non-minor child with a disability, or irrevocably to a special needs trust, established by the parties and for the sole benefit of the non-minor child with a disability, pursuant to subdivisions (d)(4)(A) or (d)(4)(c) of 42 USC 1396p, Section 1213 of the Illinois Trust Code, and applicable provisions of the Social Security Administration Program Operating Manual System. An application for support for a non-minor disabled child may be made before or after the child has attained majority. Unless an application for educational expenses is made for a mentally or physically disabled child under Section 513, the disability that is the basis for the application for support must have arisen while the child was eligible for support under Section 505 or 513 of this Act. (b)In making awards under this Section, or pursuant to a petition or motion to decrease, modify, or terminate any such award, the court shall consider all relevant factors that appear reasonable and necessary, including: (1) the present and future financial resources of both parties to meet their needs, including but*

> *not limited to, savings for retirement; (2) the standard of living the child would have enjoyed had the marriage not been dissolved. The court may consider factors that are just and equitable; (3) the financial resources of the child; and (4) any financial or other resource provided to or for the child including but not limited to, any Supplemental Security Income, any home-based support provided pursuant to the Home-Based Support Services Law for Mental Disabled Adults, and any other State, federal, or local benefit available to the non-minor child.*

750 Ill. Comp. Stat. Ann. 5/513.5 (LexisNexis through P.A. 101-631).

The terms of the statute give the Court wide latitude in making awards, which can also be frustrating because it is hard to predict what a Court will do. Often Judges follow some kind of support guideline, often defaulting to the current child support statute; however, this is not always the case. This uncertainty can cause extreme frustration with parents because it is hard to plan and budget for the future when there is no clear direction. Additionally, the terms of support under this statute only apply while there is a disability. Therefore, many Judges will only set support for a specified time frame and then require the parties to return to court to again demonstrate the continued disability. This also can be extremely frustrating for parents because depending on the disability, it could be clear that the disability will be lifelong and changes to support would only need to be made when there was some other change in the circumstances. Additionally, the statute provides that the Court is to consider any financial benefits that the disabled child receives; however, there is little guidance on how those financial benefits will impact an award. 750 Ill. Comp. Stat. Ann. 5/513.5(b)(3) (LexisNexis through P.A. 101-631). Are they simply a deduction from what the parent would normally pay or something less than a dollar for dollar credit? These undefined items tend to increase the litigation because the parents cannot agree with what a court would do. While Illinois took great strides in creating this statute, there is still a lot more work to be done to create comfort, predictability, and security for disabled non-minors.

Decision Making

Another major factor for parents to consider is that the law does not automatically recognize that your 18-year-old cannot make decisions for him/herself. Once that individual turns 18, they are presumed to be able to make decisions, including educational and medical decisions themselves. Additionally, unless other steps are taken because they are presumed to be making their own decisions, parents may be denied access to medical records and school records. In order to ensure this is not the case, the parents need to ensure that a Guardianship is established. This Guardianship would establish the decision making for non-minor children. Guardianships are discussed elsewhere, but in general, parents should be cautious when deciding whether to do a Co-Guardianship or whether it makes more sense to have one parent in charge of making the decisions. Again, conflicts between the parents can create lengthy delays in the child receiving the care and services that are needed when the courts are involved.

Another planning tool that will need to be deployed is a Special Needs Trust. As mentioned in the Statute above, the trust can be used to house the support in order to protect other government benefits. This is actually preferred in order to ensure that we maximize the resources available to the child. The logistics of special needs trusts are discussed in other sections of this book as well. The main thing for parents to remember is that the Special Needs Trust is even more important for parents who are no longer married or were never married in order to ensure that the Courts have a place to Order support without jeopardizing government benefits that are income-based. Just as with many issues with parenting a special needs child, it is also important that the Special Needs Trust is appropriately created to ensure that the parent receiving support has access to the funds in order to provide for the child while in his/her care.

TO SIGN OR NOT TO SIGN?
THE BASICS OF PRE AND POST-NUPTIAL AGREEMENTS

Getting married is a spectacular time of preparation for the future life you hope to have. In preparing for your special day, you worry about your clothing, flowers, food choices, honeymoon, rings, vows, hair, location, weather and many other exciting choices to be made. However, you should also be concerned about the future financial terms of your relationship. Even if you have very little when you embark on this journey, a time of reflection of the financial ties that will bind you should not go unnoticed.

For many, the average age of marriage has been pushed back to pursue your career or for a variety of other reasons. Americans no longer seek marriage as the first right of passage after high school. Purchase of a house, investment options, career advancement, and other financial entanglements have occurred long before the walk down the aisle.

Perhaps you have children from another relationship that will be with you when you finally decide to marry. Maybe you have been married before. Maybe there is a large difference between the wealth of yourself and your fiancé. For others, you may be considering a new life after being a widow for many years. No matter your circumstance, when planning for marriage one must look through the lens of financial entanglement.

Prenuptial agreements deal with issues and division of assets that will occur in the event of divorce or of death. The failure to consider the financial entanglements of you and your fiancé could have grave consequences on your future. As a divorce practitioner, it is always difficult to hear individuals state they had no idea of the consequence of residing in their spouses' residence owned prior to the marriage.

For example, if you've been married for 20 years but you have resided in the residence owned by your now spouse who purchased the residence prior to the marriage, the asset will remain the purchasing spouses' non-marital property even after 20 years of marriage. It is true that you might have the ability to seek a reimbursement for the marital contribution to the non-marital asset, but the consequence of not considering the impact of the ownership of the home prior to the marriage will have a serious impact upon the division of the marital estate.

In other instances, you may have a non-marital residence but upon marriage you simply add your new spouse to the title not realizing that you've converted the asset from non-marital property to marital property. This clearly may be your intent and, in that instance, it is understood. However, ten years later when looking at the possibility of a divorce and seeing that you have now gifted that residence to the marriage can have a serious financial consequence in that it is now marital property. The bottom line is that the entanglement or non-entanglement of assets can impact what will occur in the event of a future divorce. Without the advice of legal counsel and an understanding of the consequence of ownership of assets, you may blindly convert ownership without even understanding what occurred.

To rectify the situation, you should obtain legal counsel prior to walking down the aisle. For many, your first response to that statement is one of laughter or fear. After all, why would I risk my relationship or bring up a financial issue to the one I love. You are living in a state of bliss while planning for marriage. Why in the world would you risk that euphoric feeling by bringing up issues of financial consequence? The reality is that preparation for marriage should embrace both the good and the difficult. Addressing issues of your core values, what you want out of life, and what your future plans are must all be part of the process. Discussions about your future financial arrangements are a key element to embrace a good solid relationship from the beginning. Fear of bringing up the subject should be an alarm to you to understand that you and your future spouse may not have the same objectives and goals in life.

For the reader who says I don't have any assets, only debt or for the reader who says I only have a home, the answer is the same. The discussion and understanding of the impact your marriage will have on those issues must be a priority. If you embark on the journey without an understanding of the lifelong impact that could occur, you are foolish and the failure to address these matters may result in unnecessary turmoil in the future. Even if you elect not to have a written agreement governing your affairs, the knowledge you gain from understanding the potential consequences of your decision to marry grants you freedom. Life is uncertain and anything can happen but taking steps to limit uncertainty and gain understanding is worth your time. At the end of the day, everyone should consider legal advice prior to leaping into a legally binding contract called marriage.

At the end of the day, the answer to who should have a prenuptial agreement is that it depends on what you want. On the other hand, the answer to who should seek legal advice prior to marriage is clear and the answer is everyone. You do not have too little or too much to seek this answer. Formerly, the thought was that prenuptial agreements were right for only a few and particularly those who are very wealthy or those who had a prior family. Now, a prenuptial agreement is a good choice for everyone to consider. If you cannot have this conversation with your prospective spouse, then marriage is probably not the way to go. After all, if you can't pass this hurdle in your relationship, the next hurdle is sure to cause you to stumble. An open honest discussion about the financial arrangements of your relationship is one of the keys to a successful marriage.

What is a Prenuptial Agreement?

A prenuptial agreement is a contract between you and your future spouse. It is a written agreement and a tool with which you can preserve property or funds for a variety of reasons. For some, a prenuptial agreement is an essential mechanism to protect your children or grandchildren of a former marriage. For others, it is a means to protect what they built prior to the marriage. Prenuptial agreements give you some sense of predictability.

What Can a Prenuptial Agreement Do For You?

A prenuptial agreement can provide a written agreement in advance of marriage to predetermine what will happen in the event of divorce or death related to:

A. The disposal of property;
B. The award of maintenance formerly known as alimony;
C. The protection of family-owned businesses;
D. The rights of spousal claims and rights to inherit in the event of death;
E. The classification of income;
F. The issue of future attorneys' fees;
G. Matters relating to your residence;
H. Payment of expenses;
I. How to deal with tax issues;
J. Whether a will, trust, or other legal document will be created to carry out the terms of the agreement;
K. The ownership rights of the death benefits from life insurance policies;
L. The responsibility or right to a reimbursement for payment of one spouse's premarital debt;
M. Any other agreements, including personal rights and obligations, as long as they do not violate any laws;
N. Other issues unique to your circumstances.

In summary, "by entering into a premarital agreement under section 4, the parties...agreed that their enumerated rights at dissolution are no longer governed by statute to the extent that they are validly modified or waived in their agreement." *In Re Marriage of Best* 228 Ill. 2d 107, 117 (Ill. 2008). Further, a prenuptial agreement can alter one's ability to claim a portion of a spouse's estate under Illinois law known as a spouse's statutory share.

A prenuptial so long as it meets basic legal requirements can limit possible future litigation. These agreements can be simple and straightforward. Seeking a prenuptial agreement and reaching terms to govern your relationship need not be offensive and can provide clarity to a couple to understand exactly what their financial relationship will provide. On the contrary, a couple blindly getting married without understanding the difference between marital and non-marital property, the maintenance guidelines and issues of commingling property can find themselves in a situation that was not intended. You can avoid this blindness by properly setting forth the financial terms of your relationship in a prenuptial agreement.

What are the Requirements for a Valid Prenuptial Agreement?

Illinois adopted the Uniform Premarital Agreement Act, effective in January 1990 and this Act was applicable to all prenuptial agreements executed on or after that date. Section 7 of the Illinois Premarital Agreement Act governs whether a prenuptial agreement is enforceable and provides as follows:

> *(a) A premarital agreement is not enforceable if the party against whom enforcement is sought proves that:*
> *(1) that party did not execute the agreement voluntarily; or*
> *(2) the agreement was unconscionable when it was executed and, before execution of the agreement, that party:*
> *(i) was not provided a fair and reasonable disclosure of the property or financial obligations of the other party;*
> *(ii) did not voluntarily and expressly waive, in writing, any right to disclosure of the property or financial obligations of the other party beyond the disclosure provided; and*
> *(iii) did not have, or reasonably could not have had, an adequate knowledge of the property or financial obligations of the other party."*

750 Ill. Comp. Stat. Ann. 10/7(a) (LexisNexis through P.A. 101-631).

Pursuant to case law interpreting those provisions and as found in *Kranzler v. Kranzler*, there are three basic requirements of a prenuptial agreement. In that case, the Court found:

> *. . . a premarital agreement that governed property and maintenance rights was "valid and enforceable as long as three conditions are met: (1) the agreement does not create an unforeseen condition of penury due to one spouse's lack of property or employability; (2) the parties entered into the agreement with full knowledge, free of fraud, duress, or coercion; and (3) the agreement is fair and reasonable.*

Kranzler v. Kranzler, 2018 IL App. (1)st 171169, ¶63, citing *Berger v. Berger*, 357 Ill. App. 3d. 651, 656 (Ill. App. Ct. 1st Dist. 2005).

The case also stands for the holding that a prenuptial agreement is unenforceable if a party challenging the validity of the prenuptial agreement proves that

> *(1) he or she did not execute the agreement voluntarily; or (2) the agreement was unconscionable when it was executed and, before execution of the agreement, the party was not provided a fair and reasonable disclosure of the other's property, did not waive the right to such disclosure in writing, and did not have (and could not reasonably have had) an adequate knowledge of the other's property."*

In re Marriage of Kranzler, 2018 IL App (1st) 171169, ¶65, citing *In re Marriage of Heinrich*, 2014 IL App (2d) 121333, ¶49 (citing 750 ILCS 10/7(a)).

Therefore, in order to have a valid prenuptial, the following is critical:

1. **The Agreement Must Be Entered into Voluntarily**

Illinois law says that to be valid, a prenuptial agreement must be signed voluntarily by both parties. A signature obtained by duress or coercion will invalidate a prenuptial agreement. Coercion does not exist just because you state you won't marry someone because a prenuptial agreement is a precondition to marriage. A prenuptial agreement is voluntarily signed when someone has the choice to walk away from the relationship.

The best way to avoid an issue of coercion or duress is to discuss the terms of and execute the prenuptial agreement well in advance of the marriage date. The closer you sign to the actual date of the marriage, the more scrutiny there will be. An agreement signed while drunk or right before a wedding may not hold up in court. To ensure that the agreement is entered into voluntarily it is always good advice that both parties are represented by counsel with the ability to understand the terms and conditions set forth in the document. Further, the execution or signing of the agreement should be done in as formal a setting as possible, and a court reporter should be considered so that both parties can acknowledge that they are signing the document voluntarily and of their own free will.

2. **There Must Be Disclosure of All Assets, Liabilities and Income**

A prenuptial agreement requires disclosure of all assets, liabilities and income so that the other party can understand what they are agreeing to and any rights they may be waiving. There must be a "fair and reasonable" disclosure of these items. You cannot waive your interest in something you do not know about. The determination of whether a fair and reasonable disclosure has occurred can be interpreted on a case by case basis. The best practice is to disclose all assets and liabilities as well as your income by listing same and providing the best available value of each as will be discussed below. Going one step further to document or prove that the disclosure is accurate is also important to protect yourself in the future in the event of litigation.

3. The Agreement Must Be Conscionable at the Time of Execution

When determining whether a prenuptial agreement is "conscionable," the court considers the circumstances that existed when the agreement was signed; not circumstances that may have arisen since the agreement was executed or at the time the agreement is being enforced. If you meet the previous two requirements, generally the agreement is enforceable.

Nevertheless, if a prenuptial agreement eliminates or significantly modifies guideline spousal maintenance, and this would result in one spouse experiencing "undue hardship" because of circumstances that were not reasonably foreseeable when the agreement was signed, a court may choose not to enforce these terms. This is the exception rather than the rule based on experience. 750 Ill. Comp. Stat. Ann. 10/7(b) (LexisNexis through P.A. 101-631).

Are There Any Issues a Prenuptial Agreement Cannot Address?

A prenuptial agreement cannot address issues about the allocation of parental responsibilities or parenting time previously known as child custody or visitation rights. The agreement cannot govern the issue of child support. Inserting these provisions would be void for public policy reasons and the law looks at the best interests of the child at the time of its ruling. You cannot predetermine what your obligations will be if your child is disabled or what will occur as to college expenses. Additionally, provisions in your agreement regarding illegal acts or actions are prohibited as a matter of law.

Who Has the Burden of Proof to Avoid Enforcement of a Prenuptial Agreement?

In the event of a contest over the validity of a prenuptial agreement, the person who is seeking to avoid enforcement of the agreement has the burden of proof. The burden of going forward will require that you prove that the agreement did not meet the requirements under the act. Many people contest an agreement to see if the Judge hearing the case will be sympathetic to your plight if the agreement is enforced. However, smart drafting in the prenuptial agreement provides that if a contest occurs, the person who contests the validity of the agreement has to pay the attorneys' fees incurred by the party defending against the validity of the agreement. This will help avoid a contest as to the agreement just to see what a Court will do. To the contrary in the event the agreement truly does not meet the requirements to be valid, a battle would occur.

Once a Divorce Is Filed What Can You Do To Enforce The Prenuptial Agreement?

The best way to expedite your case and have the divorce court enforce your prenuptial agreement is to file a Motion for Declaratory Judgment. This Motion seeks a court order that declares the validity and enforceability of your agreement. This will expedite the process of your divorce and can save you attorneys' fees during your litigation.

When Is a Prenuptial Agreement Effective?

Illinois law says that prenuptial agreements become effective upon marriage. 750 Ill. Comp. Stat. Ann. 10/5 (LexisNexis through P.A. 101-631). If you sign a prenuptial agreement, but the marriage is called off, the agreement has no effect. As a result, a prenuptial agreement is not a wedding contract. In other words, if the wedding is called off and you incur debt and expenses related to the wedding, the prenuptial agreement will not help you. Prior to 2016, Illinois had a "breach of promise to marry" law that allowed a person to recover damages for expenditures made and debt incurred for the wedding. That is no longer the law. If you are concerned about costs and debts from a failed engagement, you need a wedding contract and not a prenuptial agreement.

What Occurs in a Prenuptial Agreement as to Federally Governed Retirement Benefits?

Unique requirements exist with regard to retirement funds and plans governed by Federal law. All "qualified" retirement plans are regulated by the Employment Retirement Income Security Act of 1974 ("ERISA"). Federal law requires that any waiver of benefits payable under ERISA, Employee Retirement Income Security Act of 1974, be subject to spousal consent. Spousal consent is effective only if certain factors exist. A spousal waiver must be in writing, must designate a beneficiary or a form of benefits that may not be changed without spousal consent or expressly permits changes in designations without further spousal consent and the consent must acknowledge the effect of the waiver. The consent must be witnessed by a plan representative or notary public and it must be made within the applicable election period.

If your agreement calls for a waiver of spousal rights, the prenuptial or postnuptial agreement will not be sufficient in and of itself to waive the benefits. That is to say, the waiver in the agreement will not be implemented by the plan nor enforceable unless it meets the requirements of ERISA, Employee Retirement Income Security Act of 1974. If you fail to follow the waiver requirements set forth in ERISA, Employee Retirement Income Security Act of 1974, then the spousal share of the plans at issue to be awarded to either the divorced spouse of the participant or the participant's surviving second spouse may not be enforced.

What is critical is that the waiver has to be signed by a "spouse." You don't become a spouse until after the marriage and therefore, for this term to be enforceable you have to execute a spousal waiver after the marriage. The way to resolve this issue is to have the prenuptial agreement signed prior to the marriage and the spousal waiver executed after the marriage.

Can a Prenuptial Agreement Be Amended or Revoked?

Prenuptial agreements may be amended. Amendments do not require consideration to be valid. Any change or update to the prenuptial agreement must be put in writing, and it must include both spouses' signatures. 750 Ill. Comp. Stat. Ann. 10/6 (LexisNexis through P.A. 101-631).

Prenuptial agreements may also be revoked, but any revocation must be in writing and signed by both parties. *Id.* Revocations of the Agreement do not require consideration to be valid. *Id.* At the same time, the agreement cannot be revoked if only one spouse wants to cancel it; both spouses have to confirm they want to end the agreement.

Prenuptial agreements may also incorporate what is known as a sunset provision. Many people are worried about a relationship that may not survive but as time passes, they agree that certain benefits such as maintenance and certain assets should be subject to division. For example, your agreement may state that a residence will be awarded to a certain spouse but after 10 years of marriage, the property will be equally divided. So, if the marriage is less than 10 years for example, the residence goes to Spouse A but if the marriage lasts more than 10 years the residence shall be sold in the event of divorce and the proceeds divided equally. Very specific and detailed language should be incorporated in that event.

Is a Prenuptial Agreement Confidential?

Prenuptial agreements are not protected by the "marital privilege." In the event of litigation, both spouses will have to testify as to the terms of the agreement and any amendment related to the agreement and the circumstances surrounding the execution of the agreement.

What Are Postnuptial Agreements?

Postnuptial agreements generally include similar provisions as prenuptial agreements. The primary difference is that prenuptial agreements are entered into in contemplation of marriage which is to say in advance of marriage; while postnuptial agreements are entered into after the couple is already legally married. A postnuptial agreement allows both sides to prepare and arrange their finances while agreeing to work to preserve the marriage. It is a way to adapt to a change in the marriage and in some cases, it can save a marriage

A postnuptial agreement can preserve a marriage during a crisis or breakdown. It is an agreement in advance as to what can occur if the divorce becomes inevitable. It is not in your best interest to get a postnuptial agreement in lieu of a prenuptial agreement. On the other hand, many people enter into a postnuptial agreement if they want to work on the marriage but they want protection in the event the marriage does not work out.

Illinois allows for postnuptial agreements to help simplify divorces and promote settled solutions to family law issues. A postnuptial agreement is similar to a prenuptial agreement, only it is entered into after a couple is married.

What Issues Can Be Addressed in a Postnuptial Agreement:

Just like a prenuptial agreement, a postnuptial agreement can address issues such as the division of marital and non-marital property and the right of reimbursement from one estate to the other. The division of debt and the allocation of earnings for items such as maintenance can also be predetermined. Solutions if a spouse becomes ill, disabled or dies can also be incorporated.

What Should You Know Before You Enter Into a Postnuptial Agreement?

The Illinois Marriage and Dissolution of Marriage Act, the same Act that governs marital settlement agreements, governs postnuptial agreements. Section 502(b) of the Illinois Marriage and Dissolution of Marriage Act (Dissolution Act) provides that a marital settlement agreement is not binding upon a trial court if "it finds, after considering the economic circumstances of the parties and other relevant evidence produced by the parties, on their own motion or on request of the court, that the agreement is unconscionable." 750 Ill. Comp. Stat. Ann. 5/502(b) (LexisNexis through P.A. 101-631). Similar to prenuptial agreements, the agreement must be entered into voluntarily and assets, liabilities and income should be disclosed to ensure the agreement was fair at the time it was entered into between spouses.

A Court in Illinois may find that an agreement is unconscionable and may refuse to enforce the agreement. Therefore, ensuring that both sides are represented by counsel and know their rights and responsibilities is critical. Knowing the finances of the marriage and rights to maintenance in terms of amount and duration are critical prior to waiving these rights in a postnuptial agreement. There are several things that can be done to make the agreement valid. First, it must be in writing. Second, it must be voluntary and not under duress. Each spouse must have the opportunity to read and understand the terms with time to consider the terms included in the agreement. The disclosures therein must be truthful and complete. There are risks associated with a postnuptial agreement. First the agreement is a legal contract and you cannot simply get out of it. You must read and understand the document If you fail to understand your rights and responsibilities, you may waive important rights that could have a significant impact on you if your marriage fails. .Make sure that you formalize the document and understand its impact.

Just like a prenuptial agreement, issues regarding the allocation of parental responsibilities, parenting time and support cannot be resolved in a postnuptial agreement. The Court must determine what is in the best interest of the children at the time it hears the case. In like manner to a prenuptial agreement, a postnuptial cannot require anything that is illegal.

Mandatory Disclosures

A prenup is to establish the property and financial rights of each party just in case it were to end with a divorce. As previously mentioned, in order for a prenuptial agreement to be valid you will need to disclose all assets, debts and income for both parties. The point of this is because if a divorce proceeding were to be filed, sometimes the 'go-to' would be to split marital property 50/50; however, your prenuptial agreement can state something different. Whether you have only one bank account or you pay off all your credit card debt from month to month, it is best to disclose more than less and your attorney can advise whether same should be listed on the Disclosure. If you choose to or have forgotten to disclose an account, there is not much your attorney can do if a divorce were to be filed down the road. That's why it's important for the parties to take this document seriously and view all aspects of your life and account for everything your name is on. This will also help you better understand your finances personally and know more about your soon to be spouse. This isn't meant to scare them away, but better understand what the both of you are getting yourself into just in case you hit a bump in the road.

What Are Assets?

Assets are something of value. Anything from a checking/savings account, investments, vehicles, stock, life insurance, retirement plans, real estate, wills or trust agreements, any business interest, inheritance, etc. if you should have any questions on what is considered an asset, consulting with your attorney is the best option.

What Are Debts?

Debt is something that is owed or due. Some examples of debt include the following but are not limited to credit cards, mortgage loans and car loans. You should also include any promissory notes or any other item you have promised to repay.

When gathering the above-mentioned documentation, it might be a good rule of thumb to provide the most recent statements for everything to your attorney so they can properly list the assets/debts in the disclosure portion of the prenuptial agreement. This does not mean that said statements will be disclosed to your soon to be spouse, but just back-up proof for your attorney.

In summary, prenuptial agreement should be taken seriously and you should analyze every aspect of your financial world to ensure all information is properly documented.

Conclusion

Prenuptial and postnuptial agreements in Illinois are complicated and require the assistance of an attorney. Care should be taken to ensure the agreement is entered into voluntarily and after full disclosure Do not sign an agreement without knowing your rights and responsibilities. Critical errors can be made if you do not understand the impact of the agreement you are executing.

AGREEMENTS WHEN COHABITING TO PROTECT A COUPLE'S INTEREST

Negotiating the legal terms of your relationship is anything but romantic for most people. However, if you're in an unmarried but serious relationship, setting out a cohabitation agreement could be one of the most important things you and your partner do together.

What Is a Cohabitation Agreement?

Cohabitation" is a legal term describing a situation in which romantic partners reside together and merge portions of their financial interests, but do not enter into a legal marriage.

Cohabitation agreements are designed to protect both parties' interests during a relationship and at the end of one, whether the end is precipitated by a breakup or a death. A legally binding cohabitation agreement is a powerful tool for solidifying a mutual understanding of what the parties expect from their relationship.

Cohabitation agreements are created between couples of all types who have decided for a variety of reasons to become partners, but not formally solidify their union as a marriage.

When two people combine their interests or assets in this way, there is no mechanism under the law, such as is the case with legal marriage, to dissolve the union in a formally equitable way. This leaves the process up to the individuals, who may be managing an acrimonious split.

With a cohabitation agreement, the two parties can set their own terms as to jointly own property, along with the consequences of its potential end.

Illinois Law Behind Cohabitation Agreements

Up until 2012, Illinois law refused cohabitation agreements as a way to encourage traditional marriage and discourage "competing" arrangements, following a decision in the case of Hewitt vs. Hewitt. *Hewitt v. Hewitt*, 394 N.E. 3d 1204 (Ill. 1979). Since the passage of the Illinois Religious Freedom Protection and Civil Union Act, the state has accepted cohabitation agreements.

Why Create a Cohabitation Agreement?

Financial considerations primarily drive couples to enter into cohabitation agreements. When two people merge lives, they often make mutual purchases; overlap financial accounts and obligations; and transfer money and property between one another.

Cohabitation agreements between unmarried partners clarify what portion of funds each person must contribute to the household's ongoing expenses such as bill payments, support for children and even groceries and household goods. Further, if the relationship ends, cohabitation agreements lay out what each person is entitled to financially and in regards to mutual assets.

Children and pets shared mutually by unmarried couples also provide another reason to create cohabitation agreements. Though couples may have a parenting or support agreement that supersedes it, their cohabitation agreement can indicate how expenses for mutual children will be divided between the parties. If the parents separate, future parenting matters and care of the children would be determined by a family court judge.

If the couple has pets together, a cohabitation agreement allows them to formally record their plans for sharing expenses related to the pet. It also, importantly, should detail what will happen with the pet if the relationship ends.

Emergency medical and end-of-life considerations are another powerful motivator for creating a cohabitation agreement. In some unfortunate situations, unmarried couples experience a terrible shock when they learn that they have no decision-making power when their partner dies or becomes incapacitated.

Couples who are legally married automatically retain certain rights over the care and legacy of their partner, while unmarried couples do not. These include making decisions about medical care for their partner if that person is unable to make a decision, what type of experience their partner will have at the end of their life, and how their final arrangements will be handled.

A cohabitation agreement can **indicate a person's wish** for their assets and property to be distributed to their unmarried partner. While wills, advanced health care directives and durable powers of attorney are powerful legal tools for securing all these rights for unmarried couples, cohabitation agreements can be used as a precursor or in addition.

What Is The Difference Between a Cohabitation Agreement And a Prenuptial Agreement?

A cohabitation agreement acts to protect the interests of unmarried parties who are mingling property and/or assets together but not necessarily intending to get married. A prenuptial agreement precipitates nuptials forged through legal means or in layperson's terms, marriage, to protect a party's premarital property and/or assets.

Conclusion

In most instances, agreements as to real property are the primary type of cohabitation agreement or at least the impetus that compels parties to address their ownership interests and obligations. What happens if one party wants to move out? What happens if one party fails to pay their share? What happens if one party moves someone else into the residence? Dealing with these issues up front can go a long way to sustain your relationship and keep the peace. Before you jointly obtain an asset consider this useful tool to protect yourself.

GLOSSARY

LEGAL GLOSSARY

Each profession adopts its own unique language and terms which may not be common knowledge to the general public. Divorce and Family Law are no different.

While this glossary is not exhaustive, it is a good reference point if you have a question about language you may find in some of our legal documents. The definitions are simplified in order to provide you a general overview of the term.

Alimony
The legal obligation of one spouse to provide support for the other; now known as maintenance and spousal support.

Allocation of Parenting Responsibilities
The division or allocation of responsibilities related to the child(ren) which can include but is not limited to medical care, education, religious training, and extra-curricular expenses.

Annuities
Investments that will pay a specified amount for a particular period of time.

Answer
Refers to a written response prepared by the party against whom a pleading was filed.

Appeal
A process to bring your case to the Appellate Court if you believe that justice was not served in a lower court.

Appearance
The filing of a document with the Court saying you want to be heard by the Court.

Appraisal
A means to obtain the fair market value of your property.

Arrearage
The sum total of payments past due for child support or other court-ordered obligations.

Attorney For The Child
An attorney appointed for the child to assist the Court in contested cases involving children who advocate for what the child wishes.

Bankruptcy
A federal court proceeding generally used to discharge debt.

Capital Gain Tax
A tax imposed upon the increased value of investments.

Child Support
The obligation of parents to contribute to the economic needs of their children.

COBRA
The Consolidated Omnibus Budget Reform Act, which gives spouses the right to continue medical coverage obtained through the other spouse's employment, for a specified period of time and with premiums being paid to the company.

Community Property
A legal term used in nine states that requires judges to equally distribute all property accumulated during the course of a marriage, this is not the law in Illinois.

Counselor
Also known as lawyer or attorney, used interchangeably to refer to a person who has passed the state bar requirements and is licensed to practice law.

Custody
No longer awarded in Illinois as of January 1, 2016 and has become known as the allocation of parental responsibilities.

Deferred Compensation
A retirement option wherein wages are deferred to also defer taxes to a later date.

Dependency Exemptions
The right to claim minor children as dependents for tax purposes, thereby reducing the total amount of tax paid, in most cases.

Deposition
A discovery tool whereby oral testimony is taken of a party or witness under oath, by an attorney of the opposing party.

Discovery
The right of one party to obtain information from the other party.

Dissolution of Marriage
Refers to the termination of a marriage, thereby ceasing all rights incident thereto.

Divorce Decree
Also known as a Judgment for Dissolution of Marriage, the court order terminating the marriage.

Domestic Violence
Also known as domestic abuse, refers to violent acts and inappropriate conduct of one spouse towards the other.

Equitable Division
The power of the court to divide the assets and liabilities of the parties as the court finds to be fair and just.

Exclusive Possession
The right to use and hold property, denying the use of that property by the other party.

Ex Parte
Actions taken by one party without notice to or the presence of the other in court.

Grounds
The legal basis or reason for the divorce, no longer used in Illinois except for Irreconcilable Differences.

Guardian
A person who manages and is legally responsible for the estate or person of an individual called a ward who is unable to manage their own affairs, especially an incompetent or disabled person or a minor child whose parents have died or are unable to provide care for the child

Guardian Ad Litem (GAL)
Refers to a person appointed to advocate for the best interests of a child and to assist the Court in contested cases involving children.

Hearing
A proceeding before a court where limited evidence and testimony may be presented by an aspect of the case while a trial is proceeding where all issues are presented.

Home Study
An investigation by a government agency of a parent's home, background, and conduct; used in disputed cases of child related issues.

In Camera
An interview of the children by a judge, traditionally in a judge's chambers without the presence of the parents.

Indemnification
A guarantee made by one party toward another that he or she will be responsible for the actions or inactions of the other.

Inheritance
Money or property given to one party following the death of another.

Injunctions
A court order prohibiting a person from doing something.

Interrogatories
Written questions sent to the opposing party regarding issues and facts relating to the matter before the Court.

IRA
Also known as Individual Retirement Account, refers to retirement investments accumulated by an individual.

Joint Custody
Formerly an award of custody to both parents but is no longer in place in Illinois as of January 1, 2016 unless you have an order entered prior to that date.

Joint Parenting Agreement
A written agreement granting both parties joint custody of the children and outlining the obligations of both parties but is no longer used in Illinois as of January 1, 2016 unless you have an order entered prior to that date.

Judgment for Dissolution of Marriage
Also known as divorce decree, refers to the written court order dissolving a marriage.

Legal Separation
A court order setting forth both parties' rights and obligations while living separate and apart, but not divorced.

Litigant
A person involved as a party in a lawsuit

Maintenance
The legal obligation of one spouse to provide support for the other, also known as alimony or spousal support.

Marital Property
Property that was accumulated during the course of the marriage.

Marital Residence
The dwelling the family resided in prior to the filing of the Petition for Dissolution of Marriage. The term does not necessarily mean that the residence is marital property.

Marital Settlement Agreement
The written agreement of the parties in a divorce distributing property and setting forth the obligations of both parties.

Mediation
The use of a third party, who attempts to assist the parties in reaching a settlement of the issues involved in the divorce.

Non-marital Property
Property that may have been purchased during the marriage, but which is not considered marital property because the acquisition of same was through the use of premarital property.

Order
The commands of the Court upon the parties of the case.

Order of Protection (OP)
A court order often used in domestic violence cases prohibiting a spouse from certain conduct toward the other spouse such as harassment, physical abuse, and intimidation. This is often referred to as a stay away order.

Paramour
The lover or illicit partner of a married person

Parenting Time
The schedule as to when a child will have time with each parent and was formerly known as visitation

Pension
Retirement benefits paid to a spouse upon certain events.

Petition for Dissolution Of Marriage (PDOM)
Also known as a Petition or Complaint for Divorce, wherein a party seeks a court order dissolving a marriage, distributing the parties' assets, and resolving issues regarding the parties' children.

Petition for Rule To Show Cause
A pleading filed with the court seeking for a party to be held in contempt of court for failure to obey a court order.

Petitioner
The person who initially files a request or petition to the court asking for specified relief.

Pleadings
Written documents filed with the court or orders entered by the Judge.

Premarital Property
Property accumulated by a spouse prior to the marriage.

Prenuptial Agreement
Also known as an antenuptial agreement, refers to a written agreement signed by both parties prior to the marriage that allocates the rights of property and maintenance in the event of divorce.

Pretrial Conference
A conference held with the Judge and the parties' attorneys wherein the court seeks to attempt to settle the case or alternatively to limit the issues at trial.

Profit Sharing Retirement Plan
A retirement fund established by many businesses for the benefit of their employees.

Pro Se
Representing yourself in court without an attorney and is now known as an unrepresented litigant or self-represented litigant.

Psychological Evaluations
Also referred to as psychiatric evaluations, refers to the use of a professional to evaluate the family and the parties' minor children to assist the court in making its decisions regarding parenting matters.

Qualified Domestic Relations Order (QDRO)
An order entered by the court to transfer retirement benefits of one spouse to another, usually payable upon the retirement date of the employee.

Qualified Medical Child Support Order
An order entered by the Court commanding the insurance provider to provide information to and to deal directly with the custodial or residential parent of the minor children.

Ruling
The order entered by a Judge after hearing the evidence presented by the parties.

Service of Process
The right to be provided notice that a case has been filed.

Spendthrift Spouse
A spouse who wastes marital assets.

Subpoena
A legal notice to appear or produce certain documents.

Temporary Order
A court order setting forth obligations for a specific period of time or prior to the entry of the divorce.

Verification
A party's affirmation that the facts and allegations outlined in the body of a pleading are true and correct to the best of the party's knowledge.

GLOSSARY OF ESTATE PLANNING TERMS

Estate Planning
The preparation of documents and planning for events that serve to manage an individual's assets in the event of their incapacity or death.

Comprehensive Estate Plan
A plan that attempts to address not only what will happen to your assets when you die, but also protect both you and your assets during times of incapacity.

Last Will and Testament
Often simply referred to as your Will, is an attestation of who you want to wrap up your affairs (called your Executor) and who you want to receive your property when you die. A Will is governed by the Probate Act within your state, and thus only receives its force and affect through court action.

Living (Revocable) Trust
A legal document, or trust, created during an individual's lifetime where a designated person, the trustee, is given responsibility for managing the trustmaker's assets for the benefit of the individual and the eventual beneficiaries. A living trust is revocable during the trustmaker's lifetime, meaning the trust can be changed or revoked by them at any time. The trustmaker generally retains complete control over all trust property while they are alive and able to do so competently.

Irrevocable Trust
A trust that cannot be revoked and that takes effect during the life of the trustmaker. Usually made to transfer wealth, protect assets, or reduce taxes. The trustmaker

generally does not maintain control over the assets once they are transferred to the Trust as they are no longer considered the owner of the assets.

Power of Attorney for Property
A legal document that allows you to give someone else the ability to handle your financial affairs on your behalf. Such powers of attorney can be "durable" (beginning when signed and terminating on death or revocation), or "springing" (beginning upon a set event, such as a determination of your incapacity and inability to make your own decisions). These powers of attorney can be very broad, or they can be limited in scope.

CLOSING

The purpose of this book is to introduce you to both the simplicity and complexity of family law and estate plan matters. The book is not to be construed as legal advice but general information about issues you may face. The book is based on Illinois law at the time of this writing and the law may have changed since it was written.

Each situation is unique and no two families look exactly alike. There are consequences for each decision you make. We urge you to seek the services of an Illinois attorney to help you and give you advice as to the specifics of your situation.

At the same time, we believe knowledge is power and we have attempted to provide a summary of what we believe to be some of the key issues in family and estate law. This attempt is just that, a summary, and should not be construed as anything more than that. Not every issue and nuance was included.

If you are embarking on this journey, we also suggest that you look beyond the legal piece and assemble a network of resources to help you move forward with your life.

Each of us has unique skills and talents and just because you need help with something you should not shy away from help because you feel embarrassed or ashamed that you don't understand something. The community is necessary because we all cannot know or understand everything.

As you are navigating the winding road of life…remember help is always just around the corner. Don't be afraid to ask for it.

www.ingramcontent.com/pod-product-compliance
Lightning Source LLC
Chambersburg PA
CBHW082110230426
43671CB00015B/2654